**State Approaches
to the Management
of Educational
Research**

State Approaches to the Management of Educational Research

The Model of MACE and Its Studies

Ronald B. Jackson
Massachusetts Advisory
Council on Education

Lexington Books
D.C. Heath and Company
Lexington, Massachusetts
Toronto   London

to a mother, Dolly Lamb Baird,
a wife, Liz,
a daughter, Sue,
and two sons, Duncan and John

Contents

Figures

Tables

Foreword

The educational enterprise, like truth itself, will one day prevail. That day, of course, is still coming and although critics say it is a far horizon we glimpse, it is nevertheless readily defined. The problems of education will be solved when men of vision and fortitude address themselves constantly to deficiencies at hand *and* those things anticipatory. The educator needed is the one who can attend to the pressing problems of the present while looking to the needs of the future. Such a man, I daresay, is Ron Jackson.

If education can be characterized by a single word now, that word is flux. The demands of a probing and sceptical society have changed the bedrock of an institution from stone to porous sand. The positive architects of change and improvement move through narrowly defined limits, but move they do. Idols have been smashed in the process and taut nerves snapped.

Jackson's strength lies in the fact he is near-completely objective. He is able with his analytical mind to set a proper perspective and move to support whatever thesis reason demands. His research, proportionately ample, buttresses arguments like so many building blocks. He is never to be taken lightly; no dilettante, he.

It is his involvement and dedication that shine through his work, this and other, and an awareness that his contribution is one of many being made today by dedicated men who have sworn, like Jefferson, eternal hostility against every form of tyranny over the mind of man. Education is his specialty, vocation and avocation alike. It rings in every page, calling attention to new perspectives, certain solutions.

The hope of any good man is for the alleviation of certain societal ills and Jackson displays sufficient evidence — he knows the cancerous spots on the educational body. Familiarity with the educational and social problems of a major city like Boston is not achieved by the light-of-heart but the bold. To propose reforms in such an urban setting, meaningful measures of reform, is a contribution of the first order and transcends ordinary contribution. His perspicacity is exceeded only by a higher moral code.

I have been particularly fascinated by his ability to analyze the federal largesse and pick at its nuances and define overt and covert strengths and weaknesses. Too often men settle for the accepted and conventional and fail to look behind gratuities for the stockpile of wealth that might be better apportioned. Not so, this author.

This work, then, is substantial, for it brings a fresh look to subjects grown old through usage, made dull by pedants and hacks. And it is comprehensive, ranging from the origin of a council and its problems, frustrations and progresses to the convoluted world of guidance. Wide-ranging, it allows exhibition of an incisive mind and stylish wit. Gentlemanly, he diminishes old fetishes not with the bludgeon but the rapier.

The problems besetting this nation will be dealt with squarely by men such as Jackson. He and others like him will have their day in court and they will bring, I rather think, more exquisite tools to the reshaping of education in particular and society in general. And the future belongs to he who prepares for it, and see to it shaping.

I consider it an honor to rank him a cohort of mine and to recommend the fruits of his labor.

Neil V. Sullivan
Commissioner of Education
Commonwealth of Massachusetts

Preface

There is a fourfold purpose in relating the story of the Massachusetts Advisory Council on Education at this time. The first is to introduce the Council and to discuss its development; the second, to relate and account for key studies conducted by the Council; third, to demonstrate that MACE is a distinctive agency which other states might well consider emulating in one form or another; and the fourth, to show the need and importance of state educational research activities.

The first chapter discusses the development and operating procedures of the Council in such a way as to furnish a guide for others interested in establishing a state research agency. The chapter illustrates how MACE operates today.

Next, the book is organized into three parts, each containing four chapters, which discuss specific Council studies. "Retooling the System," the first part, represents four studies of large systems including the State Department of Education. The second part, "Perspectives on Emerging Programs," reviews Council studies of programs needing a greater share of the state's resources and so badly organized and led that they achieve little. In the third part, "Revisiting Some Conventional Programs," three of the four chapters focus largely upon high school programs including vocational education. The fourth chapter recommends reforms in teacher education and certification.

The final chapter of the book reexamines the need and uses of state educational research and development, the impact of the Council on public education, and ends by presenting a series of proposals meant to lead to an enlarged sense of the potential of state research-sponsoring agencies.

A word about how the studies are rendered. Each is presented in a different way with attention given to those features that might catch the interest and imagination of the reader. Chapter 3, for instance, has a detailed section on developing a local educational information system. Hopefully, each study reviewed will be of interest in its own right. The researcher or student who feels he needs a more complete understanding of a given Council report is urged to read the full version.

The final chapter attempts to convey the sense that educational research and development are immensely important and need to be more central to what happens in education. An opportunity will be lost and education ultimately blighted unless educational research agencies learn to respect themselves and their role. Some proposals are made in this chapter to assist in reconstructing research and development into a central state activity.

Acknowledgements

Members of the Advisory Council who have worked so hard to develop MACE into a strong and respected state agency deserve the first round of acknowledgments. Presently, those members are: Philip C. Beals; Morton R. Godine; Shirley R. Lewis; J. Norman O'Connor; Felix de C. Pereira; Walter J. Ryan; Nina E. Scarito, M.D.; Verne W. Vance, Jr.; Mary Warner; and ex officio members, Patrick E. McCarthy, Chancellor of Higher Education; Neil V. Sullivan, Commissioner of Education.

The complete list of Council members and staff since MACE was established is given in Appendix A.

The reports upon which most of this book is based have been directed or codirected by the following persons: Burton Blatt; Courtney Cazden; Evan R. Collins; Joseph M. Cronin; Andre Daniere; Donald T. Donley; Bruce Dunsmore; Frank Garfunkel; John S. Gibson; Richard Hailer; Herbert Hoffman; Daniel Jordan; Warren King; Melvin Levin; Gordon Liddle; George Madaus; Vincent Nuccio; Lloyd S. Michael; Richard Rowe; Charlotte Ryan; Carl Schaefer; Joseph Slavet; Lindley Stiles.

Much credit falls to Mrs. Judith Pippen for her critical reading of the manuscript, for filling the gaps, and for handling manuscript details of every kind.

Typing the manuscript has been graciously and patiently done by Sharon Julius, with help from Mary Gammons, Christine Strader, Elaine Comras and Dorothy Linick.

**State Approaches
to the Management
of Educational
Research**

1 Introduction

People are always telling me to make practical suggestions. You might as well tell me to suggest what people are doing already, or at least to suggest improvements which may be incorporated with the wrong methods at present in use. - Rousseau, Preface to *Emile*

From an economy of goods, which America was as recently as World War II, we have changed into a knowledge economy. - Peter F. Drucker

Each generation must recast, and in certain instances create, educational agencies to meet emergent realities, needs and purposes. While few educational needs are new, the way they are perceived and acted upon sets a framework for the kinds of educational agencies appropriate to a given time. The federal courts, for example, require us to change our view of separate but equal educational programs and draw both blacks and whites together. An old but ignored need became new and pressing.

The problems of responding to a new need or requirement – in our example a court decision – are often compounded by in-place institutional structures with set patterns of behavior. Unless that structure is changed, implementation is often hindered and a series of ugly conditions result. Thus we maintain that established institutional structures are not always able to deliver on making the changes inherent in new conditions. The Vermont farmer (who no doubt has counterparts elsewhere) expressed the problem of matching new needs and purposes with appropriate action when he, after reflection, informed a lost driver that it was impossible to get where he wanted to go from where he was.

Similarly a case can be made for new educational research and development agencies. We are only beginning to recognize, develop and value state public agencies capable of conducting studies that guide and assist diverse groups with educational concerns. Legislators, parents, teachers, commissioners of education and students are examples of both clients and consumers of educational research. Ongoing agencies can furnish some of the research and information sought by legislators, schoolmen and other citizens. Needs are in fact crystalizing into demands. Conventional agencies and frameworks are strained to cope and often have problems merely keeping abreast of research and information requirements, let alone keeping ahead of them.

Meanwhile, the pace quickens, the needs enlarge and an inventory of new realities and purposes keeps us without rest. Even general statements of the issues in pursuit of responses show a great need for specific kinds of

1

research, study and action at the state and interstate level. Our agenda, sharpened
by court decisions and a long-overdue loss of complacency indicate needs to:

1. sense the interdependence of all levels of education;
2. understand the broadening concept of education's response to society's
    needs;
3. face the inadequacies of traditional patterns of school finance;
4. understand and act on special problems generated by the struggle for civil
    rights and social justice;
5. meet the demand for improved performance and adequate accountability
    in education;
6. achieve greater flexibility in education;
7. prepare for increasing participation of the federal government in educational
    matters;
8. face an increasing complexity and multiplicity of modern government;
9. nurture a humane society;
10. mount comprehensive programs, in or out of schools, which recognize the
    whole child;
11. sense anew the importance of education in a world moving toward new
    possibilities and new dangers, and
12. achieve more active citizen involvement in the affairs of government and
    particularly in education.

The twelve points listed lead us to at least two observations. The first is
that the challenge to the entire national educational enterprise is massive. The
second is that state agencies similar to MACE deserve careful consideration
as eminently useful in helping at the state and local level to bring about the
reforms and changes in education inferred in this agenda. State level research and
development has been for too long a minor theme even in education. Later on
we will discuss recent improvements in state research and development efforts
as a result of the federal charities.

It is not our intention to propose state advisory councils on education
which will supplant or overlap with other research endeavors. Dr. Edgar L.
Morphet, director of the Eight State Project, centered in Denver, Colorado, is
undertaking a certain look at education in the future. Adapting and acknowl-
edging UNESCO's materials from the International Institute for Educational
Planning he writes the following guidelines for new approaches to planning:

In the past decade a new kind of educational planning has become necessary
to cope with the sweeping changes in education's environment and with vastly
accelerated pace of change and growth in education itself. This new educational
planning differs from the old in five main respects:

1. A longer time perspective - which looks five, ten and fifteen years
ahead so that actions can be initiated now to meet tomorrow's anticipated
needs, allowing for education's long "promotion cycle."

2. Broader coverage - not simply piecemeal planning, but comprehensive coordination of the whole educational enterprise, including nonformal education - so that its various levels and parts will grow in balance, thereby avoiding serious wastes and maximizing education's contribution to national development.

3. Closer integration — of educational development plans with manpower needs and other requirements of economic and social development, taking realistic account also of the nation's resource limitations.

4. Accent on innovation - the fostering of research and experimentation to achieve the changes needed in educational structures, content and methods in order to keep education up to date and to match its performance to the nation's needs and resource limitations.

5. Modern educational management - improved organization and administration that will ensure not only the formulation of sound and feasible plans but their effective implementation.[1]

Dr. Morphet doesn't stop there. He then cites some institutional implications that need consideration. First, however, he expresses reservations about the objectivity of such organizations as state departments of education to conduct planning and other research functions for the many clients and consumers earlier listed. We are in no sense saying that critical R&D functions in education should not be performed by a variety of state agencies, including state departments of education. Important matters such as planning, budgeting and leadership require R&D activities by departments of education. However, it is highly questionable that the same departments, or other state executive agencies, could or should meet the wide and trying demands of the groups previously mentioned. The recognition of these diverse demands was an important influence in the establishment of the Massachusetts Advisory Council on Education. The state model Dr. Morphet offers and the way he sees it operating is expressed in three parts:

1. Establish an appropriate organization in the state to enable planning for educational improvement to be conducted in a systematic and comprehensive manner;

2. Relate the planning organization approximately to action agencies - the state legislature and executive department - so that statewide, comprehensive plans may be translated into action programs mandated by these agencies; to other educational institutions - local school districts, colleges and universities, and the private sector of education - to influence the future planning of their programs; to concerned agencies and groups - lay and professional in a state - to ensure appropriate involvement in the decision-making process;

3. Build into the planning organization the needed technical competence to enable planning to be based on systematic valid study and evaluation of education.[2]

Research needs and methods have developed and expanded in ways hardly dreamt of a generation ago. Harking back to the twelve needs cited, we see new challenges to education researchers. We will recite only a few pressing requirements which flow from our twelve-point agenda of national needs to show their implications for research and planning: education and the poor; the law and education; store-front schools; the educational implications of giving eighteen year olds voting rights; the teaching of sex; state governance of education; qualifying teachers; effective state leadership of higher education, and the design of new education agencies. While the Advisory Council has by no means addressed itself to all of these subjects it has researched some and it could, in one manner or another, conduct studies of each one. A model for an ideal state education research agency can be teased out of what has been written to this point. It looks like this:

1.   A high-level, independent research agency charged by statute with studying and advancing public education at all levels, of all kinds, from the cradle to grave;
2.   An agency free to determine, after due discussions with the relevant consumers and clients, what to study and free to determine how to proceed on a study project;
3.   An agency staffed and organized to hear, understand and meet the needs of a number of different and changing clients and consumers. This means that the agency must establish study priorities and a plan for conducting the studies;
4.   An agency staffed and organized to relate and to coordinate effectively with other agencies and groups, public and private; federal, state and local. Such allied agencies should be expected to take action based upon the findings and recommendations of the research agency;
5.   An adequately funded agency with a reliable source of income;
6.   An agency prepared to play a leadership role in establishing an agenda for state education;
7.   An agency staff with a high degree of accountability based upon its research products.

The Massachusetts Advisory Council on Education, an agency already in existence and already attempting to meet these ideal goals on a realistic basis, brings this discussion from theory into practice and such is the burden of what follows.

Forces that Shaped the Advisory Council

The 1960s were a time of troubles, much as the 1970s appear to be. Imperfections, from the international to the local scale, were being forced into view. The education scene, and not necessarily only the schooling students were receiving, reflected these larger concerns, producing strife, unrest and a new generation of critics of public school education.

A small state Department of Education, in a smaller fortresslike structure on 200 Newbury Street, Boston, found itself beset by problems and often hamstrung when it tried to rise to the occasion. The bureaucratic reflex of ignoring problems or pretending that they didn't exist seemed the wiser posture. Education was still viewed as not especially newsworthy, although Sputnik in 1957 had led to a revived interest in the sayings of basic educationalists. In Massachusetts, public education remained on a business-as-usual course.

This fitful peace was shattered by a series of telling articles, first published in the *Boston Globe* and later produced in a pamphlet entitled, "The Mess in Bay State Education."[3] Two iconoclastic, youthful authors, Ian Menzies and Ian Forman, went to work on the dysfunctioning educational corpus and found a raft of disorders, including:

1. An archaic, inequitable and miserly formula of state aid which ranked the Commonwealth forty-seventh among the states in state support of public schools;
2. A heavy reliance on local property taxes (in the absence of state aid) to fund education, a reliance which meant that "the standard of education has become geared to the accident of geographic location." That is, real estate-poor communities were unable to purchase the same level of educational services for their children as wealthier communities;
3. A large number of high school students enrolled in a so-called "general curriculum" which was neither fish nor fowl: it prepared them neither for a job nor for college;
4. A lack of leadership at the state level, and a state Department of Education, supposed to provide that leadership, which was understaffed, underfinanced and underpaid. The result, Foreman and Menzies reported, was an agency where "pencil counting dominates" and public education itself was dominated by "uniformed executives, legislators and fiscal clerks in the State House;"
5. A failure to plan and coordinate for an intelligible and comprehensive system of education, a failure endemic, "since Horace Mann first gave public education here its impetus in 1838;"
6. A tradition of "every town for itself" which severely limited the possibility of state-coordinated action.

The Menzies-Forman articles struck a responsive note. "The Mess in Bay State Education" became required reading from one end of the state to the other. In 1964, this series led to the establishment of the Massachusetts Education Study Commission, popularly called the Willis-Harrington Study.

Kevin Harrington, six feet nine inches tall and a natural leader, was a state senator who has since become the president of the senate. Senator Harrington's keen knowledge of issues in Massachusetts education contributed to his role as chairman of the commission.

In a controversial move, the commission called on Chicago's superintendent of schools, Dr. Benjamin C. Willis, to be executive director of the study. Willis was immediately criticized for "moonlighting" since he planned to continue his arduous superintendency. He carefully planned his activities in Massachusetts over weekends and Chicago public school vacations.

Using a small Boston-based staff, and calling in a group of nationally reputed consultants, Willis and the twenty-one-member commission completed and published its final, 624-page report in June 1965.[4]

Willis, the staff he assembled, and the commission with $250,000 conducted a top-to-bottom study of education policy and practices in the state. Deliberately avoiding topical controversies and designed to produce change, the final report recommended, in summary, that the state:

1. Reorganize the boards for effective use of "citizen wisdom" and reorganize the Department of Education;
2. Consolidate school districts;
3. Provide comprehensive high schools;
4. Provide regional services;
5. Establish the Massachusetts Advisory Council which, in part, would help with continuous evaluation and improvement;
6. Establish a board of higher education;
7. Expand vocational programs;
8. Revise teacher education and certification;
9. Devise ways to either (a) expand program offerings, or (b) develop new programs to serve the educational needs of citizens of all ages;
10. Increase the compulsory attendance age and the number of days a child must spend in school;
11. Expand state financial commitments to programs new and old;
12. Establish mechanisms for state education units to work in harmony.

The thrust of the recommendations was clearly towards equal educational opportunity. The report found and described in detail two different worlds in Massachusetts — one poor and one affluent. Realizing the difficulties of matching remedies to needs, the report called for an advisory Council and made it clear that the Council would likely play a role in carrying out the unfinished business of the commission. The Council, in fact, was viewed by many as a permanent version of the Willis-Harrington Commission.

Certainly the educational trends seemed to be well timed with MACE's birth. Innovations in education in the mid-sixties were discussed and written about copiously. Applications of the bag of tricks used in management were proposed for use in education. Jerome Bruner wrote the *Process of Education* and gave promise for a brave new educational world. The fruits of scholars, now intent on helping education by producing quality curriculum materials, were available in the educational market place, led by PSSC physics. Could the millennium be far distant? It was. Great expectations turned to thin hope and then to grim illusion.

These events explicitly shaped the concept of MACE. Here was to be a high-level and unorthodox agency able to view all education in Massachusetts and pull together those people, forces and resources that could help alter the balance of events in favor of equal, quality education. The Council could take advantage of the optimism of the mid-1960s and the rush of innovative programs that obviously could be plugged into public education. It was within this frame of mind that the architects of MACE saw implementation of the Council's recommendations as an automatic follow-up of a well-conceived and powerfully documented study. The legislature or the school districts, and everyone else, would surely be persuaded to act on such evidence. The Council's true character, written into the Willis-Harrington report, was in keeping with the optimistic reformist orthodoxy of the early and mid-sixties, which held that a well-conceived innovation would be automatically institutionalized by the conventional agencies.

We have briefly characterized events and illustrated some early thinking about the Massachusetts Advisory Council. A number of open-ended options still remain possible for the Council to shed one role for another, kaleidoscope the agency, while not forgetting its central obligation of improving education in the state. But such criteria for viewing and reforming education need at least one more reality: the need for education to nurture a humane society.

The Council and the Willis-Harrington Commission

A mere seven pages, constituting Chapter 11, in the Willis-Harrington report are given to describing the Advisory Council. Those few pages, however, represent one of the high points in the entire document. The Advisory Council, in fact, was seen as the perpetuation of the Willis-Harrington Commission. Stressing the strong interest the Council must manifest in all the systems of education, the commission report states that the Council is "consciously designed to perform a clear, unique and necessary function in the total organization of the Commonwealth's educational enterprise." While other boards have specialized interests and functions, "the Council enjoys — indeed, exists to exploit — a freedom to range beyond institutional and operational preoccupations." The Council must develop and maintain, the commission report continues, a "comprehensive frame of reference." The essential purpose of MACE, from the Willis-Harrington view, is to study those educational systems which, in its own judgment, require installation and/or improvement.

In order to fulfill the mission of the Council, a small, full-time, professional staff is required, who should "organize, direct and conclude" studies. This staff should not conduct its own research. Rather, the staff should convince the Council of the need for a given study. Then the professionals should make a nation-wide search for the best person to conduct the study. Curiously, the commission report does not make clear whether the Council or the person selected to conduct a study should be responsible for the final result.

The Council is to issue the study and to make appropriate recommendations. This is appropriate since the Council is better informed on how a given study report fits the needs of Massachusetts. Thus, it seems the division of responsibilities indicates that the director is fully responsible for his report but the Council has the larger obligation of relating the director's report to the comprehensive education scene.

Other operating dimensions, suggested by the Willis-Harrington report to the Council, include the temporary employment of "working parties" to serve one or any combination of the following functions:

1. Fact finders — what is happening in a particular educational area;
2. Evaluators — to assess how well a given educational system or program is doing;
3. Planners and designers — describing, designing, explaining and creating new organizations and innovations.

In all of these ventures, current and accurate information is viewed as critical. Thus, the Council must, the commission chapter on the Council relates, be able to collect information when it is needed and in the form it specifies. "Only in this way can its studies be sure of their context."

The Commission wanted to get a small, yet high level, study agency entirely free to search into and improve public education on its own terms. The "bottom line" in the commission's report, which contains brief cryptic remarks about implementation, and cites a pure form of accountability, reads:

"What the Council can do is to devise educational policy for the Commonwealth and recommend it to the two Boards as appropriate for their consideration. If the Boards find the policies and designs feasible, then, as executive agencies, they plan detailed implementation of the policies and seek their respective shares of operating expenses from the General Court. If the Advisory Council does its job and the Boards capitalize on it, the stage will be set for improvement . . . in the Commonwealth. It is for such that we have a Commonwealth."[5]

Taken as a whole, the sense of the commission's aspirations for MACE is found in the statutes.

In one significant way, Willis-Harrington and the ensuing legislation differ. Four legislators and seven private citizens were to constitute the Council in the Willis-Harrington version. Only at the last moment was it realized that the

Massachusetts Constitution barred legislators from serving on a permanent
state council or board. This last-minute discovery left the Council, a small
agency among large and expanding ones, a space craft without a mother ship.

The Council and the Law

Only after a nip-and-tuck battle, in which compromises were struck, did
the packet of "Willis-Harrington" bills reforming state education, including the
establishment of MACE, pass the legislature to be signed into law by the
governor in 1965. The Council fortuitously emerged unscathed from the conflict,
largely because opponents to the education reforms focused on other nearer-to-
home components of the proposed legislation. Legislators also tended to view
the Council as an agency capable of helping them to run a tight educational
ship at a time when costs were on the rise.

From its beginning, MACE was viewed by virtually all state officials as
one of the major state agencies dealing exclusively with matters of education.
However, it has also been argued that the Council is in the Department of
Education and therefore a part of the department. The same legal chapter,
it so happens, that establishes the Department of Education (Chapter 15 of the
General Laws Relating to Education) also contains the section establishing the
Advisory Council on Education — and the Board of Higher Education. Another
version is that the Council is somehow slightly superior to the education
boards since it was the first to be formed after the Willis-Harrington laws took
effect. The Council has wisely steered clear of such speculation and functions
as a high-ranking independent agency with close informal ties to other state
agencies, the legislature and the governor. Figure 1-1 indicates MACE's relationships. Note that other departments, such as the Department of Corrections
which conducts critical education programs for inmates, are not included but
are only represented by the bottom dotted line.

The question of the power and preorgatives of the governor, and the new
secretary of education are limited yet unclear. Traditionally, governors in
Massachusetts have tended to leave educational matters to the boards. A state
reorganization plan calls for a secretary of education but allows him only the
powers held by the governor, which are largely limited to reviewing budget
proposals. Within a two year period, the secretary, like other secretaries
established under reorganization, is to propose further oganizational changes
which are likely to increase his powers.

The law establishing MACE is straightforward, if general: "The purpose
of the Advisory Council on Education shall be to recommend policies designed
to improve the performance of all public education systems in the Commonwealth."

Given the wide span of operations covered by the phrase, "all public systems

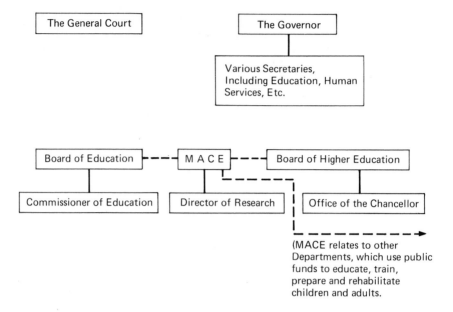

Figure 1-1. Organizational Relationships of the Advisory Council. Source: by the author.

of education," it seems wise that the Council recommend policy and stay away from details and minute specifications. The Council has enough to do without pursuing every small point or problem. The purpose thus shows the scope of the Council's work. The Council may study any matter in the state that has to do with public education. But note as well that this purpose does not state that a formal study must be conducted before any policy recommendations are made. The Council, by law, is unusually free to behave, perform and report as it sees fit.

The law establishing the functions of MACE is to the point, while requiring certain procedures and suggesting a variety of activities:

"The Council shall analyze, plan, and evaluate the programs and systems used by all agencies for public education in the Commonwealth, drawing as required on the experiences of other governments and organizations and on relevant information in other departments, divisions, authorities, and agencies of the Commonwealth.

The Council shall recommend such policies as will promote and facilitate coordination, effectiveness and efficiency in the operation of all public education systems in the Commonwealth.

The Council shall recommend to the Board of Education and the Board of Higher Education for their consideration the findings of its analyses and evaluations and the substance of its plans.

The Council may, from time to time, at its own discretion, issue public reports on education matters it is concerned with." [6]

These extracts from the law illuminate what is meant by policy recommendations and what the shaded areas are in a working process for the Council.

Begin, the law says to MACE, by revealing the Council's current interests and thrust to the relevant board or boards. In this way, some preparations can be made for absorbing and applying "the findings, analyses and evaluations" of the Council.

A special point is made in the second paragraph of the legal extract of facilitating "coordination" in the functions of "all public education systems." Here is the total array of public suppliers of education with an infinite number of ways to develop, to involve and to reinforce agency coordination. The Massachusetts education study found one weak state board of education and determined to recommend two strong state boards which, however, might need to be reminded of their coordinating responsibilities by a third agency — MACE.

The law does not point out one important intent of the commission, namely to view the educating process from the students' point of view. Students don't make the great distinction between secondary education and higher education. The Council was intended to keep an eye on this transition and to make certain the student was adequately protected.

One clear authority is given to the Council. The agency can require information, in the form and at the time it wishes, from any government agency, including local education authorities, (LEA's) supplying public education.

Organization of the Council

Nine lay members and two non-voting ex officio members, the commissioner of education and the chancellor of higher education, constitute the Council. At least one member of the Council must be a labor union official and one must be a woman. Council members serve for five years and may be reappointed once.

When a Council member has missed two consecutive meetings in a calendar year, he loses his membership and the governor is asked to appoint a member to take his place. The Council is specifically charged with making nominations to the governor to cover vacancies on the board of education, the board of higher education and the board of trustees of state colleges.

By law the Council is required to submit an annual budget request and an annual report. In such regards, the Council is not unlike other state departments in Massachusetts and elsewhere.

By law, the professional staff is limited to three, a director and two associate directors. All three professionals are appointed by the Council and serve at its pleasure. The director's salary is set by law. The director and the

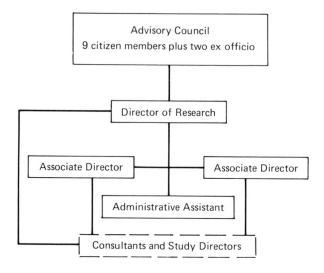

Figure 1-2. The Organization of the Advisory Council on Education. Source: by the author.

two associate directors are compensated respectively at the commissioner of education and associate commissioner levels. An administrative assistant to the professional staff is compensated at civil service grade 14. Figure 1-2 indicates the organizational arrangements of the Council.

There is no limit placed upon the number and kind of consultants the Council may employ or their length of service. Both the law and the Willis-Harrington document leave temporary augmentation of the staff as a viable alternative to the Council when requesting more professionals. In other words, those working for the Council could expand from the three professionals to 20 or more should the issue being studied require this and the Council budget contain the funds to do so.

The director is an ex officio member of the state board of education and a member of the advisory commission to the board of higher education.

There is a high level of congruence between the roles and responsibilities outlined for the Council in both the commission report and as they are stated in the statutes. Furthermore, the commission's statement is a valuable additional guide to how MACE should function, while other parts of the same report recommend a number of suitable issues and topics in need of study.

MACE can look to both the commission and to the law in interpreting its functions, particularly in its method of conducting studies.

The Trajectory of an Advisory Council Study

Where and when the idea for a study is hatched is often difficult to
ascertain. The Willis-Harrington report is stuffed with recommendations and
clues for further study. Education trends, such as the open university; neglected
domains, such as adult education, are examples of legitimate study topics.
Whatever project is developed must be viewed in light of: (a) other studies
being pressed upon MACE and what kind of priority rating makes sense; (b) the
prospects for implementation of the whole or part of a study; (c) the nature of
any support for or opposition to a study; and (d) whether the limited resources
available to the Council are up to the kind of study proposed. Consideration is
also given to what other funding might be associated with the study.

Completing in a sequential order how a study evolves, even from this point,
is still tricky. The following composite of how a study is put together and
concluded should be observed while bearing in mind our contention that there
are many other activities in which the Council ought to be involved.

Once the staff senses that a given study is appropriate to the Council,
a staff person is assigned to develop it. Some baseline concepts of the study,
its cost, and how it might be undertaken are drawn up and put to interested
individuals and groups for further refinements. Simultaneously, the project is
discussed at length with the Council, (usually it has been mentioned at earlier
Council meetings). A Council member may, at this point or a little later, be
appointed to join the staff on developing the project.

Next a search is undertaken for a study director. Usually, several likely
candidates are interviewed by the staff. The candidates may be asked to write a
brief statement as to how they view the project and they may be invited to
discuss the matter further at a regular meeting of the Council.

Typically, one or two potential study directors are requested to prepare
full proposals for formal presentation to the Council. One is chosen by the
Council, a contract is made, and the study is launched.

A study committee is next constituted to perform a variety of tasks.
This body acts as a sounding board, a communicating mechanism and, in time,
an implementation team. As an example of a study team, the actual committee
for Dr. Joseph Cronin's study, *Organizing an Urban School System for Diversity*,
is shown in Table 1-1.

Examples of the estimated budgets for Dr. Cronin's study and for a
$100,000 study of Early Childhood Education done by Dr. Richard Rowe of
Harvard University are shown in Tables 1-2 and 1-3.

The study committees meet approximately every other month to receive
progress reports, and near the completion of a study, will begin to review draft
chapters. Other interested groups are kept informed, and additional meetings
are held with Advisory Council staff. Study committees are not exclusive,
and frequently members are added after the study is underway. In some studies,

Table 1-1

Massachusetts Advisory Council on Education Study Committee, Boston Study, 1969-1970

Joseph E. Barressi. Executive Secretary of the Boston Municipal Research Bureau

Richard J. Bradley. Director, New England Association of Colleges and Secondary Schools

John Brown. Student, Dorchester High School

James E. Buckley. Assistant Superintendent of Schools, Springfield

Hon. Robert Cawley. Massachusetts State Senate

John J. Connor, Jr. Superintendent of Schools, Worcester

Michael J. Cronin. Vice President, First National Bank of Boston

Hon. Michael J. Daly. Massachusetts House of Representatives

John E. Deady. Superintendent of Schools, Springfield

Ophie A. Franklin. Executive Director, Massachusetts Experimental School System

Morton R. Godine. Vice President, Market-Forge Company

Robert R. Hind. President, Education Development Center

Ronald B. Jackson. Associate Director of Research, MACE

Paul A. Kennedy. Assistant to the Superintendent, Boston School Department

Robert T. Kenney. Director, Public Facilities Department

Reverend Paul F. McHugh. Director, Public Facilities Department

Paul E. Marsh. Education Consultant, Office of Program Planning and Coordination

Vincent C. Nuccio. Director, Center for Field Research and School Services

Theodore J. Parker. Project Director, Equal Education Opportunities, State Department of Education

Mrs. Saul Pearlman. President, League of Women Voters

Robert W. Peebles. Director, Education Collaborative for Greater Boston

John P. Reilly. President, Boston Teachers Union

Alexander M. Rodriguez. Senior Planner Associate, United Community Services

Joseph S. Slavet. Director, Division of Community Programs, Urban Institute, Boston University

Hon. Mario G. Umana. Senator, Massachusetts Senate

Francis L. Broderick. Chancellor, The University of Massachusetts, Boston.

Source: Joseph M. Cronin *Organizing an Urban School System for Diversity* October 1970, p.i.

Table 1-2

Budget Estimates for Organizing an Urban School System for Diversity, June 21, 1971

I. Staff	
Administrative (Including Fringe Benefits)	$10,000
Secretarial (Including Fringe Benefits)	8,000
Fellowships	15,000
II. Consultants	4,000
III. Data Collection & Analysis	19,000
IV. Meetings & Conferences, Travel	4,000
V. Supplies, Printing, Postage, Editing	5,041
VI. Indirect Costs	14,959
Total	$80,000

Source: by the author. From the files of the Massachusetts Advisory Council on Education.

Table 1-3
Budget Estimates for Early Childhood Education Study

1. Staff	
Rowe – Director (10.6 man months)	$19,528.00
Cazden – Assoc. Director (r.5 man months)	
Secretarial and Clerical assistance	3,444.00
Research Assistant	3,880.00
Fellowships	10,850.00
2. Consultants	8,000.00
3. Data Collection	15,000.00
4. Meetings and Conferences	4,000.00
5. Travel	1,999.00
6. Supplies, telephone, preparation of final report	7,400.00
7. Miscellaneous	4,332.00
Total Direct Costs	$78,433.00

Indirect Costs		
Operation and Maintenance of physical plant	$ 4,615.00	
Administrative Costs	11,711.00	
Library	2,027.00	
Student Services		
Use Allowances:		
Equipment	820.00	
Buildings	1,402.00	
Facilities	129.00	
Total Indirect Costs	$21,567.00	$ 21,567.00
Total Costs		$100,000.00

Source: by the author. From the files of the Massachusetts Advisory Council on Education.

other special interest groups have also been organized to collaborate with the study staff.

The director and his staff run the usual gauntlet of empirical study techniques: a literature search, a state data search, development of a questionnaire, wide-scale interviewing and occasional informal hearings. In such a process, it is obvious that there is heavy reliance upon the judgment of the study director and his staff. The leap from the evidence of shortcomings and need to the actual solutions is never easy to make. Nonetheless, after hearing all sides, the director is left free to write the report and make suitable recommendations. MACE, which hears the final report and accepts it, is free to support all, a part, or none of the report. In practice, the Council has never done less than accept most of the findings and recommendations of every report brought before it.

Now comes the sticky issue of implementation which is never the same for two studies. One interpretation of the law establishing MACE has it that the

Council should conduct a study and simply hand it over to the appropriate group for action.

The Council has stayed open on its role and responsibilities in implementation. Study committees established by the Council and consisting of Council members have, for instance, met after the completion of a study to discuss matters of implementation. The issue of implementation has generally been handled pragmatically with the Council and its staff taking those actions that seem appropriate upon completion of a report. Naturally, the Council would be pleased to find a ready audience and client prepared to implement all or at least some of the recommendations in a given report. We feel there is a kind of unreality in having the Council go lax at this point and rely solely on others for implementation. It is appropriate, of course, for the Council to inform fully, collaborate with, and finally hand over copies of a final report both to those affected and those who will be instrumental in bringing about change. But this does not mean that MACE and its staff should not work for implementation of those recommendations endorsed by the Council and others.

During the heady days when MACE was conceived by the Willis-Harrington study, it was felt that each study would, on its own merits, impel action. Such a position was naive.

As part of the wind-up of a study, the Council usually calls a news conference at which all the interested parties are asked to assemble. These sessions have helped to inform the public about issues in education and about the work of MACE. The summary report on Boston's school system, by Dr. Joseph M. Cronin, was produced in installment form in a major Boston newspaper over the course of a week, thus reaching about 100,000 readers.

The final report is produced in a full report form and in a summary report form. The number produced of each has varied considerably, but invariably, the Council runs short of copies.

There is evidence that MACE has followed a responsible format in identifying and carrying out a study. A number of formats are available, with the following version adapted from the National Center for Educational Development and Research:

1. Identify overall goals and clarify basic assumptions;
2. Identify priorities;
3. Identify research and development goals;
4. Identify specific objectives;
5. Select projects based upon 1 to 4;
6. Implement and monitor specific projects;
7. Develop and sustain communication networks to insure proper feedback;
8. Evaluate impact.

The literary polish in a final report is secondary to arranging the report for use. Thus, recommendations have been ordered in a number of ways:

A.   No-cost;
B.   Short range — long range;
C.   Legislative matters — administrative matters etc.;
D.   Local action;
E.   State action, etc.

An assessment of the impact of MACE studies will be found in the final chapter. Accountability and self-evaluation is as necessary for MACE as it is for other segments of education.

Some Observations on the Council and its Practices

A close look at how the Council actually operates and the establishment of some other guidelines should be helpful to those wishing to propose a similar agency elsewhere. This section begins with a comprehensive view of the Council, moves to a discussion of its functioning, then on to the Council members and staff, and concludes with an accounting of how MACE handles a completed study.

While the components of MACE are hardly unusual, the sum of these components make it a distinctive institution. Several elements place the Council on a unique level. First, a citizen Council is responsible for what the agency does or does not do. Second, the Council is on equal footing with other state departments, and in fact, nominates those who serve on its sister boards of education to the governor. Third, the Council has an entirely free hand to conduct studies as it sees fit, even though those studies may cross agency lines. Fourth, by statute, the Council is called upon to issue statements about educational matters of public concern. And fifth, since MACE has no raison d'être except to produce useful studies and assume coordinating and leadership roles it lives with one of the purist forms of accountability. Finally, the professional staff works at the pleasure of the Council and may be changed at any time.

We have a picture of an organization that must be lean and hungry. The performance required cannot be confused with rhetoric, and the agency cannot afford to fall back on a structured set of annual chores. One qualifier seems appropriate. Such an organization needs time. The recommendations of a study may be accepted by the legislature or operating agencies little by little, or even rejected at first. An organization such as the Council may be perceived by its sister agencies as an upstart and professional jealousy might ensue.

In turning to the functions of the Council, of first importance are its plans. The law states that the Council should reveal "the substance of its plans" to the boards. Practice has found the Council discussing individual studies with the relevant boards and agencies, including key legislators, but not in a manner that could be construed as a comprehensive plan for one or more years. The intent of

Willis-Harrington was to have the Council reveal completely its plans and purposes for all to see. The Council can hardly cast itself otherwise since it is clearly to serve as a model to others. To ask that others plan, as virtually every MACE study has found it necessary to say, is to require the same from the Council.

Of course, the chief executive officers do sit ex officio on the Council and can learn about what studies are being considered. The Council must annually present to the governor a list of the studies, and their estimated costs, for budgetary purposes. However, none of these measures serves the sense of either the Willis-Harrington statements or the law. Revealing the kinds of studies contemplated is only a part of a plan. A plan infers a comprehensive design, including a statement of what purposes the plan is to serve. Recently the Council staff has considered drawing up a two or three year general plan. In summary, it seems inconsistent for the Council to advocate good practices, such as planning, and itself not develop a coherent statement of its plans.

A key Council function has to do with interagency coordination. At present, a coordinating council, which consists of the chairmen of the boards and the Council chairman and their chief executive officers, meets more or less monthly. These meetings have served a number of useful purposes. Not only has information been exchanged, but other activities dealing with MACE studies have been generated. The Council and its staff have also held a number of meetings of an informal coordinating nature. There has been one combined meeting of the Council and the boards of education. That one meeting, the first ever held, was fruitful, but there was not time to develop any collective thoughts or effort. Attempts have been made to have a follow-up session. Clearly, two or three such planned meetings a year, would be useful in achieving what the Willis-Harrington commission called "doing the Commonwealth's business."

Other coordinating activities were suggested in the commission's report. Such a level of coordination suggests that there are others, besides the boards and other state agencies, interested in education. These constituents, which include students, have already been named.

The Council, as advocate of the student, and in the interest of improving education, must not only have full intelligence about what is happening in education but must also use a "good office" approach to keep the educational machinery working. When the machinery no longer works, for whatever reason, the Council should be the key agency in bringing about a change. The citizen Council is the heart of MACE. The more effective the citizen Council, in particular in recognizing its responsibilities to what happends in education, the more effective MACE is. Of all the ways that MACE might be considered distinctive, the citizen Council is the prevailing feature. Leadership should, with the assistance of staff, come from the Council. The Council must state its position and the Council must design itself for leadership. Who the spokesman might be is quite another story. It could be the chairman, another member of the Council or the director of research. What is important is that the spokesman represent the citizen Council.

Leadership of this stature infers an active Council and staff and a constant interplay with various study directors and task force groups. Contacts with others are also essential. Earlier in this chapter we spoke of new realities and emerging needs. The citizen Council must tease out these realities and needs and inform the public about their meaning.

By statute, the Council nominates prospective board members to the governor. This responsibility has become more critical as wider and wider representation is demanded by all.

Some Council members have been more active than others in serving on various committees and performing coordinating functions. Since not all Council members should come from one social class, not all need to work for the Council in the same way. A concern about people, particularly students, and an alert and active interest in what is happening should be enough to qualify a person to Council membership.

Perhaps the Council should be increased by two more members in order to make it more cosmopolitan and to help assure wider representation. Perhaps as well, three year appointments rather than five year appointments would bring greater freshness to the Council's deliberations.

Of vital importance to the functioning of the Council is its main tool – the professional staff. Their duties can be outlined as follows:

Planning for Research
Taking a needs assessment (formal and informal);
Convening conferences and special groups to determine needs;
Requesting and receiving information and reports designed to aid the planning process;
Attending conferences and special group meetings;
Working with consultants;
Assisting study directors in readying proposals for the Council;
Evaluating design and impact of past research interns.

On-going and Management Commitments
Monitoring MACE studies;
Attending board meetings;
Addressing matters of coordination;
Attending (and testifying before) legislative hearings;
Attending committee meetings and performing "good office" consultant roles with other government agencies;
Assisting the Council in its nominating responsibilities.

Implementation and Dissemination Activities
Planning for release of a MACE study;
Informing the various agencies, groups and individuals of the impending release of a study of interest to them;

Conducting press conferences;

Assisting in the development of legislation;

Calling conferences and special committee meetings;

Serving on implementation committees;

Preparing newsletters to inform others of the Council activities;

Developing a master list of persons to receive MACE materials (see Figure 1–3).

In referring to the entire list of activities, it makes sense to increase the regular professional staff by at least one more person and to increase the secretarial staff as well. While a staff limited to three professionals has held up reasonably well in the first two categories listed, it has somewhat overlooked the last, which demands a great deal of time and ample amounts of talent. The skills called for in attracting attention to MACE's products, in a society already overflowing with materials to consume, are of the highest order.

The Council continues to have problems with dissemination. How does one inform even the key leaders in a state of five million persons? Fifty-thousand

To	Full Verision	Summary
Boards and Departments of Education	✓	
News Media		✓
Libraries	✓	
Government Officials and Agencies		✓
Subject Supervisors	✓	
College Educators and Administrators	✓	
Elementary and Secondary School Administrators	✓	
Elementary and Secondary School Educators	✓	
Student and Faculty Councils	✓	
Professional Organizations		✓
Civic Organizations		✓
Business Organizations		✓
Labor Organizations		✓
Student Organizations		✓
Interested Individuals	✓	

Figure 1–3. Distribution of a Typical MACE Study. Source: Massachusetts Advisory Council on Education working paper.

copies of a report would only begin to do the job. The costs of printing and distributing that many copies of a single study would require MACE to double or more any given study budget. Some studies have overcome this problem. Dr. Joseph Cronin arranged to have a Boston paper publish his summaries in installments. At times, funding has been sought, unsuccessfully, by study directors to develop a television presentation. MACE is committed to making its studies available to the public. At present, however, MACE has not found any reason to be satisfied with its "delivery system." Furthermore, the Council constantly finds itself short of copies immediately after the study has been released.

These efforts to display the wares of the Council publicly have led some to object, since the law has been interpreted to mean that studies will simply be presented to the relevant boards and those boards will take it from there. Adding fuel to this issue is MACE's practice of having several thousand copies of summary versions of a study printed and disseminated around the Commonwealth and, upon request, elsewhere. These activities are sometimes perceived as forcing the hand of the public agencies involved into implementation. In such a context, the objection continues, MACE looks like the reforming angel and other public agencies are invariably found wanting. This argument could be dismissed merely by pointing out that, by law, MACE from time to time is enjoined by law to issue public statements bearing on issues in education. MACE has simply chosen to treat each report as a public statement. Yet critics abound these days, and operating agencies are understandably sensitive to another public agency that probes their purposes and functions and is therefore perceived as joining the chorus of critics. Neither the law nor the Willis-Harrington report are entirely clear as to what the role of the Council is when a given study or project is completed. Willis-Harrington has it that "the Advisory Council supplements and extends the planning functions of the two separate boards. It must persuade because it cannot command." The sense is that MACE should leave implementation to others. Yet persuade is an action word that can cover a wide variety of procedures and activities. One answer is to bring agencies being studied into the picture as much as possible without compromising the integrity of a study. On balance, awkward handling of MACE's final reports by the relevant agencies, including the Council itself, are being smoothed out. A recent illustration of such improvement is the harmonious and unified action in developing a governor's commission to study school district organization. Both the councils agreeably interlocked in producing a better organizational scheme for school district consolidation and collaboration.

A study is not the last word on a topic. The Council has the final say. In exercising its prerogative the Council has an obligation to put a study both into the larger educational context and into the context of its funding limitations.

To fund its studies MACE submits a budget request to the governor each year. This request has always been for almost twice what has been received.

The habit has become to appropriate $300,000 annually for MACE studies and for the Council task force projects. The Council has produced an impressive number of studies for this kind of funding. It may, in fact, have diffused its efforts by contracting for so many studies. At any rate, MACE is presently seeking an additional $50,000 based upon further work needed on studies already completed. Thus, MACE hopes to be funded in the future at the $350,000 level. From time to time, other monies and resources have been linked to this sum.

The total amount invested by the Council in studies from 1966 to 1972 was $842,225.

The total amount of funds contributed by other agencies has been over $300,000.

National and State Sponsorship of Educational Research and Development

A glance at state sponsorship of research gives a sense of the context of MACE in the national research field. Opening comparisons are grim: the overall national investment in R&D is three percent, while in education it amounts to two-tenths of one percent.

Only in the last half dozen years has the federal government put any appreciable amount of money into educational R&D. The funding of both not only remains woefully inadequate but has leveled off since 1965.

In 1954 the eighty-third Congress passed the Cooperative Research Act, authorizing the commissioner of education to enter into agreements with research performers (universities and other agencies prepared to conduct research), but the actual funding of the act was not forthcoming until the fiscal year 1957. At this same time, the National Science Foundation became interested in supporting institutional improvements at the secondary school level. The year 1965, with the passage of the Elementary and Secondary Education Act (ESEA) which authorized funding over an array of educational areas, seemed to be a watershed year. At that time, the Cooperative Research Act was broadened to include the funding of regional educational laboratories and to open up research in teacher education, library needs and information services. As it turned out, schoolmen and researchers were overly optimistic in believing that ESEA would be shortly followed by greater amounts of federal money supporting research, state departments of education and local education associations.

Table 1–4 shows the altering pattern of support by the U. S. Office of Education, given to various areas performing educational research. The total sum going to 50 state and local governments for R&D amounts to only slightly over 31 million dollars.

Table 1–4
Historical Analysis of USOE Support to Various Performer Categories (In thousands of dollars)

Category	Up to 1964	1965	1966	1967	1968	Totals
Regional Educational Laboratory	—	—	$ 7,336	$18,543	$22,793	$ 48,672
University-Based Research & Development Centers	$ 999	$ 3,493	6,579	14,188	15,419	40,678
College or Univ.	58,354	24,516	50,085	38,792	40,849	212,596
Policy Research Centers	—	—	—	600	999	1,599
ERIC Clearinghouses	—	—	1,768	2,050	1,762	5,580
ERIC, Other	—	—	202	1,000	1,083	2,285
Profitmaking Corporation	540	0	336	835	1,825	3,536
Nonprofit Corporation	10,735	3,717	6,552	6,821	9,393	37,218
Local Educational Agency	2,920	1,205	2,467	1,414	2,527	10,533
State Educational Agency	3,302	3,350	5,205	4,284	2,666	18,807
Other Government Agency	1,148	86	266	147	567	2,214
Total	$77,998	$36,367	$80,796	$88,674	$99,883	$383,718

Source: U.S. Dept. of Health, Education and Welfare, *Educational Research and Development in the U.S.*; Dec. 1969, p. 91.

Some show pieces have emerged from the meager amounts the national government gives to educational research. An Office of Child Development has been established within the HEW family to conduct, in part, research in early childhood education. The Educational Resource Information Center (ERIC) deals in the storage and uses of educational data. Nineteen required clearing houses have been established, each with a speciality e.g. teacher education, higher education and educational administration. Plans are almost completed for a National Educational Institute (NEI) which will be a problem-solving, mission-oriented agency with major research responsibilities. The NEI will pull together a number of federal agencies and programs, including the regional laboratories and the Office of Education research program.

It is estimated that, from all sources, about 250 million dollars were given over to R&D in 1968 for all levels and kinds of education programs. Table 1-5 documents known funds from all sources. Two hundred fifty million dollars means barely over one dollar per capita.

An HEW publication, *Educational Research and Development in the United States*, gives even more information on this subject.[8] The final chapter of that publication cites the following shortcomings in commitments to R&D.

1. *The absence of an over-all strategy.* A full view of the sponsorship and management of educational R&D reveals a bewildering variety and a diffu-

Table 1-5
Documented Minimum Base Financial Support for Educational Research and Development by Sponsoring Agency

	FY 1968
United States Office of Education	$101,967,000
National Science Foundation	23,326,000
National Institute of Mental Health	11,860,000
National Institute of Child Health and Human Development	8,377,000
Office of Economic Opportunity	12,800,000
Department of Defense	6,046,000
Other Federal Agencies (Labor; Commerce; Children's Bureau; Agriculture; Social Rehabilitation Service; Food and Drug Administration; Interior; and Endowments for Arts and Humanities)	6,725,000
Private Foundations	7,344,000
All Other (State agencies; higher education institutions; professional and academic associations; etc.)	13,845,000
Total	$192,290,000

Source: U.S. Dept. of Health, Education and Welfare, *Education Research and Development in the U.S.*, Dec. 1969, p. 117.

sion of responsibility. Efforts are simply not being linked or impelled: research and development are not hand in glove but rather hand in mouth.

2. *Inadequate financial support*. True R&D involves rich funding. We must factor into the last picture such elements as fundamental research and design, prototype testing and demonstrations, dissemination, phased evaluations, and manpower development activities. Other kinds of studies and research, costing less, are useful and necessary, such as those conducted by MACE. In many areas, however, inadequate funding results in premises as substitutes for basic research.

3. *Manpower shortage*. Those who deal in R&D express serious reservations about the poor training available to prepare talent. The range of skills necessary is considerable. Even more serious is the shortage of R&D management persons.

4. *Data Inadequacies*. Here the problems are rife. Each agency uses different definitions of research, development, experimentation and so on.

The taxonomies to describe educational R&D are incompletely developed, making the organization and analyses of studies virtually impossible. Finally, the complete reporting of R&D projects, an art in itself, is inadequately developed.

Other shortcomings can be cataloged. The annual uncertainties of federal funding are a major deterrent to research planning. The neglect of the development component of R&D is notorious. Party politics often rears its ugly head in determining what R&D activities will be funded.

A look at state involvement with educational R&D does not relfect a brighter picture. The educational responsibilities of the state are immense. School districts spend elementary and secondary school funds for teachers, administrators, programs and school buildings. Very little of what is left over is spent on R&D.

While most states report having units with a primary responsibility for educational research, few states possess a coherent approach to R&D. State commissioners are typically charged with maintaining certain fiscal and other statistical information. In addition, a few legislatures require studies, or statistical reports, on an annual basis of specific areas, such as special education. Research expenses in New Jersey in the 1960s were charged to an account known only as the "Commissioner's Office". New York's department of education administers grant programs in support of a variety of research and experimentation activities. Other states with grant programs include California, Georgia, Utah, Virginia and Washington. California and New York, however, stand out with the largest state-level research units.

A few states report innovative R&D activities, ranging from training researchers, compiling projects for doctoral dissertations, sponsoring research councils and encouraging local research and development.

Several states, New York being the latest, have conducted comprehensive state studies. The Willis-Harrington report belongs to that rubric. The Massachusetts Advisory Council and the board of education are presently conducting a state-wide study of school districting. Also, studies of the organization and structure of state higher education have been produced in almost every state in recent years.

However, there has been little, if any, effective cooperation between states over R&D matters. This is all the more disconcerting since states share a common educational responsibility, and remarkably similar problems plague every state.

An increasing realization of the common educational problems of states is bringing a few states together with some further encouragement from federal funds. The issues of poor school districts and racially imbalanced cities have found their way to the courts, and represent the leading edges of issues common to virtually every state.

Title V, ESEA, in particular, has provided opportunities for states to band together in regional and national groups to approach old problems on a broader front. One example is the Eight State Project involving Arizona, Colorado, Idaho, Montana, Nevada, New Mexico, Utah and Wyoming.[9] This project is engaged in peering into the future and has turned out a number of highly useful publications. Vocational education research funds have also fostered inter-state activites.

A word about state commissions appointed to study educational issues. Ad hoc state commissions, typically charged with looking at various systems of public education, have reported on their findings and made recommendations which have occasionally received national attention. The Fleishmann commission [10] in New York State is a case in point since the commission addressed such sensitive associations of public policy as school finance, integration and support of parochial education. A number of other state reports by special ad hoc groups, in particular those dealing with higher education, have been studied carefully for signaling trends which have spread elsewhere. The Willis-Harrington commission, which produced a loose but comprehensive "action plan" for all of public education in Massachusetts, did lead other states to appoint commissions. Such temporary commissions, it may be argued, illustrate the need for permanent state agencies able to anticipate and break out key issues for careful study. To rely upon a progressive governor or legislature to establish a commission to assist educational causes is a chancy way to operate.

Educational studies sponsored by a permanent research agency are greatly ahead of any kind of ad hoc group, be it a state legislature or a state department of education, which mounts occasional studies. A permanent educational R&D should have greater impact in a state. Such an agency, staffed by competent researchers, should have a good sense of when and what kind of study should be done and have devised ways to make the study count.

American schoolmen have been fond of pointing out that there is no national system of education but fifty different systems. A problem arises in testing such a general statement for any redeeming significance. Teachers, instructional materials, examinations and school facilities are nationally cast. However states may differ in organization, they are much the same when it comes to educational problems. States can band together to study improved communication, information needs, educational technology, teacher preparation, metropolitanization, exchange programs, instructional material, special education programs, preschool programs, and the role of state education agencies.

A number of government agencies are sponsoring or could sponsor educational research in Massachusetts. There are also regional managers and sponsors of research, such as the New England Regional Commission on Occupational Education. Some federal funds go directly to local school districts or special projects.

The following state government bodies are the typical sponsors of educational R&D in Massachusetts:

Massachusetts Advisory Council on Education: Long-range and short-term research. Nominations to boards of education

Massachusetts Board of Education: Sponsors and manages a wide variety of R&D activities using federal funding. Recently established an Educational Planning Council.

Massachusetts Board of Higher Education: The Board is a planning and coordinating Board with natural proclivities, using money from a variety of sources, for sponsoring studies as a major component of its activities.

Secretary of Education: New position, appointed in December 1971. A potential for mounting research projects is contained in the idea of a secretary of education. As yet, it is unclear how much or what kind of R&D activities the secretary might wish to sponsor.

Office of Program Planning and Coordination: This office, rested in the secretary of administration, may sponsor research. Its role is unclear under the Massachusetts state reorganization plan.

Legislative and Governor's Commissions: When necessary, a commission can be effected by the Legislature or the Governor. A recent Legislative commission looked at the problems created by the closing down of Catholic schools. A Governor's Commission, one with Council funding, is looking at school districting issues.

The Department of Education still conducts the greatest dollar volume of educational research in Massachusetts, particularly through its Educational Planning Committee and Research, Planning and Evaluation Division.

The principal information service provided by the Department is its town and city wide collection of data with respect to pupils and reimbursable expenditures. State aid to towns and cities for education depends upon the collection and verification of these data. Each school superintendent must give the Commissioner of Education by July first a sworn and certified statement on expenditures by the system (legally by the school committee). The nine accounting categories are as follows: (1) administration; (2) instruction; (3) other school services (attendance, health services, pupil transportation, food services, and other student-body activities); (4) operation and maintenance of plant; (5) fixed charges; (6) community services; (7) acquisition of fixed assets; (8) debt retirement; and (9) programs with other districts (in Massachusetts and other states). The Commissioner, in turn, must give a certified statement of these figures to the State Comptroller and the State Taxation Commission by December 31st.

Each school system superintendent also must submit a sworn statement to the Commissioner of Education by 1 December of each year on pupil statistics. This requirement is based on the annual October pupil census. The amount of state aid to towns and cities for education under Chapter 70 is determined by the Department's R&D Division and by the Commissioner on the basis of these figures. The school committees of towns and cities must assume legal responsibility for the accuracy of all figures and other data which they submit.

Information must also be gathered to assure that various minimum standards (the number of school days in a year, etc.) are being met.

Thus, the need is clear for an expanded investment in the funding of state educational research and the Advisory Council can be a useful model in meeting these freshly perceived needs.

Whether implementation has resulted from a MACE study or is a conse-quence of other factors can become an endless and futile debate. Indeed, many of the recommendations put forth by MACE have mixed origins. Past state studies of the same or similar issues, for instance, are always, and appro-priately so, reviewed by study directors for redeemable recommendations. the Council runs some risk in either unabashed credit-seeking or in fading out of sight when a study is completed and the implementation phase is called for. We are persuaded that the second course is the one that will prove of more benefit to MACE. In the final analysis, improving the educational scene and generously crediting appropriate agencies will be the surest base upon to build the credibility of MACE.

The central purpose of MACE is still to conduct studies intended to improve education in Massachusetts. To date, the Council has produced 23 and has presented these studies to other appropriate agencies for action. Thirteen of the major studies, undertaken and completed by the Council, are reviewed in the next dozen chapters (two studies of special education are reviewed together) to demonstrate some of the uses of MACE. These examples of what MACE has undertaken will show the range of its work and its approaches to study areas.

At a time when education is pressed to assume new roles and responsibilities, the Advisory Council can serve as a guide to others in coping with old educa-tional needs and new urgencies at the state level. The chapters that follow are organized into three parts, with a final chapter designed to demonstrate an increasing role and relevance for the Advisory Council.

Part I shows various treatments of traditional systems. Here, the Council was called upon to grapple with real structures that were hardly eager to embrace an outside study team and the changes they would likely recommend. Yet, the quartet of studies in Part One, dealing with the Department of Education, the business management of school districts, the organization of school districts, and the management of Boston's schools, has helped to start and guide major efforts at implementation.

Part II contains four studies of fragmented services and programs in need of elevation and expansion and proper attendance from a central agency. The national neglect of these areas, in particular adult education, early childhood services, and programs of special education, meant that MACE's consultants had virtually to invent a new system for each area.

The third part of this book involves a visit, by way of separate studies, to four conventional program packages — occupational education, guidance programs, high schools and teacher training programs — which have survived, too little changed, under the impact of studies, rhetoric and turned off students. Teacher training and certification are actually changing in a few states. Guidance still slumbers. High school administrators generally continue to pretend that a dropped dress code here and a bow in the direction of a little more flexibility there will get them off the hook. Yet, some high schools are beginning to take reform seriously and the Department of Education is encouraging these early steps on the part of a few.

Thus, the three parts will attempt to show the Council in action. An introductory section to each part will discuss (a) the directions and other details of the studies, and (b) the impacts of the studies on various areas.

Part I
Retooling the System

If you don't pay attention to organization, you soon find that it is determining the philosophy and goals of your enterprise. - John Gardner

Today, as was true close to a century ago, Massachusetts possesses an educational system full of "firsts" but it lacks ability to assemble these firsts into a first-rate educational system across the board. - Richard de Lone, 1971

Recognizing the importance of the means used to achieve an end, MACE, from May 1969 to January 1971, looked at four organization systems of inestimable importance to the Commonwealth. Two hundred thousand dollars of Council funds went into comprehensive studies of the Department of Education, Boston's public school management system, school district organization and the noninstructional functions of public schools. From these four studies, MACE came up with an overall picture of traditional systems and organizations and a body of concrete recommendations for improvement in the delivery of educational programs services.

We turn first to a study done by John S. Gibson, Director of the Lincoln-Filene Center at Tufts University, who produced a carefully documented study of the Department entitled: *The Massachusetts Department of Education: Proposals for Progress in the 70's.* His study, costing $32,000, is the most comprehensive and detailed accounting of the internal operations of that system ever undertaken.

In December 1969, under Warren King and associates, with the strong support of the Governor, MACE selected a group of top business and industrial executives to look at the noninstructional features of public schools. Their findings were written in a *Report of the Massachusetts Business Task Force for School Management*, which stresses planning, school district cooperation and an effective information system and indicates that massive savings over current school expenditures are feasible. The study cost MACE $75,000 and the loan by private companies of 36 executives was estimated as worth an additional $200,000.

This collaboration between industry and educators proved so successful that the Task Force Study Committee incorporated and continues to serve in an advisory capacity under the auspices of the Council.

Perhaps no major aspect of educational organization has been as ignored as an area of study than school districting. In *Organizing for A Child's Learning*

31

Experiences: A Report on A Study of School District Organization in Massa-chusetts, Donald T. Donley, then Dean of the School of Education at Boston College, found a pattern of school district organization more suited to the last century than the needs of the 1970s. Using $33,000 of Council funds, Donley's study was viewed as a prelude to a larger effort, which is currently underway by the Council.

To Joseph M. Cronin, recently appointed to the new Massachusetts post of Secretary of Education, fell the task of studying the Boston's public school management system in 1969. Dr. Cronin spent months in obtaining not only the consent and active interest of the Boston School Committee but also $12,000 of their funds to add to the $47,000 contracted for from MACE. In all, Dr. Cronin found a total of $91,000 to conduct his study. Sensitive to the need for a document of interest and value to other urban centers in Massa-chusetts, he produced *Organizing an Urban School System for Diversity* a compendium ranging from general guidelines to very specific recommendations meant to be useable in all of the Commonwealth's aging and troubled cities.

In its four studies of the organization of education, MACE has found common themes. For instance, the Business Task Force report gave top priority to five major needs:

1. a good information system;
2. long range planning;
3. coordination among school districts;
4. adequate financing; and
5. trained talent.

These overall themes are picked up and echoed in concrete examples of a number of other studies. As another instance, studies of compensatory education, pupil services, the State Department, and the high schools of the state, all echo the need for long-range planning, better prepared manpower and the necessity for leadership at the state level. This mutuality and reciprocity of themes is important because taken together the studies constitute a "critical mass." That is, they present an overwhelming accretion of evidence around a core of basic conclusions that urge, by their persistence and ubiquity, the need for fundamental systematic change. The recurrance of the same underlying structural flaws suggests strongly that piecemeal efforts at change are doomed to minimal success at best.

State Department of Education

Remarkable and promising changes have occurred in the Department subsequent to the release of the Gibson report. At first, Department reactions to the report were cool. Nonetheless, a blue-ribbon committee was drawn together to produce a set of goals and objectives for the Department as Gibson recommended. Other changes were slower in coming but the Department has set in motion a variety of reforms over a broad front.

The Gibson report and other Advisory Council reports, in particular the business task force report, have at least contributed to the following needed internal changes in the Department.

1. A major internal reorganization is underway. A Bureau of School District Cooperation and a Bureau of Business Management have been added to the Department.
2. A student has been added to the State Board of Education and student organizations are active under Department sponsorship.
3. Goals and objectives and a list of imperatives have been established to guide public elementary and secondary education in the state.
4. Information and regional services have been expanded.
5. Fresh key personnel have been recruited for the Department.
6. Communication between the Department and others state and local education segments has reached an all-time high.

Other changes have been pervasive, beginning with strengthening the office of the Commissioner of Education and adding one more deputy commissioner to changing the roles and responsibilities of a number of the divisions and bureaus. Figure 2-1 shows the present organization of the Department of Education. Organizational modifications are still unfolding, based upon a healthy sense of the need both to catch up and even to overtake changes in education.

Increasingly, as Gibson called for, the Department is taking a leadership role while also stepping up services to school districts. While internal changes in the Department can benefit school districts and help change the complextion of education in the Bay State, other changes, as John Gibson so well documents, will also be necessary to complete any transformation.

Gibson, ahead of all others who have studied the Department, was able to master its array of functions and present them in a lucid form. Since the Department had been a kind of house of mystery to many, Gibson's treatise on the way things work and who does what may be viewed as a high point of the study.

Business Task Force

The business task force report lighted the way to the future. The Department has acted on a number of the report's recommendations including the establishment of the Bureau of Business Management. The Bureau was established to assist school districts with management problems (see Chart 5). At the same time,

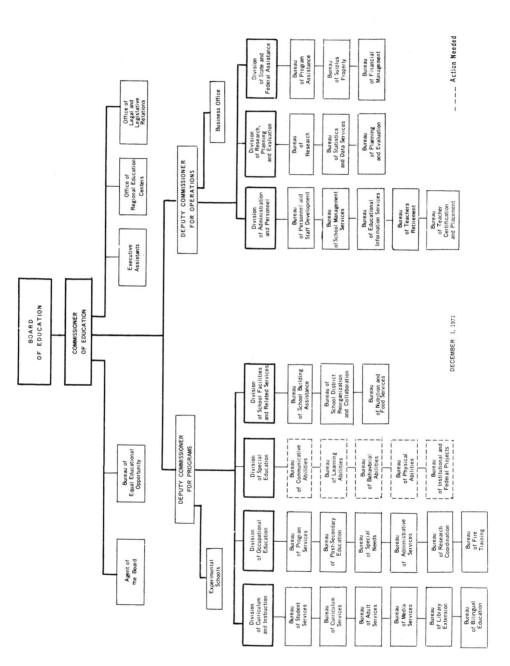

Figure 2-1. The Commonwealth of Massachusetts Department of Education. Source: Massachusetts Depart-

a federal grant has led to a district needs assessment and support program, under
the rubric of a new agency, named the Institute for Educational Services, which
will borrow heavily on the findings and recommendations of the Task Force
report.

A 15-member business task force planning committee has been working
for a year on implementation of the recommendations of the final report. One
product of this group is a directory of businesses and industries prepared
to provide management consulting of the Department and local schools in a
variety of areas and on a voluntary basis.

Because of the great interest in information systems, the task force section
which deals with a local management information system (LEMIS) is described
in its entirety in Chapter 3. LEMIS is meant to complement a proposed state-
wide information system.

Of special note in our review is the range and detail of the recommendations.
Taken on the whole, they represent a comprehensive checklist of needed modifications and reforms useable with most departments of education.

Problems remain including many cited in Advisory Council studies. The
rapidly implemented reorganization design has caused some stress and the final
work on its efficacy is not in. On balance, the changes favor the development
of a dynamic and toughened department more oriented to leadership and field
activities than to inward matters.

School Districting

Virtually every MACE study director has been perplexed and bothered by
the crazy quilt pattern of school districting in the Bay State. Massachusetts, an
urbanizing state with few significant natural barriers, has jammed almost 400
school districts within its borders. Some of these districts are beginning to
relate, but most pretend that the outside world is just that. Too often, school
districts meet only on football fields. Somehow, the state has bypassed school
districting as a problem. Where, MACE study directors and other students
of educational organization have asked themselves, has Massachusetts been?
Other states have been consolidating school districts and developing sophisticated
collaborative arrangements for almost 40 years.

Two basic approaches to school districting are recommended in Advisory
Council studies. The first calls for strengthening the state structure, while the
second emphasis is a community approach. Neither approach is proposed in a
pure form and usually the difference depends upon whether the Department of
Education is the focus of the study or the school districts themselves. For
instance, Gibson tells us to develop further the Department's regional offices
with the expectation that inter-district activities will, in time, be fostered.

The issue in such approaches revolves around the question of who will be the servant and who will be the master. This issue and others will be thrashed out in a commission on school districting which has been established as both the business task force and Donley recommended.

In a collaborative venture, the Board of Education and MACE worked out a detailed charge for a commission to study school districting and asked the governor to appoint the commission. The commission's goal is to increase equitable access to resources in public education at the elementary and secondary level. The commission will address itself not only to the benefits that may be achieved through consolidation and cooperation of school districts but will examine the whole question of the rationalization of school districting. It is charged to probe such issues as racial imbalance and metropolitanism as well as the problems of smaller and often poorer school districts which need to obtain their share of educational resources.

The commission's work will extend over a two-year period and is currently funded by MACE at the level of $200,000. Efforts are underway to add further to the funds and make other resources available to the commission. It will conduct a series of informal public hearings designed to foster communication and create visibility for these issues and to build constituencies for change. Discussions will be held with students early on in order to guide the commission in recasting school district organization for those most vitally affected by it.

As work progresses, it is expected that collaborative arrangements will be initiated by the school districts on the conviction that some important forms of collaboration need and must not wait on the final report of the commission. The commission will engage a study director and staff to produce documents basic in its deliberations.

It is not the intent of the commission to recommend a rigid, one-model organizational system to Massachusetts. Indeed, several systems will likely be recommended, with localities given the tools to help communities decide the kinds of acceptable organizational patterns that seem to suit them. Changes in the statutes may have to be proposed and it is likely that the role and responsibility of the Department will have to be shaped to ready it to assist consolidation and collaborative efforts of all kinds.

Boston School System

Many share the sense that little can be done about city school systems except through radical change. Joseph Cronin's job was to show that changes were possible and that Boston's public education system could move ahead.

Conventional wisdom has it that city schools are impervious to change. Bankrupt traditions and shallow rituals have overtaken the human and social purpose of urban education.

Boston's school system, once proudly at the summit, is in a spiral of decline. Schooling in Boston becomes yearly more expensive and less effective. Once capable of leadership and innovation, Boston schools, convulsed by crises, merely survive.

Realizing the ills of urban education in general, Joseph M. Cronin, at the request of MACE, took on the management problems of the Boston School system. He found more candor and willingness to discuss the issues on the part of key people associated with the school bureaucracy than he expected. The talk of issues led to talk about possible answers. Many able people in the system were more than ready to discuss and work for reform.

Cronin also made a major effort to pull in those outside the system who possessed resources (and needs) useful to the students of Boston. To this end, he established close working relationships with a variety of public and private institutions, including the Department of Education.

Cronin's greatest challenge and central purpose was to recommend a reorganization that would transfer more decision-making from Boston School Committee Headquarters to the school and the communities they serve. Repeatedly, Cronin found appropriate ways in his report to return to the importance and uses of decentralization.

Using an Irish softness in writing his final report, Cronin nevertheless made his point strongly that there were few things really right about the Boston system. Little was overlooked as he recommended changes in not only the composition of the school committee but also in the custodied structure.

On the day the report was released, Boston's school Superintendent, William Ohrenberger, announced a major reorganization of the Boston system, intended to decentralize decision-making. Carefully studied by many of Boston's schoolmen, a number of recommendations have been implemented throughout the system. As Cronin recommended, the funding of vocational programs has increased dramatically. Greater parental involvement with Boston's schools were encouraged by Dr. Cronin's report as were off-campus academic programs planned and begun in collaboration with local universities.

The Cronin study represents the best example to date of a MACE report which brought a wide range of organizations and groups together with Boston schoolmen. Businessmen, for instance, sat side-by-side with high officials in the Boston school system and both were able to engage in a free and frank exchange of problems and hopes centering on educational matters. Both groups were able to see that working closely together would benefit the education of children and youth.

Obviously, what Dr. Cronin has written about Boston applies in many ways to other urban school systems in Massachusetts and elsewhere. In particular, the Cronin report is a helpful guide for a badly needed change in relationships among schoolmen and others.

The following chapters will demonstrate how various MACE studies have approached on-going educational systems and organizations in need of change.

While change is a fact of life in the twentieth century, it is unattractive merely as an end in itself. To make sense, the thrust of change must be to move the educational enterprise toward an increased sense of responsibility.

Unless otherwise indicated, references are to studies conducted by the Advisory Council.

2 The State Department of Education

Clearly the time has come for this state to regain its former position as the unparalleled leader of public education in the nation. This is the challenge we offer, and we hope that this study will contribute toward that end. - John S. Gibson

What is needed are strong state boards of education, a first class chief school officer, a well-organized state staff, and good support from the Legislature. - James B. Conant

What can study directors say to inform and to inspire department of education? In what elegant design can they combine facts and feelings with perspectives and recommendations to arouse a desired response? Departments seem always to be arriving and never arrived. Swinging awkwardly between local school systems and the awesome and jealously guarded powers of the state legislature, state departments hang on tenaciously. The effects of such an uncomfortable position are described by Edwald B. Nyguist, Commissioner of Education in New York.

Budgets are usually inadequate, and restrictions in expenditures make even available funds difficult to use effectively. The conditions of employment, personnel policies, salary schedules, and travel regulations - often geared to state agencies not having comparable professional responsibilities - make hard and frustrating the recruitment and retention of qualified personnel. State superintendents of commissioners of education are seldom paid salaries as high as those paid to the large city superintendents in their own states. In the face of these conditions, state education departments have been flooded with new administrative responsibilities for federal programs. They often find themselves with more money than talent.

Internally, some state education departments are plagued by antiquated structure and organization; others operate without benefit of fully developed research and data systems or without adequate provisions for statewide study, evaluation, and planning; most lack appropriately prepared and experienced personnel in numbers sufficient to achieve and sustain desired levels of leadership and service. And without all of these, of course, there can be no vision, no ability to point to a better way or to help others see what is possible - no capacity to raise local levels of educational expectations.

Too many departments, like state legislatures, are rurally oriented and

lack the stature, inclination, and competence to deal with urban education
– the intense, concentrated problems of large cities, including high costs,
racial imbalance, organized and militant teacher groups, and the disadvantaged. And too few departments have any function in higher education,
which makes more difficult the administration of certain federal acts (the
Vocational Education Act of 1963, for one) and the fostering of cooperation between different components of the educational system.[1]

Departments of education have generally been kept weak and have been
expected to play only timid roles in local educational matters. Governors and
legislators have does little to develop sinew in debilitated departments. Given the
educational powers that reside in the states, such grudging support is both
short-sighted and educationally costly.

The times demand change. A host of tough issues have emerged that call
for dynamic leadership at the state level and for adequate resources to attack
educational problems. John Fischer, former Columbia Teachers College President,
writes "The sovereign is now called upon to be also a leader, and to some state
officers, this comes as a shock. . . ."[2]

A new sense of power and responsibility at the state level is causing hasty
reassessments of old shibboleths not only in education but elsewhere. Survival
into the twenty-first century depends in large measure upon how things
traditionally given over to the states will be handled by them. Welfare, transportation, correctional institutions, zoning and environmental controls are awesome
responsibilities for 50 states to handle. Education, always viewed as a major
state responsibility, is equally subject to a new awakening.

The Willis-Harrington report faced up to only part of the task of regrouping
the State Department of Education. Expecting revitalization to happen from
within, the report called for a lay Board of Education and for five strong
divisions: (1) research and development; (2) physical facilities; (3) curriculum
and instruction; (4) administration and personnel; and (5) federal, state and
local liaison. The changes recommended by the Willis-Harrington Commission
were in themselves inadequate and the spirit in which implementation took
place left much to be desired. The Department continued in the main to plod,
neglect, obfuscate and meander. Given more and specific powers by the
statutes developed from the Willis-Harrington Commission, things still didn't
jell. The needed resources to inform itself and to act responsibly on these
powers continued to be denied by a disenchanted legislature. As is often the
case, however, the picture was not uniformly grim. Federal funds were used
by the Department to expand the professional staff and offer localities more but
still inadequate support services. Many talented and dedicated persons in the
Department struggled to bring about improvement. Too often, achievements

went unrecognized and at times were even frowned upon by a system frozen in time.

Political scientist John S. Gibson began a study of the Massachusetts Department of Education (MDE) with less than enthusiastic support from the department's upper echelons. Some opposition was based upon doubts that MACE had the legal authority to study MDE. Another counter held that MDE had been too much studied. But many in MDE, especially the junior professionals, looked forward to a study, and "outside forces," who were made aware of the effort to study the department, urged a prompt beginning and a candid report of the results. In particular, the Massachusetts Education Conference Board, an amalgam of educational organizations, pressed for the study and gave its full support to the venture.

Still, it is doubtful that the study would have been undertaken without the arrival of a new Commissioner of Education, Dr. Neil V. Sullivan. Dr. Sullivan, fresh from victory in resolving a difficult racial imbalance problem in Berkeley, California, welcomed the study and encouraged MACE to fund the project.

In his final report, Gibson, not insensitive to skeptics, told why his report was needed and timely. First, he pointed to the need for a "five-year follow-up" of the Willis-Harrington Study which contained several sections dealing with the MDE.

He also indicated that a Secretary of Educational Affairs was soon to be appointed in Massachusetts. Finally and inevitably, he linked the state's historic past educational achievements to current unmet needs.

Once the study had been agreed upon, all members of the department cooperated fully with Gibson and his staff. The study director found that he needed all the help he could get.

Gibson was determined to learn everything he could about the department and to describe fully and carefully what he found. Easier said than done. Little that was published about MDE contributed more than general background material. Few publications by the department or others turned out to be highly useful. Gibson had to rely on primary sources which drained his resources and limited his activities. Thus, the study director and his staff found the way largely uncharted. The department was itself a landlord in an unknown world.

Gibson remained dogged in sticking with the objectives he had sketched in his proposal to MACE:

1. to examine the current internal operations and performance of external functions (leadership, service, and regulation) by the Department; and
2. to recommend how these operations and functions might translate the study's recommendations into public policy.

The Yesterdays in Massachusetts Public Education

The history of Massachusetts as a colony set the stage for educational firsts. These included the establishment of the Boston Latin School in 1635, the first public school with continuous existence. "Ye College in Cambridge" (Harvard) followed in 1636, as did the first public school (in Dorchester) supported by direct taxation of town inhabitants. The first school law was passed by the General Court in 1642 and required town officials to make certain that parents were educating their children. The local minister was given authority to license teachers, and thus the role of the church in this "Satan Deluder" law was quite evident. Five years later, every town of 50 families was ordered to construct a school, and towns of 100 families or more had to have a grammar school. Of course, many of these schools were supported by parents as well as by public funds; however, the principle of public commitment to education became well established by the middle of the seventeenth century.

As the eighteenth century emerged, the role of the church began to diminish, and each community assumed more and more authority over its schools. The Massachusetts Constitution of 1780 minced no words whatever about the function and value of education to our citizens. The following is a representative passage.

> . . . it shall be the duty of legislatures and magistrates, in all future periods of this Commonwealth, to cherish the interests of literature and the sciences, and all seminaries of them; especially the university at Cambridge, public schools and grammar schools in the towns; to encourage private societies and public institutions, rewards and immunities, for the promotion of agriculture, arts, sciences, commerce, trades, manufactures, and a natural history of the country; to countenance and inculate the principles of humanity and general benevolence, public and private charity, industry, and frugality, honesty and punctuality in their dealings; sincerity, good humor, and all social affections, and generous sentiments, among the people.[3]

The early nineteenth century witnessed passage by the Massachusetts General Court of an increasing number of laws pertaining to public education, including the first state law (1827) on the establishment of public high schools. It was now becoming increasingly clear that the expanding public educational system in the Commonwealth, accompanied by mandates and policies on education emanating from the General Court, necessitated the creation of a bureau to coordinate the state's educational program. Thus, the General Court established the first State Board of Education in 1837. Its first Secretary was Horace Mann.

The middle and end of the nineteenth century found Massachusetts riding high on a wave of educational firsts in such areas as school attendance, kindergartens, (not yet, however, fully established in the Commonwealth), teachers' salaries, antidiscrimination, classes for the mentally retarded and vocational education, among others.

In 1909, the position of Commissioner of Education was established, replacing the Secretary of the Board. Following constitutional changes in 1917, a Department of Education was established in 1919 with eight special boards and divisions.

The fabled James Michael Curley, many times mayor of Boston and governor of the state for one term, extended the last hurrah to the Board of Education. The incursion of politics weakened the Board. In 1947, the Legislature reorganized the Board, gave the commissioner several duties and virtually no power. Things began to take a slight turn for the better in the late forties. Regional districts were encouraged by a 1948 legislative act, discussed in greater length in Chapter IV. The nation's first racial imbalance law was passed, giving the Board authority to withhold funds for noncompliance.

The National Defense Education Act of 1958 and, of course, the Elementary and Secondary Education Act of 1965 brought about tremendous changes in public education in Massachusetts, as in all other states. Funds became available for adding specialists to the Department in such academic areas as English, the humanities, social studies, mathematics, and the sciences. Inservice programs for teachers, aid to libraries, school lunch assistance, special education projects and personnel, guidance specialists, and many other vital areas of education were greatly strengthened with federal funds and programs. The staff and responsibilities of the MDE rapidly expanded, and the Federal-state-local partnership in education now faced new and exciting frontiers.

On the other hand, as the impact of federal involvement in education became clear in the early 1960s, it also was evident to many that the 1947 organization for public education in the Commonwealth called for considerable overhauling. Therefore, in the early fall of 1962, the General Court of the Commonwealth established a Willis-Harrington Commission.

At least four significant points emerge from this indulgence in the annals of the past. In the first place, history demonstrates that there was never any doubt in this Commonwealth of the importance of education to the values, achievement, and life opportunities of our young people. Second, the pioneering achievements of public education in Massachusetts should give state citizens a deep pride in the past and a zest for projecting this record into the future. Third, the Bay State has from the beginning placed in the public officials of towns and cities responsibility and trust for advancing the education of young people. Fourth, it is evident that from every perspective, the power and authority for public education in the Commonwealth is vested in the General Court and the agencies delegated by that body to carry out this vital mission. History, tradition, and the concept of local authority over the lives and destinies of young and old alike cannot in any way replace the constitutional authority and responsibility of the state in education, unless, of course, the state neglects exercising appropriate power and authority. This point is vital in examining the boards and Department of Education over the past five years.

A Study of MDE

In evaluating the operations and functions of the department (MDE), six approaches to inquiry and assessment were utilized by Gibson and his study staff: (1) interviews; (2) questionnaires; (3) studies of and by the MDE and various departmental publications; (4) studies of departments of education in general; (5) studies of specific departments of education in the United States; and (6) studies of the political and legislative aspects and processes of public education.

Staff members had approximately 70 interviews with members of the staff of the MDE, and 70 interviews with some members of the General Court, professional educators, and attentive publics throughout the state. Some MDE staff members were interviewed two or three times. Most interviews lasted between thirty minutes and an hour. About 20 people were interviewed by phone. Interviews were subjected to a general content analysis allowing the staff to identify trends and patterns with respect to specific operations and functions of the MDE. Additional information was gathered at Cabinet meetings at the MDE and meetings of the Board of Education, as well as at many informal discussions with Board members and with Commissioner Sullivan, Deputy Commissioner Curtin, and the Associate and Assistant Commissioners. In October 1969, Gibson's staff also distributed 500 questionnaires to members of the department staff.

By selecting the director of the Lincoln Filene Center for Citizenship and Public Affairs to conduct the study, MACE received a bonus. The 1970 Tufts Assembly on Massachusetts government, held on March 19, 1970, was devoted to an analysis and criticism of a draft of the Gibson document. Two prominant local reporters, Ian Forman and Nina McCain, were asked to deliver critiques to the more than 200 educators and attentive citizens assembled. Later, the audience was grouped by interest for further discussions.

Gibson's preliminary report was treated roughly by many of those in attendance. It was accused, in turn, of being (1) obvious in its findings and lacking penetration; (2) less than candid in times demanding candor; (3) conventional in its solutions; and (4) without a clear focus on just who could do something to improve the department.

The occasion was used by some to express their vexation with the department. Perhaps most revealing of all was the number of persons there who showed vast ignorance about MDE or who had had trouble with one bureau in the department and were prepared to castigate the entire operation.

Gibson was able to sharpen his final report considerably after the results were in from the Assembly. The Assembly, therefore, served a purpose as a sounding board and critic.

Findings of the Report

Slightly over one half of the 560 positions in the Department are professional. Gibson found 140 vacancies with about 70 at the professional level. Such figures tell a great deal.

The vast majority of the 265 members of the professional staff of the Department come from public school systems in the Commonwealth, and most of them had held administrative or teaching positions in these school systems. It is difficult to document the reasons why educators choose to work for the Department. Certainly, it is not because the Department offers high salaries. Most superintendents of schools in the Commonwealth receive salaries equal to or higher than those of Associate and Assistant Commissioners, and other administrative and top teacher salaries in public school systems generally rank well above parallel positions in the Department (bureau directors, senior supervisors, and supervisors). At least six superintendents of schools in Massachusetts currently have higher salaries than does Commissioner Sullivan (whose annual salary is $30,000). Salary, of course, is not the only factor in attracting people of considerable talent and skill to professional positions in education and in keeping them on the job as well. The inadequate salary scales in the Department, however, coupled with lack of fiscal autonomy with respect to professional personnel, hardly permit the Department to be competitive with other private and public educational institutions in attracting and keeping a staff which can meet its many responsibilities. With approximately 28 percent the professional positions vacant, the turnover of these people from July 1968 to January 1970 amounted to 22 percent. Young, low-grade professionals were marking time for about fifteen months before securing employment elsewhere.

Gibson used the following questionnaire results to illustrate communication needs and to diagnose the implied problems and professional need. On communications within "your" division, 34 people replied *no* or *none*; 42, *very little* or *very bad*; 30, *moderately little* or *moderately bad*; 27, *satisfactory*; 20 *moderately good*; and 21, *very good*. On communications within a specific bureau, the staff replied within the above six categories as follows: *no* or *none*, 19; *very little* 18; *moderately little*, 26; *satisfactory*, 34; *moderately good*, 27; *very good*. Gibson also asked a question of "horizontal" communications where informal sharing can operate. He reports:

> This process does not take place unless there are informal communications and sharing of information among people who hold the same positions,

but serve in other bureaus and divisions. Our interviews reported this
quite heavily, as did responses from our MDE questionnaire on horizontal
communications: 59 reported *none*; 32, *very bad*; 26, *moderately little*;
27, *satisfactory;* 18, *moderately good*; 7, *very good*.

. . . Researchers tell us that lack of horizontal communications tends
to produce considerable duplication of work and repetition of duties
which could have been prevented by better administration and communications. Lack of horizontal communications also results in some tasks
never being carried out because it was "assumed" that someone else . . .
was taking care of the matter.[4]

A kind of pentagon syndrome seemed to have taken hold even among so
small a group of professionals as was found in the department. The Department
of Education, for many reasons, continues to carry out a wide variety of
mandated functions, most of which have little to do with educational leadership
or have any visible impact on improving education. The vision and recommendations of the study by the Willis-Harrington Commission in 1965, especially
those calling for leadership and quality of educational services, for the most
part have not been translated into educational policy. The Commission and the
resulting legislation did bring about many structural changes in the administration
of public education at the state level. So far as the Department of Education is
concerned, however, there have been very few improvements during the past
five years in its operations or its performance of external functions. As was
emphasized throughout this study, schools are students, and they have yet to
see the benefits of the Willis-Harrington recommendations.

The Massachusetts Department of Education is by no means solely
responsible for this remarkable lack of progress, although there is much the
Department could have done and can do to advance quality education for
students. A recurring theme throughout this study is that the executive branch
of Massachusetts government, especially the Office of Administration and
Finance (A&F), the General Court; the Board of Education, and to a lesser
extent, Massachusetts public school educators and the public at large have
all contributed to this situation. The governor has not provided the leadership
or the visibility needed by public education. The Office of Administration
and Finance, in many instances, has adversely affected conduct of internal
operations by the MDE and thus its performance of external functions. Specifically, many A&F decisions with respect to the Education Department's personnel and budget are most questionable. The General Court has imposed
upon the Department mandates and other statutory requirements without, in
many cases, giving consideration to the manifold and diffuse implications of
these mandates and without providing the Department with the resources to
perform the assigned tasks. The Board of Education, although a hard-working
group in general and inundated with a morass of problems and mandated
obligations, has not provided leverages of influence and political power needed

by the department. In particular, the Board, appointed by the governor, has not sought from the Governor and his office support for the Department on major issues. Many public school educators and the public at large feel free to criticize the department without realizing its numerous problems and obligations and without helping to muster the political and public support so essential for change and progress. The great lack of coordination, determination, initiative, and information in public school education has, more than anything else, contributed toward inequality of educational opportunity in this state and has not advanced quality education for some 1,150,000 students. Unless this situation is remedied, the present balance between the state and the local communities in the administration of public education will radically change.

Mandates given to the department by the General Court are operational in the sense that the department is called on *to perform a myriad of functions that are important, but routine and unimaginative*. There are no overall mandates to the department for educational leadership and for performing services to schools and to students which are likely to advance school achievement and thus life opportunities and options for the students. Because of legislation, policy, and traditions, the more than 500 members of the department's staff carry out bureaucratic tasks that are needed, but which do not reflect the Willis-Harrington recommendations for leadership and quality of services. These tasks include mandated functions in adult education, school lunches, health and library services, teacher retirement, collecting and processing information from the schools, and many others. Federal funds earmarked for strengthening the department are used by the division of research and development to perform functions mandated by the General Court (especially collecting and processing information and reports from the schools). *If it is the will of the General Court and the Board of Education that the Department should serve in this routine manner, then, on the whole, the Department is doing what is expected of it, but not as well as it could.*

The Gibson study leads to these overview observations about the operations and functions of the Department of Education.

A.   Problems in Operations
 1. Inadequate overall administration of the internal operations of the MDE.
 2. Lack of coordination of many operations and functions, thus resulting in duplication of effort, inefficient administration, and confusion to the publics the Department seeks to serve. Specific areas of diffusion of operations and functions are public relations and information, legislation, financial decision-making and funding, adult education, special education, and pupil services.
 3. Bureaucratic red tape and antiquated procedures in the business operations, producing inexcusable delays in reimbursement of staff for expense monies and of consultants for services rendered.

4. Poor supervision over allocation of funds within the MDE and to non-MDE agencies.

5. Totally inadequate internal and external communications and information to educational publics.

6. Inadequate procedures to collect feedback from educational publics about the Department and to utilize this feedback for improvement.

7. Remarkably little planning for one year ahead, let alone for what will take place in education during the 1970s.

8. Insufficient information about student performance from the state's public school systems in the systems' annual reports to the Department, and practically no information in these reports about nonpublic schools.

9. In the area of legislation:
   a) MDE-sponsored legislation generally not oriented toward educational needs of students.
   b) Poor coordination with educational groups and agencies.
   c) Little political muscle exercised by the Board of Education in support of legislation.
   d) Little coordination with legislation not sponsored by the Department.

10. In the area of personnel:
   a) Inadequate pay and travel money, although this is not the fault of the Department.
   b) Meaningless job titles and job specifications, again not entirely the fault of the Department.
   c) Little horizontal communication among personnel.
   d) Ineffective people occupying some important professional positions.
   e) Inadequate directions of personnel; no inservice training.
   f) Inefficient utilization of professional manpower resources.

11. MDE central office is not conducive to efficient and effective office work.

12. Overall confusion about priorities for operations which support the performance of external functions.

B. Performance of External Functions:

1. External functions (leadership, services, and regulation) appear to have little connection with services in the Commonwealth's schools which can advance student achievement and the life opportunities and options for these students.

2. Because the internal operations of the Department are poorly organized for efficient and effective performance of external functions, professional staff who should be in the field spend more than half of their time at 182 Tremont Street. Available Department services are not widely known about in the state, and the regional offices are not being utilized nearly as much as they should be.

3. The Department is not well organized to serve students in urban areas, such as Boston, Springfield, and Worcester. It places little focus on urban education as such, including racial and ethnic mixes of students in schools, teaching-learning processes, inservice education of teachers, or issues affecting dropout rates and student alienation.

4. Although the Racial Imbalance Act represents a major leadership thrust by the Department, both the Act and measures taken under the Act have not received the critical review during the past five years they deserve. In particular, the Act does not address itself to integrated education through teaching-learning processes and the imperative need for inservice education for teachers. The big question is whether social and political conditions will be stable long enough for the Boston plan for new school construction to materialize so that there will be racially balanced schools in the city's communities where there are concentrations of nonwhite students. Of greatest importance, however, is the fact that the Act does not address itself to racism and racial imbalance in communities where there are few or no nonwhite students. The basic implication of the Act is that there is poor education-race relations in schools with 50 percent or more nonwhites. Little or nothing has been done, however, to deal with poor education-race relations in schools and systems where school population is 50 percent or more white.

5. Chapter 70 of the General Laws dealing with state aid to local communities is inadequate and must be revised and fully funded.

6. Because of inadequate funding, the Division of Research and Development does little research and development. At present, it is an information collection agency and a service unit to school systems in the area of business practices.

7. The Department is ill-equipped to "regulate" in terms of enforcing mandates imposed on it and the state's public schools. School officials throughout the state know this, and their deviations from standards adversely affect the Department's status and education in general.

8. The Department's efforts to date to provide minimum standards for courses have only yielded outlines that are still in the draft stage. This might be a blessing, since we hold that the Department should have only minimal responsibilities for curriculum so far as minimum standards are concerned and that the General Court should have no role whatsoever in the content and structure of curriculum.

9. The total range of Department services and regulatory authority is not generally well known or understood among educators in the Commonwealth, and the Department, for the most part, must accept the responsibility for this situation.

10. The Department has insufficiently tapped the vast educational resources in the Commonwealth. It has not successfully adapted

many operations and functions of other departments of education in the United States for improving its own operations and functions.

Recommendations for Improving Operations and Performance of External Functions

Recommendation One. *The Department must have authority to hire, retain, and promote professional personnel at salary levels that parallel or exceed those of some of the best public schools in the Commonwealth.*

Top priority should go to giving the Department flexibility in hiring, retaining, and promoting professional personnel of high quality. Unless the Department is staffed with educators and administrators who command professional respect and esteem among public school educators and other citizens in the Commonwealth, its capacity to assume educational leadership and to provide school services of high quality will continue to be severely limited.

Many of the present personnel in the Department are educators and administrators of first rank, but our inquiries and the findings of this study convince us that the Department is not competitive with our best school systems in attracting and retaining professional educators of high quality. Therefore, it cannot carry out its many tasks satisfactorily and cannot service the school systems of the Commonwealth effectively. Without quality in professional personnel, the other recommendations which follow will be of little value.

The Board of Education and the Department should have the prime authority to make judgments about the qualifications of those applying or being considered for professional positions at the department. The Board and the Department also should have basic authority to promote personnel and to provide employment inducements so that present personnel will not be attracted to other positions because of low salaries at the department or lack of other opportunities and perquisites. As a guideline, salaries and career opportunities should parallel those found in the best school systems in Massachusetts.

Recommendation Two. *The Department must undertake a number of reforms with respect to its internal operations, especially in the area of administrative procedures. It must reduce duplication of effort and programs in certain areas, improve legislative and fiscal processes, organize specific divisions and bureaus, and train personnel, and initiate planning.*

Administrative Procedures

The internal administrative functions of the Department are, and for some time have been, poorly managed in a state of confusion. The Deputy Commissioner of Education should be vested by the Commissioner as the principal executive officer with respect to managing the internal operations of the Department and to coordinating those operations with the performance of external functions. Thus, the Associate Commissioners should be directly responsible to the Deputy Commissioner and he to the Commissioner. The Deputy Commissioner should have an executive assistant to help him with his manifold tasks and responsibilities.

Two executive assistants should serve directly under the Commissioner. One should be vested with responsibilities for making educational projections and for planning, and the other should assist and advise the Commissioner in the area of occupational education. The former should have close ties with the Division of Research and Data Systems (Gibson recommends that the present Division of Research and Development assume this new name), while the latter should coordinate his work with the new Division of Occupational Education. The Commissioner should also have whatever other administrative assistants he and the Board consider necessary. The present lack of staffing for the Board of Education could be remedied in large part by a well-staffed Commissioner's Office.

Reducing Duplication of Effort and Programs in Certain Areas

In the course of our study, Gibson found considerable duplication of operational efforts and programs. Therefore, he recommends a consolidation of the work of various bureaus such as adult education, special education, pupil services and research. Decision-making with respect to applying for and allocating federal and state funds should be tightened and placed under the authority of the (proposed) Associate Commissioner for federal and state assistance.

The Bureau of Public Information should be strengthened, and all public information programs, including publications, should emanate from this Bureau so that educators and other people in the Commonwealth may have a much better idea of the Department's role and services in public education.

Improving Legislative and Fiscal Processes

Legislative Processes.   The legislative processes of the Department leave much to be desired. Considerable effort should be made to draw upon the views of the Department's professional employees in the shaping of the annual legislative package and that more effective means be developed to utilize the expertise and advice of state educational groups and the Educational Conference

Board in developing legislative proposals. This means more meetings with members of such groups (as well as with members of the legislative Joint Committee on Education) and follow-up procedures between meetings so that such sessions are not perfunctory or window dressing. More information on specific bills submitted to the General Court should be circulated by the Department to key groups and audiences, and public progress reports should be made on how those bills are faring in the legislature. Priorities for legislation the Department wants and needs should be established. Above all, the legislation the department proposes should be articulated in terms of how it will advance student achievement and quality of education in the schools.

Improving Fiscal Processes. With respect to the Department's budget which must be submitted to the executive Office of Administration and Finance, efforts should be made to orient it toward goals rather than having it based on annual increments for each of the basic categories of the budget. This suggests developing a program and planning budget system. Goals, in turn, should be shaped within the context of legislative priorities for the Department as well as of longer-term objectives. Better communication between the Department and the Office of Administration and Finance in determining budget priorities is imperative. The deplorable fact is that it is not until well after the governor has submitted his budget (House 1) to the General Court in January that the Department can begin to learn what cuts have been made in the budget which it submitted in September. This is an intolerable situation and seriously damaging to departmental operations and planning.

With regard to other fiscal operations, it is imperative that Department personnel have more funds for travel and that business office expedite payments to staff members for expenses incurred in travel, as well as remuneration to consultants to the Department for services rendered. More effort should be made to secure federal funds and to allocate them efficiently and effectively and within the time limits established by federal legislation. The business office must be operated with modern business procedures, and it also requires additional staffing.

The services provided by the Bureau of Adult Education and Extended Services could be delivered more efficiently and thoroughly through the adoption of a revolving fund. This would mean that monies received by this Bureau from all sources, excluding monies appropriated by the General Court, could remain available to the Bureau instead of reverting to the State Treasury as of June 30th of each fiscal year.

Organization of Specific Divisions and Bureaus

The Division of Research and Development should become the Division of Research and Data Systems, with authority to supervise all research activities of the Department and to operate all data systems. It is also essential that the General Court provide greater funding by the state for the Division of Research and Data Systems rather than relying almost exclusively on the federal government to fund this vital segment of the department's operations.

The fifth recommendation of this study calls for a state-wide program for the articulation of educational goals, assessment of student performance, evaluation of school services, and accountability by educational decision makers to the publics they serve. Toward that end, Gibson recommends that the Division of Research and Data Systems should have a Bureau of Educational Assessment and Evaluation so that it may be equipped to perform these important services. The bureau would manage the state-wide student assessment program and also would conduct the evaluation processes with respect to school services that are related to student performance. This suggests that the bureau also should engage in constant research and inquiry with respect to school services that demonstrably advance student achievement and those that do not.

The Bureau of Educational Assessment and Evaluation should also be charged with responsibility for disseminating on a broad basis the findings of its assessments and evaluations so that school systems might be better informed on student performance and school services of quality. This bureau could also be of much assistance to systems and others in developing educational accountability programs.

All curricula and instructional activities and functions of the Department should come under the authority of the Division of Curriculum and Instruction. Some or all of the work of the Bureau of Elementary and Secondary Education in this division can be more effectively assigned to other bureaus in line with our recommendation on consolidation of specific areas of departmental activity.

Training of Personnel

Increased efforts should be taken by the department for training new staff with respect to the duties they will undertake, and especially for developing extensive inservice training programs for department employees. Specifically, there is a need (1) to bring all personnel working in curriculum and other rapidly changing areas of education abreast of recent developments, research, and innovations; and (2) the necessity to train certain personnel in such areas as business management (including managerial concepts and leadership skills) and pupil services (guidance, counseling, etc.). Unless the Department plans now for meeting the changes and challenges which lie ahead, its usefulness to public school education will be considerably limited. Planning should include also a continuous process of evaluation of strengths, weaknesses, and needs of the Department of Education and of public education in general so that the short-range and long-range goals of the Department may be articulated more effectively. Certainly, projections and planning will be an integral part

of the increased concern by and responsibilities of the Department in the area
of state aid to nonpublic schools.

Recommendation Three. *Strong efforts should be undertaken to increase
the Department's service role to school systems and to minimize the function
of the department as a regulator and enforcement agency with respect to the
public schools in the state.*

Leadership

Here, Gibson calls for nonauthoritarian leadership at the state level means
dealing with those things that local systems cannot do by themselves, matters
that affect the well-being and quality of all systems in the state.

State-wide areas for departmental leadership include the following:
(1) equality of educational opportunity for all Massachusetts students; (2)
state-wide educational assessment and proposals for educational accountability;
(3) assistance to disadvantaged children wherever they are; (4) promotion of
integration in education throughout the state; and provision for assistance and
leadership on the board issue of collective bargaining. It also involves (1) securing
more federal aid for all dimensions of public school education; (2) making
educational projections and providing planning directives for use by all school
systems; (3) extending many kinds of services to the schools (set forth next);
and (4) combining the best that the state and the local school systems have to
offer so that clear and current alternatives to the present structure of state-
local system cooperation will not be replaced by state or federal control and
operation of the public schools.

Services

The Department of Education should be equipped to extend or improve
school services of quality to school systems that are not providing such services
to students or that cannot provide them. School services including the following:
teachers, instructional resources, curriculum (structure and content), school
facilities, administration, libraries, facilities for physical and mental well-being,
continuing education programs, and pupil services (guidance, counseling, etc.).
School services are the very crux of education, and in Massachusetts, there is
a profound inequality among our schools and school systems in the quality and
quantity of these services available to students. We hold that services provided
by the Department to needy systems can do much to equalize educational
opportunity.

This relates to the capacity and organization of the Division of Research
and Data Services to develop programs in assessment and evaluation. We

recommend that under the aegis of the Division of Research and Data Systems, Department personnel and consultants from a number of sources compile research on positive and negative school services that demonstrably advance or impede student achievement. Such an inventory, which should be continuous, given new research and findings, will be of help to school systems and will better equip the Division of Curriculum and Instruction to organize its own resources for assisting the systems.

The Department should utilize its operations in educational television more effectively to deliver school services of quality, especially inservice teacher training and education. Significant inservice programs can do much to improve the capacity of public school teachers to advance quality education for students. This also applies to direct instructional television, or the use of this medium as an effective curricular component of all school systems in the state.

Gibson exhorts us to strengthen the capacity of the present state-local collaborative pattern of public education to advance quality of education for students, equality of educational opportunity, and equal protection of the laws for students irrespective of in what town or city they reside, or we may well expect more authoritarian processes to dominate public school education in the Commonwealth.

Regulatory Functions

Legislation enacted by the General Court requires the Board of Education, through the Department, to enforce a number of mandates or compulsory programs with respect to the public schools in the state. The most extensive listing of the mandates is to be found in Section IG of Chapter 572 of the Massachusetts General Laws of 1965. Among the mandates are length of school day (5 1/2 hours), minimum number of school days a year (180 days), minimum educational standards for all courses that public schools shall require their students to take, and maximum pupil-teacher ratios. Mandates which the Department must enforce are found in other legislation, including the racial imbalance law.

Four reasons led Gibson to this recommendation. First, mandates suggest policing and not leading. Second, the Department simply lacks the staff for consistent and effective enforcement. Third, nonpublic schools are not included. Finally, little useful purpose is served by inflexible statutory mandates when quality education is viewed as the objective.

There must be some form of minimum standards; however, they should be flexible and definitely related to student performance and achievement. A state-wide assessment program is necessary that will help to determine relationship between standards and student achievement. Research and data from other states and school systems will also contribute to finding much more about

what, if anything, should be mandated for advancing student achievement.
In this spirit, Gibson recommends more flexibility by the Department in
granting waivers to school systems with respect to compliance with present
minimum standards. Waivers should be related to pilot projects that call for
experimentation in advancing student achievement and accompanying evaluation
(fewer hours per day in school, for example, with independent study or field
work, etc.). Gibson's basic recommendation about reassessment of mandates
is dependent upon MDE's being able to provide the carrot of more effective
school services and also on a state-wide educational assessment program.

Recommendation Four. *Present regional offices of the Department should
be strengthened better to deliver school services of quality directly to school
systems; and at least two more regional offices (or service centers) should be
created, with one serving the needs of the greater Boston area.*

The regional offices should be strengthened in a number of ways, and at
least two more are needed so that a pattern of delivery of qualitative school
services can directly uplift educational standards in all schools in the Commonwealth.

This recommendation does not imply a decentralization of MDE. Rather,
it suggests a more effective organization for carrying out the leadership-service
thrust of the Department, as recommended above. The central office of the
Department should be staffed with educational specialists who can be dispatched
to the regional service centers and then to individual school systems for specific
educational programs and services. The Department's professional educators
and administrators should be much more in the field than is presently the case,
and strong regional offices, which work directly with the schools in their areas,
can provide the means to make the presence and services of SDE much more
useful to the schools. Parenthetically, we prefer the term *specialist* to *supervisor*
or *senior supervisor*, the titles of most of the Department's professional staff
members. *Supervisor* suggests regulation, while *specialist* suggests service and
leadership

The regional staff structure that should include a director; an assistant
director; specialists in teacher education, instructional resources, information
and public relations, building facilities, pupil services, and other important
school service areas. There also should be specific personnel for liaison with all
six divisions in the Department and with such bureaus as Elementary and
Secondary Education, Special Education, Adult Education and Extended
Services, Curriculum Innovation, Library Extension, School Building Assistance,
School Lunch Programs, Transportation and Program Assistance.

Gibson recommends specific services for teachers at these centers, including
advice on selection of instructional materials, collections of many kinds of
instructional resources, inservice programs for teachers, information about
curriculum innovations, listings of available paraprofessionals, and many others.
For administrators, the centers could provide all sorts of collaborative arrange-

ments and assistance for improvement of school administrative and business needs: purchasing, school construction, collective-bargaining procedures, special and occupational education services and equipment, planning and evaluation programs, personnel recruitment and placement, and so on.

The centers should organize regional task forces comprised of Department personnel and others from universities and school systems that could address themselves to specific school problems, such as special education, curriculum innovation and dissemination, and teacher inservice education. The centers could help to coordinate the many collaborative arrangements which already exist among groupings of systems in the state and could respond to requests by school systems to form such collaborative programs. The centers could provide meeting space for systems in the region, could gather research data for the Division of Research and Data Systems, could facilitate informational exchanges among systems in the area, and could develop innovative pilot programs meeting some specific needs of the schools in each area.

The establishment of a Greater Boston Regional Service Center would respond to the needs of that metropolitan area, especially as they concern inner-city students. Collaboration among the some 100 systems in the greater Boston area could do much to advance equality of educational opportunity, promote the concept of integration in education, facilitate collaboration to reduce educational costs, work closely with the already existing cooperative programs in the area (such as METCO, school volunteers, and the Title III programs), and much more.

Recommendation Five. *A program should be launched under the aegis of the Department calling for the establishment of educational goals for Massachusetts students, assessment of student achievement with respect to goals, evaluation of schools, and accountability by educators and educational decision-makers to the publics they serve for their performance with respect to students.*

Goals, assessment, evaluation, and accountability are all interrelated and are essential to any attempt by MDE to advance the quality of education in the Commonwealth. The program recommended depends upon other recommendations – improving the quality of professional personnel in the Department; improving the Department's internal operations; emphasis on leadership and services and less stress on regulation; and a pattern for more effective delivery of services to school systems.

Goals

Seneca, the Roman philosopher, said that if we do not know to which port we are sailing, no wind is favorable. Educational goals are essential in providing direction and ideals for MDE's efforts, in determining strategies for striving toward goals, and in serving as guidelines for measuring what we are doing to, for, and with the young people in the schools.

The principal goal of each school and each school system should be an increase in the potential of every student in each of five interrelated areas of educational quality: human quality, quality of skills, quality of knowledge, learning quality, and civic quality. Far too many school systems concentrate almost entirely on goals of knowledge and skills.

The National Assessment Program has set forth goals in several areas of education and is developing goals for all dimensions of education. Pennsylvania, Colorado, and several other states have by various means established educational goals for their students.

Assessment of Student Performance with
Respect to Goals

Gibson cites the need for a state-wide assessment program along the lines developed by a number of other states, such as Vermont, Colorado, New York, and Pennsylvania. The National Assessment Program can be of great assistance to Massachusetts in this respect. As a beginning, Gibson calls for a pilot assessment program on a limited state-wide basis dealing with bodies of knowledge and basic skills that can be measured and compared as among a random selection of school systems in Massachusetts.

Evaluation and Accountability

Evaluation of school services, conditions, and processes that appear to advance student achievement and those that impede student achievement is required.

For instance, there are important data on the effectiveness of differentiated staffing (efficient use of teachers and paraprofessionals) as related to student achievement. Gibson states that expansion of performance contracting (educational agencies and publishers contracting with school systems to prove the efficacy of their programs for advancing student achievement) indicates that certain inputs into school systems can improve student performance substantially. Many studies are available to prove what does work and what does not in school services, conditions, and processes; and Gibson feels that all professional educators are derelict if they do not draw upon this considerable research and experience to make our schools more serviceable to students. Again, he notes that a number of forward-looking states are moving in this direction, and we strongly recommended that Massachusetts do the same. John Gibson recommends that reports which school systems are obliged to submit each year to the

Department contain data essential to student assessment and school evaluation and that such reports include programs from all schools in the locality, public and nonpublic. Thus, school systems will account to the Department for what they are and are not doing with respect to student performance and the Department will have the data it needs better to serve systems that demonstrably are deficient. Through the regional service centers, MDE help to provide deficient systems with the services needed to advance students toward state-wide educational goals.

Finally, Gibson recommended that each school system write its annual report in layman's language and submit it to the audiences the system serves at the local level — citizens and taxpayers, parents of students, and the students themselves. He urged that local educational collaboratives be formed to consider and discuss the local reports so that accountability is not an abstraction passed on the state.

Strategies for Change

At every stage of developing his report, John Gibson sought for ways to bring about the changes he was recommending. Here, in summary form, is the way he envisioned action.

In this report, we have submitted five basic recommendations for strengthening the Massachusetts Department of Education and have suggested ways and means for translating these proposals into public policy over the next five years. Who, in addition to the Board and the Commissioner of Education, actually must take the initiative for making these recommendations a reality? Without support and favorable action by the Governor the new Secretary for Educational Affairs (in proposals with intermediate and long-run timing), and the General Court, much of what we propose may not come to pass. We therefore submit several more recommendations. A stronger Massachusetts Educational Conference Board, with expanded membership and some staffing should be the principal agency for coordinating the agents, processes, timing, and strategies for change. Obviously, the Board cannot make decisions for authoritative officials on the Board of Education, in the Department of Education, in the executive branch, and the General Court. Insofar, however, as a nonofficial group can serve as the prime mover of and catalyst for change, we feel that the Conference Board is well qualified to perform this function. Other groups, such as the League of Women Voters and the new Education Compact Council of Massachusetts, should become members of the Board, and the Board should raise funds from its constituent members on the basis of a fair funding formula enabling it to employ a competent person on a full-time basis to orchestrate the agents, processes, timing, and strategies for change.

In other words, the steps that are necessary to effect change and to implement the study's recommendations cannot be performed solely by those who volunteer time for fine causes. A staff person for the Conference Board is needed to identify all agents for change, official and unofficial, to identify and give publicity to the administrative and decision-making processes necessary to advance recommendations toward policy, to keep a careful accounting of the right timing for each recommendation, and to propose and shape strategies likely to produce the desired results. This staff person, for instance, would be able to mobilize support for the recommendations by informing influential agents of change when and where decisions are to be made by the Board and the Department of Education, in the executive branch of state government, and in the General Court, with respect to all dimensions of the recommendations. A careful flow chart for our recommendations should be developed, and all those who feel that the proposals have merit could see when and where their assistance is needed for supporting the process of change.

We cannot go into detail at this time with respect to the many things the staff person could and should do to help in implementing the recommendations. We feel sure that, without a full-time person steering the proposals toward policy through mobilizing all kinds of public and political support, we cannot expect much change to take place. We have previously noted the cycle of decision-makers on whom we must rely for official action and that it is easy to pass the responsibility or blame to others when action is or is not taken. Orchestration of the cycle and coordination of efforts to influence and to gain support can best be done by someone who is in a position to devote full energies to that cause.

The staff person naturally requires the backing of the Conference Board and its constituent members. We would hope that the unanimity ruling of the Board with respect to its own decision-making would neither preclude the employment of such a person nor hamper that person's actions and decisions. We might also add that the recommended staff person could be of great value to the Board in its many other activities and would be instrumental in strengthening the educational establishment of the Commonwealth.

Perhaps of equal importance, we recommended that the Conference Board take steps to organize in Massachusetts towns and cities as many local units of the Board as possible. A town or city educational conference board would have at the local level almost the same membership as the state Board, with representatives from the state Board's membership (teachers, principals, superintendents, organization members, and even student representation). The local boards would be the main agents for requesting accountability from the local school systems and would be of great value in mobilizing local support for the study's recommendations. The town or city board could also take steps to give publicity about the study's recommendations and other educational issues, so that representatives in the General Court would know that their respective constituencies were informed about educational affairs. Thus, the local boards would have a strong role to play in educational accountability and in promoting support at the local level for necessary state legislation and funding in the area of public education. The state Board's staff person could be instrumental in helping to organize local educational conference boards. While it may take some time for this pattern to develop, it offers a viable and realistic way to implement the study's recommendations and to advance the quality of education in the Commonwealth.

The next study we look at, concerning both local & state educational business practices, is closely interlocked into Gibson's work.

3

When Businessmen Study the Management of Education

Innovation and the systems approach are only just emerging. Their full impact is already changing man's life, society, and his world view. Peter Drucker

We must seek the highest possible efficiency in school organization. Roe L. Johns

Organizing a business task force to look at school districts and the department was a coup for the Advisory Council. Thirty-three corporation executives were loaned to the study to ferret out and form the material destined to become the heart of the report. The Associated Industries of Massachusetts (AIM), a granite-nosed but dynamic service organization, not only arranged for the seasoned executives to join the study, but contributed other talents and resources in numerous ways to the study.

In 1968, the Advisory Council thought it wise to study business practices in school systems. The going at first, however, was not easy. Some doubted that business practices could be usefully separated from education practices. Skeptics from the business world held that such a report would lead to naught. Somewhat piously, certain schoolmen questioned the motives and presumed hidden agendas lurking in the corporative mind.

AIM voted its full support of the venture. Within a few days, AIM had enlisted Governor Francis W. Sargent and the legislative leadership to lend their support to recruiting talent from corporations to help on the study.

What caused the Advisory Council to take on a project of uncertain typology and unchartered outcomes? Increasing costs and rising concerns over how efficient the education system is prepared the way for the Council in mounting this study. The public education bill, which currently comes to over one billion dollars, costs every man, woman and child $200 each year. Boston alone runs 195 schools, employs a staff of thousands and has a budget reaching for $100 million annually.

Education has become associated with costly things: people, increasingly complex school buildings and the wares of changing technologies. Nationally, the money going to schools has been increasing over the years. Table 3–1 shows that by 1971 education consumed almost eight percent of the gross national product. Another sign of the times is indicated by the amount of property taxes going to education. In 1942, 32.9 percent of local property taxes went to schools, by 1957 this was upped to 42.8 percent, and in 1969, schools were claiming one-half of property taxes.

Table 3-1

School Expenditures — Public and Private (All) as a Percent of G.N.P., 1930–1971

Year	1930	1940	1950	1960	1970	1971 (est.)
School Expenditures (in millions)	3,234	3,200	8,796	24,722	70,600	75,300
Percent of Gross National Product	3.1%	3.5%	3.4%	5.1%	7.6%	7.7%

Source: U.S. Dept. of Health, Education and Welfare, *Biennial Survey of Education in the United States*, 1971.

The Task Force vividly stated the big business syndrome accordingly:

> ... consider its massive physical plant facilities and thousands of progressional and support personnel. Think of the growing fleets of busses; inventories of supplies, books and equipment; athletic and recreation programs; maintenance and new construction; health and good services; recordkeeping and reporting requirements; and wide geographic coverage. Add to these a new era of collective bargaining and persistent demands for better and more comprehensive services.[1]

Finding huge resources pouring into education, the task force expressed concern over how things in education are managed. They reported little coordination at the state level and almost no interchange of information, formal or informal, between school districts. The Task Force found widely varying procedures. Good practices in one district were not being communicated onto neighboring districts with similar problems, because there was no organized method for exchanging information.

Effective working relationships between school committees and school administrators were found to exist in many districts, but in others, policies are vague and limits of executive authority unclear. Delegation of responsibilities and basic organizational structure simply do not exist, the Task Force reported, in some smaller systems. Day-to-day problems are dealt with on an ad hoc basis.

The Task Force also found instances where sound and useful management practices have been introduced into local school systems. Actually, no inherent obstacles were found to block initiation and application of modern business methods and management systems.

The Task Force felt that the implementation of their recommendations could result in a reduction of total expenditures (operating plus construction) equal to 6 percent of the total expenditures that would be incurred under the present system of operation.

The 6 percent reduction did not take into account the effect on total expenditures of complete school district cooperation. When that was accom-

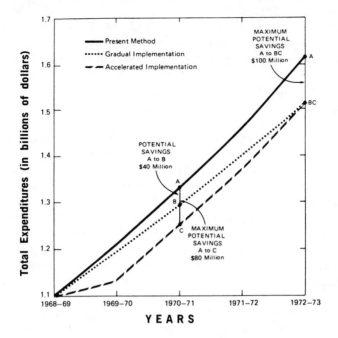

Figure 3-1. State Secondary and Primary School Total Expenditure Projections. Source: Massachusetts Advisory Council on Education, *Report of the Massachusetts Business Task for School Management,* 1970, pg. 4.

plished, a 10 percent reduction can be anticipated. These reductions would be the dollar benefits to be derived from the implementation effort.

During the past four years, the Task Force reports, public school operating expenditures increased about 13 percent per year over the preceding year, and construction costs at least 10 percent per year over the preceding year. Total expenditures for the 1968–69 school year were approximately $1.1 billion. The projected expenditures for the next four school years, assuming a conservative increase of 10 percent per year over the preceding year, is illustrated in Figure 3-1.

Thus, advocates of the study sensed from the beginning that significant savings could be made. The issue of cost was timely and has become more so. Education is big business growing bigger.

How The Task Force Operated

Warren King, chosen by the Advisory Council to conduct the study, launched the project with dispatch and elan. Telegrams were sent to 61 corporations, with a successful appeal made to Massachusetts Governor Francis W. Sargent, for his assistance. Most of those who did not respond by loaning an executive supported the study in other ways. The men volunteered were screened to assure that the appropriate range of talents were reflected by them. In a few instances, special appeals were made for specific talent needs. In a very short time, the screenings were completed, the design of the study refined and work began.

King was to be Program Director, and an Executive Committee was to advise, procure additional resources and to check on field operations. A broadly representative study committee of 47 members was named to function as a sounding board. Even at this point, the Task Force began to concern itself with implementation.

The task before them was formidable. The following domains of the public school were to be scrutinized: funding; manpower; facilities; fiscal systems; facilities-planning and acquisition system; facilities operation and maintenance; transportation; procurement; school food services; management information system; insurance; health services; library services; property and inventory control; and, finally, staff travel.

In each category, an evaluation was required from a team formed by the executive committee. This required a program of visits and intensive interviewing of school system people and among state agencies involved.

Recommendations were drawn up and cast into a set of priorities centered on: (a) "critical needs," (b) resources for public education and (c) a school business management system. A manual on transportation was also planned. The critical needs cited are in the area of planning, school districting and a management information system.

It remains to explain further the financial aspects of the coup. The talent contributed was estimated as worth at least $200,000; AIM and its affiliated corporations donated another $20,000 in office space, cash and various services; the Board of Education gave $15,000 toward printing costs.

The Report

The summary of the business task force report is a gem. A mirror of the full version, it is tightly written and not lacking in ideas to ponder. The Task Force produced the summary as one of its products. With only minor editing, it is reprinted here in its entirety. The section on a local information system is from the full report and is included as highly pertinent to the interests of schoolmen. Recommendations made by the task force conclude this chapter from the final report.

Critical Needs

Long-Range Planning. Formal long-range planning should be initiated at both the local and state levels. Five-year plans should be prepared annually because updating at least that often is essential to keep pace with changing conditions. Long-range planning is not a static function but an evolutionary process — that fact clearly is not recognized by the educational community in Massachusetts.

There are many developments which can affect the future of education. Executives must evaluate these developments and make decisions which will enable them to react to change effectively as well as to contingency and crisis. Such decisions are critical and the Task Force felt strongly that they cannot be made wisely without the kinds of information and guidance which long-range planning provides.

School District Cooperation. Optimum economic size is one important characteristic of a successful district operation. However, many local school systems in Massachusetts are not large enough to obtain the most effective educational return for the dollars expended. Inescapably, conditions today require more cooperation between school systems and on a larger scale than has been envisioned in Massachusetts. Methods of achieving this vary, but regardless of method, the Department of Education must provide a unified policy and adequate communications.

Without increased cooperation between school districts, Commonwealth taxpayers must be resigned to continued duplication of costs, competition for tax dollars and personnel, as well as an unbalanced educational system frequently favoring the better financed communities.

Local control has been traditional in Massachusetts education, but such control, as we know it today, suffers in a fragmented system. Local units often are uneconomical in operation and politically impotent. A system which combines central leadership with strong centers of local control will produce significant economies, cut waste, and offer the additional benefits of greater scholastic challenges and special programs. In addition, it will provide better facilities and management, as well as financially self-sufficient local school groupings whose voters can truly control the important aspects of their children's education.[2]

The Task Force examined and considered in great detail the history, status, problems, and benefits of school district cooperation. After a discussion of the issues at length, there is a recommendation for a transition towards larger districts in a manner which should prove beneficial and acceptable to the local communities.

Management Information System — State

There is also a need for a centrally administered information system involving the coordinated effects of the Office of Planning and Program Coordination, The Department of Education, as well as users and contributors of educational information. An Advisory Committee should be established to oversee the activities of the recommended Massachusetts Educational Management Information System, determine acceptable project priorities, and ensure that the full capabilities of the system are made avilable to its constituents.

It is imperative that the Department of Education be able to describe the current and future needs of the users of educational information. Additionally, it should have a plan for an information system to tie in with the larger state system and begin implementation where it is economically feasible as soon as possible. This will require a study of the needs for management information, the design of a data base, as well as documented computer programs.

Resources for Public School Education

Funding. Massachusetts taxpayers are plagued by the current imbalance between the support to education provided by local property taxes and the more broadly based state support. Aggravated by rising costs, taxpayers have reacted by restricting resources for local education.

The questions of state aid and local funding are complex, and involve many aspects beyond the purview of this management study. However, from a business standpoint, it is obvious that many schools are operating inefficiently because of inadequate funding. Therefore, the General Court should give prompt and serious consideration to findings of the various expert groups who have recently studied this problem.

Manpower. Manpower is an indispensable and critical resource for education. The department, as presently funded and organized, cannot make the fullest and most effective use of this resource and is not in a position to implement many of the recommendations in this report. The General Court should fund this department adequately and give it the authority to select, compensate, and classify its progessional staff within the overall limits of its budget. If not, consideration should be given to deactivating the Department of Education.

Assuming that adequate funding is made available, the department should establish an expanded Bureau of School Management Services. This organization would assist all school districts in questions of building operation and maintenance, collective bargaining, data processing, program budgeting, purchasing, transportation, and volunteer manpower.

The department should also appoint a professional administrator in the Office of the Commissioner to direct departmental communications and to plan and execute a long-range public relations program. Communications are an essential tool and function of modern management. It is vital for public under-standing and support of the educational system. Yet, the Massachusetts Department of Education now has no effective communications program.

School districts should solicit support from local business and industrial organizations to assist in special instructional areas and administrative matters. Some districts are now deriving benefits from this approach, and the practice should be expanded.

School costs have been impacted heavily in recent years by collective bargaining. In general, the bargaining units in the school system have been represented by professional negotiators. The Task Force strongly recommends that the school committees secure similar representation. In any case, the negotiations should not be conducted by inexperienced personnel.

Facilities. School building is the biggest construction business in Massachusetts — about 4-million square feet each year — but it also is the most fragmented in terms of management. Experiences gained in one community are seldom shared with another. In addition, the benefits of mass buying and standardization of methods are not realized. School building problems are being compounded as parochial schools continue to close.

Innovation in construction methods is one of the most powerful means of combating high costs. The Department of Education should promote strongly the development of modular systems construction. There is an urgent need for the Department of Education to provide coordination and expanded assistance in all areas of school construction, including cost savings analysis, site planning, building design, architectural planning, and a central data bank.

Other Task Force recommendations for reducing school building costs call for the General Court to establish a central state contracting agency and for the towns to expand the use of stabilization funds for school construction. The latter approach would eliminate or reduce expenditures for bond issues which can amount to as much as two-thirds of construction costs.

Finally, in this expensive and vital area of school construction, educational and town planners must recognize the premium on time. A three-year delay can increase the cost of a building by one-third. Long-range planning would avoid this delay, and would result in buildings being constructed when they actually are required by the local system — not two or three years later, as has been the usual experience in Massachusetts.

School Business Management System

Fiscal System. The Task Force recognized the need to modify and standardize educational budget content and preparation procedures to obtain greater public understanding of the objectives of school programs. Budgeting by objectives rather than by function provides opportunities for decision-making on the basis of priorities. In addition, uniform formats would facilitate comparisions between systems and measurements of performance against stated goals. After budget component costs and revenue sources have been properly identified, the budget should be approved as one total. This would permit the superintendent to make transfers freely within the overall budget.

The greater accountability provided by program budgeting and performance comparisons should make this increased flexibility acceptable from the standpoint of control. The temptation to make unnecessary expenditures, in order to avoid returning unspent monies to the general funds of the community would be greatly reduced.

Facilities Planning and Acquisition System.   Long-range facilities planning by the school districts must be improved, if they are to meet successfully the problems of increasing pupil population, rising construction and land costs, and parochial school closings. Figure 3-2 shows what has happened to school facility costs. The Department of Education should be funded to a level at which it can provide assistance to town school planners. As part of this assistance, the department should develop, in cooperation with the towns, standard criteria and formats for space utilization records, so that emerging space needs can be clearly identified and justified to the taxpayers.

Facilities Operation and Maintenance System.   The Task Force's review of this key area disclosed a serious lack of effective custodial training programs for establishing and maintaining adequate skill levels among the more than 6,000 custodians in the public school system. Such programs would combine on-the-job training, a custodian's handbook, and improved custodial supervision, which would incorporate comprehensive scheduling based on work measurement techniques. Performance time standards would provide uniform schedules for all custodial tasks and establish a more even distribution of work loads among employees. The Department of Education is now prepared to conduct training programs upon request from any town. Such action would bring a rapid improvement in efficiency.

Maintenance management of physical facilities in many school systems is ineffective. In some cases, this is because maintenance responsibility is assigned outside the school's authority. In other instances, maintenance management expertise among local school administrators is limited. In general, preventive maintenance programs are either inadequate or nonexistent. These conditions jeopardize the long-term serviceability of school facilities throughout the Commonwealth. Prompt action is required if this potential waste of the taxpayers' money is to be stopped.

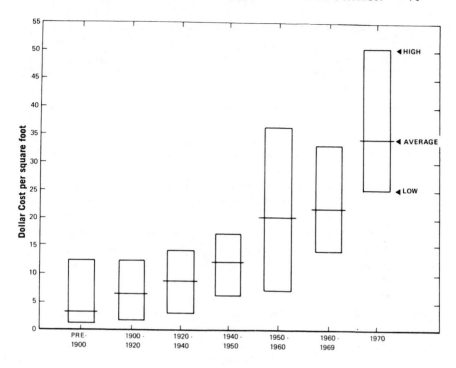

Figure 3-2. Historical Trend of School Facility Costs. Source: Massachusetts Advisory Council on Education, *Report of the Massachusetts Business Task Force for School Management*, 1970, p. 38.

Transportation System.   Review of the Commonwealth's numerous school transportation systems, which serve 500,000 pupils with more than 4,200 vehicles, disclosed opportunities for significant cost reductions. The greatest opportunity for achieving transportation economy is through combining individual school districts into larger area transportation facilities, which would be administered by transportation specialists, and through eventual public ownership and operation of bus fleets.

The Department of Education should provide expert and timely guidance to the local districts and area specialists so that effective and economical transportation systems can be implemented. Such assistance should encourage more cooperative arrangements between school districts where transportation is required for special purposes such as vocational and technical schools. Assistance in the form of centrally developed computer routing and scheduling and the establishment of pupil pick-up stations, bus and driver standards, effective service complaint processing procedures, formal rules of pupil conduct, and procedures for reporting and reviewing rule violations should also be given.

When transportation services are contracted, bids and proposed contracts should be analyzed and approved at the state level. Furthermore, state-developed forms and procedures should be utilized, and performance bonds should be required as an integral part of every request for bid and transportation contract. Moreover, legislation is required to enable school committees to negotiate contracts of longer duration to effect cost savings.

Local transportation cost reimbursement by the state should be limited to a maximum cost per pupil to ensure maximum effort to effect economical transportation. Finally, the operating manual on pupil transportation prepared by the Task Force should receive wide distribution in the school districts.

Procurement System. A uniform business system for purchasing at the local level is critically needed, so the Task Force prepared a school purchasing manual to meet day-to-day operating requirements. Furthermore, a procurement specialist position should be established in the Bureau of School Management Services to coordinate purchasing activities and disseminate information among Commonwealth school districts. Since lower prices inevitably result from higher-volume procurement and administrative cost, reductions are achieved when several schools are served by a single advertising and bidding procedure, cooperative purchasing should be developed on a regional basis.

School districts should also be informed of commodities available under state contracts, and the State Purchasing Office should encourage them to use such contracts. A serious lack of communication among local school districts and the State Purchasing Office now hinders this process; this gap should be bridged immediately. Incorporation of large-volume school requirements into state purchasing orders would result in lower prices for all state agencies. Table 3-2 indicates savings possible on certain selected items.

School Food Services System. The Task Force believes substantial improvements in the Commonwealth's school lunch program would result from the creation of a Division of Nutrition Education and School Foods Services within the Department of Education. This division would provide financial and technical assistance to the local districts, handle government commodity distribution for the schools and eventually other institutions, and provide innovative and creative nutrition education.

However, the greatest economies could be achieved by using central kitchens to serve more than one school, and the division should actively promote this concept. In addition, the state should take full advantage of government-donated commodities by contracting the processing of this food for conversion into finished products for resale to various school district systems.

Table 3-2
Cost on Selected Items – Individual Versus Unified Buying

	High Price	Low Price	Weighted Average	Total Cost	Low Price Cost	Saving	Percent Saving
Spirit duplicating paper	$ 0.99	$ 0.70	$ 0.806	$138,302	$120,171	$18,131	13.10
Construction paper	1.22	0.78	0.879	18,285	16,222	2,063	11.28
Mimeograph paper	1.15	0.71	0.842	28,510	24,039	4,471	15.68
File folders	2.00	1.21	1.432	30,009	25,358	4,651	15.49
Chalk	1.13	0.79	0.942	2,987	2,504	483	16.17
Liquid floor cleaner	3.40	1.27	2.167	34,645	27,370	7,275	20.99
Floor wax	3.85	2.00	2.813	57,257	40,712	16,545	28.89
Fluorescent bulbs	21.60	10.80	13.505	38,247	30,585	7,662	20.03
				$348,242	$286,961	$61,281	17.60

Source: Massachusetts Advisory Council on Education. *Report of the Massachusetts Business Task Force for School Business Management* 1970, p. 72.

Management Information

System — Local. It is essential that the Commonwealth have a state-wide management information system. Therefore, the local districts should participate in its development in coordination with the Department of Education, whose functions in the system have been described previously.

The Task Force suggests a one-year moratorium on the addition of data processing equipment. During this period, the Department of Education will establish the input-output configuration of the system. Thereafter, as mutually agreed, the local districts and the department should cooperate in the development testing and implementation of the system.

Interfacing Systems

The Task Force has defined interfacing systems as those which govern functions which are not generally considered in the business area, but which depend on the business area for services such as purchasing and budgeting. Such functions are insurance, attendance, health, and library services; property and inventory control; and the like.

Many disparities were observed among the school districts' vast array of insurance programs. Direction and coordination are required at the state level to ensure adequate protection of school district property and personnel and to achieve the economies that group rates provide. The cost of attendance services could be reduced by conducting the school census and street-list canvasses simultaneously. Finally, important financial and educational benefits could be achieved by coordinating the purchasing and processing of library materials on a regional basis.

A Proposed Local Information System

Because of the current high interest in information systems, the Task Force's full statement on a proposed local management information system is reproduced here. The reader will recall a Massachusetts Educational Management Information System (MEMIS) for the state outlined in the previous section.

Management Information System — Local. The study found that local school administrators are burdened by increasing requests for information from taxpayers, the school board, the Department of Education, and the legislature. Today, taxpayers want detailed building costs, program pupil costs, population and construction forecasts, and evidence of educational excellence. The school board seeks to understand the needs of an expanding school system while maintaining economic control. The Department of Education requires annual budgets from each district in a format that may be different than those the local district would prefer. The legislature tries to support education but needs information to develop intelligent legislation. Most school administrators recognize these requests but, unfortunately, the quality of response has been varied.

The study found few school districts which consider the office staff and its data handling a system. However, every school district is trying to satisfy information needs. Their methods range from well-staffed computer installations to a single clerk, under the superintendent.

Response to the increased and varied information demands are evidenced by:

(1) Development of new budgetary methods such as Planning Programming Budgetary Systems (PBBS). A budget displayed in the classical sense no longer provides the information for effective planning and measurement of school program costs.

(2) Introduction of accounting and computer machinery at the local, regional, state, and federal levels to process massive statistics.

(3) Creation of a computerized Research and Development Center in the Department of Education.

(4) Grouping by some local school districts for the sole purpose of processing data.

(5) Establishment of data processing departments within many school systems.

(6) Use of systems and computer consultants throughout education management.

(7) Commercial service bureaus processing educational data

(8) Statistical data developed as needed by the Massachusetts Teachers Association.

The single thread among these eight responses to information needs is the lack of coordinated effort amongst them.

Systems design should be based on the concept that a record be created a minimum number of times and the data it contains used frequently. The decision-maker need not be concerned with how, where, or by whom the information is produced, provided it is timely and accurate. These form the parameters for evaluating the current status of educational data processing and management information.

Evaluation. The choice and location of equipment and staff to provide information processing and long-range planning appear to be within the province of local school administrations. As a result, the degree of satisfaction is varied and has led some districts to employ specialists or consultants. Several districts have pooled resources to process data with accompanying economies.

The cost of processing data at the local level is rising. Much has been written to document the waste of dollars in uncoordinated attempts to reinvent the wheel in any area of data management. Thus, it is costly to continue on the present course of individual development. Most significantly, local school districts will continue to miss the goal of satisfying information needs at a reasonable cost.

The urgency of this problem is upon us. Some of the funds that supported local ventures into the field of data processing are drying up. It is reasonable to expect that a few local school districts will have a system meeting the demands for information as a result of their jumpin-in at the beginning. Most will not have a system and time is running out.

Recommendations. School administrations should develop and implement Local Educational Management Information Systems (LEMIS). Three factors bear on the implementation of this recommendation. First is this size of the development. This is important because development and implementation of systems must satisfy the needs of approximately 400 school districts. Second is the current status of information processing at the local level because:

(1) Costs involved in gathering, arranging, and presenting information are not available.
(2) More than 75 districts are using their own or rented electronic accounting machines/electronic data processing (EAM/EDP) equipment. Another third of the districts are using service bureaus, and many schools are sharing facilities in a neighboring district. This is done at annual rental and staff expense in excess of $2.5 million.
(3) There are approximately 400 different systems for information processing.
(4) There is no organization with the Department of Education to advise and guide local districts in areas of information processing, office systems and procedures, or date processing. The recommendation on Bureau of School Management Services, if adopted, will correct this.
(5) All local districts are involved in an information system, and the end of the year report to the Department of Education.

Third, is the level of local expertise. This problem must be considered because there are few qualified professional systems people at the district level.

For these reasons, the development and implementation of Local Educational Management Information Systems (LEMIS) must involve the following four steps to provide necessary data most economically.

Phase one, or introduction, is a one-year period that would involve, at the local level:

(6) Appointment of a local coordinator to be responsible for all data flow, including internal processing as well as service bureaus, cooperatives,

Massachusetts Educational Management Information System (MEMIS),
the Department of Education, and the community.
(7) Voluntary delay of contemplated computer additions, changes, or new data
processing involvements during the initial phase one.

This period is not one of inactivity but rather like that described in the Manpower section on Resources for Public School Education as a period of vigorous
activity at the state level establishing the links to the local level in MEMIS. The
end of year report input from the district to the Department of Education and
the annual report of the Department of Education as output from that agency
require particular attention.

The local coordinator to be selected from within the system would ideally
be a person with a background in systems analysis and data processing. Realistically, that will occur in only a few school systems. However, this should not
be considered a serious handicap. The phase one period should be used by the
coordinator to:

(8) Study and document the tab, computer, or manual information flow within
the local system.
(9) Note the deficiencies within their systems.
(10) Actively be involved in the MEMIS study of the existing information flow
such as the annual report.
(11) Participate in organizations such as Massachusetts Educational Data
Processing Association (MEDPA).
(12) Contact local industry for professional systems help.

In summary, phase one involved the moratorium on the addition of data
processing equipment, the development of a local coordinator, the understanding
of the local information system, and its relationships with other systems.

Phase two, or development, begins at the end of the first year and requires
a period of 18 months to develop and standardize adequate systems for local
information needs.

As a result of information available from the documentation of local systems
by local coordinators in phase one, MEMIS and a selected group of local
coordinators must evaluate and choose those systems best suited to information
needs. Where local systems are lacking or nonexistent, the resources of MEMIS,
local school districts, other state Department of Education, vendors, and
business would be utilized.

In this study, many manual and EDP systems were found in the local
information areas. Some of these areas of information meet legal requirements;
others are or would be helpful in managing school business. The following list
of applications indicates the diverse types of information necessary for local
school managemement.

(13) Students: Scholastic information – grades, test scores, and progress. Census information – age, date of enrollment, attendance, and class scheduling.
(14) Personnel: Staff status – qualifications, teaching experience, accomplishments, and evaluation. Financial – payroll and retirement fund.
(15) Fiscal: Budget – current budget, balances, and history. Funding – local, state and federal. Accounting; insurance.
(16) Facilities: Design and construction – date of construction, capacity, use, cost-original bid, actual cost, and replacement value. Operations and maintenance – custodial costs, building utilization, and utilities.
(17) Transportation: Vehicles – inventory, financial records, and usage. Bussing – pupil location, scheduling, algorithm, and analysis of contract versus ownership cost.
(18) Purchasing: Cost and usage data. Vendor analysis – history and performance. Order status – open, late, and balance due. Sources of supply – quality and quantity.
(19) School Lunch Program: Personnel – staff status and financial information. Procurement – source of supply and usage. Financial – cost analysis, budget, and government aid.
(20) Miscellaneous: Athletic programs. Attendance services. Collective bargaining. Computer services. Driver education. Health services. Library services. Community relations. Property and inventory control.

The systems developed for LEMIS must be suitable for manual as well as computer-based local districts. Systems must allow for a smooth transition from manual to computer operations and be suitable for more than one manufacturer's equipment configuration. There must also be standards and discipline in the systems to ensure information compatability between local districts, MEMIS, and the like, be they manual or computer based. Certain peripheral constraints, standards, and information for LEMIS should be the responsibility of the EDP service as established in the Manpower section of Resources for Public School Education. These must include:

(21) Proper computer, tab, or business machine configuration for business and educational purposes.
(22) Approved methods of equipment rental and purchase, and school discounts.
(23) Possible methods of staffing and job responsibilities in information processing areas.
(24) Available funding, both state and federal, as well as the status of all EDP or information systems projects.

MEMIS and the selected group of local coordinators would be responsible for:

(25) Documenting the standard systems.

(26) Upgrading systems to meet new and/or changed needs.

(27) Describing the multiple information needs for MEMIS as a requirement from each local school district.

(28) Describing the input-output requirements.

(29) Discouraging local districts from developing their own systems. Costs avoided by standardization are great if the previous list of applications being developed within each school district is considered.

Phase three, or testing, would begin at the end of 18 months. Its completion time would be one year to test the standardized systems. This segment would overlap the last year of phase two. It will become obvious as the local districts pass through these phases that they cannot economically solve their information needs by themselves. In addition, the larger systems may be hesitant to give up their partially established information systems for a compatible solution.

In order to avoid these problems, funding and considerable leadership will be necessary at the state level. Funding of two computer-based information systems — one for a cooperative of small school districts and the other for a large district — could provide a laboratory for testing the selected system's software. This would be done under the direction of the MEMIS staff with cooperation of the local coordinators.

A series of seminars, as these developments progress, to inform those coordinators not involved, would keep the two projects from becoming localized. The evaluation of the success of these projects should involve the coordinator's committee. That evaluation should be based on the local school's satisfaction with the information provided as well as the ease of input, timeliness, flexibility, and cost. From these two efforts, the modules of information processing systems would evolve to comprise the computer versions of LEMIS.

Phase four, or implementation, must begin no later than 30 months after the start of LEMIS and would be the implementation period for standard systems at the district level. Local systems must be implemented in a reasonable period of time in order to meet the needs surveyed in phase one. This phase will involve a flexible MEMIS staff. Their posture must endorse cooperative data processing or the joining of districts to economically process information. They must be available to local districts for adjustment to standard systems to better meet local needs and trouble-shoot any difficulties during implementation.

The success of the development of LEMIS, by the coordinators and the MEMIS staff, will be easily determined by the number of local school systems that implement standard systems. However, the ultimate test will be if the information needs of the users are fulfilled. Unless these requirements are realized, many of the benefits indicated in this report will not be attained.

The summary of the recommendations which follows reveals the scope of the study and the diligence of the task force in finding issues.

Key Recommendations of the Task Force

General Court Action

1. Consider the findings and recommendations of the various individuals and groups that have studied the school funding problem, and take appropriate action.
2. Grant the Department of Education authority to select, compensate, and classify their professional staff within overall limits of its budget.
3. Grant school committees responsibility for insurance coverage on school buildings and contents.
4. Invest full authority for purchasing supplies and services used in the school district with the school committee.
5. Authorize the school committees in all towns and cities in the Commonwealth to maintain the school buildings.
6. Permit school districts to keep their own books of account or contract this function to the parent town or city.
7. Require the town treasurer to pay promptly and without further authorization all purchase orders and requisitions on certification by the school committee or its appointed representative providing the amount due and payable is within the approved budget.
8. Authorize the school committees to delegate executive authority to the superintendent.
9. Exclude principals and assistant principals from any collective bargaining unit.
10. Establish a central state agency to contract for construction of all elementary and secondary public school buildings.
11. Use the Commonwealth's credit rating to minimize bond interest costs.
12. Require all school committees to submit budgets that are program-oriented rather than function-oriented.
13. Require school budgets to display revenue sources and contributed services, all anticipated expenditures for whatever purposes within or without the school system, and indicate the net amount to be raised by local taxation.
14. Provide for periodic destruction of records.
15. Permit school districts to advance funds in anticipation of payment by state or federal authorities for projects which have been properly approved.
16. Establish a limitation on state financial aid for school construction projects.
17. Permit the use of a base bid and alternate specifications.

18. Enable and encourage school committees to consider and negotiate bus contracts for periods of longer than the presently allowed three years.
19. Limit state reimbursements to school districts for pupil transportation costs.
20. Require municipalities which do not carry primary insurance on their buildings and contents to purchase excess-loss coverage.
21. Amend the Workmen's Compensation Act to make mandatory the provisions of the law to all local and regional district school system employees.
22. Require municipalities not insured against liability for Workmen's Compensation to carry single accident excess insurance or reinsurance.
23. Distribute the existing collective bargaining manual to all school authorities.
24. Create a division of School Construction and Facilities.
25. Establish standard criteria and records for evaluation of space utilization.
26. Provide school districts with experience records of school architects.
27. Develop procedure manuals for educational specifications, building design and construction, site selection, site development, and financial assistance.
28. Immediately implement the provision for state financial aid to rehabilitate and modernize older schools.
29. Upgrade minimum school building lighting standards to conform with the latest Illuminating Engineering Society recommended levels.
30. Require the Division of School Construction and Facilities to act as consultants to school districts on building construction to reduce operating and maintenance costs.
31. Develop bidding forms and procedures for use by school districts.
32. Develop computer-assisted routing and scheduling techniques for use by the school districts.
33. Encourage the establishment of area transportation districts in Massachusetts.
34. Develop and implement a uniform purchasing system for use by school districts.
35. Establish a state-wide continuing purchasing committee.
36. Create a Division of Nutrition Education and School Food Services.
37. Adopt criteria for measuring efficiency of individual school and district food service operations.
38. Channel available government-donated commodities to good processors for conversion into finished products for resale to various school district systems.
39. Redesign the Report and Claim for Reimbursement form by substituting a monthly balance sheet and profit-and-loss statement.
40. Publish a cafeteria personnel handbook at the state level to emphasize selection, motivation, and training of cafeteria employees.
41. Create a position of Supervisor of Insurance.
42. Promote the concept and establishment of regional instructional media centers.

43. Establish a program to provide a system of mutual support among all libraries.

School Committee Action

1. Increase solicitation of volunteers through civic organizations and local citizens to aid local school administrators.
2. Solicit volunteers from local business and industry to assist in special instructional areas and administrative matters.
3. Secure the services of a professional negotiator to represent the school committee in collective bargaining sessions.
4. Adopt a policy that the superintendent act only in an advisory capacity in collective bargaining.
5. Approve the school budget as one total.
6. Require all school superintendents to make a report at the end of each school year showing the financial results by program compared with budget and also the educational results compared with those forecast when the budget was prepared.
7. Establish security procedures for handling, counting, and depositing cash.
8. Increase use of proper long-range planning techniques.
9. Reactivate custodial training programs conducted by the Division of Occupational Education at regional vocational high schools and other locations.
10. Procure a handbook for all custodial personnel.
11. Develop cooperative maintenance arrangements between cities and towns.
12. Establish cooperative arrangements where transportation is required for special purposes such as vocational and/or technical schools, and the like.
13. Include a provision in all contracts giving the school department authority to set the conditions of bus and driver behavior.
14. Require performance bonds as an integral part of every request for Bid and Transportation Contract.
15. Develop cooperative purchasing on a regional basis with assistance from the Department of Education.
16. Organize regional committees to select and maintain lists of recommended textbooks for each subject level and establish procedures for their procurement.
17. Require the use of central kitchens to serve more than one school.
18. Coordinate the purchase and processing of materials on a regional basis.
19. Establish written policies governing travel and reimbursement regulations

for school district personnel based on guidelines to be developed by the Massachusetts Department of Education.

School Administration Action

1. Prepare, beginning in 1971, and annually submit a five-year plan to the school committee for action and forward a copy to the Department of Education for review.
2. Make special purpose areas available for other activities.
3. Improve on-the-job training for new custodians.
4. Improve the quality of custodial supervision.
5. Institute schedules for custodians using work-measurement techniques.
6. Install a suggestion system for custodian and maintenance personnel.
7. Involve the pupils in the care of their school building.
8. Limit assignment of maintenance planning and administration responsibilities to properly qualified employees.
9. Develop and implement maintenance management systems which include sound principles of preventive maintenance.
10. Analyze the school's contracted services to determine if employment of full-time craftsmen is justified.
11. Encourage custodians to perform minor maintenance jobs.
12. Establish centralized student pickup locations unless safety considerations dictate otherwise.
13. Designate a telephone number and a person to whom parents can call to obtain bus information or register complaints.
14. Issue written rules of conduct to pupils and parents every year and post the regulations in each bus.
15. Require written reports of rule violations from bus drivers and establish formal review procedures.
16. Assign responsibility for transporting handicapped students to the agency responsible for their education.
17. Expand school district purchasing under state contracts with assistance from the Department of Education.
18. Use paperback books where practical and economical.
19. Develop and implement Local Educational Management Information Systems (LEMIS).
20. Designate guidance personnel as supervisors of attendance and, where possible, shift disciplinary aspects of the position to local police departments.
21. Use nonprofessional adults on a part-time, full-time, or volunteer basis to

perform clerical and other nonprofessional work tasks which consume much
time of school nurses.
22. Improve the availability of library materials and facilities.
23. Install property control systems within each school district.

City and Town Action

1. Designate a member of the school committee and the superintendent or his
   appointee as voting members of the School Building Committee.
2. Promote the development and use of the modular systems approach to
   reduce construction costs.
3. Establish local stabilization funds for new school construction to reduce
   financing costs.
4. Make early decisions and commitments to new buildings.
5. Require the architect selected for a new school building to evaluate
   proposed new school building design technologies and methods.
6. Require the architect selected for a new school building to study alternate
   types of heating and ventilation systems prior to completion of the final
   design, and specify high-quality, easily maintained mechanical and electrical
   equipment.
7. Involve maintenance and custodial personnel in the design and planning of
   new facilities.
8. Make the local health agencies responsible for health services in all public
   schools.

While many organizations united in asking for this study, there were those
who felt that business matters could not be disassociated from instructional
aspects of education. The general sense now among the doubters is that the study
came off well and the distinction between business and instructional matters
worked.

The next study reviewed, dealing with school district organization, is knitted
in with the task force report. We will, in fact, find some of the business task
force report cited in the pages that follow.

4 What is a School District?

Massachusetts public schools are as various as municipalities. – Willis-Harrington Report

Come close and let us wake the joy
Our fathers used to know,
When to the little old school house
together we would go,
Thus neighbor's heart to neighbor warmed
in thought for common good;
We'll strike the fine old cord again –
A song of neighborhood. – George Ford

As a small, densely populated state virtually without natural barriers, Massachusetts is ideally suited to school district consolidation and collaboration. By automobile, it takes little more than two hours to travel its length from the outskirts of Boston on the coast to Pittsfield in the extreme western part of the state. North to South the state is, for the most part, a mere 50 miles wide. Except for the recent use of federal funds, under title III of the Elementary and Secondary Education Act, to encourage inter-district collaboratives, there is little evidence that the twentieth century has influenced school districting in Massachusetts. Inequality, isolation, overlap and separation are the four horsemen of school districting in Massachusetts.

The contemporary scene has brought changes on such a vast scale that they cannot continue to be ignored by schools and communities. Possibly the twentieth century can be better introduced by its predecessor, the nineteenth century, in which most people lived their lives out in one community. Unless one traveled by train, a twenty-mile journey usually required a tiresome full day on the road. Not much changed from decade to decade. Nineteenth century technology can be characterized by ingenious farm implements, the iron horse and the pervasive conviction that most things had already been invented. Six grades of education, obtained in a two or three room schoolhouse within walking distance from home, satisfied most individual, social and industrial requirements. The issues of racism and inequality were blunted or overlooked.

With greater fidelity to the last century than to the present, small and fragmented school districts seemingly thrive in the Massachusetts climate. Three-hundred and eighty-nine administrative units serve a state population of 5.4

85

million while Rhode Island has 40 administrative units for a population of 900,000. Of states wth roughly comparable population sizes, Florida, for 6.1 million residents, has 67 basic administrative units; North Carolina with 5.1 million has 160 units; Virginia with 4.6 million has 132 units. Thirty-one of the 50 states have fewer administrative units. This means that Massachusetts has fallen far behind in the national trend toward unified school districts.

Surprisingly, the topic of school district consolidation and collaboration has not been a topic for the public forum in Massachusetts. Yet, it is difficult to cite an educational problem that is not related to key aspects of school districting. Efficiency, costs, the year-around school, inservice teacher training programs, and options for students are merely a few issues associated with the character of the school district and the kinds of collaborative arrangements fostered with other districts.

The fruits of school districts joining together are not difficult to witness in other states or to imagine in the Bay State. Indeed, educational cooperatives have emerged dramatically in the last several years to the point where virtually every state can point to its version. Most states, including Massachusetts, have devised some forms of school district cooperation in addition to the old standby of consolidation. Federal money has encouraged a host of arrangements which have led school districts to link.

In joint arrangements, school districts have offered a myriad of functions. Small districts may link in order to offer programs they cannot individually perform. Others offer elaborate library and information services or inservice teacher training, or even briefings for school board members. Affiliations are often made by cooperatives with other institutions, particularly colleges and universities. Special industry-education cooperatives have been formed which again serve a variety of needs.

One of the better known and older arrangements has been the Boards of Cooperative Educational Services (BOCES) in the state of New York. Such cooperatives typically offer a central facility carrying on a span of activities according to need, location and financial status. Mobile educational laboratories are often a part of such control. Sometimes, teacher specialists work out of these facilities. Typically, conference rooms, storage areas, special equipment and other central facilities may be found in a BOCES.

The purposes of such arrangements are to provide access to services and programs not otherwise readily at hand. The supposition is made that the added services and programs are not only more readily available but are better than could otherwise be provided. A necessary purpose, as well, is to be more cost effective and to develop a system of accountability and, in the final analysis, to make rationale arrangements.

The best-known study of school district organization in Massachusetts in recent years is the Willis-Harrington report which held central comprehensive study of the problems in inequalities in education in Massachusetts at that time. One of its strongest recommendations was for reorganization of schools into larger districts and the establishment of a subcommission to implement this. As a result of the Willis-Harrington study, the School Building Assistance Bureau was established in the Department of Education as an effective instrument of implementation within the constraints of the law. Unfortunately no real, long-range master plan was developed in adequate detail in the Willis-Harrington report. Yet, many of the problems which school districts now face were either described or anticipated in the study.

In 1966, Lawrence Ovian conducted a study of school district organization in Worcester County and developed several proposals for reorganization:

1. Establishment of unified school districts, including a grade organization of 1–12.
2. Inclusion of all communities within a district maintaining and operating a high school.
3. Administration of unified districts by a single superintendent working with one district-wide school committee.
4. Establishment of minimum pupil population of 2000 (grades 1–12).
5. Location of schools so that elementary pupils spent no more than 45 minutes and secondary pupils spend no more than 45 in transit to or from school.[1]

Most other studies and reports dealing with school district organization in Massachusetts have been sponsored and published by the State Education Department or by the Council.

The Massachusetts Department of Education in 1968, issued the booklet, *Quality Education Through School District Organization,* which included a number of definitions of quality education, status and progress reports on reorganization in Massachusetts, information on reorganization procedure and available services, and guidelines for School District Organization.

1. Each community shall constitute, or be a part of, a school district maintaining and operating a complete Kindergarten-Grade 12 educational program, governed by a single school committee with one superintendent of schools.
2. Each school committee shall make provisions for participation in an approved vocational-occupational program.
3. Each school committee shall provide an educational program which meets the minimum standards mandated by the Board of Education. Each school committee shall be encouraged to exceed these minimum standards.
4. Each school district shall contain at least 2,000 pupils, unless prevented by extenuating circumstances acceptable to the Board of Education.
5. Each school committee with less than 2,000 pupils under its jurisdiction on December 31, 1968, shall submit a plan to implement these Guidelines to the Commission of Education by December 31, 1969.[2]
   The guidelines reflect the sense of the findings reported in research and the

experience of other states moving toward reorganization. However, the guidelines, even the 2000 pupils enrollment figure, tend to lie in the minimum range of research recommendations and other states' practices.

The study reports produced by the Council intensified the concerns of a growing number of people that all was not well in school districting. Gibson, who as we have seen studied the State Department of Education, reflected a need for school districting and program reform in three of his five major recommendations:

1. Strong efforts should be undertaken to increase the Department's service role to school systems and to minimize the function of the Department as a regulator and enforcement agency with respect to the public schools in the state.
2. Present regional offices of the Department should be strengthened better to deliver school services of quality directly to school systems; and at least two more regional offices (or service centers) should be created, with one serving the needs of the Greater Boston area.
3. A program should be launched under the aegis of the Department calling for the establishment of educational goals for Massachusetts students, assessment of student achievement with respect to goals, evaluation of schools, and accountability by educators and educational decision makers to the publics they serve for their performance with respect to students.

While the focus is on the Department of Education, the intent was the improvement of education state wide.

In 1969, Gordon P. Liddle and Arthur M. Kroll conducted a study, *Pupil Services in Massachusetts Schools* sponsored again by the Council. Among other findings, Liddle and Kroll report:

> Most small communities in Massachusetts have long and unique histories, and residents have not only jealously guarded their traditions and independence, but have also wanted to keep their communities at a size where town meetings could deal with all civic affairs. When asked to consolidate school districts in the interests of economy and excellence, they have frequently responded negatively. . . .
>
> The result of high degree of local autonomy in Massachusetts has been that many school systems are too small to provide a comprehensive educational program at reasonable cost. . . .This combination of poor public support and small school districts can mean substandard education opportunity for a majority of the state's children.[3]

Liddle and Kroll proceed to compare pupil services at the secondary level with a state study in 1968 which revealed that 44 percent of small high schools employed full time counselors, 9 percent part-time and 47 percent none while all regional secondary schools provided full-time counseling.

They conclude that:

Although the only comparison identified here has been that of guidance counselors, our impression is that a similar discrepancy exists for the other pupil services groups. In fact, many small districts have no psychological, social work, or speech and hearing services; thus, although existing evidence shows a lower per-pupil cost in small school districts than it does in regional units, services available to students are also considerably fewer or may even be nonexistent.[4]

Lloyd Michael, whose study of high schools is discussed in Chapter 11, was sorely concerned with the small and inadequate high schools he found. He produced the following terse summary of his findings in this regard:

On October 1, 1969, 92, or 30.2 percent of the 305 high schools in Massachusetts, had an enrollment of 500 or fewer; 89, or 29.2 percent, had between 501 and 1,000. The median enrollment in the 204 regular high schools was 1,041; in the 42 regional high schools, it was 704; in the 50 vocational-technical and trade high schools, it was 246; and in the nine regional vocational-technical high schools, it was 436.

While other MACE studies express versions of concern over the archaic patterns of school districting, no study does it better than the Business Task Force on Business Management.

Supporters of local control should be concerned about a system which so fragments the functions of communities that they have, in fact, very little control over their destiny. Some cities and towns have been forced to hand over control of important parts of their programs to bodies with which they, as communities, feel very little affinity. Therefore, local control, especially if it is considered as limiting the necessary and sometimes overforceful activities of state and federal authority, can be more effective and economically operated if the local units can call upon a larger and more diverse group of citizens to represent their interests.

The growing complexity of the educational process makes today's situation increasingly ciritcal. The concept of cooperation in education is one which has not, in the past, appealed to a large segment of the Commonwealth's citizens. However, aside from purely educational advantages, we are convinced that a system which combines central leadership with strong centers of local control will best produce economies of operation. It will minimize the wasteful and often dilatory processes of bureaucracy.

The Task Force states that cooperation between school districts produces the following specific advantages:

1. Greater challenges, higher scholastic achievement, and more efficient use of teaching staffs.
2. Construction of facilities at lowest cost to meet needs of the community.
3. Use of funds for educational purposes rather than excessive administration costs.
4. More capable business management and the resulting economies. Specific examples of this will be found elsewhere in their report, particularly in the sections dealing with transportation, purchasing, libraries, textbooks, and management information system.
5. Special programs for all children in need of them at the lowest cost.
6. School groupings which are financially self-sufficient and whose voters can truly be in control of all aspects of their childrens' education.
7. Orderly planning of future developments of the system based on financial projections.
8. Establishment of a state aid equalization system which can be easily administered and still make possible equitable results.
9. Ability to employ consultants and experts and improve general managerial effectiveness.
10. Capability of systems to appraise and employ new educational technology, including machine teaching and other purchased services which promise to free the classroom teacher for the more important problems caused by the rapidly expanding body of available knowledge. This is an area where substantial savings will be made in the near future.

The time has come when Massachusetts should not and need not be satisfied with limited objections. In recognition of this situation, the Board of Education has instructed the Department of Education to prepare legislation making mandatory the regionalization of smaller districts. This courageous attack on the basic problem is welcomed. However, the Task Force strongly questions the desirability of mandatory legislation at this time because:

• Public opinion needs a period of informed and in-depth discussion if such a program is to receive the popular support essential for its success. Some deep-seated traditional attitudes must be changed. This will require public meetings, identification of power sources within the community, involvement of citizens and legislators, gathering of relevant statistics and information, and a positive attitude that what is educationally and economically useful can take place.

• Norms that have hitherto been accepted by the Department of Education for district size need careful reexamination. It is doubtful whether a district with a pupil population of 2,000 is today adequate to support an effective and economical program.

• Possible forms of cooperation or regionalization plans have not received sufficient consideration from all concerned parties. It is vitally important that this subject be carefully studied in the light of present conditions and the solution be more than a patchwork superimposed upon existing laws and regulations. Changes that will ultimately be regarded as necessary may be so sweeping that a period of experimentation is desirable if the optimum program is to be accepted and adopted.

The Task Force envisions a gradual but steady transition in the direction of larger school districts. This process needs the complete commitment of the General Court, the Board of Education, school committees, teachers, and the general public. It should be a process by which all persons experiment and learn together with the common objective of devising the most effective and economical educational system. Such a process, which appeals to the traditional independence and good sense of the citizens of Massachusetts, is the one which has the greatest possibility of success.

The following guidelines to foster school district cooperation were adopted:

1.   Education is a function and responsibility of the Commonwealth, which it may delegate in whole or in part to other groups.
2.   Massachusetts is committed to providing an equal opportunity for a quality public education to all its children, in accordance with their abilities. This opportunity should depend on the individual's desire to learn rather than accidents of geography or local wealth.
3.   Policy-making and direction of public education beyond the authority of the local school systems should be concentrated in the Department of Education.
4.   A local school district should be the basic organizational unit as it has traditionally been. Cooperation by local school systems will serve to strengthen, rather than weaken, local control.
5.   Local cooperation must depend on factors such as destiny of population, length of travel time, local wealth, character of the communities involved, and the like. No absolute figure for the size of such groupings can be determined.
6.   Participation by a community in a proposed cooperative effort should take place with the full understanding and consent of voters in the planned district or entity.
7.   Cooperation must be guided by some form of logical planning, even though plans may be changed from time to time. If this is not done, there is substantial risk (as experience in other states has proved) that certain communities would be in a situation where all their neighbors had been preempted.
8.   There should be an equalization of the tax burden in such a way that poorer districts are able to provide an adequate education for their children, but also in a way that does not prevent any district from providing whatever level of educational services it desires and can afford.

School districting is not an issue but an amalgam of critical, related problems including inequality of educational opportunity, racial imbalance and narrow educational options. When education is unequally supported small and/or isolated school districts are bound to create more problems in an interdependent, technological society.

It fell to Donald T. Donley, the Dean of the School of Education at Boston College, and Vincent Nuccio, Director of their Center for Field Research and School Services, to make the first serious study of school districting in Massachusetts for the Advisory Council.

How the Study was Organized

The Donley-Nuccio report was understood from the beginning to be preliminary to a major additional study, probably to be done again by the Advisory Council, meant to produce a specific and detailed plan. Since the Donley-Nuccio study, this intent has become a reality with the appointment by the Governor of a commission as we reported earlier.

The procedures followed by Boston College's Center for Field Research and School Services were designed to collect pertinent information, analyze it as it relates to the problems and needs of school districting in Massachusetts, and to derive from the analysis, a set of conclusions and recommendations for effecting desirable change.

The procedures included:

1. A review of other studies conducted both in Massachusetts and other states treating with the subject of school district organization.
2. A review of the experience of other states in studying and effecting school district reorganization.
3. An historical review of educational law in Massachusetts and evaluation of current education law in terms of its appropriateness and effectiveness in relation to school district organization.
4. A comprehensive protocol of discussion meetings with representatives of all groups identified with a strong interest in education. The protocol included meetings with state education department personnel, the State Board of Education, school administrators, school committeemen and laymen representing a wide spectrum of professional and business interests. Several meetings were held in the various areas of the state to insure the input of regional thinking across the state.
5. Extensive analysis of statistical information available within the state bearing on the current status of public school systems in Massachusetts relative to quality of education, equality of educational opportunity, and financial efficiency.

Completion of the procedures necessitated seven separate but related studies, each of which is handled as a separate chapter in the full study report. In the remainder of this report, the major findings of the seven studies are digested and summarized and the major conclusions and recommendations for action presented.

The Findings

In Massachusetts, there are 351 municipalities consisting of 312 towns and 39 cities. Until recent years, there were 351 districts and each school district was coterminous with the geographical boundaries of each city and town. The schools of each municipality were managed by a school committee elected at large by the registered voters and each school committee was responsible for the education of all its resident pupils attending public schools from kindergarten through grade twelve.

The fundamental concept was that each municipality, irrespective of whether its population was 750,000 persons or 75 persons, was required to educate its own pupils without the legal means to merge with other towns.

This basic concept was satisfactory for the larger cities and towns, but was disastrous for small towns. Small towns were unable to maintain adequate schools for the education of their youth.

Massachusetts still has 51 towns with a population of less than 1,000 persons. In addition, there are 114 other towns with a population of more than 1,000 but less than 5,000 persons.

Most of these small towns were unable even to maintain a high school and were forced to send their children "on tuition" to high schools in other municipalities. In 1948, a study by the Legislature showed that 119 towns in Massachusetts had no high school at all. One hundred six additional towns maintained high schools with an enrollment of less than 200 pupils. Therefore, of the 312 towns in Massachusetts, 225 either maintained no high school at all or maintained high schools that were inadequate according to any modern educational standards.

As a result of this study, sweeping educational reforms were made by the Legislature in 1949. For the first time in Massachusetts, a new concept was developed whereby any two or more towns could create a regional school district. A regional school district is a separate body politic and corporate which may be established by vote of two or more towns for the purpose of operating a school district as one separate unit. The district is a separate legal entity and is operated by a regional district school committee consisting of members from each of the towns embracing the district. The district builds and operates its own schools and charges the capital and operating expenses to the member towns in accordance with the terms of a written agreement.

The regional school law was the first major step in Massachusetts which enabled small towns to break away from the old concept of maintaining a small, wasteful and inefficient form of school district organization.

However, it should be noted that the original purpose of the regional school law was to enable small towns to devise a method whereby they could solve their secondary educational problems. The law does not require the member towns to regionalize all the grades from kindergarten through grade 12. Towns which form a regional school district may agree in advance to operate a high school for grades nine through twelve or a junior-senior high school for grades seven through twelve, or they may operate schools for all or any of the grades from kindergarten through grade twelve. In the twenty years that the law has been in existence, considerable progress has been made in improving the educational system in small towns. Fifty-one regional school districts have actually been formed embracing 154 of the smaller towns in Massachusetts. As previously noted, these regional school districts operate schools only for the grades agreed upon in advance. The breakdown of the various grade jurisdictions of the 51 academic (as distinguished from vocational regional school districts) is as follows:

26 districts operate schools for grades 7 through 12
12 districts operate schools for grades 9 through 12
3 districts operate schools for grades 5 through 12
1 district operates schools for grades 1 through 6
1 district operates schools for kindergarten through grade 6
8 districts operate schools for all the grades from kindergarten through grade 12

From these figures, it is apparent that most of the regionalization has been accomplished at the secondary level. Only eight districts have been formed which include all the grades from kindergarten through grade twelve.

The opportunity to learn, to be educated according to his ability, is something that every child in the Commonwealth deserves. The state has long recognized the responsibility to provide equal educational opportunity and has been aware that inequities exist. A major focus of the Donley-Nuccio study was to identify differences as they relate to geographic, financial and curriculum factors — on the basis of statistical analysis of available school data. Results of the analysis, apparently the first such study of district organization, identify many inequalities in educational opportunity and confirm the opinion expressed by many Massachusetts residents that there is a need for the development of a sound state financial support program for education, designed to eliminate inequalities.

There is no master plan for school district organization, currently effective in the Commonwealth. Statutes have been passed, frequently to treat *pro tem* situations, which are too narrowly focused or unclear to be effective in achieving desirable change on a broad scale. There is no mandate for exploring a uniform state-wide procedure for planning and organizing school districts aside from leaving it to local initiative.

It should be understood that no single approach to the problems of school district organization will guarantee improvement in the quality of education in Massachusetts or any other state. However, there exists a great deal of information available from the experience of other states and from numerous studies which indicates the relationship between improvement of quality and such factors as district organization, size, legislation, and financial support. Most other states have reorganized school districts, drastically reducing the number of administrative units. Massachusetts alone has increased the number of school districts. The increase has been caused primarily in the interest of providing education through the regional vocational-technical schools to pupils not well served by the traditional academic high school. However, this has not solved the problems of the too small district and, considering the fact that regionalization of schools recently has moved so slowly, it is apparent that the 1967 guidelines "endorsed" by the State Board of Education which calls for each school district to contain at least 2000 pupils in a K-12 organization, are not an adequate answer.

Educational leadership throughout the state, including committeemen, subscribe to the importance of long-range planning as a prerequisite to quality educational programming. Long-range planning is not evident in most school districts.

There is no clearly defined concept of quality education currently accepted in the state and, consequently, there is no consensus on the steps necessary to achieve quality education. (The State Board of Education has since produced a useful set of concepts.)

By law, the responsibility of fostering and encouraging school district reorganization in Massachusetts has been assigned to the State School Building Assistance Commission and subsequently, the School Building Assistance Bureau in the State Education Department. Under the leadership of the State Education Department, much progress has been made in reducing the number of operating administrative units. However, there are still many districts which cannot provide adequate programs and which are inefficient because of administrative duplication and high cost.

However, educational statutes place authority to plan state-wide programs for education with the State Board of Education. The power to implement such plans is restricted by statute and resides in the local district. Under current state financial support and incentive provisions, it is unlikely that much implementation will occur.

Legislation designed to treat a specific problem such as lack of vocational education programs will not solve the basic educational problems of the state. A long-range master plan is needed.

Donley's team sensed a "widespread" willingness to look at school district organization, yet the problem of preconceived notions, and a stated willingness on the part of many to settle for second or third rate educational programs prevails.

Analysis of available statistical data on Massachusetts public schools provided several significant insights. While it is impossible to draw strongly definitive conclusions on the relationship of organization, enrollment, wealth and expenditure to quality (because of the data limitations described in the section dealing with facts about Massachusetts schools), the following statements can be made:

1. The concern of citizens in some K-6 districts about their school becoming part of a larger K-12 district is understandable. Some K-6 districts provide more in the way of special personnel, separate facilities, equipment, and library books than are provided to elementary grades in many K-12 districts. However, they do so at high cost.

2. The impact of federal monies and the existence of a secondary school program have benefited elementary programs more in K-12 districts than in K-6 or K-8 districts.

3. School districts which include higher grades (K-12 and K-8) provide much more program articulation than do K-6 districts.

4. K-12 school districts pay higher teacher salaries than do K-6 or K-8 districts. Generally, the level of teacher salaries seems to be most closely related to the geographic area of the state in which they teach. The implications for recruiting are clear.

5. There is evidence of geographic differences in educational vitality and probably leadership in different areas of the state. The extent to which this may be related to school district organization needs further study.

6. There are wide differences in secondary school curriculum offerings among high schools in K-12 districts. Consideration of expenditure, wealth, location, or enrollment did not reduce the variability. This factor should be studied carefully in planning for reorganization.

7. From a financial viewpoint, the K-12 school district is economically the most efficient of all types of school district organizations in Massachusetts. The K-12 organization appears to get the greatest educational benefit for every dollar spent. K-6 and K-8 districts, which represent the greatest proportion of small districts, are the least efficient.

8. K-6 and K-8 districts are being disproportionately subsidized through high percentages of state aid and other special aides, regardless of their wealth. In many such districts, over 50 percent of total current expenditure is derived directly from state support. Therefore, the current formula is encouraging financially inefficient systems.

Finally, if Massachusetts is to deal successfully with its educational problems and move toward quality education, a process must be formulated which fits the unique characteristics of the Commonwealth.

The ensuing section outlines the necessary bases to touch in discussions of access and quality in educational programing and in managing the educational enterprise.

A. Improvement of Academic Program through:

    1.-guaranteeing articulation, so that as a child moves through grades K-12 each year's experience is based sequentially on previous years' learning experiences without gaps or unnecessary repetitions

    2.-offering a wider range of course offerings

    3.-increasing vocational education opportunities

    4.-providing better pupil-teacher ratios

    5.-attracting and retaining better qualified teachers

    6.-utilizing teacher academic specialization better

    7.-reducing the number of drop outs

    8.-improving occupational preparation

    9.-eliminating too small grade enrollments − so that no teacher handles more than one grade

    10.-developing adult education programs

    11.-broadening extracurricular opportunities − such as music, drama, debate, athletics

    12.-coordinating with and supporting of community colleges.

B. Expansion of Educationally Desireable Supportive Services through:

    1.-providing special education for all kinds of exceptional children close to home

    2.-expanding organized programs of physical education

    3.-providing guidance counseling at all grade levels

    4.-providing psychological services to all age groups

    5.-securing speech therapy for students

    6.-providing health services for all children

    7.-collaborating with social workers in home-school relations where necessary

    8.-providing remedial specialists such as reading to all children who need it.

C. Improvement of financial Efficiency through:

    1.-lowering per pupil costs by creating more efficient organizational structure

    2.-lowering administrative costs per pupil

    3.-increasing economies in purchasing

    4.-broadening the tax base

    5.-gaining more state aid

    6.-equalizing property valuation over a wide area

    7.-improving possibilities of getting more federal aid

    8.-decreasing legal and business costs

    9.-increasing borrowing capacity

    10.-improving professional salaries to attract most competent personnel.

D. Improvement of the Social (or Societal) Function of the School through:
    1.-equalizing educational opportunity for all pupils regardless of geographic location or other factors
    2.-involving citizens from all participating communities in educational development
    3.-increasing public and family support of schools by providing information, involvement, and better programs for all pupils
    4.-providing a broader base for citizens to participate in policy making in a comprehensive district
    5.-achieving an adequate size school population to make possible the achievement of desireable educational goals.
E. Improvement of Operational Functions and Related Economies through:
    1.-establishing a unified and coordinated transportation system
    2.-gaining greater flexibility in the use of buildings
    3.-coordinating custodial and maintenance services with greater flexibility
    4.-unifying administration of such school responsibilities as the lunch program
    5.-providing paraprofessional assistance for clerical functions so that professionals are free to do what they are paid for.
F. Improvement of School Administration through:
    1.-coordinating educational programs and development for an area or region by one effective, representative policy-making body (school board or school committee) rather than several
    2.-coordinating supervision and evaluation of instruction on an area-wide basis
    3.-establishing one cohesive budget for an entire district
    4.-establishing a more effective program for recruiting and hiring teachers
    5.-establishing a basis for uniform reports and evaluations – making accountability more practicable
    6.-eliminating duplication (and waste) in administrative time, energy, and cost.

Recommendations

In any school, the student is the focus in the learning process. Organizing schools means organizing for learning. The major task in organizing for learning is to develop the *means* that will deliver the educational resources and services needed to assist the child in achieving – to the best of his ability – those skills, knowledges, attitudes, and values that will enable him to become a productive citizen in a democratic society.

Accomplishment of such organization implies drastic changes – not easily accomplished but, nevertheless, imperative. The most significant contribution made to the Commonwealth, aside from documenting the need for reorganization, is the formulation of a design for achieving more effective organization. The design is based on all of the information collected, including that relative to communication difficulties and political attitudes, and is intended to establish a process which can achieve more equitable allocation of educational resources and services. Ultimately, this means that all of the children of the state will have equal access to the advantages characteristic of the good, large K-12 district plus vocational or occupational education opportunities, and the state will benefit from increased economic efficiency. The following is recommended by Donley:

A. The legislature create a Commission of School District Organization to be appointed by the Governor of the Commonwealth.[5]

The Commission should be action-oriented and charged with three major responsibilities:

1. The establishment of a statewide definition of quality education for Massachusetts, based on the educational experiences which should be available to all Massachusetts youth.

2. The development of a statewide master plan for organizing the educational resources and services of the state to achieve the goals found in the definition of quality education.

3. Participation with the legally constituted educational authorities (Secretary of Educational Affairs and State Board of Education) in executing responsibilities 1 and 2.

The purpose in establishing a Commission, Donley states, is to create the machinery for broad representation, wide involvement, clear communication, and political potency to attack the problems of quality and equality of education in the state. The situation is serious and currently existing instruments (statutes and agencies) need reinforcement in developing and implementing plans for change.

He recommended that the Commission have approximately 21 members, including balanced representation from education, government and legislature, business and industry, and other interested groups. Appointment of Commission members should also provide for representation from the State Board of Education, the State Department of Education, and from the various geographic areas of the state.

The work of the Commission during the first one and one-half years would be the establishment of a master plan. It was estimated that meetings and studies necessary to completion of the task would cost about $100,000 over the one and one-half period. The Commission, in fulfilling its responsibility, should enter into agreement with the Massachusetts Advisory Council on Education whereby the Council, with the approval of the Commission, would employ competent study teams and supervise the studies required by the Commission.

The Commission will be responsible for any information releases and will submit its final report and recommendations to the General Court and governor by December 1972.

B. The Commission on School District Organization will use area task forces in developing the master plan. The task forces established in specific geographic areas of the state would each be responsible for drafting organizational plans for its own geographic area. Each task force should include area representatives from the Legislature, higher educational institutions, vocational schools, public and private schools, business, industry, civic groups, and parent groups. It should also involve the appropriate State Education Department Regional Office. The leader of each task force should be appointed by the Commission. Geographic areas display unique characteristics and the Task Force approach will provide for planning in terms of area differences as well as guaranteeing a broad base for contributions and comprehensive communication.

C. The delineation of geographic boundaries for each task force be established by the Commission.

D. Planning for school reorganization for the benefit of pupils be predicted on as sound an information base as possible.

Several steps should be taken immediately upon appointment of the Commission to strengthen the information base. Some of the procedures will terminate upon completion of the master plan; others should be incorporated into continuing state practice:

1. The Commission make a careful study of available information on school district organization in Massachusetts, including the full report of this study.

2. An inventory be taken immediately to identify specific data needs of the State Education Department so that data collection instruments can be identified or developed to gather additional information for educational decisions. The Division of Research and Development should be assisted in staff expansion to develop the needed programs of data collection and information dissemination in response to Commission requests and on a continuing basis. Such development could be part of the "Massachusetts Educational Management Information System, as recommended in the Business Task Force School Management Study.

3. The responsibility for developing a more comprehensive data processing system (as described in b. above) be supported by necessary funding and authority.

4. Data on pupil progress be systematically collected on a state-wide basis. Such data collection could be modeled after the National Assessment of Educational Progress (NAEP). Data of this type can establish a degree of accountability and made available to the Commission and the State information needed for improvement of education and organizational modification on a continuing basis.

5. Careful study be made of variations in quality among school system types and within school system types to determine the nature and possible causes of such differences. Resulting information can guide developmental decisions.

E. The Commission and Area Task Forces approach the problem of school district reorganization on the basis of a set of guidelines for developing quality education. Such guidelines need specificity in identifying the programs and services necessary to the achievement of quality education.

F. The Commission and Area Task Forces must consider the nature of a community and the role of the schools in it before recommending new district boundaries. Each task force should become familiar with what regional and metropolitan planners are doing and should draw on available expertise in such areas as political science, economic geography, sociology, anthropology, and marketing in studying its own region.

G. The state board of education, through the Commissioner of Education, designate the year 1971–72 as a Year of Educational Planning for all local school districts, urging each district to become involved in the work of its Area Task Force. The major questions to be answered at the local level:

1. How can we best organize the learning experiences for each child in accordance with the guidelines?

2. What resources and services can be provided best at the local inter-mediate or state levels (recruiting teachers, purchasing, inservice training, transportation, curriculum planning, etc.)?

H. Long-range educational planning be mandated by the legislature for all educational units, state and local, with financial assistance for planning provided by the State. Each educational unit should be required to develop and to keep current a five-year educational plan for improvement and for compliance with the master plan when adopted. Local planning should be based on careful projections of personnel, facilities and fiscal needs. Planning should be reviewed and updated annually and a report submitted to the State Education Department.

I. The legislature clarify current educational statutes and formulate new legislation to speed progress toward the solution of educational problems. Several problems need immediate attention and action through legislation:

1. The state board of education, under Chapter 15 of the General Laws, is obliged to provide school district planning services. Their authority for implementing school district organization change should be clearly established, especially for the implementation of a master plan (once it is developed and adopted). In fairness to the children of the state, educational improvement and reorganization cannot remain strictly a matter of local initiative. The State Board of Education should have the power to grant or withold construction incentives to school districts on the basis of district compliance with the master plan guide-lines at the end of five years — and of determining exceptions. Experience in other states indicates that once the process of broad-based involvement in establishing a state educational blueprint has been completed, progress toward reform has been accomplished through state mandates and protection of administrative posts in reorganized districts.

2. Financial incentives for reorganization are currently inadequate. School

districts which reorganize under current statutes should have construction aid increased to a flat grant of 75 percent of building costs. Incentives for other desirable educational purposes such as program development or staff improvement should be provided. Existing or new districts organized on a unified basis should have Chapter 70 aid increased from 15 percent to a minimum of 25 percent under current circumstances. While some inequities in financial support of schools must be corrected, the general level of state financial support for all school districts should be raised.

3. The operational responsibility for reviewing long-range plans and implementing school district reorganization should be vested in a separate bureau within the Department of Education, independent of but closely allied with the School Building Assistance Bureau.

4. To increase the effectiveness of the department in executing current and developing responsibilities, sufficient funds must be provided for the Department to recruit and retain sufficient competent personnel.

J. Immediate interim steps be taken to encourage school districts to establish new cooperative relationships to move toward the attainment of the quality characteristics in their educational programs. Aside from unified K-12 reorganization or the creation of intermediate districts, the most feasible immediate action would be the establishment of area cooperative educational resource centers. Such centers can be patterned after some of the more successful Title III programs such as the Merrimack Educational Center and Project Spoke or the functional operation of the Boards of Cooperative Educational Service in New York State. Such centers could provide, as an intermediate agency, the human and material educational resources not available to or supportable by individual school districts. Each district would contract with the center for materials or services it needed and all participating schools would provide support for the center on a per pupil assessment basis. Outside funding would probably be necessary and a formula such as 50 percent cooperative school support; 50 percent state support could be explored and worked out.

K. Coordination of publicly supported education include a range from preschool programs through public higher education. Resources available to the coordinated system should include at least one institution of higher learning offering graduate programs, research personnel, and services. A coordinated planning effort between the Commission for School District Organization and the agency developing the higher education master plan is also recommended.

L. The results of the study of current state financial support of education be utilized as soon as available and legislation drafted to correct inadequacies in baseline support of schools, equalization aid, and incentives.

M. The Commission on School District Organization, upon completion of its master plan, assume the role of an advisory committee to the State Board of Education and the Commissioner for a three- to five-year implementation period after adoption of the master plan. At the end of the specified time, the

Board and the Commissioner should review the Commissioner's function and made the decision as to its continuance.

Given Donley's limited resources and the slight interest heretofore shown in school districting as a major educational issue in the state, his study seems to achieve as much as could be expected. A Commission has since been appointed and is preparing to conduct a two-year study of school districting using $200,000 of Advisory Council funds.

Since Donley did not have the resources to look directly at Boston, it is appropriate that the next chapter, which discusses decentralization and some of the uses of metropolitanism, do so. The Commission has been charged to undertake a study of school districting which entails a hard look at urban, suburban and rural problems.

We next review a study of the most populous school district in Massachusetts.

5 Boston — Educational Reform in an Urban Setting

The society must provide school based upon quite different interpretation of the functions of schools, the social meaning of education and the importance of learning. – Thomas F. Green

The children of the city of New York need a public school system that will liberate the talents, energies and interests of parents, students, teachers and others to make common cause toward the goal of educational excellence. – Reconnection for Learning
McGeorge Bundy, Chairman

America is a nation of abondoned cities. Power, prestige and people have flowed to new centers and have taken the good schools with them. New urban centers flourish while old cities fester.

Boston has learned this lesson painfully and slowly. Still a proud and historic city, studded with public and private institutions — including the state capitol — Boston is no longer the home of the middle and upper classes.

Boston schoolmen may be among the last to learn the lesson as they tried to pretend that times hadn't changed. A sense of mission, the glories of the past and a sheltered bureaucracy artfully combined to keep reality at a distance.

Some changes did creep into the system. Teachers in Boston's schools no longer are required to reside in Boston. Since World War II and the severe teaching shortage, female teachers who marry may continue to teach. Federal funding fostered some improvements. The schools have become more open and volunteers have been working in the schools in recent years.

In the 1960s, however, the critics and the issues produced a bitter brew. Strikes, zooming tax rates, minorities, vandalism, Johnathan Kozol and student drop-outs were mixed together and with a deteriorating city made for something unpalatable.

Concern over Boston's schools is nothing new. In 1751, a citizen committee was appointed to inquire into the great expense of supporting its public schools. The citizens reported that "although this charge is very considerable and the number of schools is greater than the law requires, yet as the education of children is of the greatest importance to the community, the committee cannot be of the opinion that any saving can be made to advantage on that head."[1]

In 1883, a governor of Massachusetts in his inaugural address attacked the education system in general but particularly the Boston schools for their failure to meet the needs of the common people. This was an era in which parents of Irish-American ancestry were especially upset with the public schools and, although relatively poor, invested heavily in their own alternative schools.

Some more recent reports did produce change. Here are some examples:

1. The 1905 suggestions of Professor Paul Hanus of Harvard helped to plan the restructuring of the Boston School Committee and Department;
2. The 1944 recommendations of George D. Strayer led to the superintendent being given authority to appoint his chief assistants;
3. The 1953 study of school facilities by Cyril Sargent led to the closing and consolidation of more than three dozen antiquated school buildings.

Dr. Joseph Cronin's 1971 report for MACE on Boston schools includes several ideas which require modest funding and little legislation — school councils, school accountability profiles, more aggressive pursuit of available federal funds and the more rigorous evaluation of all programs and budget items. At the same time, some of his other recommendations require time and money — school ombudsmen, teacher grants, planning charrettes, day-care centers, and administrator retraining. Some require greater social conscience and unencumbered moral commitment.

But money, time, and legislation will not alone suffice. Although teacher leaders and top school officials in Boston revealed during the study an openness to change and improvement that every educational system needs, they, and the ideas in the report, need the enduring and vocal support of citizens, the media, the state, and other agencies of government. Any report on Boston's schools remains just a blueprint for possible action.

For example, some of the remedies suggested have indeed appeared in previous surveys.

A 1911 study admitted that one of the most perplexing problems in dealing with the health of school children is that of their proper nourishment. The truth undoubtedly is that a large number are not properly cared for, either through lack of sufficient food, or, if the quantity is sufficient, because of its poor quality or improper preparation. The study commission urged opening up the school lunch concession to all responsible bidders.

A 1916 survey suggested, "When the number of children in average daily attendance in a district exceeds 1,500, the Master (elementary principal) is to be assisted by a submaster, *who is to devote all of his time to supervision. . . .*" [2]

A 1931 report on Boston schools observed, "The kindergarten is now so a part of the elementary school that there is no good reason for continuing it as a separate department, for confining its supervisors strictly within it, for excluding the primary supervisors from it."[3]

Associate and Area Superintendents will agree with the 1931 description of their dilemma that "they are very busy men. They all complain of having so many things to do that they are prevented from doing what they themselves regard as their real professional work."[4] But their predecessors apparently did not agree with similar recommendations in 1916 as well as in 1931, that the supervisors' time-consuming centralized board (72 meetings in 1969) be abandoned. That board still interviews and rates candidates for headmaster, principal, assistant principal, director, and assistant director; it also discusses the program and budget matters.

The 1931 team recommended, "We are of the opinion that the statutory provision establishing the Board of Superintendents should be repealed; that the statutory provision establishing the Board of Superintendents should be repealed; that the responsibility, which his salary seems to indicate, should be laid squarely upon the Superintendent, and that he should be free to take counsel with many or few as he may desire. We find very little evidence that the Board of Superintendents has conducted a far-sighted program, pursued or settled policies, or has been a unifying influence."[5] Although harsh, this verdict remains pertinent in 1972.

Cronin's report favors a strengthened superintendency and stresses planning, but also advocates a transfer of considerably authority and staff to area superintendents, principals, and parent councils. Let decisions, he tells us, on people and programs be made closer to those affected. Let diverse decisions be made in different sections of the city with and for children of divergent needs and interests.

In years past, change may have been desirable. The seventies and the eighties press new events on us at an accelerating rate. Change must now become a characteristic of Boston's schools. Cronin's report points the way.

The Study Design and Methods

Schoolmen of a progressive stripe have been searching for more effective ways to evaluate and change organizations. Among the more popular and more effective approaches are what students of organizations commonly call survey feedback, action research, and organizational development. While not identical, these three approaches share important elements. Each approach has an early state devoted to data collection and analysis. The objective or focus of the project largely determines the data the researchers collect, but it invariably includes information about how members of the organization perceive and feel about their jobs, their relationships with their supervisors and colleagues, and their working evnironment. In some instances, these researchers or consultants are outside the organization; in others, members of the organization working under the direction of outside "experts" collect the data.

Rather than analyze the information and formulate recommendations themselves, field researchers tabulate or summarize the raw data and feed it back to groups in the organization they are trying to help. These groups then analyze and interpret the data. Consultants normally help in this work. Frequently, they give the task force special training in group problem solving and group leadership to help them reach better decisions and to communicate more effectively with the organizational units they are representing.

Once they have identified key problems and agreed on change goals, they formulate implementation plans, allocate responsibilities, and specify procedures for evaluating their progress. Because many parts of the organization have been involved in identifying problems and formulating change goals, members of the organization are predisposed to support change rather than to resist it.

Involving the membership of the organization in the analytic process will increase the probability of identifying key problems and of recommending effective, workable changes. No one has more information about any job than the person who does it every day. If he is given the tools and skills for collecting and analyzing that information, he can become more expert than the expert. Cronin, using McBer and Company behavioral scientists located in Cambridge, Massachusetts, adopted such a rationale and from it developed a procedure for the study. He even found sentiment for such a procedure within the Boston school system.

Both the Boston School Committee and the Massachusetts Advisory Council on Education, Dr. Joseph M. Cronin knew, insisted on useful recommendations and guidelines from the study. "We know the problems", said one school official; "Give us some answers." The Superintendent clarified this challenge, stating that "Urban school systems usually respond to problems with specific solutions and therefore piecemeal change; a report can help by offering long-range targets and specific steps to reach them." [6]

In addition to these behavioral approaches, Cronin's research and data collection techniques included:

1.   interviews with parents, teachers, students, and principals;
2.   community in-depth opinion surveys in selected sections of the city;
3.   interviews with past and present school committee members, city adminis-
     trators, associate and assistant superintendents, and most directors of
     central departments;
4.   questionnaire surveys on organizational problems, on school-community
     relations practices, and on coordination of outside resources, and
5.   a survey of the willingness of selected business to cooperate with the
     Boston schools.

Cronin's team used data which other study groups and agencies assembled on school personnel practices, high school programs, pupil services, maintenance repair contracts, school attendance, and nonacademic staff. His study did not review existing curricula, student achievements, or projected facilities needs, but it did include analysis of decision-making on these issues.

Many study recommendations reflect findings by a research team which was financed by the Danforth Foundation, St. Louis; it observed the decisions the Boston School Committee made from October 1967 through the summer of 1969. The Danforth grant included the stipulation that the study findings and insights be shared with local school officials.

The Superintendent designated two liaison staff members, and he met on six occasions with Cronin's team to outline problems and to discuss alternatives. The staff asked several school officials to review plans for a series of workshops; this team of school officials became a sounding board the staff used for their ideas before workshop plans were final.

The workshops involved more than 100 Boston school staff members from all levels in discussions of:

1. schools' relationships with outside agencies, especially health centers and medical hospitals, universities, and business firms;
2. school-community relations, emphasizing resources and policy changes necessary to deal with parent and neighborhood groups;
3. school personnel policy and procedures, especially those for searching for minority group personnel;
4. educational budget-making, emphasizing use of program budgeting, and evaluation techniques, and
5. organizational development, strategies to help the school department staff plan more effectively, to set new goals, and to develop new structures as they are needed.

Boston school staff members used these opportunities to consider long-range policies, to offer suggestions for solving complex problems, and to comment on the study team's ideas. These workshops provided an opportunity for candid discussions of obstacles and change. Cronin found that many Boston educators have ideas about how to improve the system, and he reflected their recommendations in the full report.

The budgeting workshop staff held an evening meeting, with the School Committee, Superintendent, and business manager present, to discuss PPBES (Program, Planning, Budgeting, and Evaluation System) and a federally financed study which would both benefit and assist Boston.

The workshop on outside resources stimulated several city proposals to the state for vocational education funds for health careers and other programs. Deans from Boston College, Boston State College, and MIT made more specific proposals after the university personnel session. To develop new ideas, the staff held several follow-up meetings with business leaders. White and black educators found the frank and open discussion of minority staff recruitment to be constructive and practical. The sessions on budgeting led staff members to further participation in other seminars on state and municipal budget-making. The workshops also gave the study team numerous suggestions for improving teacher training, community relations, and system reorganization. Most important, these discussions indicated how eager many of the school system staff members are to try a variety of approaches to solve educational problems.

In summary: the format of the study required not only data collection, but also a series of planned, intensive work sessions (six days total), during which all parties explained and tested ideas on each other. Therefore, Dr. Cronin was able to produce a report that contained few surprises for many school districts.

Since they had not only shared in producing the findings but had also developed a better sense of the need, school officials found that embedded in such a process is a heightened awareness of responsibility.

The Findings

Cronin renders a virtuoso performance as he weaves, dispassionately, but with telling effect, through the Boston school system, giving out messages for every interested and concerned reader. In this case a summary of the findings would only lose their intended impact. Therefore, we will give only a few selected highlights to inform and to give the flavor of the full report.

A Survey of Parents.   On the first pages of his report, Cronin illustrates the power of information by revealing the results of a professional research survey, resulting in what he calls a "parental report card" on the public schools of Boston. Table 5-1 ranks what parents feel should be included in the curriculum.

The general conclusions drawn from the concerns and opinions of parents were:

1. Parents generally expressed a moderate level of satisfaction with the system, calling it good or fair.
2. Parents with elementary school children in the system were less critical than those who did not have children in the Boston schools. However, many parents in both groups criticized Boston's junior and senior high schools.
3. Over half the parents said that if given the opportunity, they would not send their children to other schools; almost one-third said they would prefer to send their children to parochial or private schools.
4. Only 25 percent of the parents preferred to keep a five-man School Committee elected at large. Twenty-five percent favored an appointed board while 27 percent favored a larger elective board.
5. Parents expressed a willingness to consider a metropolitan school organization and to recruit administrators from both within and outside the system.

Table 5-1

Parental Preferences for Attention Given to Various Topics

| Subject | Percentage Preferring a "Great Deal" of Attention Given to the | |
	Subject	Rank
Drugs	71.0%	1
Proper behavior	41.1	2
Loyalty to the Country	39.0	3
Race relations	33.2	4
Preparation for a job	32.7	5
Good grooming	27.7	6
Pollution	27.5	7
Negro history	26.4	8
Creative Writing	22.2	9
Communism	19.9	10.5
City problems	19.9	10.5
Vietnam war	18.6	12
Religion	18.4	13
Sex education	14.6	14
Music appreciation	12.8	15
Irish history	6.0	16

Source: *Organizing an Urban School System for Learning.* Joseph M. Cronin, Massachusetts Advisory Council on Education, pg. 26, 1970.

6.   Parents expressed little confidence in their ability to control the school system; less than half agreed with the statement "you can generally trust the School Committee to do what is right." Two-thirds of the parents felt they should have more of a say in running the schools.

7.   Parents generally felt they should work in and with the schools rather than make decisions regarding budget, curriculum, or personnel. Only in the area of discipline methods did a majority of parents want a decision-making role.

8.   In open-ended discussions, greater parental support was for teachers; greatest parental complaints were for school facilities.

9.   Parents' primary goal for elementary education was to instill a "desire for learning"; in addition, they felt elementary schools should encourage "proper behavior" and "Critical thinking"; each of these ranked ahead of the 3 Rs.

Goals and Objectives.   While the Superintendent's Annual Report has been much improved recently, the 1968–69 version carried the following piece of inflated rhetoric as an objective: "to serve to the fullest all the children, youth and adults of the city." There has been no formal way established for the system to judge its own performance on these broad terms or any particularized set of goals or objectives. Not only have the standardized achievement tests used been changed, with six different tests used over a three-year period, but the method of recording reading achievement scores has been changed, making comparisons impossible.

The policies, rules and regulations which govern and guide the Boston system are often unwritten, used to block change and assure a heavy-handed central control. The rule book used was published in 1935.

The School Committee. A five-man school committee has governed Boston's schools since 1906. At one point in the nineteenth century, as many as 76 elected members, six from each ward, served on the school committee.

Meeting at least once a week, in a usually chaotic fashion in an ancient building, there may be nothing that quite compares with it. The politically ambitious who reside in Boston often run for school committee (U. S. Rep. Louise Day Hicks is a former chairman of the committee), although the position generally has not proven to lead to any major political office.

Personnel items occupy the greatest space on the School Committee's meeting agendas and most of the space in the Committee's official proceedings. The Associate Superintendent for personnel, working with the Secretary of the School Committee and his own staff, prepares for each meeting abundant background materials on all personnel appointments, professional and non-professional, and on transfers, requests for leave, and retirements. Rated lists of candidates for promotion appear at intervals. With promotions, the number of points each candidate has earned appears on a list in rank order.

The School Committee reacts to the many deadlines of other local, state and federal agencies. Under such conditions, the committee finds itself being rushed into making decisions that require time and reflection to do properly.

Each year, the staff prepares a preliminary budget. In January, the School Committee reviews the budget, suggests any additions or deletions, and sends it to the mayor to review. By early April, the Committee must review and adjust the budget, again with the limits the mayor and statute set.

State and federal agencies require another set of deadlines, according to the project and the availability of funds. Examples include the various titles (categories) of the Elementary and Secondary Education Act, Vocational Education grants, and the Education Professions Development Act. There are many more, and their appearance, primarily because of the federal appropriations cycle (action usually comes late in the year), does not often coincide with the budget timetable.

The Racial Imbalance Act sets another deadline. It requires an October 1, racial census, a report, and later, a plan of action which includes short- and long-range steps to reduce and to eliminate imbalance. The committee and staff must supply the statistical data required under the statute.

Committee members find the budget information accurate. Some of them wish there could be more information concerning those programs which are working well — information beyond school system officials' testimony. School committeemen in Boston have not yet asked for a program budget, a budget that puts a price tag on the total cost of various specific programs, including cost of teachers, materials, and textbooks. Nor has there been a demand for a program budget which includes an evaluation of *alternatives* (with the cost of each alternative matched with its effectiveness of benefits).

Committee members complain about many of the state and federal programs Often, they find a proposal must be read, approved, and signed right away to meet a federal agency deadline. The Committee lacks time to consider alternatives, and rarely is it offered choices.

Third, collective negotiations with employee groups require frequent progress reports from School Committee negotiators. The teacher contract is only one of seven employee contracts. The School Committee hires a full-time coordinator and a part-time labor relations counsel who conduct the negotiations. In each instance, they inform the Committee of initial demands for improved salaries and working conditions, and they receive the Committee's instructions, usually in executive sessions.

Legally, the teachers' salaries cannot be raised after September 1. More realistically, the School Committee should make salary decisions by the first Monday in April, the budget deadline. Although the teachers' union indicated a desire to meet this deadline, a negotiations impasse continued not only after that deadline, but also after a major strike.

The problem seems not to be one of information, but rather one of timing the decision to be part of the budgetary process. Salaries account for more than 80 percent of the total school allocations each year and 90 percent of instruction costs.

Fourth, the Committee receives requests for hearings from various employee and community groups. Employee groups can request hearings to present salary requests or to make the final step in the grievance process. Community groups can request a hearing through the Secretary of the School Committee, the Chairman, or an individual member. Any member can place a request for a hearing on the agenda.

The Committee's record as a hearing board is uneven. Some groups get a quick response. Other groups, and there are many examples, may be granted a closed hearing only after months of postponement and delay. Some groups are denied hearings on the grounds that their request or concern has been dealt with administratively.

The committee has conducted as many as four meetings a year in various sections of the city, from East Boston to Hyde Park and Roxbury, for parents and citizens whose testimony they have welcomed. Teachers, students, and state representatives have addressed the committee at some of these forums, on problems ranging from airplane noise to corporal punishment.

As an unpaid board, committee members find it difficult at times to meet on the scheduled day or to grant all requests for hearings. Nor can they visit all sections of the city each year and still transact their routine business. Nor are hearings the most efficient ways to gather information— although they are interesting and often shed light on the problem, the hearings are not one of the most efficient ways to collect information.

Fifth, the Committee approves textbooks and courses of study. Traditionally and by statute, the Committee reviews all the texts, regular and supplementary, and the course of study guides the teachers use. The initial screening of materials are made by the professional staff; they then make the books and materials available to the School Committee members so they can review them. This review of instructional materials consumes much of the Committee's time.

Often, only one member looks at all the materials, although others do try to examine potentially controversial materials. This procedure has origins in the seventeenth century when ministers and other educated men examined the teachers and students. No longer does the Committee worry about religious orthodoxy, but the school staff members are concerned over what biology texts might include or which authors can be quoted in courses on minority groups.

Ironically, the newer media like films, filmstrips, and programmed instruction are more difficult for a committee of laymen to review. Books are still the staple, but students now learn as much, if not more, from other modes of instruction.

The greatest obstacle to meeting the diverse needs of a complex system may be the pattern of one course guide for each subject. In many areas — science, English, and social studies — a variety of course guides might better serve the needs of a diverse population.

Sixth, an incredible array of problems come before the School Committee — requests for out-of-state travel by staff, permission to maintain a tavern within so many yards of a school building, problems of athlete eligibility in a league competition, and new ventures, like the proposals of the Model Cities administration which carried implications for the schools.

These are formal, established activities. In addition, the Committee can and does solicit information and advice from the Superintendent, the Board of Superintendents, the Chief Schoolhouse Custodian, and others who regularly attend School Committee meetings. The Committee may seek information from the Chief Structural Engineer or from any of the nearly three dozen directors of departments.

Informally, the Committee members learn of problems and decision opportunities in many other ways.

Each member has a secretary or staff assistant whose salary is currently $9,992. This assistant handles many requests for information and assistance. The requests he receives range from information on vacant seats, to what parents can use open enrollment, to requests for assistance in getting a teaching or secretarial job in the school department.

Dozens of reports come to the School Committee's attention. The Education Planning Center staff conducts special studies in areas like facilities needs and site locations and the best way to establish a new department — for example, one for research and evaluation. External sources for reports include federal agencies, the Massachusetts Advisory Council on Education, Massachusetts Department of Education, ABCD, (Agency for Boston Community Development), and many other agencies. A former School Committee member commented it was impossible to digest all the reports; he gave many of them to reporters, on the condition that they would give him a written summary of what he should examine. Other reports include evaluations of federal programs, some with statistics and tables that lay citizens are not trained to comprehend.

The mass media, especially newspapers and television, bring many issues to the surface and indirectly create both much of the criticism and much of the support the Committee receives. The media tend to play up conflict, controversy and confrontations; examples are the Gibson School walkout, the teachers' strike of 1970, high school accreditation decisions, school fires, and reports which criticize the system. The Committee reaction appears to be ambivalent; members resent the stress on problems and protest that progress is ignored. But they do like the public visibility controversy generates.

Court suits, always an official source of guidelines, increasingly indicate to the School Committee and other school officials a need to reexamine school department policies. Recently, litigants have challenged the continued use of corporal punishment; the right to fire nontenured teachers without a hearing; the necessity for girls to score higher on Latin School admission tests than boys; the School Committee's right to substitute its nominee for the Superintendent's nominee; the equity of special education testing and evaluation procedures, and other practices. Parents and students will continue to seek clarification of their civil rights to information, to protection from arbitrary action, to admission to programs made available to others (e.g. through tests or tracking).

In this domain, the Committee — although most of the members are attorneys — relies heavily on the Law Department of the City because of the lack of special School Department counsel.

How adequate are the existing procedures? Reviewing the evidence suggests that the Boston School Committee gets the most information and expends the greatest effort on personnel or employment matters — from hiring and transfer decisions to collective bargaining. The staff provides ample materials.

The committee gets less information on the evaluation of the total educational program — federal programs are a possible exception. But even on federal programs, the Committee does not review and select among alternative proposals; it finds it must generally decide whether or not to expand an existing program. Federal, state, and local officials may need a rapid decision, a situation which prevents the Committee from making a full, searching review of the program and its alternatives. On the other hand, Committee members often ask a great many questions about the consultants hired to assist with training or evaluation of federal and other programs. They often hold consultant contracts for further study, a feature related more to employment questions than to education program review.

As a hearing board, the committee serves an important function as a last step or last resort. At the same time, many problems concerning personnel — including the transfer of ineffective or inappropriate principals — should never get to the school committee; they could be resolved administratively.

The committee generally gets the information it needs to make decisions about specific people and specific departments on a routine basis, and about the annual cycle of personnel recruitment and selection, the budget, and selection of system wide texts and courses of study.

But the Committee is not served well in coping with changes in the school population or in changes in programs which new state and federal mandates make possible. Since 1965, the superintendent and staff have developed new ways to identify the needs for change. . .for example, in the dramatic increases in the number of minority group students. The new Office of Curriculum Development, the Bilingual Department, the Educational Planning Center, and the public information office all exist as responses to the need for new courses, new staff patterns and new facilities. But many of the Committee procedures and preferences seem stuck in the cement of tradition. The focus is on employment, not on program evolution, and on reviewing system-wide course materials, not on adapting to the special needs of rapidly expanding minorities — especially the Spanish-speaking, the black, and the Chinese.

Given the present patterns, the Committee will continue to learn of the more intense problems through litigation and through the mass media. The more fundamental remedies go beyond the mere flow of information to require a more diversified committee, a top staff more representative of the diverse population of the city, and a total reform of personnel and budgetary procedures.

Cronin conveys the helplessness of the system many times over, but he is also quick to praise promising programs and changes in the system.

His 200 recommendations are comprehensive and, taken together, represent ways to far-reaching reform.

The Major Recommendations

A. The School Committee.   The Boston School Committee must invest its energy in educational policy questions — the value of existing programs, the priorities of programs, expansion, relationships with other agencies, and the search for new ways to make education more productive. The major function of the School Committee should be to evaluate the work of the school system and make recommendations concerning the extra resources needed to help certain schools and neighborhoods reach higher standards of achievement.

The term of the School Committee members should be extended to four years, coterminous with that of the mayor. Each member would receive the sum of $500 a month for every month in which a minimum of two meetings were held.

B. The Central Departments.   Functions of the school system which should be (or continue to be) centralized are:

1.   The recruitment of all personnel; principals, teachers, and other staff should participate in staff selection.
2.   The development of an overall program in basic skills; individual schools should make decisions as to implementation, variations, materials, and alternatives.
3.   The preparation of a budget document that plans for a system, an area, and a school and that displays alternative programs with estimated costs and benefits.
4.   The furnishing of books, supplies, media, and other resources for an instructional program.
5.   The planning of buildings.
6.   The arrangement of special classes for categories of students – the bilingual, the talented, the retarded, the handicapped, the disturbed, and the unusually motivated.
7.   The coordination of vocational-technical occupational education.
8.   The coordination of testing, counseling, health and mental health services.
9.   The handling of employee negotiations, payrolls, accounts and audits, and other business support services including food, transportation, and major repairs.

C. Planning.   The planning function in the Boston schools grows more complex every year. Planning is implicit in many of the recommendations Cronin makes. The largest and most obvious need is for physical facilities. But planning is more than that. It requires:

1.   program evaluation and projections for the future to plan specialized facilities;
2.   an identification of the need for new kinds of staff or staff skills in using new technology;
3.   an analysis of regional and local demographic trends, such as the impact of the Puerto Rican migration to Boston;
4.   the survey of parent and neighborhood attitudes and an investigation of new approaches to education, such as the use of nonschool resources (cultural centers, firms, museums, hospitals, etc.);
5.   the Associate Superintendent for Planning should coordinate the work of what is now the Educational Planning Center, the Statistics Department, and the planning function of the Engineering Office; and

6.   the planning center should include statisticians, specialists on drawing up specifications, community advocate planners, and other technical specialists trained in planning and liaison work with communities and architects.

D. Curriculum Services and Program Development.   1. A brief outline of the scope and sequence of courses requiring continuity between levels should replace curriculum guides. The major activity of curriculum and supervision staff should be materials evaluation and assistance to school faculties, teaching teams, and individually needed advice and assistance.

2. Schools in each area should refine, test, and adapt alternative programs.

3. The curriculum and instructional staffs in areas such as Fine Arts and Music (aesthetics) and Physical Education should be gradually expanded.

The Boston School Department should prepare to adopt a program budgeting system to encourage more rational decision-making about resource allocation. The Superintendent should create two staff departments: the Department of Planning, Management, and Evaluation (PME) and the Department of the Budget. The central functions of analysis and evaluation should take place in the Department of Planning, Management, and Evaluation. The Department of the Budget should supply expert and up-to-date cost information and should assist in the preparation of the traditional budget, the program budget, and the display of fiscal information.

4. A new Department of Research and Evaluation should assume responsibility for individual level pupil diagnoses, Title I evaluation, and the production of profiles on each child and each school.

5. The new director, equipped with advanced doctoral training, should work closely with planning and data processing staff; he should report to the Associate Superintendent for Special Services.

E. Health Services.   The school doctor lshould be gradually phased out and his responsibilities assumed by the school nurse and personnel from local neighborhood health clinics. Also:

1. Boston should provide more resources for psychological services, for dental needs, and should expand services to areas of the city with the greatest needs.

2. A new Department of Occupational Education should be formed to plan and prepare a program for all Boston children in occupational-technical-vocational skills.

3. The Work Study Program should be expanded − to 1200 and eventually to 2000 or more high school age children − with the help of federal, state and city funds.

F. Associate Superintendents.   There should be an associate superintendent in charge of each of the following service areas:

1.   Personnel − recruitment, placement, and evaluation;
2.   Curriculum and Instruction;

3.   Educational Planning — demographic, physical, financial;
4.   Special Services and System Evaluation;
5.   Staff and Organizational Development; and
6.   Field Operations — supervision of the areas.

Each associate superintendent should have wide and full responsibilities in his area. Information-collecting, coordination and goal-setting should be major aspects of the associate superintendents. The business manager should have equal status and should continue to be the chief budgetary coordinator in charge of accounts, fiscal controls, supplies and inventories. He would assume general supervision of food service, transportation, school custodial operations, maintenance and repairs.

G. The Area Superintendents. The six area superintendents must be educational leaders and planners, must participate in the central policy-making or goal-setting process for the system as a whole and develop detailed educational plans for their areas. They should conduct regular planning meetings with their principals on problems and develop closer communication among the schools in each area. Each area superintendent should have two assistants at the level of pay of vice-principal — one assistant for program planning and one assistant for community relations.

1. Each principal should have a full-time administrative assistant for every 600 pupils in his school community. This person should be a full-time administrator and not a teacher.

2. Each satellite elementary building of more than six classrooms should be staffed by a school clerk-receptionist.

3. Responsibility for teacher evaluation and retention should be assigned to the principals and headmasters; they should request help as needed form the Area Superintendent's supervisory staff of "resource teachers."

4. The Boston Teacher's Examination should be eliminated; the National Teacher's Exam should be used instead.

5. Teachers should be recruited by the associate superintendent for Personnel, but the final selection of teachers ought to be made at the building level.

6. Master teacher positions should be created.

7. Every administrative position in the Boston School Department should have a job description, outlining the general as well as the unique qualifications essential in each specific post.

8. Notice of specific vacancies, along with position descriptions should be circulated within and outside of Boston schools.

9. The Boston School Department should conduct an ambitious national and local search for administrators.

10. Principals, headmasters, and area and associate superintendents should be hired on a six-year renewable contract basis (first two years probationary).

H. Personnel Practices. Included in a study of personnel practices by Boston College is a two-year administrative development program which future principals and headmasters would attend (except those with previous administrative experience outside the Boston schools). During the first year, they would attend classes in human relations/sensitivity training, program development/ evaluation, staff supervision, community-school relations, budget, and union relationships. Trainees would spend a ten-month period working in a school outside Boston in the central or area office, or in a community service agency.

Associate superintendents, area superintendents, and directors of central departments should not remain in their jobs more than seven years without a nine-month sabbatical to hold a similar position in another school system, enroll as a full-time student for advanced professional training, or hold a different position in the Boston School Department.

1. One of the associate superintendents should assume major responsibility for staff development (inservice training) and organizational development.

2. Administrators and staff members of new schools should learn to maximize educational uses of facilities and spaces.

3. School administrators and other specialists should be encouraged and rewarded financially for one or two-year leaves for full-time advanced study.

4. Model elementary and secondary schools should be established in each of the six school system areas. These schools should be open continuously for teacher observations; teachers should take two days a year to visit model schools.

Boston's teachers need money to work in groups or individually to develop new programs. An initial budget of $100,000 per area should be distributed in the form of grants to teachers who present valid innovative plans. Resource centers should be housed in each model school to provide a reservoir of materials for new programs and supplementary materials for existing programs.

5. Teachers should have a role in establishing the criteria for selecting principals for their schools; teachers know the school, the children, and their parents, and can give valuable ideas on what is needed in a principal.

6. Teachers should be evaluated annually at joint discussions with the master teacher and principal based on classroom visits and demonstrations. Union representatives and school officials should develop standards of accountability.

I. Differentiated Positions. The career ladder would be as follows:

1. teacher aides – community people and others helping students and teachers.
2. teacher interns – teachers in training with some teaching responsibilities.
3. assistant teachers – teachers working on a team with other teachers, counselors, and aides.
4. teachers – teachers of individual classes (e.g., some special classes) much as at present.

5.   team leaders — master or career teachers with extra responsibility for programs and teacher supervision.

Additionally, child advocates are needed who would work to protect the child's rights. They would serve in a counseling role and work closely with pupil adjustment counselors. They would be the field personnel for the special service team in their area. Child advocates should have a college degree with concentration in psychology or social work and experience in school guidance, social work, or public or private health or welfare agencies.

Boston educators should visit more and different colleges in the search for black talent; such efforts should be concentrated on schools in larger cities with a high percentage of minority students and an interest in urban education. Recruitment personnel, both black and white, should represent the most articulate, enthusiastic, persuasive, and vigorous team that Boston schools can muster. At the same time, the School Department should seek out and promote black educators to highly responsible leadership positions in the system.

J. Labor Relations.   1. Massachusetts should adopt a feature of the New York State Taylor Law which ties contract negotions of public employees to the budget cycle. It automatically recognizes an impasse and calls for outside mediation if the teacher contract is not signed by a deadline of 60 days before the budget is due.

2. The Superintendent and the Associate Superintendent for Personnel should be responsible for preparing for negotiations, involving staff in study committees, conducting negotiations, and follow-up training of staff.

The School Department should create the position of Supervisor of Civil Service (i.e., nonacademic) Personnel. This director would work under the Associate Superintendent for Personnel and would be in charge of all personnel matters relating to custodians, secretaries, attendance supervisors, cafeteria staff, and health services personnel. The Supervisor would coordinate with the Civil Service Commission to schedule examinations. He would recruit minority group personnel by developing joint programs with local agencies and neighborhood groups. He would work with the Mayor's Office of Human Rights to educate and interest people in employment opportunities offered by the School Department.

3. Councils should be formed at each school in the city at the request of ten or more parents. Councils should consist of all concerned parents and school staff members, and should have an executive board of five parents and three educators.

4. Councils should be consulted and the officers should sign annual requests for the school budget, for staff and building operations. They should develop criteria for the selection of principals and headmasters, and should review, discuss, and make recommendations on a "school achievement profile."

K. A School Profile on Problems and Performance.   Each year parent groups and school councils should see a "profile" of school resources and performances. This profile should include:

1. the number of teachers and their level of experience;
2. special programs, aides, and extra staff available;
3. known drop-out rates, college acceptance, etc.;
4. test scores by grade and subject;
5. school expenditures for teachers and counselors, custodians, books and materials, repairs and alterations, special staff, and lunches; and
6. projected enrollments for the next three years.

L. Student Relations.   1. Plans to involve students in the educational decision-making process should be developed on a school-by-school basis. Students indicating interest should receive every opportunity to develop leadership skills, group participation skills, and problem analysis and solution skills.

2. Student Councils should be established at each secondary school and should be encouraged to deal with as many questions as possible. A uniform code of eligibility for serving on Student Councils should be developed and adopted. This Council should reflect the diverse composition of the school population.

M. An Ombudsman for the Boston Schools.   1. The ombudsman should be separate from the administrative structure; it is essential that he be independent and impartial.

2. The School Committee should turn over to the ombudsman the complaints they receive during the year.

3. The ombudsman should be able to initiate investigations on the basis of individual complaints, newspaper stories, or any other form of information.

4. The ombudsman should be empowered to inspect all records and communications of the School Department, to call for explanations, and to attend any meetings or deliberations.

5. He should be able to call hearings requiring the presence of any School Department employee.

6. He should be able to visit any school.

7. The ombudsman should have final say in disputes between parent councils and aministrators. (The ombudsman should be called on only when the issue under contention involves procedures or the interpretation and application of agreements, not when it is a basic policy issue.)

8. The ombudsman should be selected by the leading attorney in the state, the Attorney General.

N. School-Community Relations – The Spanish-Speaking Child.   1. The Boston School Department, the Department of Health and Hospitals, and other relevant public agencies are urged to accept more strongly as a regular responsibility the annual survey of neighborhoods in which non-English speaking people live.

2. A Spanish-speaking registrar-secretary should be employed full-time in each elementary district in which at least 20 Spanish-speaking families have been identified.

3. All report cards, letters, and other communications to parents should be made available in Spanish as well as English.

4. As many native Spanish-speaking teachers as possible should be hired and auxiliary staff from the Spanish-speaking community should work with the children in the schools.

5. Instructional materials in Spanish should be adopted.

6. Bilingual programs for Spanish-speaking and other non-English speaking children should be opened in small-scale facilities tied closely to regular school programs to allow a flexible movement of students as their language skills and self-confidence improve.

O. University Resources and the School.   1. A school system-university forum should be reestablished to give school officials and university representatives a chance to discuss mutual criticisms.

2. The Boston School Department should continue to draw for assistance from sectors of the universities other than the Schools of Education – such as the Medical Schools, the Law Schools, and Schools of Social Work and of Public Health, the Sloan School of Management at MIT, Harvard Business School, and other centers concerned with the city, young people, and the flow of social services to urban populations.

P. Business and the Schools.   1. An industry-education council should be reestablished in Boston. It should meet frequently and should examine school needs *vis-á-vis* business cooperation. Its membership should include principals, area superintendents, business leaders, members of the Chamber of Commerce, the Associate Industries, and the Central Labor Council.

2. A member of the School Department Planning Staff should be responsible for the creation of collaborative school-business relationships.

3. The Superintendent should examine the potential for additional forms of industry-education collaboration.

4. Each school should have an activities fund to support trips and the use of outside materials and speakers. At present, schools depend on money raised in picture sales, lost book fines, and contributions from the local Home and School Association. This results in an unequal, inadequate, and uncertain amount of funds available. There should be a direct allocation from the School Department to each principal on the basis of need.

5. Institutions and cultural organizations should recruit students as volunteers or part-time staff for pay or course credit.

6. Schools and cultural centers should apply for state and federal aid authorized for cultural events.

Q. The Mayor's Office of Human Rights. 1. The Office of Human Rights should continue to assist in school problems as needed. It should be involved in plans for inservice training for principals and other staff.

2. Periodically, members of the OHR should be invited to meetings of Area Superintendents and to meetings of principals to coordinate responses and other special needs.

3. The state should be the broker and disseminator of useful ideas and exemplary methods developed by experimental schools under state support and under Title III programs; particularly of the model cities venture, with its main purpose of improving the delivery of social services, such as education and health.

R. Financing the Boston Schools in the Seventies. Even if the Boston School Committee and Massachusetts legislature adopt none of the recommendations in this report, the Boston School Department budget will increase by $8,000,000 to $10,000,000 per year or by a minimum of $40,000,000 in five years to a total in excess of $120,000,000.

1. Boston and state officials should plan for a minimum of 90 percent state financing of education by the middle or late seventies, financed by shared federal tax revenue and by a revised state income tax.

2. Massachusetts should revise the state aid formula to recognize the municipal overburden and greater costs of the central city school systems.

3. The state should, even in the absence of aid formula revision, supplement federal aid for disadvantaged children based on family income. This should be the core of a system of "urban grants" to cities for education.

By some remarkable alchemy, Cronin was able to obtain the support of Boston's school committee to conduct his study and continued to have their support after the final report was published. His report continues to produce and review policies, and to discuss preventive measures.

S. Parks and Recreation Department. 1. There should be a Parks and Recreation Council to develop plans in cooperation with the School Department, Parks and Recreation Department, the Metropolitan District Commission and private agencies concerned about recreation.

2. The School Department and the city should develop ways to prorate and share costs for community recreation — including dances, fairs, and festivals.

3. Schools should be open twenty-four hours a day, if people want to use the facilities. Too many public facilities close at 4:45 p.m.

T. Model Cities. 1. Both the Model Cities and School Department administration should arrange for substantially increased communication and coordination of ideas and plans at several levels.

2. The School Department should sponsor some Model Cities education programs and cosponsor some Model Cities education programs and cosponsor others to ensure a carry-over of innovation into the regular school program.

U. State and Metropolitan Contributions.   1. The state should strengthen its capability to serve the urban school districts and children by developing a state bureau of pupil services.

2. The state should appropriate adequate funds for programs for the academically talented, for art, music, and the humanities, for dyslexic children, and   n other needs. Most groups in the city with a general or a special interest in its schools – they number in the hundreds today – have found at least one section of the report useful to them.

In Part II, we leave on-going institutions and organizations and discuss newly emerging educational domains.

Part II
Perspectives on Emerging Programs

Education must shift into the future tense — Alvin Toffler

One of man's most urgent endeavors is to try to find some clue about what tomorrow will bring — Frank C. Jennings

The ensuing four chapters review MACE studies of special education, compensatory education, adult education and early childhood education. While each has had a long and interesting history, they have in common the fact that they are undernourished programs.

A young and talented professor at the University of Massachusetts approached the Council in 1968 about the need for a scrutiny of federally funded compensatory education, especially as to how programs were planned, evaluations were conducted and teachers were trained. Fifty thousand dollars of the Council's funds were applied to this challenge.

Intrigued by a weak, uncoordinated and leaderless lump of programs called continuing education, Melvin Levin and Joseph Slavet, undertook a comprehensive study of adult education from July 1968 to December 1969 which required $48,000 of Council funds. Their report covers not only the programs they found but recommends some new dimensions to continuing education.

An ambitious but necessary 100,000 dollar two-year study was begun for the Council in the spring of 1970 to help prepare the state for early childhood and kindergarten programs. Richard Rowe, a dean at Harvard, aided by Courtney Cazden, undertook this project which was to lead them through a maze of agencies, committees and individuals, all struggling with the pieces of the problem.

Herbert Hoffman, at Brandeis University, received $18,600 from the Advisory Council to study the costly "750" program in Massachusetts for the emotionally handicapped. Several months later, in December 1969 Burton Blatt and Frank Garfunkel successfully proposed a master plan study of special education to require $55,000 of MACE funds. Both Drs. Blatt and Garfunkel knew the state's special education programs at first hand and were naturals for the task.

Compensatory Education

In the autumn of 1968, MACE contracted with Daniel Jordan at the University of Massachusetts for a one-year investigation of compensatory

127

education programs in Massachusetts. Title I of the Elementary and Secondary Education Act of 1965 was designed to meet the special educational needs of educationally deprived children in school attendance areas having high concentration of children from low-income families. Jordan describes those in need, saying:

> The disadvantaged child . . . is clearly at a tremendous disadvantage when compared to his more affluent peers. The school then compounds the disadvantage by giving him learning tasks the prerequisites to which he has not yet mastered, thereby setting him up for a guaranteed failure. Being stuck in such an intolerable and unjust position and being forced to accumulate failures over long periods of time generate such negative emotional by-products, all associated with the formal learning situation, that effective learning within the formal context becomes impossible. Since failure in school reduces opportunities for attaining future economic security and continuing growth and development, both socially and personally, the magnitude of this problem approaches incomprehensible dimensions. Its ramifications are far-flung largely because the situation perpetuates itself through a cycle that is difficult to interrupt.[1]

While the compensatory education guidelines from Washington talk about planning and evaluation, the programs mounted in Massachusetts (and elsewhere) are case studies in bad planning and worse evaluation.

Cleaning up the mess created by bad planning over the years is a challenge in itself. Learning how to plan for new programs is another, and it is a crucial need.

Jordan's survey of compensatory education in the state pinpoints the need to have, as the study title puts it, a "blueprint for action." Compensatory education is aimed at improving the education offered students from low-income families, students who have traditionally received the weakest education, and it is a particularly good case in point for four reasons:

1. The problem is a large one, affecting most school districts, and hence representative of the overall capabilities of the state.
2. The funding for compensatory programs, with a few minor exceptions, is a product of federal monies over the last five years. Hence, the data are relevant.
3. There is a clear role for the State Department as well as for local school districts, so the entire system is tested. (Federal funds flow through the state to local districts.)
4. Compensatory education requires changes in the existing system.

These are children for whom school has usually been, by all conventional standards, a series of frustrations and failures. It is obvious then that the conventional school experience fails these children. Something different has to happen.

Yet, Jordan observes, compensatory education is usually a patchwork of remedial and "enrichment" programs. That is to say, it is "standard brand" education, only the doses are a little heavier (remedial work) and a few fringe benefits are thrown in (a trip to the orchestra.)

"This kind of education," the study concludes, "is not producing significant results of a lasting value in sufficient numbers of students fast enough to deal with a problem that has already reached vast proportions and is still growing at an alarming rate."

The Jordan data show that compensatory education programs in Massachusetts are for the most part "programs which do not focus on developing competent learners and which are, therefore, not being maximally effective." At first glance, it seems odd that any educational venture is not aimed at developing "competent learners." But a careful look at many education practices reveals a crucial distinction — one Jordan is driving at — between programs established to teach something (e.g., French, U. S. history, metal work) and programs which are aimed at helping students learn to learn, whatever the subject matter.

What does planning have to do with this? Again, by definition, planning means developing clear objectives (e.g., "competent learners"), developing strategies for achieving those objectives (e.g., well-trained teachers, sound programs) and developing and utilizing evaluation methodologies.

All this would seem as obvious and basic as the desirability of competent learners. Yet, Jordan's study concludes that the "four basic characteristics of compensatory education" in Massachusetts are:

1. lack of explicit objectives, operationally defined which deal with the basic problems of the disadvantaged child.
2. lack of sound designs for evaluating programs so that they can be continually improved.
3. lack of model compensatory education programs which demonstrate appropriate curricula and effective teaching methods, and
4. a critical shortage of well-trained compensatory education manpower.

The Department was not unaware of its problems before Jordan did his study. Indeed, the small staff assigned responsibilities for Title I were able to accomplish a good deal, although most of their achievements were clerical in substance.

Jordan's study did help to move things ahead. Since his study was completed, the number of project evaluations has increased considerably. On October 23, 1970, the Board of Education put forth the most far-reaching guidelines for Title I in the nation. Stronger than the federal recommendations, the guidelines require each school district desiring Title I funds to established elected councils in such a way as to assure parent representation from each Title I school. Appeal rights are given to the councils when they wish to exercise the option.

Adult Education

Malcolm Knowles, a national authority on adult education, wrote the Fore-
word to the Levin and Slavet work and made the following observations about
their study:

> First, it gives the clearest guidelines yet provided for the use of continuing
> education of adults as an instrument of social policy. Other documents —
> such as the Report of the President's Committee on Education Beyond the
> High School in 1957, the "Status Report on Continuing Education Programs
> in California Higher Education" by the California Coordinating Council for
> California Higher Education in 1965, and the Master Plan of the Ohio
> Board of Regents in 1966 — have proposed that continuing education is a
> potent under used weapon against social ills. But the present study provides
> the most specific step-by-step, priority-ordered, plan yet promulgated for
> any state for attacking the problems of illiteracy (and the attendant
> problems of crime, poverty, and unemployment), manpower development,
> citizen participation in democracy, and the improvement of government
> service.
>
> Second, this is the first time that the powerful new systems analysis tools
> of cost-benefit, cost-effectiveness, planning-programming-budgeting, and
> social indicators have been applied to a state's continuing education
> situation. This is a breakthrough of great importance, for until now the
> cause of continuing education has been supported almost exclusively in
> terms of its social benefits as well; and to hard-pressed tax payers, state
> agency executives, and legislators, this is the more telling argument.
>
> Third, this study provides a model for both research and planning that can
> be used in approaching other areas of social planning in Massachusetts and in
> other states. At the Galaxy Conference on Adult Education in Washington,
> I mentioned to educational leaders of several states that the study was in
> progress. They urged me to send copies of this study to them when it was
> published so they could launch a similar process in their states. I am
> convinced that this study will stimulate the improvement of the quality of
> educational planning across the country.
>
> Last, this details a plan for strengthening state administrative leadership
> and capability in continuing education that is so clear, simple, and
> feasible it promises to bring order for the first time in Massachusetts' history
> to what has heretofore been an utter morass of confusion. In one of the
> classic studies of public adult education, it was found that the single most
> critical factor, which distinguished states with strong from states with weak
> public school adult education programs, was the quality of state aid and
> leadership. In every study of the quality and volume of adult education in
> the various states that has been made, the Commonwealth of Massachusetts
> has been rated toward the bottom of the scale on both counts. This study
> provides us with a fast way up the scale. Continuing education is vastly
> better known for its promise than for its universal practice. Undernourished,

continuing education, has no place to grow except up. Consideration is presently being given to expand the role responsibility of public institutions of higher education to include a wider range of students under a variety of flexible arrangements.

The problems experienced by Levin and Slavet in collecting information and in making some sense and order out of what they found, were perhaps unmatched by any MACE study. Yet, their findings and recommendations present a comprehensive whole badly in need of action.

To this point, the MACE's look at continuing education has led to more activity then action. The Board of Higher Education became very interested in the study and, in some measure, the Board pursued its interest by commissioning two additional studies dealing with open university - external degree programs for Massachusetts. Jerrold Zacharias of M.I.T. was asked to discuss likely programs for an open-external university while James E. Allen, Jr. was asked to describe some organizational parameters. Allen, former School Commissioner of Education, states his three major points:

1. *The structure of the program should enable it to respond to the widest range of potential students.* The organizational pattern should not prevent students from participating because of their home location or other factors such as age, income level, physical handicap, or cultural background. It should provide easy accessibility for the poor and minorities, including non-English speaking groups. (In this connection, special attention should also be given to simplicity of procedures in such matters as enrollment, correspondence, fees.) It should make it easy for individuals to pursue education as a continuing process, enabling them to enter early (perhaps even before the completion of the standard high school grades), to step in and out of the Open University as circumstances and interests warrant, thus fitting the opportunities of the University into their total educational experience in ways most appropriate to their special needs and desires.

2. *The organizational pattern should serve to enhance the credibility, prestige and reputation of the program and its degree.* Extraordinary effort will be necessary to combat the "second-class" status which too often has been the public impression of the value of equivalency or extension programs.

3. *The structure should offer the utmost encouragement and opportunity for innovation.* It should accommodate nontraditional policies regarding requirements for entry, employment and use of personnel, the curriculum, course grades and credits, scheduling and location of learning experiences, etc. It should not be dominated by professional forces having special interests in maintaining the educational status quo.[1]

Meanwhile, the Board of Education has established a committee to review the Levin and Slavet report and to make a further set of recommendations. The prospects for more than token action for the years immediately ahead are not promising. Like other programs mentioned in Part II, funding into the millions of dollars is called for.

Early Childhood Care

The care and education of young children was the subject ot the Council's most recent study. *Child Care: The Public Responsibility* by Dr. Richard R. Rowe, Associate Dean at Harvard Graduate School of Education and Director of the *Program in Public Psychology at Harvard.* Dr. Rowe draws attention to the plight of both the young child and the family who are in an environment that fosters economic goals to the detriment of family life, without an extended family of grandparents, aunts, cousins, etc. to help with child care, the nuclear family is unable to alone meet the needs of young children. The study points out that adequate child care, outside the family, is simply not available in sufficient quantity.

The parents of some 90 percent of the 683,000 preschool children in Massachusetts would use some form of regular child care if it were available, inexpensive and convenient, according to the study.

The two-year study found that about 350,000 children 6 years old and under now get regular, nonparental child care – mostly in informal settings in the homes of relatives or neighbors. The study also found a huge reservoir of demand for child care, not necessarily related to the number of mothers (25 percent) who work outside the home, nor to economic necessity. Among those who can afford the option of child care (those who have incomes of $15,000 and up), almost 60 percent regularly send their children out of the home to nursery schools or other arrangements.

Demand for child care, the study concludes, "is based on fundamental, long-term changes in the functioning of the society, the composition of the labor force, the roles of women and men, changes in family life. Forceful economic and political realities underlie the marked rise in demand for child-care services. They will not go away; rather, they are on the rise and will bring with them even greater effects than we now see."

The cost of providing these services in Massachusetts – at about $1000 per child for part-time care and about $2000 for full-time care – would amount to $800 to $900 million annually, with private sources and fees paying about half and government left with a cost of $400 to $450 million.

The bulk of this money will have to come from federal sources, the study reports, since the state does not have the resources to shoulder the burdens of operating costs for child care.

But the state does have a role to play, the study continues, in licensing child-care arrangements, providing training programs for the staff and furnishing support and advice for local groups who want to set up child-care arrangements.

Rowe concludes: child-related services, now scattered among some 14 state agencies, should be centralized in a new department of child development under the Secretary of Human Services and not in the state's educational secretariat.

Human Services is presently the conduit for federal funds for early childhood. Dr. Richard R. Rowe believes even more federal money will soon be flowing to the states for early childhood programs through the Human Services agency.

Rowe said although pro-child-care forces are now disorganized and politically ineffective their potential power is great. He pointed out that Congress last year passed a comprehensive $2 billion child-care bill, only to have it vetoed by President Nixon.

Rowe emphasized the study's main conlusion – that the role of state or federal government in child care should be limited to guaranteeing the basic rights of the child (to be safe, free from abuse, etc.) and to support families by providing a range of options for child care.

"We believe that the family is a basic and necessary structure for caring for young children and meeting their needs," the study said. The government should "support families by helping parents develop their own options for child-care and early education, including direct support of families as the primary setting for child-care, supplementary child-care for those families who need it and alternative family arrangement for those children whose basic needs cannot be met."[2]

Rowe's report deals with the full range of early childhood education and child-care issues. His detailed recommendations are meant for many readers among public officials and private citizens. As this book goes to press, it is too soon to discuss the impact of the recommendations. The Governor, however, has expressed great interest in the study and proposed legislation to help bring about some of what Rowe wants. Leaders in the legislature, who encouraged and followed the study from the beginning, are also submitting legislation on early childhood matters. The prospects for at least some improvement in the crim early childhood picture are, at this writing, better than average.

Special Education

Burton Blatt's study of special education involved not only the Department of Education but also the Department of Mental Health and, to a lesser extent, several other state agencies. Able to praise only a few people and programs, Blatt basically found special education in organizational disarray. Children were stuck with labels, such as "emotionally disturbed," that helped or hindered them in epic inconsistency. Problem children in Boston are, in effect, excluded from school and not picked up in any other kind of program.

Children were a direct and intimate concern to Blatt. His "Study of Educational Opportunity for Handicapped and Disadvantaged Children," details some of the treatment received by institutionalized mentally retarded children:

Phil is taken into the bathroom where he is washed with a large towel dipped
in a two gallon bucket of soapy water. He smiles throughout the process and
tries to keep his face away from the soap. The aide hoses him off with a
garden hose and Phil laughs and smiles as if it is all a game, turning and
holding his hands above his head. The aide quickly shoves him back in the
cool dayroom after drying off his face superficially. Phil keeps trying to go
back into the bathroom, but one of the residents is guarding the door and
keeps him out. As the other residents are lined around the bathroom wall
and washed as a group, Phil paces around the dayroom till he is dry. The
residents are shuttled into the bedroom from the shower where they get into
beds without being dressed. Mr. B., the aide, locks the bedroom door and
remains in the dayroom with Phil and three others. He comments, "That
didn't take long, about 30 minutes. I like to do them in a bunch, it keeps
them from getting cold."[3]

Gibson points to much the same abuse from the distant halls of the
Department of Education:

Our inquiries within (the Department of Education) and among educators
and publics throughout the Commonwealth reveal a remarkable absence of
mention of students and of school services which can advance student
achievement and thus life opportunities and options. The Department of
Education and most other bureaucratic contrivances associated with
education in Massachusetts are simply not oriented towards the basic
premise of this study – that schools are for students.[4]

The Department has moved to remedy this situation. A high school student
now sits on the Board of Education and a new Youth Advisory Council is
establishing a state-wide representative network of students.

Two other Advisory Council studies have also dwelt upon special education –
Herbert Hoffman's study of the emotionally disturbed, which is discussed in
Chapter 9, in conjunction with the Blatt study; and Joseph Cronin's report on
Boston's schools. Cronin states that black children are rarely found or eligible for
the emotionally disturbed program (an expensive program paid for by the state)
but are often placed in retarded classes. Signaling rigid and expensive specialized
staffing, Cronin cites:

1. With rare exception, guidance counselors and advisors work without
secretarial assistance so that at least one-third of their time is spent in
clerical work.
2. Pupil adjustment counselors are paid more than $14,000 a year and yet,
by contract, work from 8:30 to *no later than 2:15,* which rules out
visits to homes, work with teachers, or inservice meetings in mid or later
afternoon.
3. Few recently trained medical doctors now will accept the itinerant school
M.D. role that Boston pioneered in the 1900s, for it now falls seriously short

of the clinic and lab technology conditions required for modern medical practice.

4. Nurses receive salaries well above R.N. scales (creating a long waiting list for school jobs), work fewer than forty weeks, administer few health services, and spend an average of 50 percent of their time on paper work.

5. Attendance workers, few with A.B. degrees, are paid more than teachers with M.A. degrees who instruct students in the classroom.

Cronin agrees with both Blatt and Hoffman in calling for more realistic staffing arrangements. In a summing statement, he writes:

> Still another problem is that of attitudes of the teachers and administrators, and of the general public. Each of us tends to attach a stigma to emotional problems. Even worse, we tend to want to exclude or exile the person who acts out his problem. The number of special classes keep growing. This is an expensive solution, and many judge it less than ideal. Many experts believe in reeducation programs, some residential, many of them involving the entire family. Others are at work developing milieu therapy that may help a child cope more adequately with himself and with his environment. All teachers and administrators must find ways to prevent a student from suffering under a stigma, from being excluded or treated in a totally separate site when perhaps counselors, psychologists, and psychiatrists can help the teacher develop strategies within the classroom. Reeducation, not separate education, is the frontier of specialized education for many students only temporarily disabled as learners.[5]

Blatt also looked at the structure for leading special education and decided he didn't like it. He recommends a new organization as does Richard Rowe for early childhood education. The Governor is presently proposing an Office for Children, which would serve both some of the interests of early childhood education and some of the interests of special education.

Included in the proposed Office for Children would be agencies for day care, foster care and adoption, child abuse and neglect, and special education. Initially, the new office would coordinate child-related programs in the Office of Human Affairs. Eventually, the Governor feels it would be responsible for all children's services provided by state government, services which are currently strewn about the various departments with little regard for planning. Under the Governor's proposed legislation:

1. All day-care centers, family day-care facilities, foster care, group care, and placement agencies would be licensed and regulated.

2. A uniform procedure for surrendering a child for adoption would be used by all 30 child-care agencies, and nonagency adoptions would be established.

3. The procedure for ending the right of parents to withhold consent to adoption would be reformed in cases where foster children have been shown to be neglected by their natural parents.

The legislation also would:

4. Provide a right to be heard for an unwed father desiring to raise his child.

5. Broaden the kinds of professionals required by law to report cases of abuse and severe neglect of children by extending immunity from civil or criminal liability.

6. Make it a requirement that School Committees have the primary responsibility for educating children with special needs, providing a reimbursement of 100 percent above any per pupil outlay.

7. Remove categorical labels such as "retarded," "disturbed," from the general laws and replace them with a single category — children with special needs.

The Governor's proposal also would require local communities to take over special education of children while the state provides $11 million of the $19 million being spent for this purpose by the cities and towns. There are about 17,000 special education children in the state now.

The proposal also would decrease the number of children who are sent to private school under Chapter 750 by emphasizing community-based programs. It costs approximately $8000 a year to send an emotionally disturbed or retarded child to private facilities, and there are some 1250 on the waiting list.

In establishing a "voice for children" and a network of services for children, the Governor states he is attempting to expose some of the "thousands" of cases of physical abuse that go undiscovered.

At present, only social workers, teachers or doctors are immune from civil or criminal liability in reporting child abuse. The new legislation would extend immunity to other professions such as police or clergy.

Part II uses five MACE studies to view special and compensatory education as well as programs for the very young child and the adult. Unless otherwise indicated, references are to studies conducted by the Advisory Council.

6

Compensatory Education: The Federal Cinderella Program

The children are where the money ain't. – A folk saying quoted by Lyndon B. Johnson

The Title (Title I) has a variety of purposes, among which are providing the quality of education in poor schools, relieving the fiscal burdens of city school districts, raising educational achievement for poor children, and improving education for disadvantaged nonpublic school students. – David K. Cohen

The past decade has seen both an increased awareness of the existence, scope and ugliness of poverty in the United States, and a greater public concern for understanding and changing socioeconomic forces that serve to capture people and perpetuate poverty. Traditionally, and somewhat optimistically, education has been regarded as the major means of gaining security and assuring success in a middle class society. Horace Mann, in fact, spoke of public education as society's balancing wheel. Utilitarian as such an aim might be, it is lost on the disadvantaged child who has different and more immediate needs. For a growing minority, the children of the poor in particular, the schools have been generally ineffective, extraneous and, for some, destructive. These children come into the schools from cultures that are markedly different from the mainstream. They frequently have neither the verbal and cognitive skills nor the expectations and motivations that are prerequisite to academic success. The school programs and schoolmen have been ill-prepared to deal constructively with these children and have, therefore, in effect, dismissed them.

Compensatory education focuses attention upon the various factors that can inhibit learning and seeks to "compensate" for the demoralizing and isolating effects of economic and social deprivation upon children and their families. Its purpose is to provide children from impoverished homes with the kinds of educational experiences that will enable them to function and compete successfully in the larger society.

Much of the recent impetus to the development of compensatory education has been provided by Title I of the Elementary Education Act of 1965 (P.L. 89–10.). Although later amendments have extended the original scope of the Title I program to include children of migratory workers, handicapped children, and neglected and delinquent children, the principal emphasis of the legislation is upon extending educational opportunities through local school districts to children living in low-income areas. The stated purpose of the program is "to provide financial assistance to local educational agencies serving areas with

137

concentration of children from low-income families to expand and improve their educational programs by various means (including preschool programs) which contribute particularly to meeting the special educational needs of educationally deprived children."[1]

Financially, and in terms of participation, Title I is the largest federal education program. Each year, it has been providing approximately one billion dollars nationally and serving nearly one million children. Collectively, Massachusetts school districts receive over $15 million and provide Title I activities for about 100,000 children annually.

The state education agencies are responsible for the administration of the program within the states. Entitlements for each school district are calculated according to a formula. School district personnel must prepare project proposals annually to apply for part or all of their entitlements; these proposals are reviewed and approved by staff in the state education agencies. Regulations regarding the geographic locations in which school districts may spend their Title I funds and the inclusion of children attending nonpublic schools are designed to ensure that the funds do reach areas where there is the greatest concentration of low-income families within each eligible community.

Evaluation is a central concern of the Title I program and has been since its inception. The legislation contains specific provisions for evaluations at the local, state, and national levels. A section of the Act stipulates that "effective procedures including provisions for appropriate objective measurements of educational achievement will be adopted for evaluating at least annually the effectiveness of the programs in meeting the special educational needs of educationally deprived children."[2] The legislation also requires local school districts to submit the results of their projects evaluations to the state education agency. In turn, state education agencies are to report annually to the U.S. Office of Education, providing information relative to state-wide operation of the Title I program. The U.S. Office of Education is then required to submit its findings regarding the national impact of Title I to the Congress and the President. The legislation further established the National Advisory Council on the Education of Disadvantaged Youth, a group that conducts outside evaluations which it presents each year directly to the Congress.

Since the beginning of the program in 1965, numerous other public and private organizations have been examining Title I programs and assessment procedures. Some are working independently; others are working under contract from the states and the U.S. Office of Education. Several of these studies have involved Massachusetts school districts or been conducted by organizations within the state. Abt Associates in Cambridge, Massachusetts, designed a study for the U.S. Office of Education in which they investigated the feasibility of applying cost-effectiveness analysis to the evaluation of Title I projects. Boston College reported on its federally funded study of the participation of nonpublic school children in Title I programs, and the Reading Studies Center of Western Reserve University has provided the U.S. Office of Education with a report on Title I reading projects throughout the country. These latter two studies included some Massachusetts projects in their samples. The USOE also contracted with the New England School Development Council (NEEDS-NESDEC) to examine the operation of Title I in New England. This study developed a statistical description of FY66 Title I activity in the region and provided findings and recommendations concerning the feasibility of programmatic evaluation and the availability of suitable data.

The Willis-Harrington Commission expressed concern with poverty and devoted much of its final report to that subject. The study produced some useful statistics regarding the extent of poverty within Massachusetts. As of the 1960 census, all but three communities in the state had families with income under $3,000. Between 25 percent and 30 percent of the total student population was considered to be in need of compensatory education services, including services for the handicapped. The Commission studied the need for extending compensatory education activities and, prior to the existence of the Elementary and Secondary Education Act, offered a series of recommendations to the Department of Education and to local school districts regarding ways in which they might improve the quality and quantity of programs for the disadvantaged child.

As the Willis-Harrington Commission was completing its broad study of Massachusetts education, and partially because of the findings and recommendations that the Commission was developing, the Massachusetts General Court authorized a state program to provide funds to public school districts for the support of compensatory education activities for disadvantaged children. Chapter 650 of the Acts of 1964 was approved in July 1964 and became effective the following September. The legislation provided state funds for reimbursement on a matching base to school districts that developed compensatory education projects approved by the Massachusetts Department of Education. The total program was small, awkwardly designed, and short-lived. After June 1967, it was not renewed. During its first year, fiscal year 1965, the legislature approved only $50,000 for the program; during its last year, that amount was increased to only $100,000. Thus, limited funding meant that few communities were able to participate, and none could receive more than a few thousand dollars. The provision that state matching fund reimbursements could be made only *after* local projects had been completed meant that the total operating costs of the approved projects had to be encumbered initially in the local budgets. This arrangement did not work to the advantage of participating school districts. Instead, it added administrative difficulties in exchange for meagre financial assistance. By this time, too, Title I of the Elementary and Secondary Education

Act was providing much larger grants to fully fund local projects. As a result, in 1967, rather than revise and strengthen Chapter 650, the legislature discontinued state support of compensatory education.

Study Procedures

To assist in the improvement of compensatory education programs in Massachusetts, the Advisory Council commissioned Daniel Jordan to recommend modifications of current programs based on evaluations specific enough to develop practical recommendations for improvement. For planning purposes, the study was originally envisaged as a three-year program with the first year's activities being undertaken as a separate unit which could provide the basis for the research activities of the subsequent years. Obviously, it is not possible to do a thorough study, collecting comparative data by using control groups, within one year. Thus, the first year's activity was devoted to an inventory of federal, state, and local programs, an evaluation of a representative sample of programs, and the formulation of recommendations for improving evaluation, for modifying the programs themselves, and for new administrative arrangements to facilitate program improvement. Primarily concerned with educational programs dealing with deprivations arising primarily from unsatisfactory economic and social conditions, Jordan's study did not deal with programs of special education for the disadvantaged. Also, other programs with direct or indirect bearing upon the effectiveness of Title I PROGRAMS (such as Model Cities Programs, Foster Grandparents, Headstart, Upward Bound, Neighborhood Youth Corps, Family Planning, etc.) were not included as a part of this study, although some attention was given to how all these efforts might be better coordinated.

Four hundred sixty Title I projects were operating in Massachusetts at the time the study was conducted. A ten percent sample was made "theoretically representative of the total state-wide Title I program."[3] Jordan's team visited each project one to six times.

The visits were made to (1) observe projects; (2) talk to the director and his staff; and (3) administer a questionnaire.

A survey form was mailed to all Massachusetts project directors seeking (1) general information on those being served; (2) express the needs of their pupils; and (3) specific project information. The information gathered was used to supplement the sample data.

A Brief Summary of the Findings

Over 135,000 school children have backgrounds which did not prepare them for successful performance in traditional school systems. Thousands of similar children not yet in school will continue to enter school at some future time unprepared and therefore disadvantaged. To guarantee these children an equal educational opportunity means that they must be provided with special learning experiences that will enable them to compensate for disadvantages created by inadequate preparation.

Needs Assessment

No systematic review of needs was found to be a part of most projects and therefore slight attention was given to establishing priorities among needs. Three of the highest ranking needs identified were: (1) reading improvement; (2) improvement of self-image; and (3) improvement of attitude toward school. Jordan reports that these identified needs were consistent with national findings.

Annual Program Modification

Almost one-third of the sample projects were repeated each year with no revisions. Most of the revisions reported concerned matters related to personnel. Evaluations, when there were any, played only a minor role in making revisions.

Planning of Staff Training

Little evidence of preservice or inservice planning for staff training was found by Jordan. When there was planning for staff training, it often did not have a focus congruent with objectives.

For all practical purposes, compensatory education in the State is financed by Title I (Elementary and Secondary Education Act of 1965) funds. In fiscal year 1968, the State received over $16 million in Title I funds to finance 466 compensatory education projects involving over 100,000 students in 305 school districts. A comparable amount was received for fiscal year 1969. Jordan's study dealt with practically every aspect of a ten percent random sample of these projects. Based on these findings, 48 recommendations for improving compensatory education in the Commonwealth were proposed.

The findings of Jordan's study are consistent with the findings of a large number of similar studies on compensatory education and on Title I programs in particular. His findings show an impressive accumulation of experience in working with disadvantaged children gained by hard-working and devoted teachers, aides, and administrators and, a growing disillusionment and frustration, frequently not readily admitted, with compensatory education as currently conceived and practiced. The reason for the frustration is clear: this kind of education is not producing significant results of lasting value in sufficient numbers of students fast enough to deal with a problem that has already reached vast proportion and is still growing at an alarming rate.

Participants in the Planning Process

Planning for Title I projects was found to be done largely by school administrative personnel. Teachers and university faculty were involved in planning in only one project in five. Community organizations were typically ignored, as were students and parents. However, a number of "cooperative" projects (9 out of the sample of 43 indicated a cooperative project) were conducted.

The Major Recommendations

All of the recommendations support four basic courses of action which are pertinent to these weaknesses and which Jordan believed would, if fully implemented, dramatically strengthen the programs in compensatory education and make them effective. They are:

(A) establish appropriate program objectives, operationally defined, and center all planning on these objectives;
(B) establish sound evaluation components in all Title I projects for use in systematic modification towards program improvement;
(C) establish several model compensatory education programs which may be adopted with appropriate modification in other localities; and
(D) take steps to fill the compensatory education manpower shortage by setting up training programs consistent with the above three courses of action.

A. Establish Appropriate Program Objectives.   During the first four or five years of their lives, most middle-class children go through a "hidden" curriculum which provides for them the kinds of basic learning competencies that are prerequisite to successful performance in school. Up to the present time, schools have based their curricula, their teaching methodology, and their grading and incentive systems upon the erroneous assumption that everyone coming into the school has had exposure to "hidden" curriculum and mastered it reasonably well. A child growing up in poverty or semipoverty will also be exposed to a "curriculum" — one that enables him to survive in his culture, to be sure, but also one that does *not* provide him with the kinds of learning competencies prerequisite for successful performance in schools as they are currently set up.

In coming to the school situation, he is clearly at a tremendous disadvantage when compared to his more affluent peers. The school then compounds the disadvantage by giving him learning tasks the prerequisites to which he has not yet mastered, thereby assuring failure. Being stuck in an intolerable and unjust position and forced to accumulate failures over long periods of time generate such negative emotional by-products, all associated with the formal learning situation, that effective learning becomes impossible. Since failure in school reduces opportunities for attaining future economic security and continuing growth and development, both socially and personally, the magnitude of this problem approaches incomprehensible dimensions. Its ramifications are far-flung largely because the situation perpetuates itself.

There are approximately 15 million children in the United States who find themselves locked in a system that is not helping, but in many cases, making things worse. Compensatory education has come to be regarded as one means of helping these children. This kind of education is intended to "compensate" for the missed "hidden" curriculum. Unfortunately, there is a widespread tendency to cast compensatory education into a remedial mold or put it in the form of general enrichment activity, neither of which can compensate for inadequate preparation for school. Both remedial work and enrichment experiences have their place, *but if they do not focus on the task of developing competent learners, they are apt to have very little permanent or even short-term effects.* The Jordan data indicate that Title I programs in Massachusetts are similar to the variety of compensatory education programs prevalent throughout the United States — programs which do not focus on developing competent learners and which are therefore not being maximally effective. It is therefore hoped that the following recommendation will be regarded as urgent and critical:

1. That the state Title I office make *the development of effective and competent learners* the required main objective of all Title I programs and that local projects be given assistance in translating this main objective into specific behavioral objectives relevant to their own programs.

In education everywhere, there is evidence of a distinction between what educators say they propose to do and what they find themselves doing. In compensatory education, this is particularly true (largely because there is a better notion of what is gained than how to achieve it). This is not a matter of willful deception, but a problem of inadequate attention to the evaluation process as it relates to objectives and priorities within objectives. Stake and Denny have expressed it succinctly:

Not only must the evaluator report the goals but he must indicate the relative importance of the goals. Goals are not equally desirable; some have priority over others. Different educators will set different priorities, and the same educator will change his priorities over time. Priorities are complex and elusive, but the evaluation responsibility includes the job of representing them. New conceptualizations and new scaling techniques are needed to take a first step toward discharging this responsibility.

The great weakness in our present representation of goals is that it does not guide the allocation of resources. Goals compete for our support, for our efforts. Relying on some explicit or implicit priority system, those who administer education decide among alternative investments, operational expenditures, and insurance. Evaluation requires an acknowledgement of priorities.[4]

Not only do the priorities need to be clear, but the objectives need to be explicit and operational. Otherwise, they cannot be communicated, will be useless as a guide, and can easily be changed without being noticed. Jordan's findings clearly indicate the need to implement the following recommendation within the context of the preceding one;

2. That the state Title I office publish guidelines on formulation of program objectives which will include an elaboration on the following suggestions:

a. objectives should be generated out of assessed needs and be feasible in terms of resources available;

b. objectives should reflect a hierarchy of priorities so that resources, time, and personnel can be allotted accordingly;

c. program objectives should be clearly stated in behavioral terms that establish performance criteria for students and specific success criteria for the program; and

d. program objectives should be disseminated to all staff members and be included as a part of their preservice and inservice training so that everyone knows how he is related to the achievement of the objectives.

In connection with "c" above, it is important to bear in mind at least two basic criteria for program success:

(1) that students achieve at a rate *above* the norm; and

(2) that students receiving compensatory education exhibit achievement levels statistically significantly higher than a comparable control group which does not have the compensatory treatment.

Anything less than this will be an indication of program ineffectiveness.

Establish Sound Evaluation Components in All Title I Projects. Once objectives have been specified and the program planned around them, there is no way of determining whether or not, or to what degree they were achieved without a carefully planned evaluation component. It is clear that good evaluation is the *sine qua non* of program improvement. There is little hope of ensuring good evaluation unless adequate time and resources are allocated for this purpose. Above all, qualified personnel are required. Given the scarcity of trained evaluators, it is all the more important for this kind of expertise to be present in the Title I Office. Although the state report for 1968 indicated to Jordan a growing sophistication in evaluation, his data nonetheless *clearly* indicate a great need for improvement of the evaluation procedures employed by project directors. He therefore recommends:

(3) that the Title I state office retain two or more full-time professionally qualified program evaluators who can be assigned the responsibility for reviewing this aspect of all proposals, monitoring the evaluation process of the programs, and for helping to mobilize evaluation resources to assist local districts as needed.

It is important to note here that one percent of the state allocation for Title I can be used by the state for administration of programs. In Massachusetts, this amounted to $167, 965 in fiscal year 1968–69. During last year, only $77,663 was used, the rest being returned to the federal government. Thus, this recommendation is not unrealistic from a financial point of view since funds exist to increase administrative activities.

Since state agencies are frequently not able to compete for adequately trained staff, particularly in the area of evaluation, Jordan suggests:

(4) that the Title I state office establish contractual agreements with business or institutions of higher learning to provide training and/or consultant services to evaluation staff members on the local level or encourage local districts to do so;

(5) that specific encouragement be given to local educational agencies to appoint paid evaluators to Title I program staffs and that it be mandatory that these evaluators be included on the planning staff, and

(6) that the state Department of Education organize a pool of university consultants who can be drawn upon by local districts for assistance in planning, implementing, and evaluating their projects.

It should be noted here that the Massachusetts Advisory Council on Education and Title I Office in the state have already acted on the recommendation that consultants from various institutions of higher learning be identified and these have been brought together for a discussion of their responsibilities. Lists of these consultants and their addresses have been made available to all Title I programs.

(7) That part of the funds for Title I programs should be made available to provide release time for potential Title I staff members for planning, evaluation, pre-service, and inservice training. Guidelines should specify this and suggest various kinds of arrangements for doing it.

With the possibility of adequate assistance being offered, it becomes reasonable to establish the requirement embodied in the recommendation:

(8) That sound evaluation designs be considered a required part of the proposal for funds and that no project be funded if it does not have an acceptable evaluation.

It is common practice for administrators to require reports of various kinds which are seldom read and rarely used. Evaluation reports are no exception and our data show that for the most part the basic purposes of evaluation reports (modification towards improvement) are frustrated by:

(a)   the design of the report forms;
(b)   the medium of the report;
(c)   the pattern of dissemination; and
(d)   the timing and frequency of dissemination.

Rather than being a vehicle for change, evaluation reports are frequently viewed as an official opportunity to justify what has been done by presenting the program in the most positive light possible. This attitude always has an effect on dissemination patterns and reduces the utility of reports considerably. Jordan believes the following recommendations are essential to the realization of the purposes of evaluation:

(9) That the state Title I office creates and adopts a new evaluation reporting system, giving attention to the use of new report forms, different media for different audiences, patterns of dissemination, and frequency and timing of dissemination, all geared to facilitate program modification for improvement. Specifically, evaluation reports coming at an end of a project should be required to include concrete recommendations for program modification, or present evidence as to why the program should be modified when repeated.

(10) The evaluation results of a previous year's program be made a mandatory source of input for the current year's planning. Proposals should therefore require some kind of evidence confirming compliance.

Establish Several Model Compensatory Education Programs.

Given the magnitude of the educational problems facing disadvantaged youngsters and the fact that deficits accumulate rapidly with passing time, it is imperative for methods of compensatory education that are highly successful to be identified as soon as possible and then put into operation as models. By providing adequate rewards and incentives, these models will be adopted in localities where evaluation demonstrates that little success is being achieved. Identifying such approaches may require a greater investment of resources initially but will pay off in the long run. Jordan recommends:

(11) That the state Title I Office collaborate with the Board of Higher Education, selected institutions of higher learning and promising school districts in the development of several carefully designed compensatory education models which can be rigorously evaluated and results from which can be disseminated to other projects. Such models should become demonstration centers where student teachers may be trained and where site visits may be made by those working in compensatory education.

Jordan suggests the kind of evaluation specified by Edward Suchman:

> The key conceptual elements in a defining of evaluation from a method-
> ological point of view are (1) a planned program of deliberate intervention,
> not just any natural or 'accidental' event; (2) an objective or goal which is
> considered desirable or has some positive value, not simply whatever change
> occurs; and (3) a method for determining the degree to which the planned
> program achieves the desired objective. Evaluation research asks about the
> *kind* of change desired, the *means* by which this change is to be brought
> about, and the signs according to which such change can be recognized.[5]

Take Steps to Fill the Compensatory Education Manpower Shortage.
According to a 1967 Yeshiva University report to the Civil Rights Commission,
only 3 percent of the 15,000 teachers graduating in 1966 from the ten major
institutions that certify public school teachers in the United States had
received any orientation in teaching disadvantaged children. Yet, it is estimated
that 20 – 30 percent of the children in the nation's schools require compensatory
education. This general lack of preparation from teaching the disadvantaged is
reflected in our data from the sample. Jordan recommends:

(12) That in order to meet a critical manpower shortage in compensatory
education the state Department of Education, in collaboration with selected
institutions of higher learning and public school systems, give top priority to the
establishment of model programs, both preservice and inservice, for training a
variety of compensatory education personnel; that these programs be based on
up-to-date research findings concerning learning and the kinds of experiences
that are prerequisite to the development of competent learners, particularly as
these experiences relate to the disadvantaged; that they include model components
on evaluation and curriculum; that the programs be selective in whom they admit
and rigorous in extent and depth of training; and, that they be carefully evaluated.

As Jordan indicates, training for compensatory education – when any
exists – is apt to consist of a narrow variety of single courses. Jordan proposes
the following content materials for use in preparing teachers for work with the
disadvantaged:

Descriptions of Contents of Training Experiences

1. Nature Of The Competent Learners
This aspect of the training involves acquiring a relatively thorough understanding of the program's main objective in terms of the capacities
characteristic of a competent learner and how these capacities insure
competence.
2. Culture And Its Relationship to Preception And Learning
Culture refers to ways of feeling, thinking, and acting that are trans-
mitted from generation to generation. Understanding a "disadvantaged"
child's prior capabilities (including knowledge, attitudes, social skills, etc.)
will necessitate understanding how culture shapes these prior capabilities.
The culture of the middle-class child provides him with a "hidden curriculum" that prepares him for the traditional school experience.
3. Kinds Of Learning And The Conditions Of Learning
One of the primary conditions of learning is the existence of prior capabilities, conditions internal to the learner; there is another category of
conditions that are external to the learner; these are matched in various
ways and make up different kinds of learning. Growing up in poverty
produces a set of prior capabilities different from what the middleclass child
will bring to the school situation.

4. How To Plan For Learning

This concerns knowledge and application of theories of planning in relationship to teaching and learning and includes defining performance criteria, behavioral objectives, and defining alternative routes to the achievement of instructional objectives on different levels.

5. Practicum in Techniques for Developing Perceptual Speed and Acuity

Students from disadvantaged backgrounds are sometimes known to have reduced perceptual spans, speeds, and acuity. Discussion will center primarily on visual and auditory modes of sensory perception. Excercises for increasing perceptual capacities (using tachistoscopes, projectors, and recorders) are demonstrated and opportunities for training disadvantaged youngsters will be provided.

6. Nature Of Cognition

This includes a review of the theories of cognitive organization and functioning, with an emphasis on the following cognitive processes, convergent processes, divergent processes, translation from one symbolic form to another, interpretation processes, formation and application of principles, analytic processes, synthesis, evaluation and judgmental processes, and forming and testing hypotheses.

7. Memory

Certain kinds of experience appear to facilitate storage of information. Forgetting is a special case of not being able to retrieve information that is stored.

8. Conceptual Behavior

One capacity which readily distinguishes a competent learner from an ineffective one is the capacity to form, identify, and utilize concepts. The chief function of conceptual behavior is to enable the organism to bring a manageable order to the inordinate complexity of the environment by classifying objects, events, ideas, behavior patterns, and feelings.

9. Transfer Of Learning

The capacity to transfer knowledge both laterally and vertically is a general factor underlying competence in learning. Certain approaches in teaching help to facilitate transferability. This is of particular importance in helping disadvantaged children "catch up." Teachers are given practical exercises in how to induce the transfer of learning as a habitual part of instruction no matter what subject is being taught.

10. The Nature Of Volition and Perseverance — Increasing the Capacity to Intend And Carry Something through to Completion

Volition and perseverance are examined in relationship to motivation, aspiration levels, sense of personal future, and self-expectations. Practical ways of helping a child to strengthen these capacities are discussed.

11. Management Of Feelings And Emotions — Principles Of Self-Control

Because of frustrations, pressures from injustice and lack of consistent patterns of reward and/or punishment, disadvantaged youngsters may find it difficult to control impulses and aggressive behaviors. This course provides basic information on how to help a student to begin to control himself in constructive ways.

12. Seminar In Motivation

One way of conceptualizing a basic problem facing all students needing compensatory education is in terms of motivation. Without motivation to attend, to pay attention, to become involved in the learning process, little learning takes place. Students who come into the public school system from a different cultural background will experience the structure of values in the public school system as perpetual criticism of them for certain "deficiencies," a focus on failure, rather than on support for positive efforts made.

13. Reward and Punishment and the Nature of Encouragement

This course reviews the practical application of research findings concerning reward-encouragement and punishment-discouragement.

14. Handling Frustration and Failure — Identifying and Individualizing Learning Experiences around Strengths and Interests

This course examines the ways in which so many remedial efforts fail because they concentrate on weaknesses where there is little interest rather than on strengths. It includes a reconceptualization of "failure" as nothing more than a useful trial which eliminates one approach and points to a potentially more promising approach to be used on a subsequent trial.

15. Seminar and Practicum in Learning Disabilities

The general psychological aspects of learning disabilities will be reviewed, the relevant research literature will be discussed, and the specific applications of principles of remediation will be formulated.

16. Anxiety and Learning in Compensatory Education

This course will enable teachers to utilize anxiety as a motivator, to create some anxiety if need be, to control it, and to utilize it in fostering attention, using its reduction as a reinforcer, and as a means of enhancing learning. This course will also be useful for counselors who would like to take advantage of mild states as a means of enabling students to gain insights into their own strengths and weaknesses, and thereby come to know themselves better.

17. Theory and Practicum in Continency Management

This practicum will be used to train contingency managers for dealing with specific problems in compensatory education where the behavioral pattern of students mitigates against maintenance of attention long enough for learning to be possible.

18. Seminar in the Development Of Self-Image

The seminar will be devoted to a review of the research literature on the formation of the self-image and its relationship to perception, motivation, emotion, confidence, and competence.

19. Role of Humor, Fun, and Laughter in Educating the Disadvantaged

This course examines the cognitive and motivational elements in humor. Practical ways of relieving the tediousness of some learning tasks by the injection of humor are discussed.

20. Developing Moral Behavior for Supportive Learning

"Morality" refers here to the aspects of behavior concerned with relationships among human beings. Certain qualities of a relationship can facilitate or impair learning. For instance, a cooperative spirit facilitates learning while a rebellious one tends to impair it. Moral behavior is learned like most everything else. Those who are cooperative in spirit help others while at the same time attracting support form them.

21. Practicum in Aesthitics in Compensatory Education

This course focuses on the practical ways of utilizing drama, music, art, and dance to develop expressive capacities of disadvantaged students, to increase their abilities to discriminate among various stimulus properties inherent in the arts, and to heighten cognitive development generally. In the past, the arts have been regarded as a nice but unessential addition to the curriculum. This course demonstrates how the arts can function as a solid core of the curriculum in a way that will support and serve intellectual and affective growth in all other areas.

22. Practicum in Selection of Media and Utilization of Different Presentation Modes

The purpose of this practicum is to provide exercise in arranging the relationship(s) between student and media so that communication is maximally effective.

23. Techniques in the Presentation of Materials for Individualizing Instruction — Utilizing the Sequential Hierarchy of Content Arrangement and the Concrete to Abstract Approach

This course will enable student-teachers to review any kind of material which students need to learn, extract the essence of it, break it down into small units, and arrange them in a sequential manner so that making errors in mastering the material is greatly reduced. Sequentially arranged information can also be used to identify the exact nature of the difficulty a student might have in comprehending a certain concept. The capacity to translate materials into a sequence of small learning tasks is crucial to a teacher's functioning as part of a compensatory educational program, particularly where the material is difficult or abstract. The course also serves as an introduction to programming material for teaching machines or other kinds of programmed instruction and for arranging explanations on a continuum ranging from concrete to abstract.

24. Techniques in Developing Study Skills, Study Habits, Ability to Take Tests and Follow Directions

This is a short course designed to explain practical means through which students may develop good study habits and skills. (This is particularly appropriate for students planning to work in secondary schools or on the college level where much of the learning is dependent upon independent study.)

25. Theories and Methods of Fostering Creative Potential

This course is a practicum in ways and means of identifying a creative person and individualizing instruction in such a way that creativity is not stifled, but, in fact, will enhance and support the child's learning efforts in all areas.

26. Theories and Techniques for Establishing Rapport

The capacity to establish and maintain rapport with students is a critical characteristic of an effective teacher, particularly a teacher who is working with disadvantaged students.

27. The Nature of Curiosity and Techniques for Developing a Demeanor of
Inquiry

This short course focuses mainly on techniques for training students how to
get information from adults. Since many disadvantaged students are
inexperienced in soliciting information from adults and, therefore, simply
"tune out" when information which they do not understand is presented in
the classroom.

28. Compensatory Education Evaluation

Material covered in this course will include explanations of the difference
between research and evaluation and how they overlap; the relationship
between program or teaching objectives and educational needs, and
comparison of objectives with actual program outcomes; discussion of various
kinds of instruments which might be used in the collection of different
kinds of data relevant to evaluation; ways of treating data; interpretation of
data; analysis of data in terms of program objectives as a means of building
evaluation components into the general program.

29. The Principles of Behavioral Cybernetics Applied to Compensatory
Education

Performance and learning are analyzed in terms of the controlled relationships between a human operator and an instrumental situation. The concept
of the behaving individual as a closed-loop or cybernetic system utilizing the
processes of sensory feedback in the continuous control of behavior is
explored and applications of the concept to specific learning situations
pertinent to compensatory education are discussed. According to behavioral
cybernetics, learning as well as other aspects of behavior organization are
determined primarily by the nature of the feedback-control processes
available to the behaving individual. Therefore, practical experience will be
gained in this course in the designing of learning situations to fit the control
capabilities of the learner. Grading philosophies and examination procedures
as feedback systems are also examined.

30. Techniques in the Analysis of Child Behavior

This course will focus on the description and ecology of behavior, how to
record behavior in its context, and the utilization of different instruments
for describing psychosocial situations and specimens of different kinds of
behavior.

31. Tests and Measurements for Disadvantaged Students

This course reviews the basic theories behind testing programs and offers
practical experience in selecting or devising tests designed to assist in the
collection of data appropriate to a sound determination of whether or not
the goals of any given part of a compensatory education program are being
achieved. Students will acquire adequate knowledge for evaluating specific
teaching efforts and for monitoring the teaching-learning process going on in
the classroom so that modifications for improvement can be introduced at
any time. The need for careful interpretation of tests results in the light of
their built-in cultural biases is discussed.

32. Techniques of Self-Evaluation

This course is designed to enable teachers to analyze verbal and nonverbal feedback from students as a means of ascertaining their own effectiveness as teachers. Approaches to self-observation in the analysis of subjective feelings arising out of different situations are discussed and applied. Experience will be gained in the interpretation of feedback data, both from students and self-observation, with the aim of identifying modes of behavior that may be tried out as modifications of approaches judged to be ineffective.

33. Seminar and Practicum on Family Resources in Compensatory Education

The school can no longer be regarded as a socializing agent independent from the families of its students or the community in which it is located. This course centers upon ways and means of identifying and utilizing family resources to assist in the educational program of disadvantaged students.

34. Supplementary Services in Compensatory Education

When working with severely disadvantaged populations, compensatory educational programs are not complete without supplementary services which help to fulfill more basic needs. This short course discusses various kinds of supplementary services such as provision of dental care, medical care, vitamin supplements, vaccinations, eye care, psychiatric help, and, in some cases, legal assistance. Discussions will include ways and means by which school programs can be integrated with welfare services and other kinds of assistance from community agencies.

35. Practicum in Preparation of Home Environments for Cognitive Stimulation

One of the disadvantages experienced by many students from low-income families is the discontinuity between home and school. This course provides a discussion of, and gives the student experience in, planning with parents and alteration of home environment which will help reduce discontinuity and also provide for cognitive stimulation appropriate to the development of the children living in the home.

36. Practicum In Utilization Of Nonprofessional Personnel

As educational systems begin to differentiate their staffs, the classroom teacher will be supervising the efforts of the paraprofessional, the teacher aide, and other kinds of supporting personnel. This practicum focuses on ways of analyzing tasks and defining roles for the paraprofessional so that the teaching-learning process is maximally efficient.

37. Practicum in the Utilization of Members of the Peer Group as Teachers and Planners

This practicum is devoted to training student teachers in the techniques of utilizing other class members as teachers and as planners of activities consistent with the basic curriculum. Research evidence indicates that peer group members used as teachers can often communicate very effectively to their peers, thereby facilitating the learning of their peers, but they themselves also improve in their knowledge and motivation. This is frequently neglected as a classroom resource which could be very effective if properly organized and utilized.

38. Curriculum Theory and Curriculum Development

This course examines the current theories in curriculum development and includes a practicum in creating curricula on different levels for a variety of purposes.

39. Training for Specific Curriculum Area

Master teachers may have one or more areas of expertise in a given curriculum area, such as language arts and reading, math, physical science, behavioral science, biological science, art, dance, music, theatre arts, literature, technology, etc. Basic training in most of these areas would be ordinarily undertaken in the appropriate department of a university or college.

40. Computer-Aided Instruction for Disadvantaged Students

This course will focus on the adaptation of computer education instruction techniques for students who require compensatory education. Special units will be prepared in which the computer will be utilized in presentation of information and the explanation of any operations in utilizing the information which the student needs to know.

41. Seminar and Practicum in Psycholinguistics

This course will cover the basic field of psycholinguistics including the following aspects: linguistic models and functions units of language behavior; mediation theory and grammatical behavior; grammatical models and language learning; theory and practice of verbal conditioning; covert habit systems; memory transformations of verbal units; semantic generalization; and forgetting theory. Experience will be gained in diagnosing psycholinguistic problems and in basic research techniques related to psycholinguistics. The above list is not complete and is only meant to serve as a general indication of the contents of the core.

42. Seminar in Administration of Compensatory Education Programs

This seminar will systematically deal with basic problems in the administration of compensatory education programs; staff selection; creating differentiated staffing patterns for large programs; preservice and inservice training for staff; creating efficient communication channels among staff, students, community people, and parents; integration of the compensatory education program with the regular program; and on-going modification and evaluation for improvement.

43. The Nature-Nurture Controversy

This course focuses upon the relationship between this controversy and compensatory education. It will involve a review of the research literature on adopted children, studies of twins, the difference in effects of living in isolation or in institutions, and the effects of nursery school attendance. Related animal research will be examined.

44. Race Relations

Difficulties among various racial groups in American society have been perpetuated by its major institutions, including the school. This course focuses upon several aspects of race relations problems: history; the dynamics of prejudice and the psychology of attitude change; human rights and the law; and an exploration of the means by which educational institutions and teachers transmit prejudice from one generation to another through their attitudes, school policies, and learning materials. This course has a practical aspect in that every student participates in small encounter groups during which time he is afforded the opportunity to be confronted with his own attitudes and feelings about all aspects of the racial issue so that he may have a conscious knowledge of how his feelings are altering his perception. Once this process begins, attitudes are able to be modified and insights can be applied to the teaching-learning situation.

45. Desegregation and Integration: Factors in Compensatory Education
Students will review the literature on desegregation and integration and discuss the ways in which the institutionalization of discrimination has made compensatory education necessary as a part of the public responsibility in a modern democratic society. The effects of integration on educational progress will be examined. This course will enable candidates to experience the nature of relevance and irrelevance as it pertains to the teaching and development of materials for black students and those from other racial backgrounds, and to be able to identify either in materials, attitudes, and behavior.

At the moment, compensatory education is almost entirely federally funded from Title I monies. While the sources of future funding are uncertain, and the characteristics of compensatory education programs of the future subject to considerable change, widening definitions of the disadvantaged dictates a continuation of such programs. The disadvantaged child, identified as early as possible, needs special assistance. But the problem is by no means limited to the child. Inept teachers and shallow programs, often in pursuit of middle-class values, exacerbate the situation.

We turn next to another kind of disadvantaged person: the adult needing continuing education.

7 New Realities for Continuing Education

His official R.C.A. biography listed 27 honorary college degrees and devoted nine single-spaced pages to only a partial listing of his awards and decorations.

Among these were the Legion of Merit and doctoral degrees from Columbia and New York Universities. But on one occasion, Mr. Sarnoff said he most cherished the high school diploma that Stuyvesant High School awarded him in 1958, when he was 67 years old. He had never gone beyond elementary school. — New York Times, December 13, 1971.

. . .continuing education can no longer be treated as a hapless orphan if only because modern state government cannot work properly without it. — Melvin R. Levin & Joseph S. Slavet

Adult education is another social program that is nine-tenths iridescent dream and one-tenth reality. It has been piously argued that adult education is largely unnecessary in a nation which makes a free high school education available to all youngsters. The argument is specious. Take Massachusetts. Almost one half of its citizens over 25 years of age have less than a high school education. Melvin R. Levin, in his study for the Council, is able to locate a need for continuing education so great that he knows the state at best will only cope with it a little at a time. Levin says,

> For at least a generation, the persistent neglect of continuing education-part-time schooling for adults — has made it one of the few remaining orphans in the educational spectrum. A former principal role, providing compensatory and citizenship education for foreign born, non-English speaking adults, has declined in importance (although recent changes in immigration legislation have revived the need for such training); once a major activity, agricultural extension for a relatively small and diminishing farm population is of declining interest. More surprisingly, until the early 1960s, the vocational education needs of adults received scant attention. Despite the poverty and manpower programs of the 1960s, however, continuing education still occupies a secondary or tertiary place in the educational priorities of most states.
>
> There has been increasing interest in new approaches to continuing education in Massachusetts as elsewhere in the nation in recent years because of two unrelated developments. The first was the rediscovery in the late 1960s of the festering problems of poverty and racial discrimination. This recognition has resulted in a growing emphasis on the need for compensatory

education and training for disadvantaged youth and adults, including parent education, consumer education and other activities designed to assist disadvantaged adults to complex urban life. Increasing concern for the employment problems of the disadvantaged has therefore given fresh impetus to a traditional function since, in one form or another, low-cost, part-time schooling for poor adults has been a primary thrust in education programs in the United States and foreign countries for at least a century.

At a time when it is estimated that an M.I.T. education is obsolete in five years, we find a mere five percent of Massachusetts' four million adults enrolled in any kind of continuing education program. The danger that technology will thrust us forward and make us all obsolete — with or without M.I.T. degrees — is real.

In any case, vast numbers of Massachusetts citizens are not touched by any kind of formal continuing education, to paraphrase Mark Twain (a risky prospect at best); everybody knows that life-long education is important but no one does anything about it. Continuing education is not built into the life style of most individuals. Schools are institutions to graduate from and leave. Firms train or retrain only when they must. Levin writes:

> Continuing education has historically played a somewhat more important role in the process of skill renovation. This function may become indispensable as the pace of change quickens in many occupations and as workers are confronted with the recurrent threat that their skills will become obsolete. A federal study indicates that employment in eighty sizable occupational groups decreased during the 1950s. These not only included jobs in declining industries such as construction (decline in paper hangers, brick layers and plasterers), but also workers in printing trades, laundry workers, tailors and the growing trade and service industries. Moreover, while most occupations are not experiencing similar declines in overall manpower needs, their skill demands are constantly changing. Even from a narrow occupational standpoint, education is becoming recognized as a lifelong process in which formal diploma and degree courses represent a stage rather than a terminus. Education, and training continuing beyond the full time day school has become a necessity. Taking into account all of its aspects — cultural, avocational activities and so on — there is a surging growth in continuing education which has led to predictions that, by the turn of the century, it will be one of the nation's biggest businesses.

The glowing projections of things to come are based, Levin and Slavet are convinced, in large degree on a shaky foundation. There is much disagreement over the objectives and content of continuing education curricula and charges of program irrelevancy are not only frequent but are apparently justified. Partly because education is dominated by concepts and approaches designed for the young, continuing education has displayed an infuriating tendency to treat pragmatic, problem-centered adult students as dependent children. Up to the present, Levin and Slavet tell us, educators have found it difficult to design curricula and teaching techniques suitable for the special requirements of adult audiences. This deficiency may be attributed to the idea that continuing education is offered as a major field of study in only a relative handful of university schools and education. Education majors have concentrated on the learning needs of children and adolescents. Continuing education is given a generalized tripartite definition by an authority in the field who sees it as a process of lifelong learning after completion of formal schooling, a set of organized activities including classes, workshops, lectures, and courses and a movement which combines the two. Knowles forecasts continuing education emerging as: ". . .the largest and most significant dimension of our national education enterprise. . .the size of the adult student body would grow to be at least twice the size of the youth student body in numbers and probably of about equal size in volume of attendance hours."

In any expansion of continuing education, a number of questions must be answered. One already mentioned has to do with the role of the external/open university proposed by Dr. James E. Allen, Jr. and Professor Jerrold R. Zacharias.[1] Another relates to the public-private interface which could lead to duplication and slight gain for anyone. Levin and Slavet feel that the question of who will furnish leadership for continuing education looms above all others.

Writing a report for the Massachusetts Board of Higher Education, Dr. Jerrold R. Zacharias, whose chore was to propose programs for a new university concept, indicates some concerns and some promise for the disadvantaged adult:

> While a heterogeneous student body is a commendable on paper, it is not easy to achieve in practice. Britain's Open University, for example, has discovered that unfortunately the majority of its students are not heterogeneous, and that students from the working class in particular are not well represented.

At the same time, Zacharias' choice of programs opens up some exciting prospects for the disadvantaged adult to study:

Social Welfare
    Day-care
    Welfare case work
    Labor relations
    Drug addiction
    State and Municipal services
Pre- and Para-Law
    Legal aid
    Police
    Municipal and State legislative aides
    Prisons

Pre- and Paramedicine and Health
   Nursing
   Technicians
   Physician's aides
   Medical management

Procedures Followed in the Study

As with so many other weak and fragmental social programs, Levin and
Slavet found data on continuing education very difficult to come by or of very
limited use. Accordingly, they found themselves using primary sources, in
particular, personal interviews and visits, to collect information and to assess the
strengths and weaknesses in the various systems delivering continuing education.
The study directors did a state-by-state search in vain, hoping to find a suitable
adult education program model to adapt to Massachusetts.

Levin and Slavet realized a need for a broader operational concept of adult
education and accordingly produced their own statement indicating the seven
major functions of continuing education:

(1) Adult Basic Education (ABE), which includes programs for persons with
less than the equivalent of an eighth grade education.

(2) High School Equivalency, which provides education from the completion
of the eighth grade level up through high school.

(3) Adult Civic Education (ACE), which is designed to prepare aliens for
U.S. citizenship, and may, in addition, include ABE and high school
equivalency education.

(4) Occupational Training, which includes preemployment and skill training
and occupational upgrading. For disadvantaged adults, this usually includes
ABE and possibly high school equivalency education.

(5) Avocational and Cultural Education, which covers leisure time instruction. Largely because of more pressing priorities in other areas of continuing
education, this area has received little attention in this study.

(6) Staff Training and Career Development of State Officials and Employees,
a critical, neglected area which has not normally been included under the
continuing education umbrella, but is considered sufficiently important and
relevant to be accorded high priority.

(7) Citizen-Client Education, which refers to the educational responsibilities
which all state agencies have for informing and educating the public about
agency goals and problems. It also concerns agency responsibility for
developing and implementing education and communication techniques to
be used as strategies for achieving agency goals.

Levin and Slavet developed the supply and demand for continuing
education, only after a massive sleuthing effort. A final chapter sets forth the

recommendations which evolved from a number of conferences with groups and individuals.

The Findings of the Report

"Cost-benefit analysis," state Levin and Slavet, "is generally defined as a measurement technique in which total costs of a given project or program are compared with probable total benefits." Several factors point to the considerable benefit from investment in programs of continuing education.

(1) Continuing education can yield substantial benefits by capitalizing on past educational experience. It must be viewed as an essential stage in a continuing process of education, in which the rewards for each additional stage tend to be increasingly larger than the previous increment of investment. The financial gains for acquiring additional education beyond the high school level seems to be particularly pronounced.

(2) In comparing investments in public continuing education with allocations for other types of schooling, foregone earnings must be considered. A young person not attending high school or college would presumably be employed; he would have to give up the opportunity for such earnings in favor of attending most types of schools. However, in the case of most types of continuing education, there is no interruption in the flow of earnings and in some newer programs, the act of initiating a course of work-training generates a flow of earnings – and taxes. Moreover, there is an obvious advantage from the standpoint of the student. No lost "opportunity costs" are normally involved because he is not giving up opportunities for employment while he is continuing his education.

(3) Some form of continuing education, in a sense, can be viewed as a necessity to protect large, previous investments in the student's education. Since the pace of technological change is accelerating and the future is unpredictable, the recent graduate embarks on his career with a store of accumulated knowledge which is certain to become partially obsolescent fairly quickly.

(4) Continuing education may provide the missing diploma, license or certificate which has become increasingly necessary for entry and/or advancement. This may be particularly true of the disadvantaged who, by reason of lack of motivation or environmental and family circumstances, failed as children and adolescents to take full advantage of elementary and secondary schooling. Grown to maturity, perhaps with military service and a few years of distasteful menial labor and periods of joblessness behind them, the adults with the help of such life experience have developed the incentive and wider horizons necessary to profit from education and training useful to their needs.

(5) Assuming that one of the principal functions of continuing education is alleviation of poverty problems through such activities as remedial education and high school equivalency education, federal programs offer the possibility of

doing more with relatively little additional expense. Therefore, from the stand-point of state policy, one dimension of the cost-benefit approach relates to attacking as many state and local problems as possible with maximum use of federal funds, using scarce state funds for nonfederally aided programs only when absolutely necessary. It is the responsibility of the state, however, to ensure that the educational and training needs of its adult residents are met regardless of the availability of federal assistance. As a guiding principle, continuing programs should be designed on the basis of need rather than in response to the stimulus of federal grants-in-aid.

(6) In the area of citizen-client education, considerable payoffs can be noted in such programs as driver safety education, conservation education, and air and water pollution.

Meanwhile the gap between the earnings of the ill-educated and the well-educated seems to be widening. The estimated lifetime earnings differential between elementary school graduates and high school graduates was just under $75,000 in 1956 but had spread to over $90,000 in 1966. There is a clear-cut implication for continuing education, especially for adult basic education and high school equivalency programs, in these enormous earnings differentials. This is shown on Table 7-1.

The dollar costs and benefits allocatable to elementary and high school programs for adults can be considered under two headings. First from the standpoint of the individual, the out-of-pocket costs are extremely small. The only personal costs, which can be included in this column, come under the heading of "psychic" losses through a reduction in leisure time. Second, a part-time investment, which requires little more than persistence, cannot only be anticipated to bring in a substantial immediate gain in annual income and a

Table 7-1

Mean Income in 1966 of Men 25 Years Old and Over, and Estimated Lifetime Income for Men by Years of School Completed, for the United States

	Annual Earnings	*Annual Differential*	*Lifetime Earnings*	*Lifetime Differential*
Elementary				
Less than 8 years	$3,520	$1,347	$188,659	$57,866
8 years	4,867		246,525	
High School				
1 to 3 years	6,294	1,200	283,718	56,802
			340,520	

Source: U.S. Department of Commerce, Bureau of the Census, *Annual Mean Income, Lifetime Income, and Educational Attainment of Men in the United States, For Selected Years, 1956 to 1966*, Current Population Reports Series P-60, No. 56, 1968, Tables A and F. Also: Melvin R. Levin & Joseph S. Slavet *Continuing Education* (D.C. Heath & Co. 1970) p. 38.

long-term increase in life-time earnings, but it also opens up options for further
education, training, promotion and pay increases.

The principal governmental gains, on the other hand, come under the
category of improved social stability and social justice, but there are also major
monetary advantages. Adult basic education costs per trainee are estimated to
run between $400 and $700 through completion, and high school completion
education is roughly the same. The federal share of these costs runs up to 90
percent for adult basic education. In contrast, except for persons who qualify
under the poverty program or related manpower programs, additional high school
education is financed from state and local revenue sources. Simply through
higher income taxes alone, the federal outlay would be recovered fairly rapidly.

In gaining perspective, Levin and his team feel it may be helpful to
visualize the potential demand for continuing education as an "expanding
universe." The word "universe" is used frequently in continuing education to
identify that portion of the population which is already, or depending on public
policy, could become a target for the various types of continuing education
programs delineated in this study. Originally, this universe consisted of a small
portion of the state's population, served by traditional programs of citizenship
education, basic education and occupational skill training, but it has grown into a
network of continuing education activities serving a wide variety of interests and
markets and involving many segments of the state's adult population. With the
rapid upgrading in recent years of standards for education, job skills and the
quality of public services, existing and potential markets for continuing education
are growing at an accelerating pace.

Since continuing education, in its broadest sense, is identified as any form
of learning undertaken by or provided for persons who have completed their
formal full-time education, quantification is a singularly difficult task since
continuing education can be said to begin where formal childhood education
leaves off, and continues virtually to the grave. For the illiterate and the high
school dropout, the need for continuing education can begin as early as late
adolescence. At the lower end of the scale, adult basic education concerned with
those who have not completed an eighth grade education is a prerequisite to
vocational and skill training. For the high school dropout and the high school
graduate alike, continuing education is associated most closely with an improvement in learning power aimed directly at satisfying changing job requirements.
Adults enroll in continuing education from their early twenties through their
retirement years.

Traditional Programs

Adult basic education represents a large potential market for state inter-
vention partly because of the migration to Massachusetts of poorly educated

persons from other parts of the nation. Because of the state's foreign-born who have little formal education, a significant proportion of its adolescents leave school well before completing high school or are "socially promoted" and learn little or nothing in school. It is estimated that, depending on definition, Massachusetts contains between 600,000 and 700,000 functional illiterates who need basic education before they are eligible to seek any but the most menial types of occupation.

1. High School Equivalency Education. Based on the level of educational attainment, Massachusetts is a leader among the states. Half of the state's population over 25 years of age in 1960 had completed more than 11.6 years of schooling. If an exception is made for those who have not gone beyond the eighth grade and the elderly, the market for high school equivalency education can be estimated at some 500,000 persons who have completed grade school and are probably young enough to be motivated to obtain a high school diploma or equivalency certificate.

2. Citizenship education, long a hallmark of continuing education, lacks the vigor that it had during the early part of this century when large-scale migration from non-English speaking countries was at its peak. During the past forty years, immigrants have been fewer in number and, until recently, were more apt to have some English skills. Recent changes in immigration legislation have increased the annual number of immigrants to Massachusetts to about 20,000 and allocated larger immigration quotas to non-English speaking nations. At present, there are about 150,000 aliens residing in Massachusetts. Consequently, there is a substantial and growing need for citizenship education, and more effective and creative state action is needed.

3. Occupational training for adults has become a critical component of national economic and manpower policy. In part, this focus relates to the accelerating pace of technological change which is generating sweeping revisions in manpower needs and standards. It is also linked to making the chronically unemployed employable through training and to upgrading the subemployed population. Most adults participate in some kind of occupational training at some time during their lifetime. Special emphasis should be given to training young persons (high school dropouts or graduates), older persons, the handicapped and prison inmates.

4. Avocational education is one of the most difficult markets to identify and serve. Increased leisure and affluence have broadened the potential market for this type of education. The state has already begun to establish a role for itself through courses at the community colleges, education for outdoor recreation and programs of the new Council on the Arts and Humanities, but it has yet to realize its full potential for leadership in this area.

5. Staff Training and Career Development for Governmental Personnel. State and local government personnel represent a sizable, well-defined market and also one of the areas where there is an urgent need for state action. State employment totalled 49,000 persons in 1966 while local government employment was 164,000. The chronic weakness in the staff capability of state and local government relates mostly to the recruitment, retention and upgrading of competent personnel. Aside from the practical value of in-service training at all levels, including benefits to both employees and agencies, progressive in-service training programs have become one of the most significant factors in attracting and retaining qualified persons in government employment.

6. Citizen-Client Education. The market for programs of citizen-client education includes the entire state population, and in some cases, the market extends well beyond the state's borders. Markets can be specialized, such as in driver safety education, or be directed at all adults, as in the case of environmental education. The difficult choice between educating citizens or policing them must be made. Ecology, safety and population concerns press us to better understandings and wiser decisions about everyday and long range events.

Four issues keep unbridged the gaps among needs, proposals, programs and delivery of services. These are relevant for continuing education activities around the nation.

First is the relatively low priority given to continuing education. No segment of government recognizes and responds to the need that is daily growing greater.

Second, there is a lack of leadership on the national and state levels. No one has the authority or prestige to lead and those who need leadership are divided a thousand different ways. Levin and Slavet declare budgeting for adult education to be "only an afterthought." There is, they feel, no substitute for leadership.

Third, the continuing education mandate is confused and limited. There is a stark contrast between the narrow limitations of Massachusetts efforts in public continuing education and demonstrable needs. Massachusetts will continue to lag behind unless it increases its budgetary commitment and revises its staffing patterns and its administrative structures. In addition, there is a need for clearer jurisdictional lines and, in particular, a greatly strengthened capability in program leadership, planning and technical assistance.

Finally, the demands of a postindustrial age in America are making it increasingly difficult to keep from being overwhelmed by the new sets of problems inherent in a post industrial society. Resources to do the job must be found. Many people, who never dreamt the day would come, must be lured back into the classroom to learn both new skills and new behaviors more in consonance with the phenomenon of postindustrialism.

Recommendations:

Continuing Education: A Program For The Seventies

An examination of continuing education in Massachusetts, Levin and Slavet write, has revealed patterns, problems and potentials which can be duplicated in most urban states. In Massachusetts, as elsewhere, continuing education is treated as a neglected orphan which understandably falls far short of its great promise in meeting increasingly cirtical needs. The difficulty is that continuing education seems to fall in between the interstices of power; unlike elementary and secondary education, vocational education and higher education, continuing education suffers from the fact that its outside constituencies tend to be weak and that it cannot rely on strong internal support within the governmental bureaucracy.

The recommendations in the Levin and Slavet report call for significant commitment to a balanced program of continuing education designed to enable the state to cope with a growing backlog of neglected needs in the education and training of adults and to equalize the educational opportunities offered to adults with those available to children. These are minimal objectives. The recommended priorities have been selected with a view toward allocating limited state financial resources to programs which are likely to result in higher personal and family incomes, a portion of which will be returned to the state in higher tax revenues, reduced dependency costs, and improved services. These recommendations also recognize the importance and desirability of flexibility to serve demands and needs which can fluctuate considerably. In addition, the recommendations would go a long way toward translating into reality the state goal of equal opportunity for all by providing a second chance for adults to fulfill their potential. The social consequences of continuing education are particularly important to the disadvantaged segments of the population, many of whom require specially designed opportunities for adult education and training.

The report declares that if a realistic and workable program in continuing education is to be established, the following steps need to be taken:

A. Declaration of Policy

The Governor should issue a declaration of policy with respect to continuing education for adults which should be incorporated in the preambles of implementing legislation and which embodies the following major principles:

1. Extending the right of free public education through the high school level, now effectively limited to children and adolescents enrolled in public elementary and secondary schools, to all adults regardless of age.

2. Extending the principle of minimum-cost postsecondary education and training to adults by equalizing tuition rates at public institutions of higher

education for part-time undergraduate students with tuition rates for full-time students; in addittion the present system of state-supported scholarships, now listed in practice to full-time, day school students, should be extended to adults enrolled in part-time postsecondary education. No qualified adult should be barred from taking advantage of continuing education opportunities because of financial need.

3. Extending the principle of staff training and career development for state employees by expanding into a comprehensive program the present limited activities in this critical area of continuing education (as part of a broader commitment for improving the quality of state service as well as the effectiveness and efficiency of state employees).

The declaration of policy should incorporate specific program targets to be achieved over specific periods of time. Both the targets and the programs should be reviewed annually by the Governor and Legislature and appropriate revisions should be made as required and disseminated in a public report.

B. Program Recommendations

To translate the declaration of policy into reality, the following program recommendations, based in large measure on the markets and needs identified in the previous chapter, should be put into effect. (The estimated costs of these programs are based on 1969 price levels; allowances have not been made for future price changes.)

1. **Adult Basic Education.** During the next ten years, a minimum of 250,000 persons of the estimated 600,000 to 700,000 in the state with less than an eighth grade education should be enrolled in programs of elementary level instruction in the skills of reading, writing, arithmetic and speaking English, with subject matter drawn from the fields of civic education, health practices, consumer education, human relations and family and home life. Priority in recruitment should be given to persons 18–44 years of age who are unemployed, underemployed, public assistance recipients and heads of households, and the program should be concentrated in those communities with relatively large numbers and proportions of adult residents in these groups.

A new Bureau of Continuing Basic Education in a proposed Bureau of Continuing Education in the State Department of Education should provide the state-wide leadership and guidance for expanding adult level education along the lines recommended in the above blueprint. Public and private agencies conducting adult basic education projects with state funds should use appropriate outreach techniques to attract previously neglected elements of the population. Some of these techniques — storefront facilities in target neighborhoods, the use of indigenous aides and other subprofessionals for door-to-door recruitment, and continued counseling and other supportive services — have proved effective in antipoverty programs.

2. Adult High School Education.   During the next ten years, a minimum of 300,000 persons of the estimated 1,300,000 in the state over 17 years of age with between eight and twelve years of education should be enrolled in programs of high school level instruction with a high school diploma as the goal or with successful passing of high school equivalency examinations as the objective for the enrollees.

The recommended target of 300,000 adults in high school education over a ten-year period is reasonable. It should be drawn from an existing pool of about 500,000 persons with nine to eleven years of schooling, to which must be added 150,000 – 200,000 high school dropouts during the next ten years. However, it does not include persons over 50 years of age in this educational category, most of whom are not likely to be attracted to a high school education program. On the other hand, a significant but unknown proportion of persons completing the adult basic education program must also be considered part of the market for high school education.

As part of the broadening of state responsibility for high school level education of adults, the present system of course fees, covering courses offered by the State Bureau of Adult Education and Extended Services and which now range from $7 to $26 depending upon the number of sessions, should be eliminated. Students should be charged only for registration ($1,000) and for high school equivalency applications and examinations.

3. Adult Citizenship Education.   Total enrollments in adult civic education should be increased from the present annual total of just over 6,000 to a new target of just 8,000. The annual enrollment should thereafter be gradually expanded to reach a peak of 20,000 by the fifth year, after which it would decline to a level-off total of about 15,000.

A new Bureau of Special Continuing Education in the proposed Division of Continuing Education of the State Department of Education would absorb the activities of the present Division of Immigration and Americanization and assume responsibility for the recommended expansion of adult citizenship education.

4. Adult Occupational Training.   The state should significantly expand the range of opportunities which are currently available in preemployment training, retraining and occupational upgrading mainly under a variety of federally subsidized programs which focus for the most part on the unemployed and underemployed disadvantaged population. This expansion should be in the form of a state commitment to supplement existing public and private programs of occupational training. The state should fund that portion of the state's training needs which have been designated in the annual Massachusetts Comprehensive

Manpower Plan as needs which cannot be met from funds available to the state under the 1) Manpower Development and Training Act; 2) the Vocation Education Act; 3) other federal legislation; and 4) training not meeting the criteria of federal aid programs.

One recommended priority for this new state program should be to stimulate a significant increase in the number of apprentices in Massachusetts. The expansion of apprenticeship training should be made in occupations where economic growth, technological changes and replacement for natural causes indicate continuing shortages of skilled craftsmen. Particular attention should be given in this expanded apprentice training program to increasing the relatively low number and low proportion of black apprentices. To this end, state funds should also be used for aggressive outreach activities to stimulate the interest of black youth, who either lack information about apprenticeship or do not consider it a realistic goal. In addition, tutorial assistance should be provided to applicants for apprenticeship to help them in passing the qualifying examinations.

In addition, two other target populations — prison inmates and older workers — should receive priority for training in view of the limited numbers from these groups being trained under federally assisted programs. There are an average of over 5,000 inmates in state and county correctional institutions in Massachusetts. Appropriate education and training to equip these persons for decent jobs when they return to society is an indispensable component of a modern program of correctional rehabilitation. Although all the recommendations of the Sub-Committee on Education of the Governor's Task Force on Correctional Industries deserve implementation, two suggestions should be given particular priority.

Through joint arrangements of the State Department of Correction and the Board of Regional Community Colleges, designated regional community colleges should provide the leadership for developing broad-gauged educational and training programs for correctional institutions in their areas of interest and for providing the instructors and other educational resources as required to carry out correctional institutional educational and training objectives. These arrangements should include joint appointments by the State Department of Correction and the cooperating regional community colleges of qualified persons to direct the planning and conduct of inmate education and training programs and correctional staff training programs.

Provisions of the law governing "work release" or "day work programs" in the state and county correctional institutions should be broadened to cover release time for training and education.

Occupational training for older workers, classified as persons 45 years of age and older, is also a relatively neglected area of training because of higher training priorities for lower age groups and because of physical and educational handicaps which often accompany and exacerbate occupational handicaps of age and discrimination on the basis of age.

An expanded state program of occupational training should also give serious consideration to supplementary funding of two program approaches which have been receiving greater priority as federally assisted manpower strategies: (1) the manpower training skills center; and (2) the Work Incentive Program.

Manpower training skills centers are self-contained, separately administered facilities offering comprehensive programs of educational counseling, basic education, prevocational training, communications skills, work orientation, skill training, and supportive services. They operate during the prime daylight hours and have full-time as well as part-time staff. Only one training facility in Massachusetts qualifies under federal standards as an officially designated skills training center. Additional centers are needed, particularly in central locations of disadvantaged urban communities.

The Work Incentive Program (WIN) is a relatively new federally assisted program of training and supportive services for persons who are receiving assistance under Aid to Families with Department Children. The current federal grant of $2.5 million which Massachusetts receives under WIN covers the cost of less than 3,000 trainees. Since the State Department of Public Welfare estimates that there are 13,100 adults classified as high-priority prospects for WIN, substantial financing in excess of the available federal authorization is required to cut more deeply into the backlog of AFDC recipients needing training and to keep up with the growing AFDC caseload.

The annual cost for this recommended state program of adult occupational training is estimated at about $3 million a year and would fluctuate in accordance with the cost of training not otherwise met from nonstate funds. An alternative to state funding would be to extend state tax incentives to employers who would accept for training persons who would meet state criteria for persons not trainable without such subsidy.

B. Strengthening State Administrative Leadership and Capability in Continuing Education below the Collegiate Level Should Be Undertaken

The Legislature should give to the Board of Education clear-cut, unequivocal responsibility for continuing education below the university or college level of adults beyond legal school age, including the approval of standards for all aspects of such education conducted by the local public schools and by private institutions conducting programs with state funds.

The Legislature should establish a Commission on Continuing Education within the Board of Education, representing state agencies as well as the private sector. This should be a 15 member commission consisting of six persons appointed by the Board of Education, six persons appointed by the Board of Higher Education and three persons each representing and appointed, respectively, by the Secretary of Human Services, the Secretary of Manpower Affairs and the Secretary of Administration.

A major role of the Commission should be to recommend which state agencies should be assigned the planning and implementation of specific continuing education programs and research tasks. The Commission should focus its attention on identifying state-wide continuing education needs and on recommending goals, priorities, criteria and standards for promulgation by appropriate operating agencies.

The Legislature should establish a new Division of Continuing Education (raising it from the present Bureau level) in the Department of Education as a strong center of state leadership for continuing education below the college level, thereby demonstrating that the state is committed to equalizing educational opportunities for the adults of Massachusetts with those of its children. It should be headed by an Assistant Commissioner, responsible to the Associate Commissioner of Curriculum and Instruction, who should be a person of outstanding academic and professional credentials in the field of adult education.

In accordance with the principle that the State Department of Education should place primary emphasis on its policy and leadership role, the proposed division should gradually divest itself and its constituent agencies of direct operating responsibilities for the organization and conduct of all adult classes. These classes may be transferred to local school departments, regional community colleges, state colleges or other appropriate jurisdictions. No fees should be charged for courses below the college level. Current statutory requirements that adult classes be self-supporting should be eliminated. The new division should concentrate on providing state-wide leadership and extending program counseling, consultation and advice in continuing education below the collegiate level. Much of the division's staff should be assigned to the regional centers of the State Department of Education to work closely with and to assist local school officials responsible for continuing education and related services and representatives of the increasing number of nonprofit and private organizations concerned with the general and special needs of adults, particularly disadvantaged adults.

The proposed new division should be organized into three bureaus:

a. The Bureau of General Continuing Education should work with local public and private school and agency administrators to assist them in organizing, operating and extending their general programs of continuing education, particularly high school level education or its equivalency for adults.

b. The Bureau of Basic Continuing Education would be assigned responsibilities similar to those of the Bureau of General Continuing Education for literacy, functional literacy and other types of basic education programs for adults.

c. The Bureau of Special Continuing Education would be assigned similar supervisory and counseling responsibilities in specialized areas of continuing education, specialized from the point of view of client groups or subject matter: e.g., civil defense education, citizenship education, correspondence courses below the college level, leisure time and avocational education, special programs for the aging, consumer education, and family life education. This Bureau would have particular concern for experimental, demonstration and research programs of continuing education. It would also be responsible for exercising the state's statutory responsibility for licensing correspondence schools.

The Division of Immigration and Americanization, which is a major source of recruits for English language, citizenship and related adult education programs, should be transferred from the Board of Higher Education to the proposed Bureau of Special Continuing Education in the new Division of Continuing Education.

The Legislature should also remove from the Board of Higher Education its unused legal responsibilities for establishing and operating citizenship classes for the foreign-born, thereby eliminating overlapping jurisdiction in this area.

Staff of the Bureau of Adult Education and Extended Services and staff assigned to the adult programs of the Bureau of Civic Education would serve as nuclei for the proposed new Bureaus. Operating responsibility for correspondence courses of college level, legally under jurisdiction of the Board of Higher Education, should be delegated to the University of Massachusetts as part of its continuing education functions. Audiovisual services should be allocated either to the Bureau of Library Extension or retained within the Division of Curriculum and Instruction.

To ensure that the expanded programs of adult basic education, high school level education or its equivalency and citizenship education achieve their prescribed goals, both in terms of persons served and of quality, the new State Division of Continuing Education should establish comprehensive criteria to guide its approval of contractural arrangements with appropriate institutions for carrying out these programs. It is recommended that such contracts be made available to private institutions as well as to the local public schools and other public agencies. Division standards for approving applications should extend beyond program components (curriculum, facilities, instructional staff, etc.) and cover organizational capability. Citizen and/or client participation in program planning is also important since the programs should reflect community needs and interests and since low-income residents, who will constitute large proportions of the clients, can make significant contributions to program directions and ideas.

A recent study confirms the general impression that continuing education in the local public schools of most cities and towns in Massachusetts fails to meet reasonable standards in terms of enrolling a significant proportion of the potential market, program variety and program relevance. Continuing education at the local level is generally underfinanced; and as a rule, it is administered by part-time staff. These recommendations represent an opportunity for local public schools to strengthen their general capability in continuing education and to focus their attention on critical areas of adult education without imposing burdens on their hard-pressed local tax resources. To give further encouragement to local public schools to participate in the expanded programs of continuing education and to provide them with opportunities to recruit full-time qualified leadership for continuing education, the state should pay two-thirds of the annual salary, up to a maximum state grant of $10,000 a year, for local full-time directors of continuing education who meet state personnel standards. Responses from 85 local public school systems showed that only six of the local directors of adult education were full-time; none had degrees in adult education.

The state should encourage efforts under way in a growing number of cities and towns to establish community school facilities. These have proved to be promising vehicles, particularly in low-income communities, for creating stronger links between the school and the community it serves. Community schools are designed to serve adults as well as children with a variety of activities in education, recreation, social service and civic action. Such schools are usually open from early morning until late in the evening, six days a week, throughout the year. They have been particularly effective in some communities in reviving long dormant programs of continuing education for adults and in reaffirming the principle that school responsibilities include education of people of all ages.

The State Department of Education can stimulate the adoption of the community school concept by encouraging local departments to convert existing school buildings where feasible to community schools by liberally interpreting program and facility requirements for new schools designed along community school lines and by approving school building assistance for such plans. The legislature, in turn, should give serious consideration to encouraging extension of the community school idea throughout the state by increasing state aid for new school facilities meeting community school standards from 40 – 50 percent of the approved cost (65 percent for regional schools) up to 75 percent of the approved cost of construction.

D. Strengthening the State-wide System of Public Continuing Higher Education

The following steps, which should be undertaken in two stages over a three-year period, are recommended for strengthening the state-wide system of public continuing higher education.

The first two steps should be implemented in 1970 in order to provide the Board of Higher Education and the upper echelons of its major systems with the necessary capability in continuing education to carry out the subsequent recommendations.

1. The Board of Higher Education should receive an initial appropriation for general supervision and coordinating of continuing education throughout the state systems of higher education. Part of this appropriation can cover the matching requirements for the $25,000 in federal funds available for administration of Title I of the Higher Education Act, the federally assisted program of continuing education and community service. Until now, the required matching has been met by the institutions receiving project grants under the program. These new state funds would not only enable the Board of Higher Education to provide technical assistance and program guidance to colleges and universities in

the state in continuing education and community service, but it would strengthen state leadership and capability in continuing education and ensure proper management and evaluation of the Title I program.

2. The office of the President of the Board of Regional Community Colleges and the Division of State Colleges should each be allocated an initial appropriation to finance the operation of a nucleus staff which will provide technical assistance and work cooperatively with the continuing education staff of their institutions in developing master plans in continuing education and community service and in planning, implementing and evaluating their over-all and individual programs.

3. Each of the 13 community colleges should be allocated an initial appropriation to finance the operation of a nucleus staff to provide leadership and coordination for the college in the planning and development of continuing education and community service programs and to supervise the operation of such programs.

This basic budget for administration, program development and counseling in continuing education should be financed from the State General Fund. The present statutory requirement that evening classes be self-supporting should be eliminated. The cost of instruction and related expenses of continuing education courses and programs, which would also be financed from the General Fund, would be partially offset by tuition fees, federal grants and private funds.

The Legislature should make continuing education a mandatory function of community colleges and broaden its definition to include "community service." These additional funds would also enable more regional community colleges to follow the lead of North Shore Community College in extending continuing education and community services to off-campus facilities, particularly in low-income neighborhoods.

4. The nine state colleges should each be allocated a basic budget similar to that recommended for the community colleges and under the same conditions.

5. The University of Massachusetts at Amherst should be allocated an initial appropriation from the State General Fund to lay the groundwork for university-wide leadership, administration, program development and coordination in continuing education, an area of University concern which has gone generally undeveloped although specialized physical facilities for continuing education have been provided in the new Campus Center.

6. The University of Massachusetts at Boston should be allocated an initial appropriation from the State General Fund to provide leadership and coordination in the planning and development of continuing education and community service programs.

E. Scholarships for Continuing Higher Education

The state should equalize opportunities in institutions of higher education between full-time students enrolled in part-time programs (mainly in the evening and designated as continuing education or continuing studies). As an initial step toward reducing the glaring inequity in tuition (persons registered in evening classes of public institutions, for example, pay tuition at a rate which is 2½ to 3 times the day division rate of tuition), the state should reduce the tuition rates for part-time evening undergraduate students who are state residents, which currently range from $10 to $18 per credit hour, to the full-time day school tuition rate of just under $7 per hour. To effect this equalization, the statutory requirement that evening classes be operated on a self-supporting basis should be eliminated.

In addition, the state should increase the annual appropriation for general scholarships by $500,000 and reserve it entirely for students enrolled in continuing higher education.

F. A State-wide Network of Public Education – Public Information Officers

The tentative state modernization plan calls for the appointment of a Public Relations Officer as a key member of the staff for each Secretary. These nine Public Relations Officers would be in addition to the Public Relations Office already in existence in the various state agencies. It is recommended that a different approach be adopted calling for a new concept of the public information involving a recasting of this function to place more emphasis on public education. The public education officer would be expected to provide the leadership in citizen-client education within each Secretariat and would work closely with agency officials in developing over-all citizen-client education plans and programs. This innovation in staffing implies the creation of a new profession blending related skills in public administration, continuing education, and public communications as well as familiarity with the substance of agency programs. The Board of Higher Education in cooperation with operating agency officials should consult with appropriate universities to arrange for both short-term and degree-credit educational programs for these purposes. The short-term programs would be aimed at providing retraining for existing staff while the degree programs would be aimed at turning out a continuing supply of public education officers, not only for the Secretary offices but in all major state agencies.

G. Staff Training and Career Development for State Employees

A review of alternative approaches to establishing an effective staff training and career development program for the employees of the Commonwealth of Massachusetts indicates that the system being used by the United States government offers an appropriate framework and model.

In essence, the recommended legislation, which would amend the state's Training Act of 1954, broadens the scope of employee training, emphasizes executive and career development as essential components and delineates strong

Table 7-2

Summary of Increased State Costs for Proposed Programs of Continuing Education (1970)

Program	First-Year Cost	Fifth-Year Cost	Tenth-Year Cost
Adult Basic Education	$ 1,200,000	$ 6,200,000	$ 1,200,000
Adult High School Education	1,000,000	9,000,000	1,000,000
Adult Citizenship Education	250,000	1,750,000	1,125,000
Adult Occupational Education and Training	3,000,000	3,000,000	3,000,000
Continuing Education Below Collegiate Level – Administration, Supervision, and Program Development	400,000[a]	550,000[a]	700,000[a]
State Aid for Local Directors of Continuing Education	800,000	1,000,000	1,200,000
Continuing Higher Education – Administration, Supervison, Program Development, and Counseling	1,530,000	1,850,000	2,200,000
Continuing Higher Education – Instructional Programs	2,550,000[b]	[c]	[c]
Scholarships for Continuing Higher Education	500,000	750,000	1,000,000
Staff Training and Career Development for State Employees	2,000,000	8,000,000	8,000,000
Totals	$13,230,000	$32,100,000	$19,425,000

[a]Includes loss of $250,000 a year in classroom receipts from elimination of high school class fees charged by the state.

[b]These costs will be partially offset by tuition payments, based on the 1969 ratios of tuition to per pupil costs. Figure excludes reduction in tuition receipts estimated at $1 million during the first year as a result of equalizing tuition rates of part-time with full-time programs. Figure based on an estimated instructional cost of $204 per evening school pupil and 12,500 pupils (8,000 in community colleges and 4,500 in undergraduate courses of state colleges). The instructional cost is derived from the estimate that the per pupil cost of a day school student is $850 and that the instructional costs account for about 80% of this total or $680. Since the average evening school student enrolls in 1½ courses per semester (equivalent to 9 hours over a full academic year), this is about 30% of the 30 hours of a full-time day school student. The cost per pupil of an evening school student is based on this proportion.

[c]An estimate is not possible because of a number of unknowns: total enrollment of evening school students; changes in per pupil cost due to upgrading of standards in pupil-teacher ratios (for example, the Board of Regional Community Colleges has requested a pupil-teacher ratio for technical-vocational programs of 13 to 1 versus the 18 to 1 in the 1969–70 academic year), and to higher salary standards and future drastic increases in tuition rates.

Source: Melvin R. Levin, *Continuing Education*, Summary Report, Massachusetts Advisory Council on Education, Jan. 1970, p. 28.

and complementary training roles for the central personnel agency and for all state agencies. The new act calls for specific commitment by all state agencies to broad and intensive training activities. At present, only a few state agencies in Massachusetts, mainly those administering programs such as corrections and police in which most of the positions are unique to government, are required by law to provide staff training. Following the precedent in the federal legislation, each agency would be required to develop a comprehensive plan for training employees under its jurisdiction based upon a review of its current and future training needs and would be required to update such plan periodically.

Under the new legislation, the central personnel agency would have the following specific assignments:

1. To advise the Governor in policies and procedures for extending and strengthening staff training, executive development and career development programs;

2. To identify areas in which interagency training is required, to conduct such training or to arrange for other agencies to do so, and to coordinate such interagency training; a high-priority area for interagency training should be the training of Staff Training Officers;

3. To provide information on and to encourage the appropriate use of non-state training facilities and programs on the basis of established criteria;

4. To develop and operate a system of training information and data required for the performance of the above duties.

Finally, the Secretary of each state agency would have responsibility for planning, operating and evaluating training programs in accordance with training standards and guidelines prescribed by the central personnel agency. This comprehensive plan would take into consideration projected manpower forecasts, career and subcareer executive systems, reward systems, expansion of interagency training, establishment of training facilities and maximum use of existing future sources of federal aid for training and education. The 1970 costs of the various programs recommended is outlined in Table 7-2.

In a manner speaking, Levin and Slavet have taken us to the mountain top and shown us a new view of adult education. The new view contains both new prospects and new challenges. They show us how so well-placed investments can pay off handsomely. At the same time, they point to past neglects and emerging needs.

Educational equity should apply to adults as well as children and youth. Few citizens are able to pursue happiness or enjoy domestic tranquility with a grammar school education or a bag of obsolete skills.

From the adult we turn our attention to early childhood education and the curious position of kindergartens in the Bay State.

8

The Early Education of Children

The child-care I propose is more than custodial. This administration is committed to a new emphasis on child development in the first five years of life . . .(which) . . . would break the poverty cycle for the new generation. – Richard Milhaus Nixon

The needs of the child are parcelled out among a hopeless confusion of agencies with diverse objectives, conflicting jurisdiction, and imperfect channels of communication. – Urie Bronfenbrenner

Child-care has become a public issue. A number of long-term economic and social forces have dramatically increased the demand for child-care and early education. Nationally, nearly half of all mothers with children under 18 years are now in the labor force, compared with 18 percent in 1948. Nearly a third of mothers with children under six are now working outside the home, and this percentage is increasing. The economic conditions which have lead parents of young children to enter the labor force rather than remain at home with their children are not likely to be reversed. Their affects upon the need for child-care are likely to be permanent.

A further consideration in the increased demand for child-care and early education is the press for equality of opportunity among the disadvantaged. At the same time, the steadily rising costs of welfare and its manifest ineffectiveness have led to a search for ways to help those who are poor, since almost every welfare plan proposed involves some kind of child-care.

The growing recognition of the importance of the first few years of life has also had an effect upon the politics of children. Although much of the pressure for increasing publicly supported child-care is based on economic and political forces centered on the needs of adults, there is also growing support for responding to the needs of all children and ensuring them a healthy and stimulating beginning in life.

At the same time, the family unit has been changing and affecting child-rearing practices. First, fathers, other male relatives and hired laborers left the household for a different work place, thus sharply decreasing the care, training and supervision available to older children. In the last two decades, mothers, older daughters, and other relatives have increasingly left the household for paying work, thus sharply decreasing the supply of parental and nonparental child-care at the same time that demand has increased. The increased social acceptability and economic necessity for women to work outside the home, the desire of educated mothers to use their training in a paying job, the changing roles of women are all overlapping and cumulative in their effect.

With these factors looming on the horizon, the Advisory Council in May 1970 commissioned Dr. Richard R. Rowe of Harvard University to do a comprehensive 2-year research project on child-care and early education. The report, *Child Care in Massachusetts: The Public Responsibility,* established three general goals for its work: (1) to investigate and describe the current status of early education and child-care in Massachusetts; (2) to ascertain the extent of need of Massachusetts families with young children for support and assistance in their nurturing, child-rearing and education activities; and (3) to develop a public perspective for the care and education of young children which could serve as the foundation for an integrated and comprehensive state plan for child-care and early education in the Bay State. That plan was to integrate new programs for young children, such as kindergarten, with the first few years of elementary school; to provide parents and children with the aid they need and want; to be congruent with the modernized structure of state government; and to be politically and economically feasible.

Dr. Rowe based his study on the premise that the family is a basic and necessary structure for caring for young children and meeting their needs. Thus, programs for children, as he saw them, should facilitate and promote families, including the needs of parents as well as of children. Well-designed programs for children offering a number of options should be a significant force for strengthening the family unit. Furthermore, Rowe contends, children have rights and every child should be able to begin life in a healthy and accepting environment which enables him to develop into a healthy and mature adult.

In the process of the study, Rowe and his team concluded that the role of government concerning children should be twofold. First, to prevent the basic rights of children from being violated and second, to support families by helping parents develop their own options for child-care and early education, including both direct support to families as the primary setting for child-care and the provision supplementary or alternative child-care for those families who choose it. With the increasing involvement of government in supporting children's services, it is extremely important to guard against the development of sterile uniformity, requiring arrangements with inadvertently or otherwise inhibit variety in child-care programs. In order to prevent such premature narrowing into one kind of care, Rowe recommends a deliberate policy of promoting diversity in child-care and early education arrangements.

As the study team saw it, the family is and will be the primary setting in which child-care occurs. Nevertheless, in their preamble to their report on the status of families in our society, the 1970 White House Conference on Children concluded:

"Our national rhetoric notwithstanding, the actual patterns of life in America today are such that children and families come last." The study team looked and saw that the economic sector is given priority over family life, leaving the family as an underdeveloped social institution; children and adults are isolated from each other in a wide variety of ways and segregated into age groups, and that social institutions, other than the family, are having increasing influence on children and adults, especially through peer groups, media, child-care specialists, and government.

Industry's need for a specialized labor force was incompatible with the large extended kinship networks common in earlier families. As a result, the family unit adapted itself by becoming smaller and more mobile. Adapting itself in response to economic changes, the nuclear family, small and economically independent of the parents' original families, has replaced the extended family. The size, complexity and power of the economic sphere relative to the family is accurately reflected in the pressures family members feel impinging on themselves, and in the ways in which they respond to those pressures. For example, the economic survival of most families is dependent on the occupational performance of breadwinners. As a result, occupational demands placed on breadwinners take precedence in the daily life of most families. If Dad or Mom must work late at the office, be transferred to the new plant in Rochester, be laid off without pay for the slow season, or take inventory on Saturdays, in most circumstances, the family must simply adjust. When there is a serious conflict between the demands of our occupations and the demands of our family, almost inevitably, the family gives way.

Participation in the economy Rowe tells us, is more than an issue of survival, because it also shapes the major dimensions of individual and family lives. Since some occupations are viewed in our society as more valuable than others, occupation is the key to status, and beyond that to social class. Economic status affects family life, the ties of kinship, friendship, neighborhood, and participation in clubs and organizations. The occupation of the primary breadwinner, together with the specific demands for time, energy, training, and education which that occupation requires, is probably one of the most important determinants of a family's pace, style, values, structure, and social reputation.

As a result of economic priorities, fathers are further from the center of family life, especially the raising of children, than mothers. The literature on the detrimental effects of the total absence of the father is considerable and persuasive. Unfortunately, the effects of the "normal," i.e., occupationally caused absence of the father has been less well studied.

Occupational roles often influence the qualities parents hope to instill in their children. The values underlying these qualities are often the values motivating economic activity. Since successful economic activity is necessary to survival, parents would be somewhat irresponsible if they did not prepare their children emotionally and intellectually for future roles. Yet, when socialization practices are excessively oriented to existing or future occupational roles, attention to the kinds of attitudes, beliefs, values, and character traits characteristic of emotional health and maturity may be sacrificed. Given the importance of work in our society, the temptation is to answer that we cannot talk about "emotional health" or "maturity" apart from the successful performance of an occupational role. That it is so difficult to separate these issues is further evidence of how dedication to economic tasks shapes understanding of what it means to be a healthy individual in our society.

Another detriment to healthy family life was the isolation of children from their parents and other adults. Common forms of isolation of contempory American families include:

1. the isolation of wage earners from spouses and children, caused by their absorption into the world of work;

2. the complementary isolation of young children from the occupational world of parents and other adults;

3. the general isolation of young children from persons of different ages, both adults and older children;

4. the residential isolation of families from persons of different social or ethnic, religious, or racial background; and

5. the isolation of family members from kin and neighbors.

The segregation of children from adults has a number of serious consequences, recently described by Bronfenbrenner[1] among others. Parents are discouraged from becoming involved in major aspects of their children's lives. Both young children and youth are growing up without the benefit of a variety of adult role models. Children are becoming increasingly ignorant about the world of paid work. Parents are rapidly being replaced by other socializing agents, such as the schools, the peer group, and the mass media. Child-care specialists are increasingly professionalizing "parenting," and are providing it as a purchasable service. Finally, government is assuming a greater role in the nurture and socialization function of the family through child-care programs and the schools.

In studying the need for child-care, Rowe concludes that families feel they need more (and more adequate) options for child-rearing. There are, in fact, widespread and growing demands for greatly expanding services to all children.

There are many different kinds of child care arrangements in Massachusetts. Public and private nursery schools, day care centers, Head Start programs, and private kindergartens have programs which are mostly half day or less. Only day care centers and some Head Start programs regularly provide formal program care for children more than three or four hours a day.

Data indicate that over 60,000 families with over 100,000 children age 0-6 report difficulty in making child care arrangements. Adding those families who report having difficulty sometimes shows that underlying this definition are the assumptions that:

1.   There is no generally agreed upon or objective definition of "good care";
2.   Within the limits of nonabusive care parents have the right to choose from available options the kind of care their children will receive, and

3. In the long run, most parents will choose styles of child-rearing that are beneficial to children, adults and society, if they feel they have adequate options.

In general, parents want child-care that is free or inexpensive; near their homes; at the right hours for the right lengths of time; properly sponsored and with adequate facilities and program and qualified personnel. Parents say they would pay more than they now spend if they could choose the child-care they want. The price of child-care is critical in determining demand. When parents were asked, "How much would you be able to pay for the child-care of your choice?" they answered as follows, in Table 8-1.

Patterns of use of child-care arrangements make very clear that finances, geographical convenience and appropriateness of hours of child-care are of necessity the parent's first concern. When these primary needs are met, parents can and do express their strong preferences for various program types and elements. Given a choice, some parents would always choose large, school-like centers; some would seek tiny, neighborhood centers, others would always choose cozy home substitutes. Most want an educational environment, that at the least corresponds to the responsive stimulation of middle-class homes.

The following list of 16 program characteristics were shown to parents who were asked to select those they found "most important" and "least important" in a children's program:

1. Would provide meals;
2. Would provide health care;
3. Close to home;
4. A program your child could be in as long as you want;
5. Would involve parents;
6. Would teach children how to read;
7. Would provide special toys;
8. Speak many languages;
9. Available anytime day or night;
10. Staffed by men teachers as well as women;
11. Close to place of work;
12. Program with children like mine;
13. Would provide TV;
14. Racially integrated with children of various backgrounds;
15. Give children chance to learn about community.

Parents' answers are recorded in Table 8-2.

For these reasons, diversity of programs seems a critical element of demand, even after distance, financial need and appropriate hours have been taken into consideration, and provided, according to parental wishes. Rowe's study estimates that 75 to 90 percent of all parents might be expected to use free,

Table 8-1
How Much Would You be Able to Pay for the Child Care of Your Choice?[a]

	"I want the services I've got"	Nothing	$1–10/week	$10–20/week	$20+/week	DK	
For one child							
(%):	36	8	22	17	9	8	(100%)
(No.):	140,000 families	31,000	86,000	66,000	35,000	31,000	
For all the children							
(%):	36	2	14	14	18	15	(99%)
(No.):	140,000	8,000	55,000	55,000	70,000	59,000	

(N = 390,000 families with children 0–6.

[a]Figures rounded to nearest thousand and may not add up to totals.

Source: Richard R. Rowe, *Child Care in Massachusetts* Massachusetts Advisory Council on Education, 1972, p. 3–19.

Table 8–2

Most Important Characteristics of Child Care Programs According to Massachusetts Parents

	Percent	Number of Families[a]
1. Help children get along better with each other	57	222,000
2. Close to home	41	160,000
3. Provide health care	38	148,000
4. Provide meals	36	140,000
5. Racially integrated	25	90,000
6. Involve parents	22	86,000

Least Important Characteristics of Child Care Programs According to Massachusetts Parents

1. Provide TV	68	265,000
2. Speak many languages	49	191,000
3. Provide special toys	33	129,000

[a]Figures rounded to nearest thousand.

Source: Richard R. Rowe *Child Care in Massachusetts* Massachusetts Advisory Council on Education 1972. p. 3–26.

nearby or in home child-care of the "right" kind, at hours corresponding to their work day. Conversely, fewer than 1 percent of all parents say they would use well-staffed child-care for which they must pay full costs.

A growing child needs the following basic elements of good care: prompt, regular and caring attention to his physical and psychological needs; a responsive person-animated environment, and at least one consistent relationship with a trustworthy grown-up over time. Well-designed, competently staffed, parent-involved, well-funded programs for the care of our youngest can provide options for families and help them fullfill their child-rearing responsibilities. Present frameworks for providing such options include family day-care homes, which regularly care for children other than those living in the home, and family day-care systems which provide a caring and supportive network of persons concerned with child- and family-care. Center-based programs, which differ from home-based programs in the hours of care, curricula, and child development model, have as their principal goal the provisions of a safe, warm responsive environment for the children who are cared for in the center and for the staff who are paid or who volunteer to work in the program.

Programs for young children, either home-based or center-based, provide both care and education. The important issue is not care *or* education; but rather what *kinds* of care and education. There are many kinds of acceptable programs for young children now in planning, operation or conception.

Kindergarten

On the issue of kindergartens, however, Rowe's study specifically concludes that kindergartens should be made available to every child in the Bay State. Dr. Rowe makes his recommendation on two grounds.

First, we feel it is reasonable to assume that five-year olds can significantly benefit from a kindergarten program. Despite the lack of unequivocal research evidence, the case for the benefits of kindergarten on empirical grounds is at least as good as the case for any other school program. Second, for us the most compelling argument is the one of equal educational opportunity. We have found no persuasive argument based on child development considerations for beginning school at any particular age. Individual differences in development make any chronological age highly arbitrary and the child development case for four-year-olds, fives, or sixes probably can be made equally well. Nationally, age five is becoming the convention. What does seem compelling is the constitutional requirement for equal protection and the principles of good educational opportunity. If substantial public funds are used to provide kindergarten for one group of the population, especially for communities with a relatively strong financial base, then this opportunity should be available to all children in the Commonwealth. Wherever the dividing line is finally drawn by the courts, it seems self-evident to us that offering a full year of schooling to one child and not another is unequal opportunity. If, in addition, the child without the opportunity for attending public kindergarten comes from a poorer home, the inequality becomes manifestly unjust. If the courts find unconstitutional inequality when there are significant differences in per pupil expenditures in schools, they would almost certainly find the absence of the opportunity to go to school an even grosser inequality.
Thus, we conclude that, given the fact that a majority of the school districts in the Commonwealth provide kindergarten, this opportunity must be made available to all children in the state.

Can the Board of Education maintain acceptable levels of kindergarten quality while still promoting a wide diversity of program types? Thus far, the Board of Education has been reluctant to offer any but a few basic quality guidelines for kindergartens. Its strategy has been to establish a "floor" for program quality — setting a few guidelines which define basic program dimensions — and otherwise to assume that communities will design their own programs according to local needs and local convictions about how five-year-olds are best served. A state curriculum guide also has been prepared, but only to suggest a range of possible classroom activities. The Board has not told local school committees how the program should be run, but, rather, has tried to ensure certain essential elements of pupil-teacher ratio, teacher certification, facilities, length of program, and eligibility of children.
Even these few state guidelines, necessary though they may be, have had a

powerful effect on program definition. Once a district has been told, for instance, that in order to qualify for state aid it must have a 25 to 1 pupil-teacher ratio; must house the program in a facility which meets school safety standards; must hire teachers with at least elementary school accreditiation; and must offer the program for 180 days each year with a minimum of two and one-half hours each day, program variation is already clearly delimited.

Study Methods

The study staff visited towns and cities across Massachusetts, talking with and learning from parents, program operators, school officials, and local leaders' about existing and needed services for young children in urban, suburban and rural areas in Massachusetts. In July 1970, the staff convened a conference of nationally known child development specialists to discuss some of the psychological and social issues in child-care and early education.

Dr. Rowe's staff, working with persons in the Department of Education, Public Health, Public Welfare, Mental Health, Community Affairs, Public Safety, and in the Office of Program and Planning Coordination discovered many and often overlapping efforts of state government to assist families and young children in Massachusetts. They contributed to and received help from members of the Governor's Advisory Committee on Child Development and were aided by members and staff of the Advisory Council.

A study committee met regularly and advised the staff of possibilities and pitfalls. After tackling the voluminous literature on child development, programs for young children, planning and implementation of human services and education programs, the staff sought experts in the state to guide their efforts.

At the beginning of the study, Dr. Rowe and his staff designed and commissioned a major survey of Massachusetts families with children 0 to 6, interviewing mothers and fathers about their child-care arrangements, problems, attitudes, needs and desires. They organized a conference on licensing attended by representatives of state and federal government, and planned and led a series of ten Regional Child-Care Meetings where over 600 parents, program operators, and citizens from each of the eight regions in the state voiced their child care and early education needs, concerns, and hopes. Questionaires were sent to school officials in every school district in the Commonwealth to gather data on plans for implementation of the Department of Education's kindergarten mandate. Regional meetings were held with school officials in each region of the state to enable teachers, principals, and superintendents to participate in developing the related recommendations. All training institutions for early education and child-care teachers were queried and information was gathered on their training, their plans and their needs.

The early child-care staff watched children play in homes, schools and centers all over the Commonwealth, hearing requests for aid and assistance —

some loud and others timid and shy. Teachers and parents are constrained in asking certain fundamental questions about general program characteristics, such as whether it would be wise to offer a "kindergarten without walls," or a program for three days a week, or a program taught by unaccredited paraprofessionals.

The study recommends that the Board continue its policy of establishing only minimal protective regulations for kindergarten, leaving the maximum possible flexibility to individual school districts. It should be possible to suspend even the limited guidelines in cases where responsible alternative programs are proposed. The Board should systematically encourage and support diverse kinds of programs which are or have been carefully evaluated.

The guidelines should not become so deeply engrained that teachers and parents forget the tentative basis on which they are established. Contrary to the popular impression, there is no real certainty about which educational experiences are best for young children. Therefore, it seems better to keep as open a mind as possible toward different kinds of programs rather than to accept some particular orthodoxy on insufficient grounds.

But most current attempts at diversity will not require suspension of state kindergarten guidelines. At present, there are school districts in which fundamentally different programs are being attempted without any special dispensation. This practice should continue. Some schools, for example, are experimenting with the full-year kindergarten.

Findings, Conclusions, Recommendations

A. Agency Program Functions

The four functions described below all have one element in common: they entail some form of direct involvement with ongoing programs for children at the local level. Consequently, they are termed "program functions." The first of these programs functions – licensing – is a regular function of state government, while the latter three – program responsibility, consultation, and monitoring – theoretically provide actual service to programs. There is considerable overlap among these functions as they are actually provided by state agencies.

1. Licensing. Licensing is the process by which the state permits and regulates the operation of programs which meet minimum quality standards. There are two state agencies currently involved, eighteen state professionals chiefly providing this function; and 1050 licensed institutions serving approximately 37,183 children.

2. Program Responsibility. The state assumes various forms of administrative control over total programs or aspects of programs funded with public monies. There are seven state agencies, approximately 88,000 preschool children; funding from at least thirteen federal programs, and five state programs, in addition to local and private sources.

3. Program Consultation. The state provides technical and programmatic assistance to ongoing program personnel. Five agencies provide some degree of consultation, twenty professionals chiefly serving this function; areas include: health, nutrition, education, child-rearing, training, and program development.

4. Program Monitoring. Program monitoring is the process by which funding agencies ensure responsible fiscal administration by local program operators.

B. Agency Support Functions

Four other functions relate less to the specific needs of ongoing programs and more to state-wide concerns and a broader "clientele," both professionals and the general public. These "support functions" are also shared in various ways by numerous individuals and agencies. However, to the degree that they are fulfilled by state agencies, they are often provided on a more informal basis than was the case with the first four functions.

1. New Program Development. The state provides technical and planning assistance to individuals and groups at the local level who desire to initiate new programs or services.

2. Informational Services. The state provides informational assistance to parents and professionals regarding programs for child placement, opportunities for training and job referral, agency responsibilities and procedures, and developments in the early childhood field.

3. Training and Education. State activity is also directed toward developing or providing inservice and academic opportunities for staff development.

4. Planning and Coordination. Agencies spend a significant part of their time on state-wide resource planning and interagency coordination.

By way of summary, the functions of the thirteen agencies involved with child-care are listed in Table 8-3

Conclusions

In concluding his report, Dr. Rowe writes:

The Commonwealth of Massachusetts currently provides a wide range of limited services to program personnel and others involved in care and

Table 8-3

Summary of Agency Functions

Agency	Licensing	Program Responsibility	Consultation	Monitoring	New Program Development	Information Service	Training & Education	Planning & Coordination
Health (DPH)	f	f	f	f	f	i	f	
Welfare (DPW)	f	f	f(1)	f	f(1)	i	i	
Public Safety (DPS)	f							
Mental Health (DMH)		f	f(1)	f	f(1)	i	i	
Education (DOE)		f	f(1)	f	f(1)	i	f	
Department of Community Affairs		f	f(1)	f	i	i	i	
Mass. Comm. for Children & Youth						i		f
Committee for Child Development						i		f
Off. Planning, Programs & Coord'n					i	i		f
Communities and Dev. (CAD)								
Ed. Higher Ed. (BHE)							f	f
Dir. Empl. Sec. (DES)		f						
Rehab. Comm. (REC)								
Comm. for Blindness (CFB)		i				i		

f = formal agency responsibility.

i = informally provided by agency personnel.

(1) = limited to agency programs.

Source: Richard R. Rowe *Child Care in Massachusetts* Massachusetts Advisory Council on Education 1972 p. 9-12.

educational programs for young children. In addition, many different programs for children are currently operating in Massachusetts, although they do not exist in sufficient quantity to meet state-wide needs. The majority of programs for children — particularly those receiving public support — were created for the benefit of specific clienteles among parents and children. As a result, the bulk of early childhood services provided by the state have been "program-specific" and consequently have been developed and allocated through an array of different state agencies. These agencies develop and provide often similar services independently from one another, and subject to no over-all coordination or extensive planning. It is difficult to determine how constructive this fragmentation of state responsibilities may have been in the past. However, the system is seriously dysfunctional today and will be even more so in the future, particularly since the public is developing an increased commitment to care and educational programs for all its young children, not solely for specific sub-populations. The major dysfunctions in the present system appear to be the following:

. Early childhood resources are misallocated, as the result of duplication and lack of effective coordination at the central level.

. Critical support services not directly related to ongoing program operation are generally not provided, owing to the "program-specific" character of the existing system.

. Local efforts to develop new programs or to coordinate existing programs are severely handicapped by the current fragmentation of responsibilities at the state (and federal) level.

. No effective mechanisms for state-wide planning or coordination of early childhood services have been utilized, although a large proportion of available professional energies are taken up in negotiating between groups with overlapping interests and mandates. In addition, it is hypothesized that the current system, lacking any major agency which has young children as its primary concern, reflects a history of ineffective political action on behalf of young children. The development of support for all young children has not been a political priority. As the demand for more and better services leads to more effective efforts by the public, one can expect services for children to become increasingly supported. In the meantime, a rare opportunity exists for state government to establish an effective and accountable structure for children's services that will anticipate future demand and be capable of becoming responsible to the greatly increasing needs of children and families.

Recommendations

At some future date, the present period of heightened concern for early childhood may be perceived as a time of major transition regarding governmental services for young children. In any event, the current structure of Massachusetts services reflects the assumptions of the past more than those which are to shape the future.

A. The Responsibilities of State Government

The study of early child care proposes some basic policies regarding children and their rights.

1. *Every child* has an inalienable, natural right to a living arrangement which provides not only for his physical needs but also for an accepting, responsive and stable setting in which to grow.

2. The family is normally the desired structure for meeting the basic needs of children in our society.

3. There is no one correct way to raise children and government should encourage and facilitate the development of a maximum amount of diversity in child-care arrangements, providing the basic needs of the child are met.

4. Innovative family patterns which may be responsive to children's needs, including efforts to reduce the isolation of families and to facilitate changes in family roles, should be supported.

5. In order to meet the basic needs of each child, it is the responsibility of government to assist families by providing:

a.   support to families as the primary setting for child-care;

b.   supplementary child-care for those families who need it;

c.   alternative family, and familylike arrangements for those children whose basic needs are not being met by their family.

The implications of accepting such a set of policies are substantial and should be thought through carefully. The notion that a child has an inalienable natural right to an environment that enables him to thrive has not generally been accepted. Not long ago, children were commonly seen as the chattel or property of parents with no basic rights of their own. Changes in these attitudes have been developing slowly. Just in the last hundred years have we asserted that all children must attend some school, regardless of their parents' wishes. Child labor laws designed to protect children from exploitation by businesses are a product of this century. Only in the last few years have we had adequate child abuse laws and these are still poorly enforced today. We are now on the verge of establishing the legal right of retarded and mentally defective children to appropriate educational opportunities.

Dr. Rowe and his staff believe that the policies they suggest should now be explicitly established in this society. The implication of such a policy for the role of government, however, are such a policy for the role of government, however, are substantial.

With a total of 683,000 children in Massachusetts aged 0–6, perhaps 90 percent of whom would use part-time or full-time care in the 1970s (at an estimated cost of $800 – $1,000 worth of resources per child for part-time care and $2,000 per child for full-time care) the budget for this age group would be between $800 and $900 million a year. These needed resources would not all be in the form of money. Donations and volunteer services should account for 25 percent of these resources, and parent fees and support from private agencies and organizations should account for another 25 percent. Even so, federal, state and local governments would have to provide some $400 – $450 million annually for recurrent operational costs alone. This would not include the costs of state support services or construction costs.

Thus, in order, to implement the preceding policies, the cost at the federal, state and local levels will be substantial over time. The needs for child-care are such that it is only a matter of time before the public demand becomes sufficiently organized and is an effective political force, for it to lead to the development of services of the magnitude described in the child-care report.

It should be plain that the demand for child-care is not just one more well-intended, liberal call for a bigger welfare state. The demand is based on fundamental, long-term changes in the functioning of the society, the composition of the labor force, the roles of women and men, changes in family life. Forceful economic and political realities underlie the marked rise in demand for child-care services. They will not go away; rather, they are on the rise and will bring with them even greater effects than we now see.

Rowe writes that it is crucial at this time, before the inevitable pressure overwhelms us, to improve radically our capacity to respond to the needs of families and children. Such an investment should provide a base for sound long-term development and should assist individuals and local groups to develop services responsive to their own changing needs.

B. Problems of State Government Involvement in Child-Care

Rowe recognizes that the kinds of services envisioned by his report will not be provided immediately. Many constraints upon state government make it difficult to develop such services immediately.

Most important of these constraints is the fact that the advocates of improved child-care services, including those who are in direct need of them, have not effectively made their case in the political arena. Consumers, providers, professionals, bureaucrats and legislators are all poorly organized for effective lobbying when it comes to children's services. A great deal of effort is spent in squabbling between groups. Despite a number of groups which could potentially become a focus of effective lobbying, none has emerged. New groups come and go regularly, but there is no continuity or accumulative thrust in the efforts to improve child-care services.

A second difficulty is the fact that within state government there is no centrally accountable structure responsible for developing comprehensive children's services. Several groups, each wanting some if not all of the action, tend to cancel each other out, just as they do in the private sphere.

A third factor is that state government is in a serious fiscal pinch and new programs are not easy to establish, even with broad support. Lacking a clear public demand, it is easy to postpone the development of expensive child-care services.

A fourth factor is that since the federal government appears continuously on the brink of doing something in the child-care field, there is a tendency to wait and see what will happen at the federal level before moving at the state level, using the logic that whatever is done at the federal level may determine the state's roles and responsibility.

A fifth factor is the widespread reluctance, on the part of the public and their elected representatives, to include government deeply in areas that traditionally have been considered the private affairs of a citizen. Many feel that such involvement may be necessary in extreme cases of poverty, illness or abuse but should not become the norm of society.

C. Guidelines for the Next Step

On the other hand, the federal government will very likely provide major new program funds in the near future. Congress passed major comprehensive child development legislation in 1971 (vetoed by Mr. Nixon). Several legislative bills, including the Nixon Administration's welfare reform proposal (Family Assistance Plan), are before the Congress in its 1972 session and approval of some kind of assistance seems probable. Indeed, it can be assumed that if significant new program monies become available, they will be federally funded.

It is unclear what impact future federal legislation will have on planning for the state's role. There is no consensus in Washington as to what mechanisms would be most desirable for allocating new funds. It has been suggested that the most likely funding arrangements will be from federal to local, at least with regard to the larger cities. If this pattern becomes established, the potential "support" functions of state government will receive additional emphasis.

There are a number of essential state functions which will be required under any federal plan: licensing, consultation, planning and coordination, training, research and evaluation. No matter what delivery system for operational support is devised by the federal government, the state must be in a position to be responsive to federal initiatives and must not be forced to throw together a makeshift organization overnight to cope with the likely substantial increase in federal aid for children's programs. Hesitation and delay at the federal level provides the state with an opportunity to become better organized and more capable of utilizing federal assistance wisely when it does become available. It is quite possible to establish a framework and pattern of state-level functions which will be needed no matter what support the federal government provides, and at reasonable cost.

D. Modernization of Massachusetts

In Spring 1971, the first stage of a two-phased modernization plan for Massachusetts government was implemented. During the first phase, all existing state agencies were brought within a cabinet structure composed of ten secretariats. During the second phase according to the plan, these secretariats will be reorganized internally along what are intended to be "functional" lines of authority and structure. Although the state's modernization plan is primarily directed toward change at the central state level, it is also hoped that all agency services provided through field offices will eventually be allocated within the recommended uniform system of regional and subregional areas.

Proposals for changing governmental structures with regard to early childhood services should be made within this overall modernization plan.

E. Increased Program Responsibility at Local Communities and Program Levels

The focus is on the role of state government in providing early childhood services. However, it must be emphasized that the state is only one of the actors — perhaps ideally only a *supporting* actor — in the delivery of these services. Most decisions regarding the aims, content and clientele of programs should be made in the communities served by the actual programs.

It should be pointed out, however, that there is not presently, nor should there be in the future, any single vehicle for decision-making at the local level. Public school kindergartens are under the traditional jurisdiction of local school committees; however, the wide array of other programs — private nurseries, Head Start programs, day-care centers, family day-care services, and publicly supported programs for special populations (handicapped, retarded, blind, deaf) — all maintain somewhat differing processes for decision-making and review. If sensitive to local needs, this pattern of program diversification would appear to hold great future potential: Unlike the consensus-oriented decision-making process in local school districts, there is potential in this diversity for developing significant program *options* for the individual parent and child.

Attention must also be given, however, to the *community-wide* pattern of services, in addition to the specific needs of on-going programs, to ensure that local needs are being met. In theory, the 4-C concept discussed earlier would provide one such form of community planning in 38 substate areas, although this concept has yet to be tested or supported in the field.

There is a clear need, however, for encouraging the development of vehicles at the local level which first would identify and specify currently unmet community needs for programs and services and then inform agencies of the importance of helping to meet these needs. At the state (and federal) level, ways must be found to loosen rigid program funding guidelines which unnecessarily restrict the options of local program coordinators and planners.

F. A Client-Centered Approach to Early Childhood Services.

One of the primary characteristics of current state services for children is that they are divided along types of specialized services: health, mental health, welfare, education, etc. Depending upon the particular need, a child is sent to one or another agency for help. This kind of need-specific approach is not satisfactory for early childhood services.

Children from different backgrounds and socioeconomic groups should have opportunities to be together and learn to know and understand each other. This is not only good social policy, but it is also what most parents in the state want. So long as it is good care, most parents want their children to have contact with other children from different backgrounds.

There is growing consensus that children with special needs can often be effectively served in regular settings with other children rather than separated into special classes or institutions. Again, specialized care may be necessary, but the objective should be to keep different kinds of children mixed together rather than separated. Programs which in the past have separated out the "handicapped" or the "disadvantaged" for special treatment have often had the effect of widening the distance between these persons and others even more, creating an even deeper and more permanent alienation than would have been the case with no special program. There is today a general move toward more individualized care for all children stemming from the notions that every child has special needs and *for the notion* that it is important to be familiar with and supportive of wide differences among us. Properly organized, there is no reason why most blind, deaf, retarded, and emotionally distrubed children should not spend major portions of the time they spend under formal supervision in child-care programs with other children who do not have these special needs. Likewise, there is little justification for keeping poor children in separate "compensatory" programs isolated from children of other backgrounds, especially since mixing seems to be related positively to school achievement.

G. Government Provided State-wide, Early Childhood "Supportive Services."

It appears that Massachusetts is now ready to develop more early childhood services in its communities. These same supportive services – providing technical assistance to new groups, referral assistance to parents and professionals, developing adequate training vehicles, and state-wide planning – are the very services which are likely to be most needed.

The guidelines for future change proposed above essentially recommend new thrusts for Massachusetts government – strengthening the local community role, and developing state structures which have as their primary function early childhood services (support throughout the Commonwealth). This particular recommendation, on the other hand, suggests changes in the current pattern of existing agency services.

Not all existing services should be reorganized into one governmental unit, even if such an occurance were politically feasible, but there are some principles by which state resources for early childhood services can be more effectively and responsibly organized and delivered.

Coordination of categorical programs should be strengthened at the state level. The diversity of children's programs existing at the community level should be balanced by effective local coordination. The coordinating function should be consolidated and strengthened by being brought into the actual system of services; a major thrust of such a coordinating unit would be to seek ways of developing interagency and interprogram coordination which would improve the decision-making role of local and state agency personnel.

Where appropriate, duplicated services and personnel should be consolidated. To achieve a more efficient utilization of scarce resources and to clarify agency roles, overlapping functions should be consolidated. On the other hand, those agencies which have developed consultative services to meet the unique needs of special subpopulations, such as handicapped and retarded children, should maintain these unique services.

Field services should be coordinated and should conform to a uniform system. If, as has been suggested, a major responsibility of state government is to provide support for local early childhood efforts, one key procedural problem is the delivery of these services. There is a clear need to develop a regional system which could incorporate and coordinate both existing services and those which may be created in the future.

The planning function should be restructured to relate directly to operating units. Currently, the sole official responsible for state-wide planning is, in effect, removed from the actual service system; consequently, data for planning are extremely difficult to obtain, and those agencies which should be most responsive to planning outcomes are under little obligation to so respond. If the planning role is to be viable, it must be incorporated into this service system. Since responsibilities for services may be shared at different governmental levels, the planning function must correspond to these different levels.

Parents and local community groups should be able to decide how to allocate resources available to them for children's services. A major conclusion of the report is that parents and local groups should be able to have meaningful options about the kinds of services to be developed for their children. Local coordination of resources is vitally important since it is only at that level that the mulitple sources and types of resources needed in a healthy system of services for children can be brought together to meet the needs of individual children, parents and communities.

Table 8–4
Changes of Service Functions

Function	Current	Proposed
Structure of Services	need-specific	age-specific
Delivery of Services	fragmented	coordinated
Program Services	major emphasis	deemphasized
licensing	shared by several agencies	consolidated
program responsibility	shared by several agencies	coordinated
consultation	shared by several agencies	largely consolidated
monitoring	shared by several agencies	coordinated
Support Services	largely not provided	major emphasis
new program dev.	informally provided	formal responsibility
information service	informally provided	formal responsibility
training and education	minimally provided by several agencies	consolidated, strengthened
planning and coordination	fragmented, disconnected	consolidated, connected to services

Source: Richard R. Rowe *Child Care in Massachusetts* Massachusetts Advisory Council on Education 1972 p. 9–34.

A central task of state government should be to assist responsive and representative local groups concerned with child-care to become organized throughout the state. The study does not recommend a single local coordinating structure at this time but suggested that the state support a diversity of local arrangements. In some communities, the School Committee may appropriately assume responsibility for child-care programs; in another, the City Council may establish a procedure; in other locations, several communities may wish to band together as a coordinating group. The state's role at this time should be supportive of such developments provided they are clearly accountable to parents and responsibly reflect their needs.

It may be useful to briefly compare these guidelines with the characteristics of the current state system. In addition to structural characteristics, the eight service functions which provided the framework for the prior analysis are compared in Table 8–4.

Summary. The basic objectives which seem important as goals for state services to children should be to:

1. facilitate child care options for parents, within basic protective limits;
2. involve parents in policy development at all levels of government;
3. facilitate rather than inhibit family development;
4. minimize administrative structure and cost, particularly at the federal, state and regional levels;

5. encourage the effective utilization of existing and new resources for children from all government and private sources, and
6. provide basic state-level program and support services.

H. Recommended State Structure for Children and Families

For a state government more responsive to the needs of children and families the following legislation are recommended in *child-care: The Public Responsibility*

1. create a Department of Child Development in the Human Services Secretariat that shall be responsible for facilitating the local development of services for infants and preschool children through decentralized licensing and consultation teams;

2. create a Council for Children which shall be responsible for reviewing programs, advising on government policies, including rules, regulations and licensing standards concerning programs for infants and preschool children;

3. assign to the Secretary of Educational Affairs responsibility for state-wide planning and coordination of comprehensive programs to meet the full range of needs of school-age children.

4. create an Interagency Coordinating Committee for Children and Families which shall be a body for state-wide planning and coordination services concerning children and families and which shall annually report to the Legislature and the Governor.

Figure 8-1 shows the organization of the proposed Office of Child Development and Table 8-5 outlines the budget for the Department for Child Development. The Department for Child Development should provide essential support services to assist parents and communities to meet their child-care needs. It would emphasize the development, coordination and delivery of support services for persons at the local level through a network of regional offices. The primary roles of the central staff would be to set state-wide regulatory standards and to assist regional support efforts, subject to the review and leadership of the Council for Children. The success of the Department will depend in large measure on its ability to decentralize its services in such a way as to be responsive to local needs and to be publicly accountable to lay and professional review.

A major child-care goal for state government should be to facilitate initiative, responsibility and accountability for effective delivery of services at the local level where programs are actually operated. It is recommended in the study that a set of eight regional offices be established which would fulfill the major functions of the Department by facilitating the development of local child-care services and in addition would coordinate the field services of other state agencies.

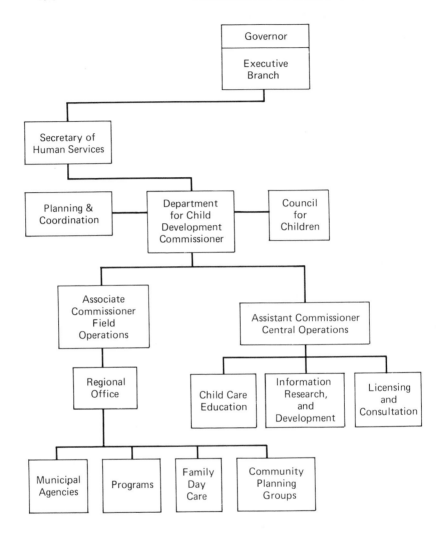

Figure 8-1. Organization Chart for Office of Child Department.
Source: Richard R. Rowe, *Child Care in Massachusetts*, Massachusetts
Advisory Council on Education, 1972, p. 9-59.

The jurisdictions of these eight offices would conform to the recommended
uniform substate regions; the offices could conceivably be housed in local
colleges and universities which provide training and education to early childhood
personnel. Although the proposed system of eight regional offices is currently
utilized solely by the Department of Mental Health, the regional systems of
several of the other agencies roughly correspond to the same geographic and
population boundaries, easing the logistics of coordination. It is recommended

Table 8-5

Department for Child Development Budget (in thousands)

	State Job Group	Approx. Salary Step 1	Sub-Totals	Totals
I. Personnel – Professional Position				
Central Office				
1 Commissioner		$30	$ 30	
1 Assistant to Commissioner	19	11	11	
1 Associate Commissioner, Field		23	23	
1 Associate Commissioner, Central	31	20	20	
1 Executive Director, Planning and Coordination	26	16	16	
3 Directors (Program Development, RD&D, Educ. for Child Care)	24	15	45	
5 Assistant Directors (P & C, PD, RD&D, Educ. for CC)	19	11	55	
4 Staff (P&C, PD, RD&D)	16	8.5	34	
Regional Offices				
8 Regional Coordinators	31	20	160	
8 Assistant Regional Coordinators	24	15	120	
16 Staff-Program Development	17	9	144	
8 Staff-Community Organization	17	9	72	
8 Staff-Education for Childcare	17	9	72	
			$802	
66 Total Professional Positions				$ 802
II. Personnel – Non-Professional				
Clerical				
1 Chief Officer	14	8	8	
2 Assoc. & Assistant CO	11	7	14	
12 Regional Offices	11	7	84	
6 Central Units	11	7	42	
21			$148	
Maintenance				
1 Central Office	11	7	7	
4 Regional Offices – 1/2FTE	11	7	28	
5			$ 35	
26 Total Non-professional positions				$ 183
Personnel Total				$ 985

	Breakdown	Sub-Totals	Totals
III. Other – Program Support			
Item			
1. Research, Evaluation Innovation, Development	5,900 per region	40	
	30,000 system evaluation	30	
		$ 70	
2. Staff Development – Contracted services	15,000 per region	120	
3. Travel – long distance		5	
in-state	(34 x 2000 @ 10 cents/mile)	7	
		$ 12	
4. Conferences and Dissemination		30	$ 232

Table 8-5 cont.

	Breakdown	Sub-Totals	Totals
IV. Other – Miscellaneous			
1. Materials and supplies		28	
2. Equipment (1st year)		35	
3. Telephone		20	
		$ 83	$ 83
"Other" Total			$ 315
Combined Total (Personnel & Other)			$1,300

Source: Richard R. Rowe *Child Care in Massachusetts* Massachusetts Advisory Council on Education 1972 p. 9–61.

that all agencies involved in the provision of services for children adopt the uniform state region and area for their operations. This recommendation especially applies to Education, Public Health and Public Welfare since the Mental Health regions and areas already correspond with the Governor's executive order.

Staffed initially by three child-care specialists who together combine skill and knowledge of human development, public health, institutional and community organization, mental health, and work with young children, the regional offices would aid parents and local groups to determine their needs and the availability of resources, and would license child-care programs.

Despite the best of intentions, bureaucracies appear to exhibit a tendency increasingly to centralize power and responsibility. If the proposed department is to fulfill its mandate for focusing its services in the field, safeguards against unwarranted centralization must be developed.

The basic functions of the regional offices should be as follows: It is recommended that licensing and consultation be provided by professional child-care staff at the regional level. There should be an active consultation group, separate from the licensing staff, which actively seeks out local groups needing help in establishing or improving child-care services. The proposed staff levels would call for an individual case load averaging thirty child-care programs.

Rowe recommends that the department consolidate the early childhood licensing function in Massachusetts, incorporating the current responsibilities shared by Public Health and Public Welfare. The Department for Child Development (DCD) would have responsibility for establishing basic standards, subject to review and comment by the Council for Children. Licensing should be done by specially trained staff who spend a significant proportion of their work in child-care licensing and consultation. Operators of child-care programs have made it clear that they much prefer a state licensing official who knows child-care thoroughly to a local official who knows very little about child-care.

Rowe suggests that one staff member in each regional office be responsible for providing technical assistance to groups and individuals at the local level to encourage the development of new programs and care services. The person charged with this task would require two related kinds of expertise; first, an informed view of the existing needs for services in the region's various communities; and second, an ability to provide and obtain sound technical and informational service to local groups. As local coordinating groups develop, this person would be particularly responsible for aiding these groups.

One staff member in each region should be assigned responsibility for encouraging and assisting the development of local education and training "networks" to serve the needs of present and prospective early childhood personnel, including program professionals and paraprofessionals, and family day-care operators. Such training would be both preservice and inservice. Included in these networks would be colleges, universities, manpower training programs, and appropriate services provided by other state agencies, notably the departments of Education and Public Health. In addition, this staff member would work particularly closely with regional units of the Cooperative Area Manpower Planning System, a federally funded effort to coordinate the use of public training funds in the state.

There is a widespread need for information concerning child-care, especially for information on funding sources and regulations.The regional office staffs would share responsibilities for providing effective information services to concerned individuals and groups in the field. These services would actually bridge several areas of regional staff functions outlined above. The following types of information would be included: listings of programs and other care services at the local level for parents; listings of available work opportunities, both paid and volunteer; early childhood training and educational programs for interested adults, both lay and professional; a guide describing early childhood state and regional resources, responsibilities, and procedures; information on available funds for child-care; significant writings in the early childhood field. The central DCD staff should provide substantial assistance in rendering this service, to be discussed shortly. Methods of communication should include mailings to key groups, individuals, programs, and municipal agencies and telephone information service. In addition, local libraries should be used as an up-to-date source of local child-care information.

I. Department for Child Development

Planning and coordination.   One unit in the central state office would be responsible for coordinating at the state level the operations of the department with all other state agencies providing related services. This unit would provide support for the staff of the Interagency Coordinating Committee for Children and Families. It would be responsible for coordinating state programs with the federal Regional Office of HEW and with all federal programs concerning children, through the Interagency Coordinating Committee for Children and Families. Second, they would provide appropriate planning services: regular status reports on the level of state-wide services, anticipated new developments, unmet state needs, and alternative responses. To fulfill this latter role, effective information collection mechanisms must be established; other agencies should be legally required to submit periodic updated reports on the status of their early childhood services through the Interagency Coordinating Committee for Children and Families to the Legislature.

In effect, the planning and coordinating unit is a key staff arm of the top administration. Consequently, this staff would report directly to the highest administrator for central operations.

This unit would serve primarily to support appropriate personnel at the regional level. Support activities of this nature would include: the interpretation of licensing standards and guidance regarding their enforcements; development of licensing guidelines for dissemination to the local level through the regional offices; guidance to program consultants, both through written materials and on-site visits. In addition, their unit would be responsible for collecting and interpreting licensing and consultation information from other levels and states for the Department and Council.

This unit would be responsible for providing state-wide leadership regarding the development of adequate training and education services in the state. It would coordinate the provision of state-level training resources for field needs; it would obtain information regarding current training practices for dissemination to the field; it would be responsible for the training of all departmental staff. In addition, the unit would advise the Department and the Council on priorities for federal and state funding of training programs.

The major responsibility of this unit will be to develop and maintain the information dissemination system so essential to the success of the proposed Department. Its staff will collect and process materials provided by the other central units and the regional offices. It will need to maintain particularly close communication with the regional offices to ensure that the information services are meeting perceived needs; consequently, it can play a vital role in communicating these developmental needs to other appropriate central units. In addition, if public funds can be obtained for such a purpose, this unit would also advise the Department and Council regarding needs and priorities for the evaluation of current early childhood programs.

J. The Council for Children

The report recommends the creation of a Council for Children which will exercise strong advisory leadership over the review and evaluation of existing services for young children and the development of state-level child-care policies.

The Council should serve in an advisory capacity regarding the total range of services for infants and preschool children, including recommendations concerning program priorities, coordination of services, and the development of systems for the delivery of child-care services which are locally controlled and coordinated. The Council should develop procedures by which parents and local community groups can make decisions and recommendations regarding the allocation of funds for their children.

The Council should review and comment on state rules and regulations, including all licensing regulations, concerning child-care. It should be responsible for reviewing and commenting on requirements for the certification of child-care personnel to the extent that such certification is needed. In addition, it should annually review and advise on the management goals and policies for the operations of the Department for Child Development. It should not be responsible for approving the budget of the Department for Child Development but should be required to review and comment on that budget prior to its submission to the Legislature.

The study further recommends that the responsibility for approving rules and regulations and certification requirements be explicitly vested in the Commissioner for Child Development rather than with the Council for Children. Although it should be legally required for the Commissioner to present suggested rules and regulations to public meetings throughout the Commonwealth, to report to the Council for Children the results of such meetings, and to have the recommendations formally reviewed by the Council, the final responsibility for the regulations should rest with the Commissioner and he should be held publicly accountable for them.

The Council should supercede the Governor's Advisory Committee on Child Development, although the Council may wish to establish a larger advisory body similar to the Governor's Advisory Committee, representative of the interests of parents, providers of child-care and relevant government agencies, which could meet periodically to assist in the planning and coordination of services.

The Council should report annually to the governor and the Legislature on the status of services to young children in Massachusetts and should publish and widely disseminate its findings and recommendations.

There should be nine members on the Council, appointed by the governor, six of whom shall be parent's of children aged six or less at the time of their appointment. Members should serve staggered three-year terms. The Council shall meet no fewer than six times each year and any member missing three regularly scheduled meetings over any twelve-month period should be terminated as a member automatically. Council members should receive no salary for their services but should be reimbursed for their direct expenses, including the cost of child-care.

K. The Role of the Educational Affairs Secretariat.

Having established the need for increased infant and preschool services, serious attention was given to determining the most appropriate secretariat for

the Department. The study team considered Educational Affairs and Human
Services to be the two most appropriate agencies.

In many ways Educational Affairs is conceptually the most appropriate
location for comprehensive services to little children, and Rowe seriously
considered recommending that Educational Affairs be given that responsibility.
With infant and preschool services within Education, one agency would be
responsible for educational and developmental services for all ages. The notion
of providing continuing educational experiences from "the cradle to the grave"
is an appealing and worthy goal.

Yet the Department of Education is heavily taxed to meet its current
responsibilities, and, given the real possibility that through court action or new
legislation, the state may soon be required to assume substantially increased
financing of local schools, it seems unlikely that the development of services for
infants and preschool children could be given priority in the Department of
Education over the next few years.

The study concludes that the Department of Education should concentrate
its resources on increasing the effectiveness and comprehensiveness of services for
children of school age. Beginning with kindergarten through secondary school,
priorities should be given to exploring ways to increase the quality of existing
programs, especially increasing their sensitivity to special needs of children.
Integration of children of varying ages, backgrounds, and needs into common
settings, combined with greater individualization of instruction is needed.
Comprehensive services including after-school programs for children whose
parents work full-time, weekend summer programs, and programs which involve
parents with their children in and out of the school setting, should be expanded.
These needs pose a massive task for the Department of Education and should be
given priority over programs for preschool children.

This recommendation should not be understood to mean that individual
school districts throughout the Commonwealth should not undertake early
childhood programs. In those communities where such programs are seen to be
of high priority and have the support of local citizens, they may be quite
appropriate. Such is the case in Brookline where a major experiment in early
childhood education is underway.

Support for those schools which decide to develop preschool programs
should be made available to them through the Department for Child Development.

The primary disadvantage of Educational Affairs as a location for such a new
department are as follows. First, most of the resources for child-care programs
are now within the Human Services secretariat. It would be politically difficult
to transfer funds and personnel from one secretariat to another. Second, given the
other pressures upon education, it seems unlikely that, even with a separate
department, services for preschool children would receive the kind of fiscal
priority that is needed.

Rowe believes it would be a serious mistake to extend didactic education downward to include four- and three-year-olds. Despite the theories and practices of individual educators, it is a fact of history that inclusion of kindergartens within the public education domain in Massachusetts during the nineteenth century narrowed the goals of the kindergarten year to a more didactic, pre-primary emphasis.

The alternative of placing the new department in Human Services seems to Rowe to be a sounder option. The perspective of human services is broader than education and in many respects is closer to the kinds of services little children need.

The study continues that it would be desirable to develop services for young children in that part of the state structure that sees its mission as more related to the total life experience, including health, nutrition, and family services, as well as education. In addition, most of the funds and personnel supporting these services are now within the Human Services area. Additional federal funds for child-care are likely to come through Human Services and Manpower, not through Education.

The problems of school-age children are of major concern to parents and the public at large and the state needs to increase its capacity to respond to those needs.

They recommend that the governor charge the Secretary of Educational Affairs with the responsibility of being the lead Secretary in the over-all state planning and coordination of services to school-age children. The Secretary should be charged with regularly convening representatives of the state agencies with major programs for school-age children, including the Departments of Youth Services, Mental Health, Public Health, as well as representatives from Education. The Secretary should be responsible for preparing an annual report through the Interagency Coordinating Committee for Children and Families (described below) to the governor and Legislature, concerning the status, needs and priorities for comprehensive services for school-age children.

Implementation

These recommendations were developed within the context of current fiscal and political constraints which affect development and expansion of any kind of state program at least in Massachusetts. They provide for a modest but greatly needed improvement in the ability of state government to respond to the rapidly growing need for more and better child-care services.

The recommendations limit the burden on state resources primarily to the provision of local support, regulatory, and coordinating services. The expectation is the funding for the continuing operation of child-care programs will be drawn in the main from parent fees, voluntary contributions and federal sources.

The total (incremental) annual cost for the proposed DCD approximates

$1.3 million, basing personnel costs on what appear to be equivalent ratings in the current civil service register for Massachusetts. The cost of the regional services total $925,000, and of central office operations $375,000. A breakdown by type of expense is as follows:

Professional personnel	$802,000
Nonprofessional personnel	183,000
Support services and materials	315,000
	$1,300,000

This study has recommended that current state agency program responsibilities remain under the administrative jurisdiction of these units, allowing the Department for Child Development to focus its resources on providing coordination, regulatory and support services. However, if new federal legislation provides "day-care" funds not restricted to the limited mandates of any of the existing agencies, and if the state government is allotted these funds for distribution, the Department and Council for Children should probably undertake the responsibility.

It is recommended, however, that the key decisions regarding the allocation of these funds be shared by personnel at the local and regional levels, according to the following general procedures: funding should be equitably allocated on a regional basis; where responsible local (area or community) coordinating agencies exist and have been so recognized by the Council; these agencies should develop proposals recommending local allocation of funds which would be reviewed by regional office personnel and submitted to the Council for Children for approval; where such agencies do not exist, prospective local grantees should submit proposals directly to their regional offices for review and subsequent action by the Council. Regional offices must be well-informed regarding local community needs if they are to discharge their duties responsibly.

A. Executive Action Needed.

Recommendations concerning state structure and the role of government, while not expensive, are extensive and will require time to be considered, amended and implemented. Many of the key recommendations will require joint executive and legislative action. However, some action can and should be taken by the governor and his cabinet immediately to facilitate more effective development of services for children.

The governor should immediately create by executive order an Interagency Coordinating Committee for Child Development, chaired by the Secretary of Human Services, with the Secretary of Educational Affairs as Vice Chariman. The Human Services secretariat should be designated the lead agency in state government for services to infants and preschool children. The Education secretariat should be designated the lead agency in state government for services to school-age children. The Interagency Committee should be responsible for state-federal coordinating.

The Governor's Advisory Committee for Child Development should be transferred from the Office of Program Planning and Coordination to the Office of the Secretary of Human Services until such time as a reconstituted body, such as the proposed Council for Children, has been agreed upon and appointed.

B. Legislative Action Needed

The major recommendations concerning the organization of state government which we have made will require legislative action to change existing statutes and to provide the necessary funds.

The committees on Social Welfare and Education are considering proposed legislation in this area. They should be encouraged to develop a comprehensive bill concerning services for children rather than acting piecemeal on individual issues such as licensing.

There is encouragement from the bipartisan support for improving children's services which was observed in the executive and legislative branches of state government, and there is hope that such support will be translated into action.

C. Public Action Needed

There is an undeniable need for improved services to children in Massachusetts, and it is our judgment that there is strong and widespread public support for action. The fact that a major comprehensive child-care bill which would have involved billions of federal dollars passed Congress in 1971 is evidence of that support at the national level. There was not enough support, however, to override Mr. Nixon's veto.

It is clear, therefore, that developing programs of the kind proposed will require extensive bipartisan efforts, including a concerted effort by citizen groups. Parents and communities have not yet persuaded the leaders of state government that improved children's services are essential, rather than merely desirable. Groups concerned with children have reduced their potential effectiveness by fighting among themselves rather than working for common goals. Although several such groups exist, they tend either to be advocates for special kinds of children or of special programs, or to represent a special perspective, such as that of educators or mental health professionals. An effective, state-wide children's lobby concerned with the development of comprehensive services for all children does not exist and is greatly needed.

The increasing need for more and improved services to children is the result of long-term permanent changes in our society, the effects of which are just beginning to be recognized in the public sector. There are two choices; to try to delay action until the mounting pressures can no longer be resisted, or provide leadership responsive to the needs of our children.

The study concludes that "The demand for child services is based on fundamental, long term changes in the functioning of society, the composition of the labor force, the roles of women and men and changes in family life. Forceful economic and political realities underlie the marked rise in demand for child care services. They will not go away. . . ."[2]

In the final analysis, we learn most about our children, their needs and capabilities by sensitive observation and interaction. Intelligently planned and decently funding programs for young children and families, drawing on the hearts, minds, and experiences of the many people willing to learn from young children and each other, will, in the words of Dr. Rowe, "continue to grow as colorful and joyous flowers in our midst."[3]

Next we look at two studies sponsored by the Council of special education.

9 Educating the Special Student

So let's stop pushing them around and give them a chance. – John Holt

The quality of society depends on the extent to which it protects the people who can't fend for themselves. – Jean Mayer

The Advisory Council has conducted two studies in the murky area of special education: *Take A Giant Step: Evaluation of Selected Aspects of Project 750* by Herbert Hoffman, and Massachusetts study of *Educational Opportunities for Handicapped & Disadvantaged Children* by Burton Blatt & Frank Garfunkel. Herbert Hoffman looked at a program for the emotionally disturbed in his evaluation of selected aspects of Project 750. In their study of special education, Burton Blatt & Frank Garfunkel looked into three major areas:

> (1) the identification and description of those children who are known to have special needs, but were not being served by 'official' agencies; (2) descriptions of life in classrooms, institutions, and other special settings for the handicapped; and (3) the development of programs, recommendations and legislative proposals leading to a preliminary master plan designed to bring into more workable and useful juxtaposition our current capability for delivering services and the need for the modification, improvement, and extention of such services.[1]

Neither study director liked what he found. Hoffman concluded that major changes were necessary to correct some obvious inadequacies. Among his recommendations was one concerned with the development of more in-state alternatives to the current practice of out-of-state placements. Such a network of private and public programs would be coordinated by highly trained regional administrators, qualified in special education and clinical assessment. Blatt describes a Kafkaesque world with the child as the victim. When Blatt and Garfunkel look at children ostracized from school they state:

> Many of these decisions to exclude, exempt or suspend have never been adjudicated; in other cases, children have been placed in private settings or in some type of institution or care facility. In still other cases (many of which have been studied intensively here), children have been denied formal schooling because of their adjudged 'incorrigibility,' truancy, or 'maladaptive' behavior.[2]

While the approach has been piecemeal, the Massachusetts legislation has been generous in funding certain special education programs. A landmark study completed in 1966, *Massachusetts Plans for Its Retarded,* involved hundreds of professional and citizen groups who, together, provided the wisdom and political clout to insure the establishment of a Bureau of Retardation. This bureau was charged with the development of long-range state policies for the retarded as well as the integration of research, programs, and agency personnel devoted to the care and treatment of the mentally retarded. That same legislation reorganized mental health-mental retardation services in the Commonwealth and deserves recognition as among the most progressive developments on behalf of the handicapped in the Commonwealth's long and often pioneering history of human services. The way was paved for regional and local participation in the promotion and extension of services for the mentally ill and mentally retarded. Further, it established, at least in principle, the necessity to develop community alternatives to institutionalization and, most importantly, the responsibility of the Mental Health Department to guarantee the development of such community alternatives. On September 1, 1970, Governor Francis Sargent signed into law a bill, updating terminology, statutory definitions, regulatory standards for services, and other commitment provisions contained in Chapter 123. The new law is a great liberalizing achievement for those who have long agitated for greater guarantees of "due process" for all citizens of the Commonwealth.

The program studied by Hoffman, the "750" program for emotionally disturbed, is another indication of the easy generosity of the Great and General Court of Massachusetts when it comes to funding special education. Begun in the early sixties and costing about one million dollars, the "750" program has escalated in cost while serving less than half the children who need major help with problems of an emotional nature. Tragically, a number of gaps exist between the legislative act and the administrative deed. Inadequacies of every nature appear. The programs go from the hand to the mouth; who is awarded money for what and why is moot; what leadership there is often appears to serve everyone but the child. Yet exemplary programs do exist, as Blatt points out. In program delivery, in his judgment, Massachusetts is, no better or worse than most other states. And some professionals are cracking good, if outnumbered.

Other issues, those dealing with pedagogical matters, appear destined to endless but not timeless debate: the uses of regional arrangements; small versus large institutions; the necessary qualifications for those working in speical education. Both Blatt and Hoffman will be seen making their choices among such issues.

Both Drs. Hoffman and Blatt find a great deal about which to be critical. The first found a creaky, unchanging and unaccounting administrative system and the second deplores the shoddy treatment given to many of the children in special education.

In Massachusetts, Chapter 750 has become a problem of major proportions.

In a program whose initial state allocation of $1 million now devours ten times that amount, just a few years later, the waiting lists of eligible children expand as local communities increasingly resist pressures to inaugurate community based, publicly supported curricula for the handicapped. And, as disturbed children are sent to private schools under the provisions of Chapter 750 — rather than to community public school programs — they appear to remain there years longer than originally thought necessary. Boards of education and their constituencies in the meantime continue to neglect developing facilities and programs that might have permitted those children to remain at home in a normal community environment. In effect, what was originally intended to be positive and liberal legislation on behalf of handicapped children may have become the instrument that now prevents, or discourages, local communities from meeting their obvious responsibilities to these children and their families.

In New York state, the Greenberg Law has, de facto, encouraged many communities to discontinue their special programs for the handicapped by permitting families to "purchase" private or other publicly supported educational programs for their children. However, as the New York legislation allows not more than $2,000 per year for each child in such a program — and as quality private schools for the handicapped cost considerably more than that — poor families have great difficulty participating in and benefitting from this legislation; at the same time, public educational alternatives are decreasing. In effect, the New York State legislation — as the Massachusetts legislation — encourages institutionalization, the removal of children from their homes, the abrogation of heretofore community-accepted responsibilities for the education of *all* children, and the further stigmatization of children and their families.

It is possible that the right to public education is a principle of a higher order and consequently of a higher priority than whatever principles were the under-pinnings of the Massachusetts, New York and other "free choice" legislation. Blatt states:

> If we examined our state and federal constitutions, we would find that there are clear mandates for local governments to provide suitable educa-tional programs for all children within their geographic-political boundaries. Discrepancies have been found to exist between the expectations held by the sponsors of "free choice" legislation — wrongfully assuming that all people have the freedom to take advantage of it is discriminatory legislation at best and, at the extreme, illegal or abusive.[3]

Procedures & Findings

The Advisory Council provided Blatt with $55,400 to do the study. O.P.P.C. Bureau of Retardation gave $5,000 for (1) the development of an analysis of Massachusetts statutes and regulations pertaining to special education of the handicapped; (2) a review of special education statutes from several other states; (3) a final report submitting draft legislation which recodifies all special education statutes in Massachusetts.

Dr. Blatt conveys his essential message in four of his seven chapters. Diricting a team of twenty-five, he uses a variety of techniques and task forces to obtain his data with protocoled observations being central to his approach. Hoffman doing a briefer report and focused on one program, relies largely on interviews for his information.

In Chapter 1, Blatt seeks to tease out what he can from "exemplary" programs. "Exemplary" was operationally defined in terms of integration of agents — children, teachers, parents — and activities. Not every program designated as "exemplary" was expected to include all aspects of integration. The term "exemplary" was applied to those programs which, in some way, had gone beyond the conventional isolated special class model.

Four graduate students screened 68 recommended public school systems; of these, 18 were chosen as "exemplary". The project utilized participant observation and nonstructured interviews to obtain data. The observers entered a wide range of special programs with a deliberate humanistic orientation, viewing the *total* setting rather than a limited aspect of it. Programs visited ranged from sheltered workshops to preschool Homestart programs, and served a wide range of children with special needs.

Observations focused on the educational setting, the general attitude within the system, the degree of integration, curriculum innovation, the role of the teacher, parent and community involvement, and the use of ancillary services and consultants. From the findings, Blatt was led to making a number of recommendations concerning teacher training and the treatment of special education children.

Another of Blatt's teams — he had seven in all — looked at special programs for the mentally retarded in Massachusetts. Using an observational schedule designed especially for application in special programs for the mentally retarded, a sample of 80 public school (55 educable and 25 trainable), five day-care, eight preschool and ten institutional programs were surveyed by five trained observers and Dr. Blatt. In keeping with the schedule format, the observers noted (1) summary rating of children in learning environment; (2) details of observed lesson and general learning environment; (3) summary rating of diagnostic and placement procedures and extent of consultative and supervisory assistance; (4) summary of quality of observed lesson(s) and curriculum emphasis; and (5) percent of daily distribution of time. In addition, information about the teachers' training and certification was gathered.

Hoffman's study, directed more to administration rather than clinical matters (and thus complementary to Burton Blatt's project), followed four basic approaches: (1) abstraction of records available at the Bureau of Special Education regarding each child in the sample; (2) interviewing a parent of each child in the sample; (3) interviewing a selected sample of public and private school administrators who have had extensive experience with the 750 program; and (4) surveying by mail all private schools approved to accept 750 children. Priorities had to be set in terms of which program features would be studied. Since the bulk of the money is spent on the private school provisions and majority of the 750 children attend these private schools, it was decided to focus on this aspect of Project 750.

Hoffman furnishes an encouraging note:

> In the process of gathering data, it became gratifying to hear high praise of this program from the parents of the children who have participated or still are participating in a 750 placement: 'If our family life has been saved, it 750 has saved it,' said one of the parents. 'Everyone was just wonderful — this 750 should be available to all the kids who need it,' said another parent. Such sentiments were echoed by many other parents. The pioneering quality of the program — the provision of services where before there were none — further adds to the perception of the program as successful.[4]

The perception of the program's relative success receives additional support from his findings: 57 percent of those children who have participated in 750 and have not yet reached their 16th birthday are back in regular public school classes. The parents perceived 44 percent of the children as improved in social adjustment, 39 percent as improved academically and 55 percent as improved in over-all adjustment. He was able to trace the current activities of 74 percent of the children in the primary sample of 160 youngsters who had terminated. His follow-up indicated that approximately 72 percent of these youngsters have what could be termed a "successful" outcome. Hoffman qualifies this rosy picture:

> It is my opinion, however, that the apparent success rate is inflated and that the true rate of success is much lower. This assertion is based on the recent knowledge that approximately 220 youngsters have been enrolled in approved private schools for more than four years and for the large majority of them the prognoses are pessimistic. The existence of this group, which is not represented in our sample, produces in our findings a strong positive bias. In addition, since the research did not employ a design with appropriate control groups, we cannot scientifically affirm that the results are directly related to the 750 program.[5]

A review of Blatt's major findings reveals the following points.

1. Teacher certification — the high percentage of noncertified special class teachers and the lack of teacher certification requirements for institutional, preschool and day-care programs.

2. Chronological age ranges in 42 percent of the classes observed were found to be incompatible with special educational practice and legislation generally agreed to be acceptable. This was especially notable in classes for the trainable mentally retarded.
3. Although observers noted that the learning environment encountered in the classes observed was pleasant and conducive to productive education, there was a dearth of teacher proficiency data which might be attributed to any of a number of factors, e.g., poor teacher preparation, lack of administrative know-how, lack of supervision, etc. Although curriculum content was generally good, deficiencies in delivery were apparent.
4. Diagnostic and placement procedures were recorded as quantitatively sufficient, i.e., they met the letter of Commonwealth law. But, data suggested that these procedures were not useful to teachers in program planning.
5. Consultative and supervisory assistance data suggested that personnel involved in special education organization and consultation were not oriented to curriculum development. This finding was especially noticeable in trainable, preschool and day-care programs, as well as in institutions. Although teacher supportive services were more prevalent in these programs, observers were unimpressed with their quality.
6. There were not enough secondary school programs for educable retarded children.
7. More than 50 percent of the trainable classes functioned without the assistance of teacher aides who are generally considered necessary in these programs.
8. Seventeen percent of the classes observed met for less than five hours daily, and ten percent for only three hours. No classes in institutions met for more than three hours daily.
9. Only 48 percent of all the classes observed received consistent and planned supervision from specialized personnel.

Until recently, children out of school were virtually ignored. Blatt's study team focused on children who were (1) culturally different e.g., Spanish speaking; (2) physically different e.g., crippled; and (3) mentally and behaviorally different e.g., mentally retarded, emotionally disturbed. To attest to the magnitude of the problem, another study stated the following.

> A minimum of 4,000 school age children are excluded from the Boston Public Schools; the likely number ranges as high as 10,700. The majority of these children remain out of school because the School Department provides no educational programs for them . . . another group of children − between 2,800 and 4,800 − go to school but are excluded from the regular educational process. Many of these children are misclassified and isolated. They are assigned labels denoting inability to participate in normal school activities.[6]

In an area in which it is difficult to produce solid data, Blatt sought his information from interviews with school administrators, social service and mental health professionals, parents and community leaders, as well as with researchers engaged in similar investigations. He frequently quotes a child, or others such as his parents, to present a reign of errors resulting in yet another excluded child.

One of the preliminary hypotheses for the project was based on recent findings that public schools do not have adequate facilities for emotionally disturbed children and are, by and large, neither equipped nor willing to deal with those who are severely retarded, multiply handicapped or severely disturbed. It was anticipated that the sample of excluded children would fit some of the above categories, or a combination of them. But, as the data clearly show, there are children out of school who do not have these severe handicaps. Many have above average intelligence, no physical handicaps and do not meet any of the three legal criteria for exclusion: (1) the child is incapable of caring for bodily needs; (2) the child is unable to communicate adequately and to understand directions; or (3) the child is a danger, physically or morally, to himself or to others.

Considering all factors, e.g., family and socioeconomic status, and physical and emotional problems, it became clear that the single most important influence in the process of exclusion is the school system. Some definite trends emerged from the data.

(1) A relationship exists between the attitude of the administration and faculty and the number of exclusions from a system. This became clear from interviews with faculty and administration, i.e., the child was seen as a "trouble-maker" or "potential legal problem." On the other hand, some denied the existence of the problem and therefore accepted no responsibility. Comments such as, "We have 800 children to account for," or "We have to protect our teachers," were typical. Teachers often justified their role in exclusion and lack of follow-up after hooky playing incidents with an excuse such as responsibility to the other children. Schools employing personnel who made these comments had relatively high incidences of exclusion.

(2) The more rigid the school system in terms of curriculum and discipline, the higher the incidence of exclusion. Most of the children interviewed complained of teacher inflexibility.

(3) In most of the schools where exclusions were prevalent, the guidance, adjustment counselors and principals evidenced little sympathy and understanding for the child and seldom offered counseling services to children prior to exclusion.

When a child has been excluded, the school's constructive relationship to him is usually terminated. The data show the following.

(1) Many exclusions occur when a child has been suspended and the school has failed to take follow-up measures to have him reinstated.

(2) There was little evidence of active cooperation between the excluding school and an agency attempting to find new placement for a child.

(3) There was little direct contact between the school and the family of the excluded child. The school rarely offered to aid a family in finding placement.

(4) The attitude was often conveyed by the administration of a school following exclusion which implied that the child, rather than the school, was at fault.

(5) In several cases, a child was not permitted entry into another school within the same system, even though he expressed a definite desire to return to school

As has been documented in this section of the project, the school system has many opportunities to play an influential and positive role in the exclusion process. But, for those systems in which there are comparatively high incidences of exclusion, they apparently fail at all or most stages. They fail to be sensitive; they fail to become actively involved; they fail to take the responsibility that is often legally and morally theirs.

However, the school should not be given total responsibility for what happens during the exclusion process; social agencies must take over where the schools leave off. Unfortunately, these agencies usually lack the information necessary for proper school placement. In fact, two of the most intelligent children in the sample were placed in a remedial school as a result of an agency referral. One boy was placed in an institution for the mentally retarded on an agency's recommendation because he "looked retarded and acted retarded." Testing later indicated low normal intelligence. Some cases remained in limbo between the schools and the agencies for long periods, with neither taking action.

The excluded child's family was often rather unsupportive of the child during and after the exclusion process. Many families were reluctant to even admit their child had been excluded. When given advice and direction, however, parents tended to respond positively and become actively involved.

Finally, Blatt, with legal aid, analyzed the laws relating to special education. The purpose of this analysis was to lay the groundwork for revisions. Analysis and recommendations were derived from a number of sources: (1) complete review of existing Commonwealth legislation and comparison with statutes of other states; (2) interviews with administrators, teachers, legislators, attorneys, parents and many others concerned with the provision of services to children with special needs; and (3) review of previous related Commonwealth studies.

In his section on recommendations, Blatt proposes either revision of present laws or an entirely new governmental agency. Since revisions are common and proposals for new agencies a little less so, I will present the latter recommendations in my next section.

Hoffman's thrust was directed more to the system and how it functioned than to the observations of classroom and institutional behaviors. He found shortages of staff, leadership and information. No traces could be found of program objectives, shared decision-making, or program evaluations.

Children, he found, were often being sent to and released from expensive residential programs in ways and for reasons not easily understood. Funds were being eaten up on a few children in a few programs with no effort being made to develop alternatives.

Hoffman's 23 recommendations deal with (1) changing the orientation of special education programs to make them more family focused; (2) stressing a child's strengths instead of his weaknesses; (3) developing community and regional involvement in special education; and (4) detailing central office needs. Thus, Hoffman's interest centers on philosophy and the delivery of programs. Blatt is more concerned with observing program segments. He asks, what actually happens inside various institutions handling the special education child?

Dr. Blatt's recommendations run more to teacher training and institutional treatment of children. He also finds and reports on exemplary programs and performs an analysis of the stacks of state laws pertinent to special education in Massachusetts.

A New State Agency

In the space we have, it is perhaps best to lay out, in Blatt's original legal terminology, the major and most far-reaching of the recommendations: a new state agency for serving the special child. What this follows is a new model, state regional and local — that would scrap the fragmented jungle of statutes on special education still burdening the student, the parent and the educational administrator. We have deleted sections on the formal qualifications of staff excepting only those of the commissions. The annual cost of the recommended governmental structure would be just under $1.2 million a year.

Purpose

The purpose of the act is to create a new state department which will have authority and responsibility for all special services for children with special needs. By placing such services within the jurisdiction of a single agency, the act recognizes that the developmental needs of children are many faceted and that a child who is not developing to his fullest potential because of temporary or permanent adjustment difficulties generally needs assistance in many aspects of his total development. The act also recognizes that the past fragmentation in a myriad of agencies of special services for children with special needs has resulted in frustration and anxiety for parents attempting to utilize those services, stigmatization of children and their families, inferior services for such children, and duplication and irresponsible waste of limited resources. The department of child development is designed to remedy these past inadequacies and to modernize and streamline special services for children with special needs. In view of the remedial purpose of this act, its provisions shall be liberally construed.

Department of Child Development: Commissioner,
Powers & Duties

There shall be a department of child development, in this chapter called
the department, which shall be under the authority and responsibility of a
commissioner of child development. All actions of the department shall be
taken by the commissioner, or under his direction, by such agents and
subordinate officers as he shall determine.

The department shall regulate and control all matters affecting the
provision of special services for children with special needs. Its powers and
duties shall include the following:

(a) it shall regulate, consult with and assist school committees in the
identification, classification and referral of children with special needs;

(b) it shall regulate all aspects and assist with the development of all special
services for children with special needs;

(c) it shall coordinate the expertise of professionals from different
disciplines both within and outside of the department in order to provide the most comprehensive special services, at both the state and
local levels, to children with special needs;

(d) it shall collect, compile and make available to the public for the purpose
of evaluating special services, data on all children with special needs who
reside in the Commonwealth;

(e) it shall develop public information programs to inform the public about
the nature and extent of the special needs of children resident in the
Commonwealth and about the availability of special services which exist
to meet those needs;

(f) it shall develop and coordinate primary and secondary preventive
programs to reduce the incidence of special needs in children;

(g) it shall develop and regulate a comprehensive system of certification for
teachers, psychologists and other professional and paraprofessional
personnel who work either part- or full-time administering special
services for children with special needs. Further, it shall assist medical,
nursing, social work and other professional and paraprofessional
societies and agencies in developing appropriate preparation and performance standards;

(h) it shall coordinate the efforts of and assist public and private colleges
and universities within the Commonwealth in developing courses and
programs best designed to prepare graduates to serve children with
special needs;

(i) it shall receive and investigate complaints on behalf of an individual
child or group of children with special needs about any aspect of any
special service and may initiate its own investigation without a complaint;

(j) it shall be the state agency designated to receive and allocate federal
and state funds for children with special needs;

(k) it shall make such rules, regulations and guidelines and shall issue such
directives as are necessary to carry out the purpose of this chapter and

to execute other provisions of law relative to the administration of special services for children with special needs;

(1) it may withhold state and federal funds from public or private agencies which fail to comply with the provisions of law relative to the administration of special services for children with special needs or any regulation, guideline or directive of the department authorized in this chapter.

Commissioner: Appointment by the Governor

The governor shall appoint a commissioner of child development for a term coterminous with that of a governor. Said commissioner shall, at the time of his appointment, be qualified by having earned from an accredited institution the highest professional degree offered in education, medicine, nursing, psychology, social work or related science fields and by having no less than seven years professional or administrative experience in work related to the problems of child development. He shall devote his full time during business hours to the duties of his office, shall be the executive head of the department, and shall have full responsibility for the formulation and execution of all of its policies and the coordination of all of its functions. He shall appoint and may remove all employees in the department and may establish such divisions and bureaus in the department as he deems appropriate.

Deputy Commissioner

The commissioner shall appoint a deputy commissioner who shall possess the same qualifications required of the commissioner, except that he shall have had not less than five years experience in work related to the problems of child development, of which at least two shall have been as an administrator. Said deputy commissioner shall serve at the pleasure of the commissioner, and shall devote his full time during business hours to the duties of his office. He shall exercise such authority and shall discharge such duties of the commissioner as the commissioner may from time to time delegate to him and, in the absence or incapacity of the commissioner, or in the event of a vacancy of the office of the commissioner, shall act as the commissioner until the absence or incapacity shall have terminated or the vacancy shall have been filled.

Assistant Commissioner for Education

The commissioner in consultation with the commissioner of the department of education shall appoint an assistant commissioner for education who shall supervise and consult with the other assistant commissioners on the educational aspects of all special services for children with special needs.

Assistant Commissioner for Mental Health

The commissioner, in consultation with the commissioner of the department of mental health, shall appoint an assistant commissioner for mental health who shall supervise and consult with the other assistant commissioners on the psychological and emotional aspects of special services for children with special needs.

Assistant Commissioner for Health

The commissioner, in consultation with the commissioner of the department of public health, shall appoint an assistant commissioner for health who shall supervise and consult with the other assistant commissioners on the health aspects of special services for children with special needs.

Assistant Commissioner for Social Health
& Welfare

The commissioner, in consultation with the commissioners of the departments of education and welfare, shall appoint an assistant commissioner for social health and welfare who shall supervise and consult with the other assistant commissioners on the social and family aspects of special services for children with special needs.

Assistant Commissioner for Linguistic
Development

The commissioner shall appoint an assistant commissioner for linguistic development who shall supervise and consult with the other assistant commissioners on the problems of children with special needs arising from cultural or linguistic factors and on the special services designed to meet those needs.

Administrative Assistant Commissioner

The commissioner shall appoint an administrative assistant commissioner who shall meet regularly with all of the assistant commissioners to assure that all regulations, guidelines, directives, and informal assistance by the department reflect, to the fullest possible extent, the views and ideas of the members of the different professional disciplines on the department's staff. Said assistant commissioner shall be responsible for coordinating the efforts of the department's staff and for assuring that all members of the department's staff are fully informed of all matters before the department which are within or intimately related to their particular area of expertise. He shall also be responsible for facilitating communication on common problems between staff members of different disciplines.

Assistant Commissioner for Research

The commissioner shall appoint an assistant commissioner for research who shall collect, compile and make available to the public, for the purpose of evaluating special services, data and information on all children with special needs who have received, are receiving or will receive special services under the regulation and authority of the department. He shall also conduct research and compile information on innovative and exemplary programs, within or outside of the Commonwealth, for children with special needs.

Assistant Commissioner for Public Information

The commissioner shall appoint an assistant commissioner for public information who shall be responsible for informing the public about special needs of children and about the availability of the special services which exist to meet those needs. Said assistant commissioner shall also coordinate the services of the department with those of other agencies and groups which have programs designed to prevent or minimize the incidence of special needs in children and shall inform the public of the existence of such preventive programs.

Assistant Commissioner for Personnel
Recruitment & Certification

The commissioner shall appoint an assistant commissioner for personnel recruitment and certification who shall develop and supervise a comprehensive system or recruitment, certification, and employment standards for professional and paraprofessional personnel who work either part or full time in carrying out any special service for children with special needs. Said assistant commissioner shall also cooperate with and assist public and private colleges and universities within the Commonwealth in developing courses and programs designed to achieve the best possible preparation of graduates who will serve children with special needs.

Assistant Commissioner for Investigation &
Review

The commissioner shall appoint an assistant commissioner for investigation and review who shall hear complaints brought on behalf of individual children or a group of children eligible for or receiving special services about any aspect of such special services which is alleged to be denied or to be detrimental to the fullest development of such children.

Regional Branches of the Department

The department shall establish in each of the seven mental health regions, a regional branch of the department which shall be composed of a supervisor and such other persons as the department shall deem necessary to perform the services enumerated in section 17 of this chapter. The department shall fix the terms of office and compensation of the supervisor and the other employees of each such regional branch team and their salaries shall be paid in the same manner as other state salaries. Each regional supervisor shall report to the deputy commissioner and shall consult with other regional supervisors.

Powers & Duties of the Regional Branches

Each regional branch shall have the following functions:
(1) it shall consult with and assist school committees in satisfying the requirements contained in the department's regulations, guidelines and directives;
(2) it shall directly assist school committees in identifying and diagnosing children with special needs and in developing special services to meet those needs;
(3) it shall be a central referral agency in all cases where children with special needs require special services outside of school;
(4) it shall assist and encourage the formation of agreements between two or more school committees to jointly provide special services;
(5) it shall investigate any special service at the request of the department;
(6) it shall engage in cooperative action with other regional branches and with any parent or community organizations whose purpose is to improve the services available to children with special needs;
(7) it shall have such other responsibilities as may be delegated to it by the department.

Regional Child Development Advisory Councils:
State Child Development Advisory Commission

There shall be established in each region a child development advisory
council consisting of at least 16 members appointed by the department in
consultation with the supervisor of the regional branch to which such
advisory council shall be attached. At least half of the members of each
such council shall be parents or guardians residing in the region, whose
children are enrolled in any special service, provided, however, that no less
than three parents or guardians on each such advisory council shall be
parents of children who are resident of institutions under the control of the
Commonwealth. Each advisory council shall advise the regional branch to
which it is attached, with respect to all aspects of all special services within
the region and shall submit a written report, annually, on the quality of such
programs, to the state advisory commission created under this section. In
addition to its other powers and duties, the regional advisory council shall
hear and transmit to such state advisory commission, complaints and
suggestions of persons interested in special services in the region. Members of
each regional advisory council shall be granted access to special education
programs and information, subject to restrictions regarding confidentiality,
and shall be assisted in carrying out their duties by the regional branch of the
department. Members of the regional advisory councils shall be reimbursed
by the Commonwealth for expenses necessarily incurred in the performance
of their duties.

Each regional advisory council shall elect two representatives to a state
advisory commission at least one of whom shall be a parent or guardian
whose child is receiving a special service. Such state advisory commission
shall submit a report, annually, to the department evaluating the quality of
special services in the Commonwealth and recommending improvements in
those services. The department shall implement the recommendations of the
state advisory commission or shall state in a written reply why such recommendations cannot or should not be implemented.

Duties of School Committees

(1) In accordance with the regulations, guidelines and directives of the
department and with the assistance of the regional branch of its region,
the school committee of each town shall identify all school-age children
with special needs, diagnose the needs of such children, prescribe a
special service to meet those needs, maintain a record of such identification, diagnosis and special service and make such reports as the
commissioner may require. No school-age child with special needs shall
be excluded, exempted or suspended from school without the written
approval of the commissioner.

(2) Within ten days after a referral of a child by a teacher or other person for purposes of determining whether such child has special needs, the school committee shall notify the parent or guardian of such child, by certified mail, that such referral has been made. Such notification shall include a statement advising such parent or guardian of the right to consult, with or without counsel, at the discretion of such parent or guardian, with one or more representatives of the school committee, including the teacher or other person who has referred the child. Such consultation shall be held promptly after a request by such parent or guardian and shall be for the purpose of explaining the basis for the referral, the procedures involved in making a final determination of whether a child should be placed in a special service, the specific nature of the courses and activities offered in such special service and the possible future placements of a child following termination of his placement in such special service.

If, within ten days after such consultation, said parent or guardian believes that an improper referral has been made, he may file a written objection with the school committee. The filing of such written objection shall stay a final determination regarding placement until the parent or guardian has had a reasonable opportunity, not to exceed sixty days from the filing of the objection, to present evidence in opposition to such placement. The school committee shall consider such evidence prior to making a final determination regarding such placement.

If, after objection by a parent or guardian, the school committee nevertheless decides to place the child in a special service, said school committee shall issue a written decision explaining the basis for such placement. A copy of such written decision shall be sent forthwith, by certified mail, to the child and his parent or guardian. Included with such copy shall be a notification of the right of the parent or guardian within thirty days after receipt of such notification, to file a complaint with the department. The filing of such complaint shall automatically stay the placement of a child into a special service until the department has rendered a decision on the complaint. The decision of the department shall be final.

After a child has been placed in a special service, the parent or guardian of such child may object to such placement by the same procedures established by this section for objecting to an initial referral, provided, however, that such objection shall be initiated by a complaint to the school committee and that subsequent post-placement complaints shall not be made until a period of at least nine months has elapsed since the decision of the department on the print complaint.

(3) In accordance with the regulations, guidelines and directives of the department the school committee of each town shall:

    (a) provide or arrange for special services for all resident school-age children with special needs.

    (b) provide or arrange for special services for children with special needs who have not attained school age, but whose development will be irreparably diminished without special services at an early age. The department shall define the criteria by which the school committee shall determine whether a child is eligible for special services pursuant to this subdivision. Such determination shall be made by the department when requested by a parent or guardian, or upon referral by a clinic, day-care center, social worker, or physician provided the parent or guardian so permits.

(c) provide or arrange for special services for children with special needs who have attained the age at which the legal duty to attend school has terminated but whose development can be substantially improved by the provision of such services. The department shall define the criteria by which the school committee shall determine whether a child is eligible for special services pursuant to this subdivision. Such determination shall not be made without the express consent of the child and his parent or guardian.

(4) To meet its obligations under this section, any school committee may make arrangements with any other school committee or, subject to the consent of the parent or guardian affected thereby and to constitutional limitations, may make an agreement with any public or private school, agency or institution to provide the necessary programs or services. No expenditures made pursuant to a contract with such school, agency or institution for such special programs or services shall be reimburseable under the provisions of section 5, if the needs of the child for whom such special programs or services are being provided can be met, in the opinion of the commissioner, by a special service within the public school. Before granting approval of said contract for purposes of reimbursable the commissioner shall consider such factors as the needs of the child, the suitability of the special service offered by such school, agency or institution and the feasibility of comparable alternatives. Any school committee may, subject to constitutional limitations, enter into a contract with the owners and operators of any workshop, training or rehabilitation center for provision of an educational or occupational training program for children with special needs who are at least sixteen years of age, provided such center shall have been approved by the department.

(5) any school committee which provides or arranges for special services pursuant to this section, shall provide such transportation, tuition, room and board, and other items as are necessary to the provision of such special services. The department shall determine when a parent or guardian shall be liable for costs incurred by a school committee for the provision of such special services.

Such a stress on the legal proposals contained in Blatt's final report do an injustice to the wide variety of topics he addresses. A number of his recommendations, for instance, bear on teacher education both for the special education child and exactly how he is being handled.

Special education is still in its infancy. Of the few children in special programs, many are making little or no progress. Yet, a good education is all important to the child in need of special programs.

We turn now to four studies sponsored by MACE which deal with well-established programs that are not always conducting their affairs in the most sensible manner.

Part III
Revisiting Some
Conventional Programs

Knowledge will not keep any better than fish. – Alfred North Whitehead

The real quarrel between the conservatives and the liberals in education is about the kind of society they wish to live in. The conservatives want more control over children and more stability in society; the liberals want more freedom and more change. – Harold Taylor

We have chosen four studies as examples of how study directors, working with the Council, have treated traditional programs. In each case, as we shall see, reforms are recommended.

The first study reviewed deals with a restructuring of occupational education. In 1967, the Council contracted with Dr. Carl Schaefer of Rutgers University and Jacob Kaufman of the University of Pennsylvania for $93,400 to spend a year studying the relevance to students of occupational education.

Partly as a follow-up on the Schaefer-Kaufman report, Lloyd Michael's proposal to conduct a study of the comprehensive high school, at a cost of $100,000 was accepted by the Council. Dr. Lloyd Michael, Professor of Education at Northwestern University and for 20 years Superintendent of Evanston Township High School, Evanston, Illinois, kept his recommendations fairly conservative since he was persuaded that radical change in high schools was an unlikely event.

Just what kinds of programs and services are available to students was studied further in a report on guidance pupil services done for the Council from July 1968 to June 1969. *Pupil Services For Massachusetts Schools,* funded by the Council at $75,000, is one of the most extensive survey and planning projects of pupil services undertaken in any of the 50 states.

The study staff was headed by Dr. Gordon P. Liddle, who was also Executive Director, Interprofessional Research Commission on Pupil Personnel Services, and Dr. Arthur M. Kroll, Associate Director and then Assistant Professor of Education, Clark University.

The certification and preparation of educational personnel is the topic of the fourth study treated in this section. *Teacher Certification and Preparation* was one of the Council's first major studies, done from November 1966 through May 1967 at a cost of $73,000. The Council chose Dr. Lindley J. Stiles, Professor of Education for interdisciplinary studies at Northwestern University and former dean of the School of Education at the University of Wisconsin.

Ongoing programs need to be examined at various times. Deciding which ones to scrutinize and how far to go in recommending modifications in them is never easy and often hazardous. The past has a way of tyrannizing the present. It is impossible to study ongoing programs in any significant way and not disturb some people — if the recommendations are implemented. Matters of understanding, attitudes and philosophy must be faced. Premises must be smoked out.

The question of what constitutes a program and what parts of it might, if adjusted, effect real change is also at risk. There is a temptation to tinker, to suggest management changes, to attack the latest listing of shibboleths.

The unadorned truth is that to define and locate a problem in any enterprise is vastly different from knowing what solution matches the problem. We in education often ignore this truism because we think it impedes us. Education as a process is more art and imagination than science and logic.

MACE undertook studies of programs of vocational education and teacher certification and education, largely at the urging of the Willis-Harrington Report. A look at the high school came about under the rubric of studying education in the frames and levels in which it exists. (There is some thought that the junior high school should be viewed next.) The study of guidance programs and activities was given high priority since they seemed so incomplete and shrouded in mystery as they moved into the 1970s.

Vocational Education

One of MACE'S first studies reviewed occupational education to evaluate the present system and recommend a master plan for the development, coordination, and expansion of vocational and technical education, including recommendations for the preparation of teachers in this area.

The report was to be concerned with the following:

(1) the objectives of and a philosophical basis for a comprehensive offering of vocational and technical education in Massachusetts, at the secondary and postsecondary levels;
(2) some estimates of the changes in and future occupational needs of students and communities and the extent to which vocational and technical education can make adjustments in its programs to meet these needs;
(3) an evaluation of vocational and technical education in Massachusetts in relation to its objectives;
(4) a proposed master plan for vocational and technical education at the secondary and postsecondary levels;
(5) a proposed plan for the preparation of the education of teachers and administrators, and
(6) a proposed plan for the organization and administration of vocational and technical education, at the state level.

The Advisory Council selected Carl J. Schaefer and Jacob J. Kaufman to undertake the study. The 296-page final report makes a case for major reform in occupational education and in secondary schools. Urging a major expansion of occupational programs, the report is critical of current practice. Shaefer and Kaufman found, for instance, at least fifty percent of the students currently enrolled in vocational programs (some 25,000) lack either the interest or the aptitude to benefit from specific career training. In part, this may be a result of their finding that vocational students receive the least counseling of any group of students. But it also suggests, as they conclude, that many teenagers simply are not ready to make a career choice — particularly if that choice is thrust upon them at the ninth or tenth grade level.

Schaefer and Kaufman advocate a career development program which, in addition to providing students with a broader range of options during their school years, assists them in keeping their options open after school. Efforts to gear vocational training to actual labor market demands are usually quite primitive. Even if they are sophisticated, they are doomed to limited efficacy: economic conditions change, employers switch locations, existing industries become obsolete and new ones take their place. The schools are left with expensive shops, without the capital outlay required to convert them to newer occupations. Machine tool operators keep getting trained after the tool-making companies leave town. Partly as a result of this factor, only about half of the vocational graduates in the state actually end up employed in the trade for which they were prepared.

Given these facts, Schaefer and Kaufman urge a dramatic shift in the nature of the regional-vocational-technical high schools which now provide the bulk of occupational education in the Commonwealth. Instead of four-year vocational preparation, they suggest that these institutions form a network of "Institutes for Educational Development." With some modifications, the 30 regional vocational-technical schools planned for the Commonwealth could become 30 institutes, with at least one within 30 miles of every student in the state.

The institutes would provide intensive and specific career training in the final two years of high school for those students with definite career plans. In addition, they could become resource centers for teacher-training and development of curricular approaches needed to strengthen the occupational and career development of offerings of comprehensive high schools.

Schaefer and Kaufman made their recommendations in 1968. At that time, there were six regional schools in operation. Today, there are 12. The careers development concept has the strong support of an energetic new Commissioner of Occupational Education in the State Department of Education, but neither it nor the full-fledged comprehensive high school have yet to make significant inroads. Among many Bay State vocational-technical educators, Schaefer-Kaufman is a dirty word. So are the words "comprehensive high school."

It would be a mistake to blame this seeming recalcitrance solely on the attitudes of the vocational education establishment. Rigidities in the legislation (federal and state) financing vocational education make it difficult to fund a broad and flexible vocational education program. The legislation needs to be changed. Furthermore, there is abundant evidence that the professionals running so-called "comprehensive" high schools frequently give vocational education short shrift. Schaefer and Kaufman report that vocational students frequently feel teachers and their classmates have a "condescending" attitude towards them. An indication of this is that they receive less counseling. The image of vocational education as a "dumping ground" is still in evidence.

Schaefer and Kaufman warn, in fact, that the ideal of the comprehensive school — a microcosm of a truly democratic society where students from diverse backgrounds with diverse interests and talents meet and rub shoulders in an atmosphere of mutual respect — is far more frequently found in speeches and pamphlets than in reality. A careers development program or a truly comprehensive high school, however they are structured, both seek to establish this ideal as actual. To do so is to take a first step toward maximizing student options.

The need for a state policy on vocational education is impelling. The questions to be raised in enunciating a policy include:

1. Who will make the state policy?
2. Who will be served and how?
3. What public purposes will be served?
4. Who will make decisions and at what level?
5. How will vocational education be organized and administered?
6. How will vocational education continue to be judged germane?
7. How can personnel needs be met?
8. How and on what evidence will changes be made?

Shaefer and Kaufman do deal with these issues excepting one and three.

Dr. Charles Buzzell, a new associate commissioner in the Department of Education, has sparked impressive changes in vocational education in the short time he has been on the job. Where appropriate, use has been made of the Shaefer-Kaufman report by Dr. Buzzell. However, the need for expanding vocational education is so great that it will take years and a great deal more money to achieve the goals laid out by Shaefer and Kaufman and others.

Comprehensive High School

Closely linked to the occupational education report by Drs. Schaefer and Kaufman is a study of the uses of comprehensive high schools by Lloyd S. Michael. Michael's final recommendations echo the occupational report on matters of organization and in the need to expand vocational programs.

The general tone of Michael's study, however, is somewhat cautious. After much consideration, Dr. Michael was persuaded that the high school of the future will be little changed. He also felt that secondary schools in Massachusetts could profit from a variety of suggestions and recommendations merely to bring them up to the 1970s. He strikes hard at rigidities, de Lone notes, and narrowly conceived programs.

Most of the high schools of Massachusetts are well organized and administered to have students scheduled uniformly and to have those in the same courses follow similar patterns of study. The evidence from the study indicates, however, that administrators, teachers and students would welcome less uniformity and increased diversity in patterns of study. More than half of the 2,748 student respondents reported 'there is little freedom, much regimentation' for them . . . to exercise initiative to work independently by pursuing a variety of learning opportunities . . . One-third of the 1,821 teacher respondents characterized the time available to work with individual pupils as "negative" or "very negative."[1]

Michael also found that 44 percent of students were "frequently indifferent" about going to school, while another 30 percent said they often "dread" or "always dislike" going to school.

Michael was perhaps most disturbed to find so many small public high schools still in operation. He judges a comprehensive high school to need a minimum of 1,200 students and to obtain such a student population requires school district consolidation. Michael relates the present situation as handicapping the development of comprehensive secondary schools.

The high schools in the Commonwealth have the responsibility to provide an appropriate and a challenging education for all youth. It is the conviction of the Study staff that a comprehensive high school of adequate enrollment and resources can most effectively and economically meet the educational needs of the youth of the community. A high school that is widely comprehensive has the breadth of program to meet the diverse needs of all students and the depth of program to assist in the fullest development of each individual student. Comprehensive high schools of adequate size and resources have the flexibility to permit the organization of students, personnel, and facilities in various groupings to realize the greatest educational effectiveness and economy. These schools are much more likely to have adequate supportive services, such as guidance and counseling, administrative and supervisory services, (457) and development services.

The low enrollments in many of the high schools in Massachusetts make it impossible for them to provide a comprehensive program on an economical basis. Ninety-two, or 30 percent, of the 305 high schools had, on October 1, 1969, enrollments of 500 or fewer students; 89, or 29 percent, between 501–1,000; a total of 181, or 59 percent with 1,000 or less. The median enrollment of the 204 regular high schools was 1,041; of the 42 regional high schools, it was 704; of the 50 vocational-technical and trade high schools, it was 246; and of the nine regional vocational-technical high schools, it was 436.

More than one-fourth of the 1,821 teacher respondents evaluated ' . . . the adequacy of the program and services in your school in providing the various types of offerings needed by all of the students' as 'Negative' or 'Very Negative.' Approximately the same percentage of the 2,748 student respondents said that most of the subjects they were taking seemed un-related to their ' . . . future interests and needs.' More than half of the students indicated they 'Very Frequently' or 'Frequently' had opportunities to study, as a part of their course work, the things they wanted to learn, the things that puzzled them; nearly half reported they 'Rarely' had such opportunities.[2]

Only slight progress can be reported as a result of Michael's study, although it was endorsed by the Massachusetts Secondary School Principals Association. Some local changes have been made, based upon the report and the Department of Education is working on implementing those recommendations which fall within its jurisdiction.

Pupil Services

While a structure of sorts can be claimed for both vocational and other secondary school programs, guidance programs have been loosely appended to schools with little attention given to a structural rationale.

A particularly clear, almost archetypal, example of a random growth pattern is provided in a 1969 MACE study of *Pupil Services for Massachusetts Schools,* a study directed by Gordon P. Liddle and Arthur M. Kroll.

Liddle and Kroll trace the growth of pupil services in Massachusetts back to their origins, over a century ago, to the rise of attendance officers, better known as "truant officers."

The motivating force for growth of these services, they point out, has usually been one social concern or another. Schools have responded on a hit-or-miss basis to those pressures, failing either to plan ahead and lead in the development of such services or, once the pressure does exist, failing to integrate new services into a coherent plan or organizational framework.

The original truant officers, for instance, were a response to reformers concern over the exploitation of child labor. Massachusetts passed the first compulsory school attendance act in the nation to get children out of sweatshops and into schools. It was the job of the truant officer to see that the law was carried out.

Over the years, many truant officers have abandoned their "dog-catcher" image and tend now to operate more as counselors, working with family problems that keep children from attending school. What the attendance officer actually does, however, and how or whether he relates to a whole host of other pupil services is a matter of local accident.

Those other services grew out of spasms of public interest as well. Health services were added to the schools in another pioneering Massachusetts step, under direction of the state Department of Health, which created the school nurse.

The immigrant tide of the first two decades of this century, combined with increasing urbanization, stimulated the social conscience of some citizens and alarmed others. This was "fertile ground for the creation of additional services," Liddle and Kroll suggest, and in 1915, a Department of Vocational Guidance was established in the Boston School Department — again, a national first. The same year saw creation in the State Department of Health of a Division of Hygiene, responsible for infant mortality, child welfare, industrial hygiene, health instruction and medical examination of school children. Liddle and Kroll remark: "The accumulation of separate agencies responsible for the needs of school children was definitely underway." [3]

And so it continued, decade by decade.

In the Depression, Federal funds stimulated creation of vocational counseling in the public schools, funds administered by an autonomous division of the state Department of Education. Later in the 1930s, the state Department of Education approinted a supervisor for special education, responsible for education of the physically handicapped and mentally retarded. However, traveling teams certified as school psychologists by the Department of Mental Health were responsible for diagnosing retardation, and frequently that certification was on the basis of a couple of college psychology courses.

In the forties, the state Department of Education created an office for Occupational Placement and Follow-Up — which had no formal relationship to the previously established office for Occupational Information and Vocational Guidance.

In the 1950s, the state's Youth Services Board was created, and a new kind of counselor emerged — the school adjustment counselor who worked with troubled elementary school pupils. Then, Sputnik gave rise to the National Defense Education Act and more funds were available for counseling. Pearl Buck's book, *The Child That Never Grew,* and the formation of the National Association for Retarded Children, were among forces that led to creation of a Division of Special Education within the state Department — in Massachusetts and elsewhere.

The fifties and sixties saw some sporadic efforts to pull this maze of agencies together, efforts which generally stalled when General Court action was required. Even special educaton, which has had a strong and effective lobby, is handicapped by vagueness in the law which results in untrained guidance counselors, under the direction of other branches of the Department, performing the job of psychologists. Furthermore, Liddle and Kroll state, "staff growth on the state level has not kept pace with local needs, and the necessity for spending the major proportion of their time approving local reimbursement has greatly limited their influence in the sphere of improvement and innovation." [4]

Guidance programs, on the whole, have not had the impact upon schools that seems necessary. Guidance staff are simply not boat-rockers. They have been satisfied with minor roles and laboring in the shadows.

Until the attitudes of "pupil personnel" staff are changed, exhortations to work in the cause of human dignity and to help clear up the state environment of schools will fall on deaf ears. Guidance people must live closer to the issues and to the youngsters who are caught up in a world they are close to rejecting. It is not possible to make an accurate statement about what has happened as a result of Liddle and Kroll's study. We think a number of school systems have used their report in revamping local guidance systems but cannot prove this. Action at the state level, in spite of Department of Education efforts, has led nowhere.

Teacher Certification

The Willis-Harrington Commission looked at the certification of schoolmen in the Bay State and declared it badly in need of change. A house is not necessarily a home, and a school does not always give an education: Teachers make the difference.

In part, the need to change teacher education reflects the need for other changes. The career development approach is a case in point. It requires teachers, Schaefer and Kaufman point out, who can accept and approve of the students on their own merits. Most teachers evaluate youngsters on their ability to do college work. This standard is, of course, totally inappropriate to the large proportion of students who require an occupationally oriented curriculum." [5] Similarly, Blatt's recommendation to integrate handicapped youngsters into the normal life of schools requires that teachers become more sensitive to the needs and particular learning requirements of such children. And the same can be said, as Jordan urgently says it, for a large number of students who stand to benefit from compensatory education.

The state — and specifically the state Department of Education — has a major role to play in improving the quality of teacher education. It is in the best position to influence the state colleges and other institutions preparing teachers. It has the power to influence teacher training programs. Individual school districts do not! It can (in theory) provide the coordination and guidance that relate the needs of school systems to the programs of colleges and universities. Most important, it has the legal authority through its responsibility for certifying teachers.

In developing laws governing teacher certification, Massachusetts abandoned custom; rather than being the first in the nation, it was the last. The state's first legislation requiring certification of teachers was passed in 1951. (However, Massachusetts was the first state to offer college programs aimed at preparation of teachers.)

A MACE study directed by Dr. Lindley J. Stiles has three harsh words to say about the certification policies that have developed in the last 20 years.

> Present standards and procedures for certifying educational personnel in Massachusetts are inadequate. They fail to guarantee that all licensed to practice in various educational positions will be competent. Nor do they differentiate between levels of professional performance. No provision is made to protect against professional obsolescence. The emphasis on specific course requirements tends to block experimental efforts to improve teacher education in colleges and also repels some able persons from entering educational work. Some qualified and experienced teachers from other states and countries find it difficult or impossible to be licensed in Massachusetts. The existing system of certification may operate, at least in public schools where licenses are required, to reduce the supply and in some ways the quality of educational personnel — an outcome the opposite of its intended purpose.[6]

The Stiles' report emphasizes two basic flaws in current certification practices. First, the criteria for certification are purely bureaucratic. They consist of course-counting. Enough of the courses with the proper name and you are a certified teacher — without regard to actual teaching ability or, for that matter, without regard for the quality of the courses. Secondly, certification embraces the twin fallacies that "once a teacher, always a teacher," and "a teacher is a teacher is a teacher."

In other words, a teacher who receives certification at age 22 on the basis of course credits is certified for life — whether or not at age 55, for example, he has kept abreast of the developments of the last three decades. Furthermore, while certification does differentiate between specialities (e.g., secondary English teacher, elementary teacher, guidance counselor, special education teacher), there is no effort to discriminate between teachers of differing ability.

Emphasis on prescribed courses discourages innovation in teacher education institutions and, most important, ignores the demonstrable fact that the best way to learn to teach is to teach. Stiles urges much more stress on practice teaching during preservice preparation. Certification itself should be based, ultimately, on demonstrated teaching performance as well as on knowledge.

The "once a teacher, always a teacher" syndrome ignores the need for teachers to change and grow in the course of their careers. Stiles recommends therefore, that certification be for limited periods of time, with renewal required periodically. To make this recommendation effective, the renewal requirement would have to be supplemented by collaborative efforts of local school districts, the state Department of Education, and colleges and universities, to increase and upgrade inservice education for teachers.

It is the state which must establish minimum standards. "In general," Stiles writes, "states that maintain the highest standards for professional practice attract the greatest numbers of talented persons seeking employment."[7]

But, as Stiles also remarks, the state cannot do it alone. State officials are farthest from the day-to-day situation where teachers actually teach. Thus, local school districts (as well as university and college supervisors) must take responsibility for evaluating the actual quality of performance. Stiles suggests they can do so through the use of trained observers, forming committees that might include teachers, laymen, college faculty, and others.

Certification procedures, in addition to attempting some kind of quality control, also provide a quantitative control. Certification is the valve through which all manpower passes into the education system.

Therefore, it is urgent that the certification process be more than a flood control gate. It should be designed to meet manpower needs intelligently. But the tendency has been, as Stiles points out, to view the manpower need in education simply as a need for more teachers and smaller classes. This is the result of "a teacher is a teacher is a teacher" thinking. It completely ignores both economic and professional realities.

Economically, the reality is that under present staffing patterns, "there will never be a sufficient supply of high ability professional teachers to staff all class-rooms." In fact, as the Stiles' report continues, teaching is "the only field that has not substantially increased the number of clients per professional over the past 30 years."[8] Professionally, the reality is that different teachers have different skills and some teachers have more skills than others.

Taking these two realities into account, Stiles concludes that "a reasonable goal is not more but better prepared teachers." Secondly, he concludes that a differentiated staffing pattern should be adopted by the state and reflected in levels of certification. Differentiated staffing requires sane standards for pupil-staff ratios. For instance, what sort of ratios should prevail in schools with handicapped children or children requiring compensatory education? Furthermore, Stiles suggests, the long-standing educational habit of maintaining smaller teacher-pupil ratios at the secondary school level needs to be questioned: "Simple logic raises doubts about this pattern of increasing the amount of teacher time available as students develop greater capacity for independent study."[9]

Each year since the Stiles' study, bills have been filed to make limited changes in certification without success. A small group of teachers and the lack of strong support in the senate have kept successive bills from passing. Meanwhile other states, some using the Stiles' report, have made changes in certification. California actually borrowed from Bay State bills proposed to the legislature to alter the certification process.

The reader should sense a close relationship between the high school and the occupational education studies. Michael studied the Shaefer and Kaufman recommendations and found himself in close agreement. The pupil personnel study shows some kinds of kinship to the special education studies and to the child care study conducted by Rowe. All of these studies advocate more comprehensive approaches to working with children.

The Stiles report leads the reader to think of not only certification but of teacher education. Dr. Stiles also conveys a new sense of reality by indicating the need for differentiated staffing. All of the studies in Part III recommend that the programs they represent live closer to their communities. Community and citizen involvement, in fact, is one of the major themes expressed in MACE studies.

Unless otherwise indicated, references are to Advisory Council studies.

shows some kinds of kinship to the special education studies and to the child care study conducted by Rowe. All of these studies advocate more comprehensive approaches to working with children.

The Stiles report leads the reader to think of not only certification but of teacher education. Dr. Stiles also conveys a new sense of reality by indicating the need for differentiated staffing. All of the studies in Part III recommend that the programs they represent live closer to their communities. Community and citizen involvement, in fact, is one of the major themes expressed in MACE studies.

Unless otherwise indicated, references are to Advisory Council studies.

10 Centering Vocational Education

Our school system is gravely defective in so far as it puts a premium upon merely literacy training and tends therefore to train the boy away from the farm and the workshop. — Theodore Roosevelt

Since all education today is, and must be, both liberal and vocational, the task is not that of finding the appropriate proportion of each but rather of reappraising and redefining all courses so they contribute to both. — Paul L. Dressel

High schools are training grounds for colleges. Even students who don't expect to attend college can only achieve status by signing up, when they qualify, for college prep programs. Students learn quickly that favors and high school resources flow to the talented. Those who aspire to college inherit better teachers, better programs and what there is of guidance. Yet, only twenty percent of all high school graduates ever make it through a four-year college, with many never even applying for college admission.

Seemingly unable to change, high schools continue to offer preparation for college as their main function. In a real sense, therefore, many secondary school students are presented with incomplete educations. They must enter and matriculate from college to make any of it worthwhile. Accountability in the community and state becomes a function of many seniors who enter college.

It doesn't take a John Dewey to see through such mindlessness. Students hardly out of elementary school are aware of it and often even their teachers and school administrators. Still, the college curriculum goes on and on and the school revolves around it.

One of the problems with changing the habits of high schools is a lack of alternate ways to educate youth. Problems, as we earlier indicated, do not always lead to appropriate solutions.

Advocates of occupational education feel they have found a large part of the solution. Occupational education is relevant, they say, and the student who avails himself of an occupational education will find himself either prepared to enter the world of work or equipped to go on to certain kinds of post secondary education. Federal money has followed this line of reasoning and, comparatively speaking, there is a good deal of it available to develop and proliferate vocational programs.

Yet, as can be seen at a glance in Table 10-1, Massachusetts does not enroll enough students in vocational education programs.

Table 10-1
Enrollment in Federally Supported Technical and Other Vocational Education Programs in Selected States and Aggregate United States, 1959 through 1965

| State | Population (in millions) | | Enrollments (in thousands) | | | | | | | | | | | | | | |
| | | | Technical education | | | | | | | Other vocational education | | | | | | |
	1960	1965	1959	1960	1961	1962	1963	1964	1965	1959	1960	1961	1962	1963	1964	1965
Connecticut	2.5	2.8	8.9	6.7	8.3	4.4	5.7	7.8	9.3	20.6	16.2	22.8	26.4	26.8	25.3	24.4
Massachusetts	5.1	5.3	0.6	0.8	1.2	1.4	1.6	1.6	1.7	68.7	64.4	66.4	68.0	70.9	70.4	70.3
Missouri	4.3	4.5	0.2	0.9	1.4	1.5	1.8	2.1	2.4	66.4	62.5	65.5	66.0	70.0	67.8	79.1
New York	16.8	18.0	1.0	1.7	2.6	3.3	6.2	9.0	13.2	207	196	185	192	239	323	448
North Carolina	4.6	4.9	–	1.1	1.6	2.0	3.3	5.9	4.8	128	134	142	164	171	182	195
Virginia	4.0	4.5	1.2	0.6	0.7	0.7	1.4	2.3	1.9	100	101	106	106	115	113	187
Washington	2.9	3.0	4.5	9.8	10.0	11.3	13.8	10.8	9.6	110	96.6	96.3	111	111	111	134
Aggregate U.S.	179	194	49	101	123	149	185	221	226	3652	3667	3733	3924	4032	4345	5205

Source: U. S. Department of Health, Education, and Welfare, Office of Education, *Digest of Annual Reports of State Boards for Vocational Education* (Washington, 1959, 1960, 1961, 1962, 1963, 1964, 1965).

Ever since the development of the first vocational programs, their status and who should take them have been in hot debate. Schaefer and Kaufman are advocates of the promise, need and relevance of vocational education. While realizing that secondary schools have been tempered by the college preparation syndrome, Schaefer and Kaufman find it easier to attach the "general education" high school track from which students, without occupational education, are expected to end their schooling with high school graduation. These students, Schaefer and Kaufman declare, could profit from occupational career programs. The study directors also want many of the more able youngsters in high school technological programs, thus widening offerings and options for those interested in post-secondary education. Schaefer and Kaufman hold that forty to sixty percent of our high schoolers should, in fact, be in occupational career programs.

But the problems remain. The kinds of programs and the proper training of teachers for these students are far from resolved. If the Schaefer-Kaufman recommendations are followed, a major upheaval in our high schools will ensue. Much of what has passed as vocational education (and most high schools offer something) would also need major modifications.

Institutional changes must also be undertaken. Vocational education is best offered in a comprehensive institution, whether that institution be a secondary or post-secondary institution. This is true, because separation of students according to curriculum results in socioeconomic segregation, which translates out into inferior education.

Vocational education should be offered at the high school level. It motivates a sizeable proportion of pupils to learn other school subjects, and it eases the transition from school to work. Even if it were desirable to postpone vocational education until after high school graduation, post-secondary institutions could accommodate a very small proportion of the students who need vocational education.

Indeed, vocational education must expand in the secondary school. It and the college preparatory program must replace the general curriculum, and remain as our two basic curricula, in the context of diverse offerings and arrangements, until the philosophers' stone betters our current guesses.

Method

Schaefer and Kaufman used three approaches to collecting data for their study of vocational and technical education: (1) a series of planned consultations and visits, culminating in a conference of social and behavioral scientists; (2) the production of special papers on issues in vocational education; and (3) the use of a questionnaire. Each of the three approaches interfaced with the visits and consultations, lasting throughout the lifetime of the study.

The questionnaire survey was, by far, the most elaborate feature of the data collecting process. Questionnaires were sent to schools, recent school graduates, parents, teachers, employers and union officials to help (1) evaluate the present system of vocational and technical education as meeting the occupational needs of students and the manpower needs in Massachusetts; and (2) to examine the image of vocational education held by four groups: employers, teachers, parents and union officials. A control group was established for comparing the question-naire responses of vocation school graduates to those of general and college preparatory curricula.

All but one of the 33 schools randomly selected for the school fulfilled their commitment. Returns from the individuals contacted were deemed by the authors as adequate enough to be considered valid.

The questionnaires probed seven areas, devoting a chapter to each: the ade-quacy of vocational education in preparing youth for employment; vocational education in the private sector; the image of vocational education; the training and certification of vocational teachers; financing vocational education; the educational media and vocational education; and the economy and vocational education in the state.

The Findings

The first area surveyed, the adequacy of vocational education in preparing youth for employment, found a "pay off" for students completing vocational education programs. The general curriculum student was least satisfied with the secondary schools in this regard. One out of every three vocational school gradu-ates continued in education in one way or another. The occupation of parents seemingly influenced the educational decision of the student. Finally, students in vocational education sensed that they and their courses were often looked down upon.

Table 10-2 indicates attitudes of various groups towards vocational education.

Occupational education and the private sector, the second area studied, yielded information on private schools and industrial training programs. Private schools were found to be attractive to high school graduates able to pay tuition and forego immediate earnings. On the other hand, company-sponsored training programs had quite different clientele with one-fourth of their trainees high school drop-outs. Such industrial programs, usually conducted in an onschool on-the-job atmosphere, allow for instant use of learned skills. The private sector as an occupational trainer has some serious limitations. Many trades and skills are not represented and those that are sometimes suffer from narrow viewpoints, or limited facilities, minimal investments, or all three. Openings exist for only a few students.

Schaefer and Kaufman next turned to the image of occupational education. Collected and studied were the attitudes of parents, vocational teachers, other teachers, labor officials and industry representatives. Parents of college-bound students expressed an either-or view of academic and occupational education, with

Table 10-2
Attitudes toward Vocational Education in the High School for the
Seven Groups as Indicated Across All 28 Attitude Scale Items

	Favorable[a]	Unfavorable	
Teachers of Vocational Subjects	86%	14%	n = 134
Parents of Vocational Students	85	15	n = 117
Teachers of Vocationally-related Subjects	83	17	n = 62
Teachers of Academic Subjects	79	21	n = 119
Parents of College Prep Students	74	26	n = 32
Industry Representatives	69	31	n = 765
Union Officials	64	36	n = 57

$x^2 = 34.63$
df = 6
P < .01

[a]Computed as the average across the 28 items of the number of respondents indicating strong agreement or agreement on the positive items and strong disagreement or disagreement on the negative items. Neutral judgments were included with the unfavorable.

Source: Carl J. Schaefer & Jacob J. Kaufman *Occupational Education for Massachusetts* Massachusetts Advisory Council on Education, June 1968 p. 108.

a strong preference for the former. They viewed occupational education as expensive, would like to see less of it, and found "the product of vocational education is 'fair' — neither very good nor very bad." On the other hand, parents of vocational students were found to be "positive and favorable" to vocational education. Teachers of vocational education subjects were also, not surprisingly, satisfied with their own program and products. Other teachers generally looked with favor on vocational course work but did not view the vocational education student as a promising student.

Labor officials and industry representatives were considerably more reserved in their feelings about the efficacy of vocational programs. Labor officials, in particular, were skeptical of vocational education for reasons not known to Schaefer and Kaufman.

Schaefer and Kaufman also entered the realm of teacher education, where they found programs rigid and narrow and humdrum regulatory requirements prevailing. Eight years' of occupational experience are required to teach certain specialities. An age requirement associated with some specialists virtually eliminates those over forty and male teachers must teach boys and female teachers must teach girls. Finally, requirements differ significantly from special field to special field, making a crazy quilt of certification regulations. Massachusetts is one of the states which has the Department of Education responsible for "preparing" trade and industrial teachers. In this arrangement, these teachers must take such courses as Interest and Interest Factors, Character Training, Teacher's Ethics and Building Good Will for Vocational Education.

The community colleges in Massachusetts next came under the scrutiny of Schaefer and Kaufman and they did not like what they saw. Since their late beginning in Massachusetts, public community colleges have favored the dubious prestige of transfer programs over terminal programs. The Department of Education did not help the situation by being the only department in the nation not allocating some federal vocational funds to post-secondary programs.

Chapter Eleven, dealing with the economy and occupational requirements of Massachusetts, cites a change in the Bay State's economy from textiles, shoes, leather and apparel production to technomanufacturing and service industries. Massachusetts must produce, Schaefer and Kaufman state, highly skilled people in order to compensate for a poor location and a lack of natural resources.

Their projections of occupational requirements over the next ten years appear in Table 10-3.

Recommendations

Schaefer and Kaufman develop 49 separate recommendations which, if fully implemented, will reshape the approach to secondary school education in the Commonwealth.

The recommendations cover eight areas. They are presented here with

Table 10-3
Projections of Occupational Requirements Massachusetts, 1980

	November 1980	Percent 1980	Absolute Change 1960-1980 (000)
Professional	412	15.5	155
Management	226	8.5	65
Clerical	466	17.5	140
Sales	173	6.5	27
Craftsman	346	13.0	67
Operative	452	17.0	16
Services	346	13.0	147
Laborers	106	4.0	27
Misc.	133	5.0	16
Totals	2,660	100.0	660

Source: Carl J. Schaefer, Jacob J. Kaufman, *Occupational Education for Massachusetts* Massachusetts Advisory Council on Education June 1968 p. 226.

explanations of the major recommendations. Other important recommendations are listed briefly. Those interested in the complete proposals and the supporting data should refer to the complete study.

Careers Development

The realignment within the state's high schools should revolve around the establishment of a careers development curriculum that, Schaefer and Kaufman write, would make schools truly comprehensive. The study directors write:

"Too often, the debate over how to provide comprehensive secondary education centers on the schoolhouse rather than on the curriculum. The advantages claimed for the comprehensive high school stem mainly from the opportunities for youngsters from all segments of the community to know and appreciate one another as individuals. It is questionable whether such individual interaction occurs under the present system."[1]

The modified track system in most secondary schools tends to reflect class structure in the communities. Those who gravitate to neither college preparatory nor vocational curricula either end up in some type of general curriculum through default or they escape it by selecting vocational education as a lesser evil.

The careers development curriculum would attempt to broaden, not narrow, the options open to students. Present general curricula limit exploration within school and opportunities beyond school. The careers development curriculum would stress exploration and arrange classes so that a student could pursue interests as far as they lead him.

As discussed at length in the full report, students in general curricula and many in vocational programs constitute a large number who do not really benefit from their school experiences. The principle of "relevance" to the lives of students is at the heart of the careers development curriculum that would serve these students. These "gray" area youngsters would have a chance to explore the nature of many occupations. Through team teaching and emphasis on overlapping clusters of subjects, students would learn more clearly the relationship between occupational goals and basic academic skills. The occupational orientation would embrace numerous fields and skills, thus widening post high school opportunities. The educational process would no longer be seen as teaching, but as providing the conditions for learning.

Teachers and Students

Teachers of traditional subjects in the "careers development curriculum" which they propose would act as resource persons in their areas of expertise and would guide students along self-selected lines of interest. Students would proceed at their own pace towards goals they had chosen for themselves. The student's program would be project-oriented, producing the potential for a sense of accomplishment that is rare for many in the subject-oriented academic classroom.

In the judgment of Schaefer and Kaufman, a relaxed and informal learning environment would be critical to the success of the careers development curriculum. It should operate in an environment where favorable reinforcements could emerge as the student completes difficult tasks and receives approval for his efforts.

The student for whom school is not now relevant seldom receives any signals of reward for his activities. If he is not academically adept, approval tends to be withheld and he does not feel satisfied with his own work. The careers development curriculum would spur internal reinforcement through self-selected interests that become a central part of school activity. The external reinforcement would be expected to come from the kind of teachers who can accept and approve of students on their own merits. The standard, say our study directors, of evaluating youngsters on their ability to do college work is totally inappropriate to students who require an occupationally oriented curriculum.

Teachers and administrators must see that the needs of students in this curriculum are better served if the school discards such traditional goals as teaching toward improved performance on standardized tests. Many teachers believe that if students would only try a little harder they would accomplish the goals the school administration has set for them. The students, in turn, are aware of the low regard in which teachers sometimes hold them. Often, it is neither the teacher nor the student, but the inappropriate curriculum and rigid system that are at fault — maintaining this destructive cycle of negative reinforcements.

The proper teachers to guide the careers development curriculum are not necessarily to be found in the ranks of the traditional vocational educators where highly skilled tradesmen assume much of the teaching burden. These teachers would be better employed in the Institutes for Educational Development where their specialized skill is needed.

In the careers development curriculum, broader, less specialized teachers would be more suitable; teachers who could work together to capitalize on the opportunities for relevance offered by occupational orientation rather than skills training.

The New Framework

The changes recommended here cannot simply be legislated. An administrative framework must be established to provide support and encouragement on the local level and to assure that the mandated changes become reality.

A new Bureau of Careers Development should be established, administered by an Assistant Commissioner of Curriculum and Instruction. This bureau would serve that large percentage of students who attend local comprehensive high schools and who plan to work upon graduation.

In addition, a new Division of Manpower, Research and Development should replace the present Bureau of Vocational Education. It would be charged with the training and retraining of youth and adults through its three bureaus: manpower, research and development.

The Manpower Bureau would be responsible for the Institutes for Educational Development and would control all phases of operation from staff selection to curriculum.

The Institutes for Educational Development should not in any way compete with the technical training function that should be developed on the community college level in Massachusetts. The Institutes should restrict programs to those for students, either young people or adults, who do not have the equivalent of a high school education. The community colleges are urged to continue development of two-year post-high school technical programs. Thus far, their development has been heavily academic.

Organization

The approximately 30 Regional Vocational-Technical schools being planned (including those now operating) should become state-operated Institutes for Educational Development. More of them should be located in the large metropolitan areas.

Conversion of the Institutes into state-operated schools is not intended to contradict the principle of a single education system with "home rule" for all school-age youngsters. This report advocates that students remain under the control of their local schools for all purposes except their vocational and technical course work.

The Institutes would provide the service but the local communities retain responsibility for those who attend. Among the advantages of such an arrangement are (1) cost of the Institutes is shared equally by all taxpayers; (2) opportunity for occupational education becomes equalized; (3) curricula can be developed through state-wide planning; (4) educational leadership and teacher competency can be centrally regulated; and (5) a substantial program of adult, nondegree offerings can be more precisely planned.

Steps should be taken immediately to reallocate a larger percentage of local school resources to meet the occupational needs of those students not going on to advanced formal education. Major emphasis must be provided by local schools and appropriate financial incentives must be made available for implementing a careers development curriculum in grades 9 through 12 for that large portion of the student body — up to 40 to 60 percent in a given school — who need it.

geographic plan for location of the regional vocational-technical schools (to be
called Institutes for Educational Development) should be developed and should
ensure that there is a facility within 30 miles of every boy and girl in the
Commonwealth.

The Curriculum

. All occupationally oriented curricula should be classified into two broad
categories: Careers Development and Vocational Preparation.

Careers Development Curriculum.   The Careers Development Curriculum
would serve the great mid-group of students presently on a secondary school
treadmill to nowhere. This is the pool of students that produces the most drop-
outs. They could be identified early and by ninth grade it is usually clear which
students should be contained in this large grouping.

The Careers Development Curriculum should be nongraded, should involve
an occupational cluster system and should be elected by students from grades 9
through 12. Some of these students will surely spin-off into the Institutes for
Educational Development, which would train highly skilled specialists.

The occupations to be considered in the Careers Development Curriculum
should include:

building construction	industrial and fabrications
transportation and power	foods and kindred
business and office	agricultural occupations
distributions occupations	communications, information
health occupations	storage and retrieval

Team teaching should prevail throughout the curriculum.

Vocational Preparation.   This curriculum would be directed toward the
truly vocationally talented student who possesses academic ability and manipula-
tive dexterity and identifies with a particular occupational skill area. The program
should be limited to the upper two years of high school, with students entering
from either the college preparatory course or the Careers Development program.

The vocational preparatory curricula would be made more exclusive and
selective than such programs have been in the past. The teaching setting would be
the network of Institutes for Educational Development and the curricula would
be designed and taught by technologically oriented teachers. These graduates
would form the kind of highly skilled pool of potential employees from which the
future craftsmen and foremen could be recruited.

The adult curricula of the Institutes for Educational Development should be
limited to those of less than associate degree nature and to those not requiring
post-secondary education as a basis for their mastery. It should be the task of the
community college program to serve post-secondary needs in a variety of technical
and vocational areas.

All high schools should offer the Careers Development Curriculum, and all high schools should have access to the services of a nearby Institute for Educational Development. The relevance of technology should be made significant to all students by introducing new materials and programs starting at elementary level. The "introductions to occupations" area should be explored in junior high school.

Teachers entering the Careers Development Curriculum should be awarded a state stipend of $500 during their first year.

Institutes for Educational Development

. A network of thirty Institutes for Educational Development should be established throughout the Commonwealth, each within thirty miles of every school district and community.

The Institutes would be highly selective — only an estimated fifty percent of the current vocational school enrollment would qualify for the proposed new schools. The rest would be served by the Careers Development Curriculum in their comprehensive high school — still provided with an occupational orientation.

. The Institutes for Educational Development should be established, financed and operated by the state Department of Education through a separate division.

The present regional vocational-technical high school structure functions as a quasistate establishment. The state already exercises effective controls over building plans, curriculum and staff certification.

. The Institutes for Educational Development should offer high school programs at the 11th and 12th grade levels and should admit only those who meet superior requirements.

This would reduce enrollments in purely vocational education but would produce a highly skilled student group sought after by employers who require young people with special talent.

. High school students at the Institutes would remain affiliated with their local, "sending" high schools for purposes of graduation, athletics, extra-curricula activities and state required subjects.

. Institute students would divide their days between their local schools and the Institute.

Ancillary services of guidance counseling, diagnostic testing, placement, technical libraries and follow-up should be provided by the Institutes.

. Consideration should be given to providing other kinds of programs and services in the Institutes. Among these may be special classes for the severely mentally and physically handicapped, the academically precocious and inservice teacher education.

. The present Regional Vocational High Schools should assume this new role immediately and gradually return the responsibility for the marginal vocationally talented student to the local schools.

Administration. . The Careers Development Curriculum should be under the general supervision of the State's Associate Commissioner of Curriculum and Instruction and should be administered by a separate Bureau of Careers Development.

The Bureau's major challenge will be to promote change and reallocation of a major portion of the funds to implement the proposed program.

. The Bureau for Careers Development should be headed by an educational generalist.

. The present Bureau of Vocational Education should be reconstituted as a Division of Manpower, Research and Development, administered jointly by the State Department of Education and the State Department of Labor.

The Bureau of Manpower would have as its responsibility operation of the Institutes of Educational Development.

The Bureau of Research would be responsible for collection of data and conduct of in-depth studies to assure accurate measures of the number and type of job vacancies throughout the state.

The Bureau of Development would be concerned with the short-range and long-range planning necessary to implement the research findings.

The Division of Manpower, Research and Development would report to the Commissioner of Education for operational and developmental activities and to the Commissioner of Labor for Research activities.

. The Division of Manpower, Research and Development should have a legally designated advisory committee appointed by the Governor and representing industry, business, labor, education, the behavioral sciences, and the federal government.

. The Director of the Division of Manpower, Research and Development would serve on the staffs of both the Commissioners of Education and Labor as Assistant Commissioner to each.

Financing. . The state should assume a greater financial responsibility in providing occupationally oriented education.

Current estimated average cost is $584, compared to the estimated average cost of $850 per pupil in approved vocational programs. If a Careers Development Curriculum were established, the per pupil cost would increase to a point somewhere between these figures to about $700. New formulas would have to be established for state reimbursement.

Extra costs for providing the programs recommended in this report are estimated on Table 10-4.

. The state should assume the extra cost per pupil for the Careers Development Curriculum in local high schools on the basis of one hundred percent reimbursement.

. Extra costs per pupil for the vocational programs at the Institutes of Educational Development should be supported by the state. Local schools who send students to the Institutes should allocate a portion of the per pupil operating

Table 10-4

Vocational Programs – Grades 11 and 12

By 1970, 9,240 talented vocational students enrolled in Institutes or 6 percent of total enrollment of 154,053 at an increased per pupil cost of $266	$ 2.5 million
By 1975, 10,715 students	2.8 million
By 1980, 12,192 students	3.2 million

Careers Development – Grades 9–12

By 1970, 123,240 Careers Development students, or 40 percent of total enrollment of 308,107 at increased per pupil cost of $116	14 million
By 1975, 143,040 students	16.5 million
By 1980, 162,560 students	18.7 million

Estimates for both programs combined:
1970 – $16.5 million
1975 – $19.3 million
1980 – $21.9 million

Source: Carl J. Schaefer, Jacob J. Kaufman *Occupational Education for Massachusetts* Massachusetts Advisory Council on Education June 1968 p. 268.

cost to the Institute on a "charge back" basis. If half the student's day is spent at the Institute, half the local per pupil cost should go to the Institute. Transportation costs should be assumed by the sending school.

. Federal funds for vocational-technical education support construction of facilities on a matching basis with the state and should support operation programs at the Institutes for Educational Development. Community Colleges should receive similar support to construct facilities and operate post secondary programs.

. There should be an additional state reimbursement to those schools whose performance achieves the appropriate objectives of the programs.

. Capital costs for construction of Institutes for Educational Development should come totally from state and federal funds.

. The thirty recommended Institutes would cost an estimated $90 million. They would be constructed on a timetable of three to four a year. Communities that have already constructed facilities and join this system should have their construction funds returned to them.

. Costs for providing physical facilities for the Careers Development Curriculum in local high schools should be borne locally.

Legislation. . The General Laws of Massachusetts, as amended, should be rewritten to reflect the need for the redirection of occupationally oriented education proposed in this report.

. When this legislation is rewritten and approved, the present handbook to guide schoolmen and others should be replaced.

Teacher Education. . Undergraduate programs of teacher preparation should be instituted to provide humanistically oriented teachers to staff classrooms, shops and laboratories of the Careers Development Curriculum and Technology.

The new breed of teacher envisioned for the Careers Development Curriculum should be occupationally oriented, but should also relate strongly to the sociological and psychological needs of students.

. A graduate program, offering up to the Ed.D. degree, with a major in vocational-technical education, should be established at a leading university in the state.

. The updating of teachers in both technology and pedagogy should become an integral part of the occupational teachers' professional development and a Technology-Resources Center should be established.

. A Center for Community College Teacher Preparation, Research and Development should be established at either Lowell Technological Institute or the University of Massachusetts.

. A course in "technology for children" should be added as a requirement in the preparation of all elementary school teachers.

. Preparation of teachers for industrial arts should be oriented towards "introduction to occupations" in junior high school and toward "understanding technology" in senior high school.

. A Director of Occupational Teacher Education should be given a joint appointment in the Division of Higher Education, the Division of Manpower, Research and Development and the Bureau of Careers Development of the state Department of Education.

Public Support. A public relations program involving business, industry, labor and schools should be directly responsible for public relations.

Community Colleges. . The master plan for providing Community Colleges throughout the Commonwealth should be implemented as soon as possible.

. Greater emphasis should be placed on high-level, technology-oriented Community College curricula.

. The Associate Degree should be awarded for satisfactory completion of the post-secondary program at the Community College and the Associate in Applied Science Degree should be awarded for semiprofessional and paraprofessional programs as they are added to the college offerings.

Shortly after Schaefer and Kaufman's study was completed, a committee met to review the study recommendations and to look for ways to implement the report. While the committee supported virtually all of the study recommendations, they did make some refinements which should be recorded.

The aim of the Careers Development Curriculum, this committee felt, was essentially the same as for any good education — the fullest development of the student. The fullest development requires free lateral movement, open options.

Therefore, the committee recommended that there be as few limitations as possible to the movement of students from one curriculum or program to another — from college preparation to careers development programs and back to college preparation.

Free lateral movement was suggested to break down the rigid requirements and standards of the various curriculums or tracks. Ideally, the course of study for each student in the high school should be tailored to his needs. Community colleges accept reasonably promising students into their transfer programs whether or not they have had foreign languages, laboratory sciences or algebra and geometry. Some four year colleges will accept such students. If the individual tailoring of study is adopted as recommended for the Careers Development Curriculums, some students in them may be qualified to go directly into four year colleges. Hopefully, the same condition would pertain in the Occupational Institutes and Centers discussed in later items.

Next, the study committee described the key attributes of an occupational institute and the kinds of programs which should be developed in each:

1. Occupational programs including academic work in preparation for a specific occupation similar to the programs now in operation — and of course, new programs. On comprehensive campuses, academic work should be in classes with students from other programs of comparable ability and achievement.
2. Short, concentrated, purely vocational programs of from a few weeks to several months as terminal for high school students who will not continue in any program to graduation, and for adults needing upgrading and retraining.
3. Vocational education resources of teachers, counselors, materials and equipment to assist Careers Development Programs in the high school, individual adults and business and industry.
4. Programs for the occupational training of the handicapped.
5. Adult education programs offering the types of education listed under one and two above or combinations of them.
6. Post-secondary, nondegree programs for high school graduates which can best be offered by the centers and which do not unnecessarily duplicate community college programs. These will be extensive.
7. Where desirable, at least as a temporary measure, cooperative programs with Community Colleges leading to the associate degree. Planning for these programs and their facilities must be approved in advance by the Board of Higher Education, the Board of Education concurring that the resources can be spared from the other purposes. The programs themselves would be conducted under the authority of the Board of Regional Community Colleges. [2]

The committee concerned itself with the kinds of schoolmen needed. They wrote:

The specialized faculty for each of these programs should be headed by a chairman who acts as teaching team leader for all the instructors involved in the particular program. They should be specialized occupational instructors, many of whom may be drawn from existing programs of industrial arts, home economics, business education, etc. and instructors from the academic disciplines. The assistant principal or director and the team leaders should have early and intensive, specialized instruction as to the aims of the curriculum and as to the aims, skills, materials and equipment of their particular program. They should have intensive instruction concerning individualized scheduling and instruction and how to lead the teams of teachers in the various modern methods of instruction. Where possible paraprofessionals and specialists outside the school should be used, including personnel from Occupational Centers and Institutes. [3]

A final section in the committee's report furnished by President James Hammond of Fitchburg State College deals entirely with teacher education.

The college or university engaged in teacher education should involve itself in "real school situations in such a way that it advances knowledge on the one hand and performs service on the other." It cannot operate effectively in isolation. Schools and institutes are not only the testing ground for application of theory; they are a setting for generating new ideas. They provide the feedback out of which refinements, extensions or revisions are made. Each agency has a basic contribution to make to the program of teacher education. The role of each is different and a careful delineation of roles and functions is necessary.

There is "nearly universal agreement" that a clinical approach to teacher education in appropriate. It is also generally accepted that such an approach requires a more thorough, systematic analysis of the teaching process than what is feasible under the conventional observation, participation and student teaching syndrome. Clinical experiences, Hammond states, can be strengthened considerably through the partner relationship of colleges, schools, institutes, the state department and pertinent professional agencies. While direct experiences are essential, the appropriate kind and amount are too frequently not available at a given time and place. Furthermore, the number of variables is such that it is a matter of chance or happenstance that a given student obtains the kind and amount of experience he needs. Selected experiences must be accumulated so that the data to be studied and analyzed are comprehensive, varied and typical. Thus, it is very likely that the clinical experiences will rely heavily on simulated activity using such means as videotapes and audiotapes as the "prepared" material for study. Prospective teachers must be involved in the collection of these materials and in the analysis, application and evaluation of their use.

Experimental pilot programs should be established as soon as possible. There should be pilot programs for each level (e.g., elementary school, middle and/or junior high school, senior high school, career or occupational institute, community college, four-year college and university). These programs should also be cooperative ventures.

The division between knowing and doing must disappear. Twentieth century technologies no not admit distinctions between the universe of matter and the universe of the mind. "It is a serious error to consider technology as separate and outside of the culture rather than as an integral part of it. Likewise, it is a serious error to confine the investigation of knowledge-based occupations to shops and laboratories, to skills and techniques, to procedures and practices. An interdisciplinary concept is a natural for occupational education and especially so at the teacher education level."[4] Occupations cannot be defined in terms of the traditional disciplines or standard school subject titles. The spread of the interdisciplinary approach is a symptom of the shift in the meaning of knowledge from an end in itself to a resource, a means to a result. End results are inter-disciplinary of necessity.

Teacher education and certification is addressed in several MACE studies. The final study reviewed in this book involves a year-long look at the training and qualifying of teachers.

Our next chapter focuses on public secondary schools and finds them wanting even by conserative measures.

11 How Does the Comprehensive High School?

. . .we offer children Algebra, from which nothing follows; Geometry, from which nothing follows; History, from which nothing follows; a couple of Languages, never mastered; and lastly, most dreary of all, Literature. . .Can such a list be said to represent Life. . . — Alfred North Whitehead

. . . I conclude by addressing this final work to citizens who are concerned with public education: avoid generalizations, recognize the necessity of diversity, get the facts about your local situation, elect a good school board, and support the efforts of the board to improve the schools. — James B. Conant

Criticism of the American high school is a flourishing phenomenon that has virtually become its own reward. Secondary schools present a ready target not only to those given to extremism in whatever cause but also to many sensible people relatively difficult to arouse. As a result, little has gone unquestioned in high schools, although only recently have certain issues appeared. Taken in the whole, those things questioned include: runaway costs, the treatment of students, the quality of teachers, morality both as taught and practiced, poor textbooks, frills, shoddy programs, vocational education and compulsory education. Each segment of the population can add to this sample of concerns.

Many of the critics have been fellow schoolmen or professionals with kinship. The findings of an eight year study,[1] completed and thus obscured during World War II, implied that high schools had grown rigid without reason. When universities, the eight-year study disclosed, agreed to accept high school graduates matriculating from progressive and otherwise nonconventional schools, these students proved to be as good, and in some ways better, than a matched group who graduated from conventional secondary schools. Many other studies have raised doubts and issues about the way high schools function, including several Council studies. Schaefer and Kaufman, for example, find high schools adjusting inadequately to a technological society. Their vocational study roundly condemns the shortage of high school career programs. Liddle and Kroll's study of guidance activities, the subject of the next chapter, took to task ritualistic and narrow secondary school guidance programs.

The last fifteen years have seen simultaneous social, economic and technological revolutions. Yet, change comes hard to schools.

By 1957 and Sputnik, American secondary schools — and other educational segments — were long overdue for major change. The message was heard and educators began to toughen, especially in high schools. By 1963, both James

Conant and James Koerner had books on the market widely read and discussed, indicating changes each felt to be necessary in high schools. Other critics rushed into print and education, for the first time, entered the general stream of consciousness in America and became a topic worthy of mention in the news media.

In the mid-sixties, hope for high schools was being reinvented. Federal funds had begun to support educational innovations and all thought it would increase. Scholars, sensing a responsibility, even before Sputnik, began recasting parts of the curriculum. Technology promised much. A shift from a process of schooling to a process of learning was in the air. Teachers employed during the great depression were retiring. New blood eagerly entered the educational field.

But it wasn't enough. Maybe such things just whetted the appetite.

Then, the critics did an astounding thing. They became everymen. The traditional critics were drowned out by new voices representing vast numbers of people including those ordinarily passive students and teachers.

An the criticisms themselves changed. Now schools, particularly high schools, were attacked as unreal and anemic social institutions serving the needs of only a handful of students. Everymen's statements were articulate, their activities dramatic and their motivations sometimes destructive. Even members of the educational establishment became sharp critics of their own kind.

Thus, the Advisory Council had ample reason to study the high school scene in Massachusetts.

Others were found to agree with the Advisory Council, including the Massachusetts Secondary School Principals' Association and the Massachusetts Conference Board. In July 1969, Dr. Lloyd Michael made a presentation to the Council, which was approved, and the $100,000, one-year study was launched.

The Plan of the Study

While the report contains a number of assumptions — a preliminary broadside announcement contained thirteen — the key assumption was that, properly put together, comprehensive high schools offered the best promise for students. It was also apparent from the beginning that vocational education, since it had earlier been studied by the Council, would be afforded a prominent part in the study.

The study developed along four phases. First, a survey instrument, a questionnaire, was developed and sent to every high school in Massachusetts. The forty-page questionnaire probed particularly comprehensiveness of program offerings and recent changes, or "blocks" to changes. Information was collected in the following areas: general information, institutional objectives and philosophy. Subject areas, guidance services, student withdrawals and career intentions, school staff and administration, student activities program, media services, school facilities, school community relations and financial resources.

The second phase called for a detailed study of 33 high schools chosen to be representative of high schools in Massachusetts and visited by "two or more" consultants. At these meetings, the following points were covered:

1. Administrator comments concerning major problems, issues, and needs of the high school were obtained from questionnaires and interviews.
2. Teacher attitudes and perceptions of their role in the school and how the school might be improved were obtained from questionnaires and interviews.
3. Student attitudes and aspirations about themselves, and perceptions about their school experiences and the need for change and improvements which they believed would be of help to them were obtained from questionnaires and interviews.
4. Parent expectations for their children and their satisfaction and dissatisfaction with the program of the school in meeting these expectations were obtained from questionnaires.
5. Significant political, social and economic factors in the community, which affected an understanding and support of the school, were obtained from interviews with administrators and teachers and, to some extent, from questionnaires from them.

Each of the selected high schools was visited by at least two members of the staff and consultants. Typical schedules followed by the staff and consultants follow.

Third, a series of regional conferences, five in all, were scheduled to engage people in all walks of life in the study's progress and to present position papers given by prominent educators associated with the study. Two papers were given at each conference which became a part of the final document.

Finally, tentative recommendations were drafted and shared with many schoolmen and others for reactions.

A brief description of the report follows. We have dropped or combined some recommendations in the interest of conciseness.

The Findings and Recommendations

Philosophy and Objectives

Most high schools reported having written statements of "objectives and philosophy" prepared in the last five years. Teachers and administration did the lion's share of the work, while students, parents and school committee members were engaged to assist in only a few instances. It was, therefore, recommended that the Massachusetts Board of Education should establish broad educational goals which can serve as a standard for its public schools. These goals should be publicized as a statement policy.

Each school system and each school should evolve specific goals with the involvement of all persons, schoolmen, students and others, who have a stake in what the school system or school does.

High School Comprehensiveness

The low enrollments in many of the high schools in Massachusetts make it impossible for them to provide comprehensive programs on an economical basis. Ninety-two, or 30 percent, of the 305 high schools had, on October 1, 1969, enrollments of 500 or fewer students; 89, or 29 percent, between 501–1,000; a total of 181, or 59 percent with 1,000 or less. The median enrollment of the 204 regular high schools was 1,041; of the 42 regional high schools, it was 704; of the 50 vocational-technical and trade high schools it was 246; and of the nine regional vocational-technical high schools it was 436.

More than one-fourth of the 1,821 teacher respondents evaluated ". . . the adequacy of the program and services in your school in providing the various types of offerings needed by all of the students" as "Negative" or "Very Negative." Approximately, the same percentage of the 2,748 student respondents said that most of the subjects they were taking seemed unrelated to their ". . . future interests and needs." More than half of the students indicated they "Very Frequently" or "Frequently" had opportunities to study, as a part of their course work, the things they wanted to learn, the things that puzzled them; nearly half reported they "Rarely" had such opportunities.

A key serious weakness in attaining comprehensiveness in most high schools was in the lack of adequate provisions for vocational and special education.

A. High School Programs

1. The high school that is widely comprehensive and provides quality education for all of its students should have the following programs:
   a. a general education for all students;
   b. for students who plan to further their formal education in college or other post-secondary institutions;
   c. of occupational education for those students who plan to terminate their formal education with graduation from high school;
   d. a special education for handicapped students and remedial programs for students with academic deficiencies;
   e. pupil personnel services;
   f. of school activities; and
   g. with a high degree of flexibility and adaptability.
2. High schools, with enrollments of 1,200 students or more and having 100 or more students electing vocational courses, should provide for comprehensive programs including specific vocational offerings.

3. Other regular and regional high schools should extend their programs and services to become more comprehensive. When limitations of enrollment and/or resources are operative, they should have cooperative affiliation with another school to effect greater comprehensiveness in program and services.

4. Municipal and regional vocational schools should function as program centers providing vocational education. They should enroll vocationally able students from constituent schools during the upper two years of high school. These students should have made a decision to pursue a particular occupational area.

5. Vocational students should be scheduled in academic classes with other students to minimize socio-economic segregation. Students should retain their membership in the home school and should be graduated there.

6. Admission and transfer policies and practices between municipal and regional vocational schools and their constituent schools must recognize the need for students to have multiple choices and permit them to move in and out of vocational and academic programs if their educational and vocational plans change.

B. School Organization and Administration

Administrators, teachers, and students would welcome less uniformity and increased diversity in patterns of study. More than half of the 2,748 student respondents reported "There is little freedom, much regimentation" for them ". . . to exercise initiative to work independently by pursuing a variety of learning opportunities (using the library, labs, seeing teachers, etc.)." One-third of the 1,821 teacher respondents characterized the time available to work with individual pupils as "Negative" or "Very Negative."

1. Organizational and administrative decisions must have as their purpose the facilitation of effective teaching and learning.

2. Superintendents should recommend and school committees should adopt policies which clarify the role of the principal and define clearly his authority and responsibilities as the executive head of the school.

3. The principal, who must be an educational leader, should be responsible for the formulation of policy at the school level and should participate in policy-making at the district level when such policies affect the school's operation.

4. Lines of administrative and supervisory authority between the central office and the administration of the school should be clearly delineated.

5. There must be greater involvement of the faculty of the school in the development and implementation of school policies and procedures. More decisions must be made at the source of effective action.

6. School committees and teachers' associations in collective bargaining must

recognize the need in the high school for substantial autonomy, particularly in curriculum and instruction. The entire faculty must work as a professional team in individual and cooperative effort to improve the educational program.

7. The principal and his staff should share decision-making with students, parents, and other citizens when their involvement is appropriate and can contribute to better understanding and school improvement.

8. The organizational structure of the school must be released from the lock-step of time and space. Opportunities must be afforded students for self-direction and responsibility in their educational endeavors. Organizational alternatives include: flexible schedule, independent study, work-experience programs, community-service programs, extended school day and school year, classrooms without walls, and open campus plans.

9. The State Board of Education should initiate a study of the diploma requirements for graduation from high school. Emphasis upon performance criteria as measures of competence and learning rather than time spent in formal classes should be the focus of the study.

10. Organizational changes should be made that will provide teachers with adequate time during the school week to prepare for their professional tasks, to keep up to date in their subject field, to work with colleagues on instructional improvement, to confer with students and parents, and to improve evaluation techniques and reporting.

11. Alternative models to the departmental organization, such as instructional coordinators, division heads, subject and interdisciplinary team leaders, merit increased study and experimentation.

12. Schools should employ at least one-third of their teachers on a twelve-month contract because of the increasing need to have staff members operate extended year programs, to supervise special educational programs, to engage in curriculum development and research, material production, and inservice activities.

13. Schools should extend the length of the school day to increase the number and variety of educational programs and services available to students. In a number of schools, and extended day would relieve overcrowded facilities.

14. Summer school, on a tuition-free basis, should be available to all students in their local school or on a regional arrangement. The state should share the cost of summer schools.

15. The state should encourage the development of year-round programs and should finance a large part of the cost of pilot programs to determine the dimensions of the year-round school.

C. Schoolmen

Primary emphasis must be given to the preparation and the performance of schoolmen. It is essential that schools continue their search for the highest possible dividend from their investment in schoolmen and staff.

Inadequate space for teaching and for essential planning by individual teachers and groups of teachers, inadequate funds for teaching materials and equipment, a very rigid and inflexible schedule, and a limited number of teachers in some subject areas which led to excessive class size were among the major obstacles to change and improvement in one or more subject areas which were cited by the schools.

More than one-third of the 251 schools reported that the time available to the principal and the school staff for effecting change and innovation in the improvement of the curriculum and instruction was "Inadequate." Nearly one-fifth said the resources needed to effect improvements were "Inadequate." However, almost nine-tenths of the schools reported the degree of responsibility which the principal and school staff had for effecting change was either "Very Adequate" or "Adequate" and approximately the same number indicated their authority was likewise "Very Adequate" or "Adequate."

1. School committees, administrators, and teacher organizations in cooperative effort should develop staff policies and procedures that stimulate and reward increased levels of professional competence and performance.

2. Improved means of deploying staff, more differential systems of compensation, and clearer recognition of professional performance are needed areas of change.

3. Differentiation in the roles of staff members is a trend that should continue. The school should study and evaluate various models of differentiated staffing in terms of their potential to improve the quality of instruction and provide more individualized learning programs for learners.

4. Teachers must be actively involved in the development, implementation, and evaluation of any plan of differentiated staffing.

5. Every teacher should have regular access to clerical help for those routine tasks that should be assigned to clerks.

6. Deterrents to the effective performance of professional duties by individuals and groups, such as lack of time, schedule conflicts, inadequate resources, and limited work spaces should be carefully examined by the faculty. Appropriate steps to alleviate the problems should be taken at the school and/or the district level.

7. Improved communication and more effective articulation procedures among staff members in the schools and with colleagues in other schools should be instituted.

8. Each school should have an effective program of inservice education. It should be designed for the self-improvement of the faculty and the general improvement of the school. The staff should be involved in the development, functioning and evaluation of the program.

9. Inservice education should also be designed to help staff members perform more effectively their roles in the process of educational change.

10. The Department of Education must improve significantly its leadership and

service functions in professional development programs in the schools.

Schools should request and receive more assistance from the regional offices of the Department.

D. Curriculum

The over-all purpose of the educational program in our high schools is the development of a curriculum which is relevant to the student's needs, his aspirations, and to the adult roles that he may play. An adequate program affords each student a number of options for his future — a job, college entry, further vocational training, or a combined work-study program. In addition, it helps him develop his greatest potential as a person, and prepares him to assume the duties and responsibilities of an effective citizen. Recognizing the breadth of the educational needs and interests which the unselected student body in the typical school possesses, the multipurpose curriculum in the comprehensive high school can best meet the common, integrating needs of all students, and the specialized needs of the individual student.

Many promising curricular changes and innovations are underway in a large number of schools. Special programs designed to individualize instruction were reported, particularly in remedial and honors work. In English, for example, approximately half of the regular and regional high schools reported remedial and honors programs and about one-third of the vocational-technical and trade and regional vocational-technical schools indicated they were offering remedial programs.

The most significant changes in subject matter content during the past five years seemed to be related directly to improvements in comprehensiveness, quality, and relevance. The most significant changes in the instructional materials used centered on the increased use of audio-visual aids.

Taking into consideration the entire program of the school, from one-half to nine-tenths of the 251 schools assessed the effectiveness of various provisions for articulation as either "Very Effective" or "Effective." When, however, the various subject areas were considered the picture changed somewhat. In English, to cite one illustration, 45 percent of the regular high schools reported that articulation with post secondary educational institutions was "Ineffective" or "No Provisions"; 38 percent indicated that articulation with feeder schools was likewise "Ineffective" or "No Provisions."

1. The priority goals and the specific objectives of the school should give direction and purpose to curriculum planning and improvement.
2. All high schools should provide a curriculum that has these components:
    a. a program of common education for all students;

    b. a program of college preparation; and

    c. a program of occupational education, including cooperative work-study education.

In addition, all students in the last two years of high school should have access to a variety of vocational offerings in their school or at a regional center for vocational education.

3. The general education program of all students should be improved to meet more effectively the common needs of youth for competence as a person and as a citizen. Schools should define and require those areas of "common" competence which they determine are essential and should be attainable, at least at a minimum level, by all students.

4. Segments of the general education should be integral parts of the college preparatory and occupational education curricula. The extent to which an individual student takes work in general education beyond that required of all students should depend upon his abilities and interests.

5. The "general" curriculum, not general education but an alternative program to the college preparatory and the occupational education curricula, is included in the program of most high schools and enrolls many students. This curriculum must be phased out. Mounting evidence indicates that students in this curriculum would be better served by enrollment in a functional program of occupational education or in a curriculum preparatory to further education.

6. The Careers Development Curriculum is recommended by the Schaefer-Kaufman Study — Occupational Education in Massachusetts — and the MACE Advisory Committee on the Study, as the Educational program that can best realize the unmet vocational needs of many students.

7. Cooperative work-education programs should be developed in all high schools. These programs should be designed, through partnership with business and industry, to give students work experience and related education in jobs closely allied to their educational and career goals.

8. The major thrust in curriculum improvement and innovation in most high schools has been in the college preparatory program. Continued efforts aimed at the development of new offerings, including minicourses, multidisciplinary programs, and revisions in the structure and content of existing courses are recommended. The focus should be increasingly on the quality and authenticity of instructional content organized around basic concepts of themes in the various curriculum areas and on its relevance to the needs and concerns of students.

9. Many high schools should extend their offerings in the arts and humanities. In too many schools, the emphasis in the performing arts is on the development of the talents of a limited number of students.

10. Programs in independent study which afford opportunities for students to work individually or on special projects should be offered more extensively. Such programs to be effective require careful planning and active participation of the staff.
11. Programs in special education should be improved and extended in many schools. Where this is not economically feasible, state-supported schools must be established on a regional basis.
12. There should be sufficient elective offerings to permit all students to pursue in depth their academic, cultural, and vocational interests.
13. Each curriculum area should be under continuous study and evaluation, not only to determine what should be offered but what is being learned.
14. Regional centers, adequately staffed and supported by the Department of Education, and various universities should work in partnership with the schools to initiate innovations and to conduct experimentation and research aimed at the improvement of the instructional program in the schools.
15. The school should establish a program of youth volunteer activities as a part of the school's service to the community and as a means of furthering the relevance of youth education.
16. The summer school curriculum should include remedial, accelerated, and enrichment offerings. In addition, many other options should be open to students, including a variety of courses to develop specific skills and expand interest areas, work experience programs, and volunteer service-oriented activities.
17. Articulation must be improved with feeder schools within a department of the school, within a department of the high schools in the district, among departments in the school, with post-secondary educational institutions, and with business and industry.

E. Educational Media Program

The findings disclosed a number of serious weaknesses and shortcomings in the educational media program of many high schools. One illustration will highlight this point. The level of adequacy of the educational media staff to serve the needs of students and teachers was reported by the 251 schools as "Inadequate" or "Not Available" for educational media (supervisor or director) in 48 percent of the schools, for librarians in 33 percent, for library clerks in 59 percent, for audio-visual clerks in 72 percent, for audio-visual technicians in 67 percent, and for student aides in 33 percent.

Other weaknesses and shortcomings which were cited by numerous schools pertained to the inadequacy of physical facilities, deficiencies in the quantity and quality of media materials and equipment, inaccessibility of services to teachers and students, and lack of effective organization and coordination of the program.

The extent to which teachers require students to use the library should be reviewed. More than half of the 2,748 student respondents said this requirement obtained "Less Often" than "2 or 3 times a month."

1. An extended and coordinated media program should be developed in the Department of Education. Regional centers can then provide numerous resources and services to the schools.
2. Each high school should have the facilities, resources, and services essential to an effective media center. This center should have a full complement of print material and audio-visual media, necessary equipment, and services from media specialists.
3. Budgetary allotments for staffing, for the purchase of printed and audio-visual materials, and for the purchase and repair of equipment must be increased considerably in most high schools to ensure quality educational media services.

F. Guidance Program

Improved organization and coordination of the guidance program are needed in many high schools and school systems. Approximately 60 percent of the schools reported a student-counselor ratio of one counselor per 300 students or more. Many counselors are involved in numerous quasiadministrative and clerical tasks with the result that they do not have sufficient time to perform their professional responsibilities. The number and quality of consultative and referral resources in the school system and in the community are often inadequate, and services which are available are frequently not used effectively. Sixty-eight percent of the parent respondents stated that additional information about the guidance program in their school would be of particular interest to them. Fifty-five percent of the students indicated the counseling and guidance they had received was "Extremely Helpful" or "Some Help," and 44 percent reported "Very Little Help," "Not Helpful at All," or "Haven't Received Any in This School." About one-third of the students said they would like to talk to someone more often than now concerning ". . . such matters as selecting courses, going to college, getting a job."

1. The State Board of Education has approved the establishment of a Bureau of Pupil Personnel Services. This Bureau should have adequate staffing and resources to provide leadership and services in the implementation of many of the recommendations proposed in the MACE study, "Pupil Services for Massachusetts Schools."
2. Guidance is more than an auxiliary service. It should function as an essential school service rather than on the periphery of the school's educational program. The guidance staff should cooperate with teachers in the develop-

ment of an instructional program that is responsive to the needs and interests of all students. Similarly, teachers should be involved in the improvement of the functions and services of the guidance program.

3. There should be a clarification of the roles and functions of the guidance staff, including differentiated assignments to counseling, group work, consulting, and research responsibilities. The counselor is a staff specialist and should only perform those services expected of a professional worker.

4. Guidance programs purport to serve all students. Each school should continually assess the adequacy and effectiveness of individual and small group counseling. Improved services in vocational information, occupational counseling and placement must be available.

5. Systematic follow-up studies of students after they leave school must be conducted. Results of these studies should be analyzed, not only to appraise the guidance program but to supply important data relative to needed curriculum changes and the degree to which the educational goals of the school have been achieved.

G. Student Involvement

With more freedom and encouragement to express their opinions, students in our high schools are increasingly articulate concerning what they like and dislike about their education. From the student questionnaires and from group conferences in the 33 representative schools, the Study staff learned a great deal about how many students felt and what they thought. Above all else, the students wanted to be respected for what they were. They wanted to be involved in more meaningful ways in the school and in the community. They wanted to learn what they consider relevant and important. Their concerns about the school were identified with (1) the breadth and relevancy of the curriculum; (2) the adequacy of the staff; (3) the scope and quality of the student activity program; (4) administrative rules and regulations, particularly those related to dress codes and discipline; and (5) the machinery for participation in school government.

1. The State Board of Education approved Guidelines for Student Rights and Responsibilities. These suggested guidelines should be carefully studied and appropriate policies and procedures adopted in the individual school and school system.

2. School committee policies should clarify and delineate the authority and responsibility of the principal in sharing decision-making with students.

3. Administrative regulations and procedures should reflect a greater concern and sensitivity to the need to involve students in the development, revision, and execution of such regulations and procedures.

4. Policies and procedures for handling student activism should be established with participation by school committee members, administrators, teachers, parents, and students.
5. Students should become more active in learning, more self-directive, and more involved in planning their own education.
6. Faculty-parent-student advisory councils are functioning very successfully in many schools. The organization of such groups should be extended. The study found that there are many serious concerns and numerous problems related to the administration and supervision of the S.A. program. The expansion or reduction of the program is an issue that continues to confront most administrators and their staff. Sixty-three percent of the schools reported that from 61–100 percent of the students participated in at least one activity. The schools reported the major deterrents to student participation were the work schedules of students, limited physical facilities, lack of student interest, and bus schedules.

Thirty-five percent of the student respondents indicated they considered participation in student activities to be "Very Valuable and Useful" or "Valuable and Useful," and 41 percent said "Perhaps of Some Value." The students freely expressed their opinions about the deficiencies and limitations in the programs in their schools. They cited the lack of diversity and balance in the program, the need for wider student participation, and the necessity for greater student involvement and responsibility in the development, organization, and supervision of the program.

1. The program of school activities should be designed to contribute to the optimum development of students. They should be afforded the maximum opportunity to plan, direct, and evaluate the activitivities program.
2. The program should be so diversified and comprehensive that each student has an opportunity to pursue in depth existing interests and talents and to develop new ones.
3. The program should be extended to include more community-service activities.
4. Activities should be supervised by qualified sponsors who are employees of the school.
5. An appraisal study in each school is recommended to determine the present status of the program, the study team should have representatives from the administration, staff, students, parents, and persons from youth-serving agencies in the community.
6. More financial support from school district funds should be provided in many schools to ensure the achievement of a more diversified and balanced program of student activities.

H. School Community Relations

There is a widening communication gap in many communities between what the school people seek to achieve in the education of youth and what the public think the schools are accomplishing. There is an increasing concern on the part of the public about higher educational expenditures and how these increased costs are related to improved programs and services. Parent respondents in the Study stated that they are largely dependent upon local and area newspapers for their information about education. More than two-thirds of the parents surveyed stated they would welcome more information about the guidance program. Approximately half of the parents said they would welcome more information about courses offered and their content, major problems in the school and district, and recent changes and improvements.

Less than five percent of the parent respondents indicated that they were "Very Frequently" or "Frequently" involved in programs conducted by the school, including planning and evaluation. Yet, significantly, approximately three-fourths of the parents stated that the quality of their high school was either good or excellent.

Thirty-five percent of the 251 schools reported they sponsored, in their programs of community-school-parent relations, special advisory committees, 29 percent a Parent-Teacher Association, and 22 percent a Lay Advisory Council.

At a time when many writers are outdoing themselves in proposing alternatives to or radical changes in secondary schools, Michael choses to advocate, as did James Conant some years' earlier, what he perceives as the tried and the true.

The reader will find some of the same issues raised, using the context of guidance, in the next chapter.

12 Guidance: An Unguided Program

Such attitudes have caused Jerry Hannah, the family counselor for the Center, to conclude that "there's more so-called delinquency caused by teachers, parents and social workers than by children themselves." – Tom Wicker

The public has come to expect therapy to reduce tension and improve adjustment. Many professional workers concur . . . but this has never been the function of therapy; it is the precise opposite. Therapy arose rather to help people maintain a taut psychic balance. . . – Edgar Z. Friedenberg

Counseling by whatever name is important in the lives of students. The complexities of a world, reeling under a variety of changes and living close to future shock, intensify that importance. Students today spend longer in school, consequently invest more in schooling, and yet end up being increasingly uncertain about what lies ahead of them. Counseling is intended to help the student take on the present and gird him for the future.

Those on the pupil personnel circuit find the abyss between intent and performance awesome. Reasons for this condition differ or, more likely, are ignored. While no one argues the importance of student counseling and guidance, all bedlam breaks loose when the discussion turns to how the counseling function is to be performed.

Almost every Advisory Council study director has found it necessary to look at those who teach in our schools. Reform in schools means reform in teacher preservice and inservice activities.

Even definitions, functions and processes are obscure or tenuous in the pupil personnel world. Much to their credit, Drs. Gordon P. Liddle and Arthur M. Kroll make an effort to produce some workable guidelines for the reader:

> Within education the two complementary functions of instruction and pupil personnel services have emerged, each working from a different point of reference. The teacher seeks to communicate the experiences of others as they relate to the child. Pupil services seeks to involve the child in an examination and analysis of his own experiences as they relate to his feelings and to the decisions he is making.

A further word of clarification is in order to avoid leaving any unnecessary impression of a separation between the instructional and pupil services programs. As it is true that teachers and administrators are also concerned with the person-

271

ality development of the child and therefore also contribute to the aims of the pupil services program, so also does the pupil personnel worker frequently influence the instructional program. Yet, *central* responsibility for the development of intellectual power and cognitive growth rests with the instructional program; *central* responsibility for adequate self-concept development by pupils rests with the pupil services workers. It is important to restate the fact that the pupil personnel services are designed for *all* pupils and are not limited to — although they do include — work in remedial, corrective, disadvantaged, and crisis-oriented situations.

The various services that meet the aforementioned criteria, and thus are grouped under the pupil personnel services 'umbrella,' work in different ways. As Edward Landy has phrased it:

> Essentially the ways in which pupil personnel services workers have tried to accomplish their mission are three: first, the direct person to person approach in which counseling, therapy, persuasion, advice and authority are used; second, the special group approach for instruction about occupational and educational opportunities, for instruction in self-appraisal, for orientation to the school, for counseling about normal developmental problems, and for other group therapy; third, an effort to use the total personnel and machinery of the school to create a school climate conducive to the development of good mental health and strengths within the individual pupil which will enable him more readily to meet and overcome constructively those problems and difficulties in the process of growing up which might otherwise lead to his acquiring antisocial, or neurotic, or even psychotic solutions.[1]

Even to express the guidance function as Liddle and Kroll have so well done is not to resolve how guidance should be carried out. Regular teachers continue to be viewed by many as the only counselors who make sense, with teaching and guidance considered as inseparable acts. Given the propensity of schoolmen to develop educational specialities, it should not surprise us that pupil services, including guidance, became (1) a set of specialties; (2) full-time functions; and (3) something performed mostly in high schools. The authors point out that in their visits they heard much about titles, status and training and little discussion of objectives, program effectiveness and basic issues.

It would help in better understanding this chapter to state the professional orientation of the authors in a somewhat detailed way. At close to the end of their report, they write:

1. Pupil services must expand beyond the present problem-centered emphasis and intensify its efforts in problem prevention, research, and the application of social and human science findings to school programs.
2. Expansion of pupil services should be approached from simultaneous examination of needs at all levels (preschool, elementary, secondary, and post-secondary) rather than from a separate examination of needs at

each level. Current program development in Massachusetts reflects concern for student development at distinct age levels; e.g., school counseling has been restricted largely to secondary school levels.

3. Although the data on planning and organization of early child development programs are unclear and incomplete, there seems to be sufficient evidence to justify increased emphasis on program development in the preschool and early school years. Certain developmental and corrective measures should be available to families before their children reach school age.

4. Pupil services workers have two major functions: (1) the facilitation of classroom efforts to educate children; and (2) the development of personality and good mental health. Although the schools have traditionally concentrated on the former, the development of cognitive abilities, they must also be concerned with affective and interpersonal growth (including capacities for effective human relations, decision-making, flexibility, and adaptability, etc.).

5. Schools should consider incorporating more extensive segments of the social and behavioral sciences (sociology, psychology, anthropology, etc.) into the school curriculum. Pupil services workers should explore ways in which they might influence such development. They might serve, for instance, as resource persons to teachers, enter into curriculum discussions, or lead semiinstructional groups; throughout such instruction, student needs should be a major focus.

What should pupil personnel services include? Early in their report, Liddle and Kroll offer nine operant services which are necessary in the pupil personnel family.

1. Child Study Service
2. Pupil Admission and Placement Services
3. Pupil Progress Monitoring Service
4. Student Guidance Service
5. Student Counseling Service
6. Remedial and Special Help Service
7. Staff Consultation Service
8. Parent Consultation Service
9. Feedback to the System, Research, and Experimentation

Liddle and Kroll feel these services should commence with the school's first contact with the child and his parents during the second or, at the latest, the third year of life. Parents, particularly those whose education has been limited, need to be assisted in becoming a more positive influence in the education of their children. At present, this pattern has not been widely accepted, except in the case of extremely handicapped children such as the blind or the deaf, but with the growth of kindergartens, Head Start programs, and experimental programs in disadvantaged areas, a precedent is being set. Society is moving in the direction of preventing learning and mental health problems in the first years of the child's life when children and families are most amenable to change.

Some crude screening of a pupil typically takes place in the most enlightened schools when the child first becomes a pupil, roughly at the age of five. If at that time or subsequently, someone sees signs of learning difficulties in human relationships, a more careful study of the child can begin. Information needed to understand the child would be gathered and evaluated, a method of proceeding established, and periodic follow-ups made to check progress and to make modifications in plans. While the pupil services team would have a major responsibility in this process, instructional and administrative personnel, and others, would also be involved.

Dr. Richard Rowe's study (Chapter 8) for the Council on Early Childhood Education, the family and child-care, explores other aspects of early services for children. We suggest you read his report for his thoughts on the need and uses of early screening of children. Agreement over the need to pay attention to children far earlier than we have hitherto done is apparent in both Rowe's position and the position of Liddle and Kroll.

The Study Methods

Three major approaches were employed. First, individual interviews were held with a wide cross-section of practitioners and administrators. Second, questionnaire surveys of two types were distributed to investigate organizational/ supervisory relationships and practitioner background and functions. Third, a number of regional conferences for practitioners and other interested persons were held around the state.

Many individuals and small groups across the state met with the study staff to discuss issues confronting pupil services and to share varying opinions on further development of programs. Later, these people and others were asked to react to a tentative set of recommendations.

A random sample of school districts, stratified on the basis of (1) size of pupil enrollment; and (2) per pupil expenditure, was selected for investigation. Liddle and Kroll wanted to examine pupil services programs in large, average, and small communities with high, average, and low per pupil expenditures.

A survey of all school personnel employed in New England was conducted during 1966–67 by the New England Educational Assessment Project. Data collected on Massachusetts pupil services personnel from this study were made available by the Research Division of the State Department of Education. While useful, there are limitations in the value of the data. It is apparent that many pupil services workers did not respond, and no analysis was done to determine how representative the final respondent group is. Also, no category for school adjustment counselors existed, so those workers either selected counselor or social work categories. The project funding ended in June 1969, with little liklihood that further analysis of these raw data will take place, particularly if no spokesman for pupil services exists to point out the need for such work.

Other recently completed studies have extended the understanding of guidance practice in the state. Leonard Farrey, of Worcester State College, in late 1968 compiled data on the organization of guidance programs throughout the state. David Armor, of Harvard University, has similarly assembled extensive interview and questionnaire data on a sample of 100 counselors in the metropolitan Boston area in his recently published book, *The American School Counselor.* [2]

The superintendent of schools in each of the 26 districts sampled was asked to cooperate with the study staff by designating a liaison person and asking his pupil services staff to complete the questionnaires. A questionnaire, oriented toward investigating organizational and supervisory relationships, was sent to all 493 pupil services workers in the sample districts. The return was over 70 percent. A second questionnaire, specifically oriented to each counselor's background and functions, was sent to a 25 percent random sampling of all counselors in Massachusetts. Sample districts were visited at least once by project staff members, and six districts were selected for more intensive visits and interviewing of teachers, administrators, students and pupil services staff.

No attempts were made to evaluate either the performance or effectiveness of individual staff members or the relative effectiveness of district programs. Instead, Liddle and Kroll sought to understand the purposes of the services in each setting and the program organized to fulfill these purposes. Particular emphasis was placed on understanding the most effective means of utilizing the various pupil services specialists involved.

Four regional conferences were held in eastern, western, southern, and northern Massachusetts. Each conference assembled from 65 to 120 persons, representing the various pupil services groups, school committee members, principals, superintendents, representatives from state agencies and professional associations, and other interested persons from the area school districts. The conference format typically included an opening presentation of the study, a panel-audience discussion, and small group discussions. The study staff also corresponded with persons in over fifty of the most active and progressive cities and states to determine what pupil services investigations or developments were underway or had recently taken place in their areas.

Finally, the proposed recommendations were sent in tentative form to over 2,500 pupil services workers, all school superintendents and school committee chairmen, and other interested persons in Massachusetts for their reaction and comments. The revised recommendations reflect many of the comments returned by these people.

Liddle and Kroll viewed the following specialties as composing pupil services:

1. Attendance supervisors — who should identify and help children with problems.
2. Counselors — who should be counseling generalists in elementary and secondary schools.
3. School adjustment counselors/social workers — who should combat delinquency.
4. Speech and hearing therapists — who should work with children with impairments in speech, language and hearing.
5. Psychologists — who should perform a variety of roles and specialties are useful in schools.
6. Nurses — who should represent preventive medicine and help with health education programs.

Findings

Exact figures being unobtainable, Liddle and Kroll made the following estimates of those involved in pupil services:

Supervisors of attendance, 75;
School psychologists, 125;
School adjustment counselors, 188;
School counselors, 1, 360;
Speech and hearing therapists, 325; and
School nurses, 1,000.

Since the state has almost 400 school districts, it is apparent that only two categories of pupil service workers potentially could be available in every school system. The estimated raw numbers reveal a state-wide "worker-pupil" ratio of 1 to 455 while the National Association of Pupil Personnel Administrators advocate a ratio of 1 to 125.

The backgrounds of counselors, school psychologists and adjustment counselors, as reflected by experience and education, were found to be markedly similar. Most began their careers as teachers and had a master's degree in education. Liddle and Kroll felt that their present positions, therefore, were job switches which represented promotions.

Pupil personnel workers, while expressing no deep-seated concerns with their jobs, did not appreciate the amount of clerical and supervisory obligations assigned them. More seriously, they revealed a lack of guidelines and policy formulations to assist them in their tasks. In conversations with the authors, pupil services workers typically discussed status, roles and procedural matters rather than performance, evaluation and other difficult issues facing them. In short, Liddle and Kroll sensed complacency and superficiality.

A particularly useful section in the final report to the Advisory Council bears approximate recapitulation. The section deals with how the functions of various state agencies relate to pupil services. Because it is unusual for guidance studies to encompass the activities of such agencies, that section, in an abreviated form, follows.

Department of Labor and Industries

The Department of Labor and Industries contains two divisions whose functions are relevant to pupil services. The first is the Division of Apprenticeship Training which is responsible for apprenticeship training and for manpower development and training: the former function involves cooperating with industry in developing, expanding, and improving training standards so that the Commonwealth's industrial needs for skills will be met; the latter function provides on-the-job training and experience other than apprenticeship. The second division is the Division of Industrial Safety which is responsible for the enforcement of labor standards and administers the labor laws governing, among other things, child labor.

Department of Mental Health

Numerous functions related to pupil services are performed within the Department of Mental Health. The Division of Mental Health Clinics provides evaluation and diagnostic services for children, including assessment of the type and degree of a child's emotional illness by means of interviews with the child and his parents, and recommendations for treatment; psychiatric treatment services for children, including short-term or long-term psychotherapy, sometimes accompanied by drug therapy, for the child and/or his parents; group therapy services for children, involving psychotherapy in a group setting for the child who needs help in his peer relationships; services for severely disturbed children, including residential placement which provides the child with supervised activity and therapy by placing him full time in a combination home-school-hospital; day-care centers, involving the profusion of daily remedial education, psychiatric treatment, and supervised activities.

Within the Division of Legal Medicine, Liddle and Kroll found two relevant programs. First, the Court Clinic provides psychiatric services to the courts in order to (a) practice and develop in the court setting techniques for the treatment of offenders; (b) investigate the psychiatric meaning and sources of antisoical behavior; (c) train psychiatrists and other professional persons so that they may provide service to the courts and work in a judicial setting; psychiatric services within courts; and (d) raise the professional level of probation and help increase its efficiency and scope. Second, the Youth Service Program provides evaluative services, consultation services, and treatment to the Youth Service Board, and renders youth after-care treatment and case work services at its clinics.

The Mental Health Education Service of the Department of Mental Health provides an educational therapy center which has programs for children and adolescents as well as programs which enable adult inpatients to continue their education. Teachers on the staff have regular consultation with psychiatrists, psychiatric social workers, and nurses. The Mental Retardation Services include diagnostic evaluation, treatment, and educational and recreational programs on both an inpatient and an outpatient basis; services to families of the mentally retarded; consultation services to community agencies serving the retardees; and staffing, including services of all helping disciplines. The Consultation Service makes consultants from the disciplines of psychiatry, social work, and psychology available for integrating and promoting community mental health.

Other related programs within the Department of Mental Health are: the Drug Unit, a small diagnostic, evaluation, and intensive treatment program which provides inpatient and follow-up care and treatment to drug addicts; the Screening Unit, a crisis-oriented program that offers 24-hour emergency help with referrals and follow-up treatment when necessary; the Adolescent Unit, an educational, vocational, and social program which includes diagnosis, evaluation, and treatment for patients up to 18 years of age; the Social and Recreational Programs, including summer camp, athletic, and recreational programs and social clubs.

Department of Public Health

Functions related to pupil services are performed in a number of the programs of the Department of Public Health. Several of those programs are in Maternal and Child Health Services:

a. Services for Crippled Children which provides financial assistance, case finding and complete medical services and care — orthopedic, cardiac surgery, plastic surgery, speech therapy, cerebral palsy, chronic diseases, etc. — for all Massachusetts children with crippling or potentially crippling conditions;

b. Child Health Supervision which develops guidelines for local programs, provides inservice training and consultation, conducts special projects for children, and compiles statistical data;

c. School Health Program which provides inservice education, leadership for developing guidelines for local programs, and consultation, assists in accreditation, coordinates agency efforts, and compiles statistical data;

d. Habilitation Centers for Preschool Hard-of-Hearing and Deaf Children which helps children develop normal speech at an early age so that when they reach school age they may attend a regular public school rather tha a residential school for the deaf; and

e. School Vision and Hearing Conservation Program which, being preventive in character, seeks to discover slight but real differences in vision and hearing so that proper medical attention can be arranged.

The Division of Food and Drugs in the Department of Public Health maintains a Drug Control program largely concerned with the enforcement of harmful and narcotic drugs, wholesalers, and nonmedical users of hypodermic needles; and arrest and prosecution of drug law violators. A comprehensive dental program is also available. Finally, the Massachusetts Committee on Children and Youth has a Delinquency Project which reports to the Governor on action that is needed with regard to juvenile delinquents.

Department of Public Welfare

The Division of Public Assistance in the Department of Public Welfare maintains two programs which have particular relevance to pupil services. The first, Aid to Families with Dependent Children, provides, with federal funds, financial assistance, medical care, and social services to needy families with dependent children (up to 21, if in school − up to 18, if not in school). Financial assistance includes cash payments for food, clothing, shelter, etc.; medical care includes any such care recognized under state law and is provided through direct payments to hospitals, physicians, dentists, etc.; social services include counseling, help in finding better housing, referral to community resources, and homemaker services.

The purpose of the second program, the Work Experience Training Program, is to help prepare the people on welfare, by such means as vocational testing, guidance, and placement, to become self-supporting through gainful employment.

Division of Employment Security

Many programs of the Division of Employment Security relate to the operation of pupil services programs in schools. The General Job Placement function provides a complete placement service for all individuals who are seeking employment and includes occupational counseling, testing referral to manpower training courses, or selective placement services when they are indicated. Job openings for all types of job skills are solicited from employers. General Youth Services provides selection for and referral to job openings, testing, counseling, referral to manpower training courses, and other special services for youths between the ages of 16 and 22. This service is available in all the employment offices of the Division. The Summer Camp Placement function, centralized in the Boston Professional Employment office, provides selection and referral of applicants for summer employment at summer camps. It accepts applications from qualified camp counselors and instructors and job openings from any summer camp.

The General Employment Counseling Program provides individualized or group counseling sessions for individuals, among whom might be school drop-outs, parolees, or the physically, mentally, or emotionally handicapped, with the objective of helping these individuals to become more employable. The Employment Counseling School Program maintains cooperation between the local offices of the Division of Employment Security and the local school systems throughout Massachusetts in providing employment counseling, job referral and placement, or referral to manpower training courses to students who are entering the labor force either on a full-time or part-time basis.

For those so disadvantaged in the labor market that they are, or are likely to become, habitually unemployed, the Human Resources Development Program offers specialized services such as identification of those persons and their needs, referrals for training or education, rehabilitation and medical aid, counseling and placement, and supportive on-the-job and follow-up services. Human Resources Centers, located in several large Massachusetts cities, provide intensive and individualized services, including counseling, testing, and manpower training.

The Apprenticeship Training Program promotes and develops apprenticeship training programs for the youth of the Commonwealth and for its industries. It promotes standards necessary to assure the proper training of apprentices and brings together management and labor for the development of formal apprentice-ship programs. The Division of Employment Security cooperates with the Division of Apprenticeship Training in interviewing and placing qualified appren-ticeship applicants.

The Experimental and Demonstration Projects Program is integrated with the Community Action Program and other social service organizations to provide counseling, case work, and other special training assistance for disadvantaged youths who have patterns of delinquent behavior and other groups who are alienated from normal manpower institutions in order that they may adapt to the work environment and hold gainful employment. The TIDE (Testing, Inform-ing, Development, and Evaluation) Program is designed to encourage potential school drop-outs either to continue in school or to prepare for a gainful occupa-tion. Accepted trainees are paid to attend a concentrated group counseling course which aims at helping them to understand the problems that dropouts face:

> The Neighborhood Youth Corps . . . provides federal funds and technical assistance to nonfederal governmental agencies or departments and to provide nonprofit organizations for establishment of work training programs for unemployed youths 16 through 21 years of age who need work experience to qualify them for full-time employment. The federal government will defray up to 90 percent of the costs of these programs, including wages paid to enrollees.

The Job Corps, by providing vocational training, remedial education, and work experience, helps to develop in disadvantaged youth the attitudes and skills necessary for finding and holding gainful employment and for becoming productive citizens.

Professional Roles and Responsibilities

Liddle and Kroll found pupil services staff far more passive than, in their judgment, they had any right to be. Counselors were reacting to problems and not playing a preventive role. More individual work with students, and less screening and diagnostic testing, appeared necessary. Pupil services workers should be more in evidence in the classrooms and in helping to establish the "climate" of schools. They should be more involved in curriculum development especially in the behavior and social sciences and in health. Counselors should thrust themselves more into current issues, such as racism, sexual mores and drugs.

In short, Liddle and Kroll raise fundamental issues concerning the professional role and responsibilities of guidance and health workers. Not only should the specific tasks of pupil service workers be recast, but their general impact on how schools are run and what happens in them should also concern them.

Pupil Services for Massachusetts Schools

The study directors discuss the scope of pupil services by expressing the need.

Growing up in the Bay State is not the same experience for all children. Her rural youth often lived isolated from the mainstream of thought and the diversity of values and opportunities; her suburban youth often lived under pressure from high educational-vocational aspirations and competitiveness; her urban youth often live in a climate of hopelessness surrounded by overexposure to the negative aspects of life. The instructional programs provided by the public school systems were meant to equalize opportunities for all these children by transmitting to them the experiences of others and the precepts of their society and by promoting cognitive growth. However, the report states, as society became more complex and as the need for a highly educated citizenry grew, it became more apparent that the accomplishment of this goal had grown beyond the scope of the instructional program alone. What was needed was a program that would complement, facilitate, and help equalize the instructional program by individualizing the educational process where needed and by fostering healthy personality development. To this end, the various services that have been incorporated into the pupil services program were gradually introduced into the school, a process in which Massachusetts often took the lead.

Pupil services fulfills a facilitating function within the school by helping each student to achieve his maximum personal and educational development. It provides both preventive and corrective services designed to meet the unique needs of each student regardless of his level of ability, achievement, or adjustment. A coordinated pupil services program provides organization, direction, and leadership to a group of more-or-less related professionals who, each in his own area of competency, are attempting to assist the student in identifying, clarifying, and perhaps modifying his understandings of himself, of the world he lives in, and of his relationships to this world and the others who live in it. Pupil services workers help the student to assess himself, to make suitable decisions regarding his educational and vocational plans, to overcome personality defects, and to develop strengths that will enable him to live with himself and others in positive, constructive ways. Among the specialists who perform this function are attendance supervisors, counselors, social workers and adjustment counselors, speech and hearing therapists, psychologists, and nurses.

Liddle and Kroll describe the necessary role of the school counselor. By providing an accepting, nonevaluative relationship and sometimes information which is personally relevant, the school counselor in the secondary schools helps the student to understand himself better in his interactions with his environment and the people in it.

The counselor in the elementary school has similar aims but typically spends a larger share of his time working with the primary help-givers, the parents and teachers, rather than with the pupils themselves.

Next, they define the tasks of the school Adjustment Counselor/Social Worker. In Massachusetts, the school adjustment counselor performs the services that are done by specialists with titles of "school social worker" and "visiting teacher" in other states. This function was initiated to combat delinquency by developing preventive programs for predelinquent children and their families.

The speech and hearing therapist, Liddle and Kroll continue, works with children who have an impairment in speech, hearing, or language. The therapist teaches a series of skills that will enable each child to communicate as normally as possible.

Psychologists, the study directors point out, were introduced into the schools for the purpose of testing children for placement in special education classes. That role may now be filled by a psychometrist, while the psychologist performs such tasks as individual counseling with seriously distrubed children, developing preventive mental health programs, providing staff consultation services aimed at individualizing instruction on the basis of students' learning styles, establishing with teachers attainable behavioral objectives and methods of reaching them, and conducting research on school climate and pupil progress.

And what about the school nurse? She is concerned with the preventive aspects of medicine and the health education program. She is concerned with all students and, when a problem comes to her attention, she acts as a referral agent to other members of the pupil services team. Moreover, as a nonthreatening communicator with parents, the nurse is often the school's best liaison with the home.

Principal Recommendations

The following twenty recommendations for the improvement of pupil services in Massachusetts have been drawn from the original list of 69. The scope of their study did not permit them to deal with every issue facing pupil services; Liddle and Kroll, instead, concentrate on several primary areas of concern and on realistic, feasible courses of action.

A. State Department of Education (SDE)

1. The State Department of Education should establish a Bureau of Pupil Services within the Division of Curriculum and Instruction.

2. The State Department of Education should develop a consulting structure whereby leaders from exemplary school districts and universities, employed by the state on a per diem basis for up to 30 days per year, would be available to school districts.

Leadership in the form of strong State Department of Education representation has never been available to pupil services in Massachusetts. One of the main causes of this lack has been the diffusion of responsibility for the various services, a diffusion that extends not only throughout the SDE, but also into several other state departments. A Bureau of Pupil Services, Liddle and Kroll state, would unify state-level leadership and would thereby engender cooperative efforts toward improvement of pupil services in Massachusetts. The functions of this Bureau would include regulation, such as guidelines stressing desired outcomes rather than rigid standards; service, such as provision of consultation, newsletters, and in-service training; development, such as implementation of a long-term master plan for pupil services in Massachusetts; and public support, such as political activity, general public relations, and interagency relations. Included in this new Bureau should be:

a. School counseling — transferred from the Bureau of Elementary and Secondary Education — the guidance and counseling function has unique aspects which warrant leadership separate from the instructional functions;

b. Speech and hearing — transferred from the Bureau of Special Education — since these services are already included in pupil services structures at the local level, such a transfer at the state level would facilitate communications and cooperation on and between the state and local levels;

c. School Psychology — transferred from the Bureau of Special Education —

responsibility for school psychology is presently extremely vague, and it is vital that definite leadership be designated.

d. School adjustment counseling – transferred from the Division of Youth Service – those persons currently responsible for state-level leadership should also be transferred and given similar responsibilities since it is important that this program retain its unique identity and purpose and not be merged with elementary guidance;

e. Vocational-technical school counseling – transferred from the Bureau of Vocational Education – this service should be considered part of the larger school counseling function since separation encourages fragmentation in terms of professional identity;

f. School nursing – in cooperation with the Department of Public Health – several public health personnel must be assigned to the new Bureau on a part-time basis of substantial proportions so that they will interact as fully participating colleagues on the staff of the Bureau in integrating health services and health education with the other pupil services and with education;

g. Attendance – at present there is no individual on the state level who has responsibility for this service, and definite leadership must be assigned.

Since the Department will probably never be able to employ the most expert administrators and practitioners in pupil services, a structure whereby individual leaders throughout the state are hired by the state on a short-term consultative basis would enable the state to serve as a clearing house in providing those communities desiring program development with access to creative leaders. University personnel might be employed for field services for the equivalent of one day per week. Program directors and practitioners in school settings might be released for a week or two per year to be loaned to communities where programs are in early stages of development in order that they might serve as resource personnel. In these and similar ways, the SDE could circumvent the lack of staff and expertise that its inadequate personnel policies necessitate.

As soon as services in the proposed Bureau become more fully developed, the Commissioner of Education should elevate the Bureau to Division status, on an equal level with the Division of Curriculum and Instruction.

B. Organization of Services

1. Every school district, regardless of size, should assign to one person the responsibility for administration of the various pupil services.

2. School districts should develop a master calendar which presents the sequential steps involved in initiating and staffing a pupil services program.

3. Liddle and Kroll strongly support the state trend toward unification of school districts, but recommend that the minimum size be 5,000 students.

In Massachusetts, only about thirty of the 389 districts have begun to move toward coordination of pupil services by assigning a director or coordinator of these services; in New York, over 250 of the 760 districts have already appointed directors.

If a school district is to realize optimum return for its investment in pupil services for its youth, administrative coordination and management are required to facilitate effective functioning, and leadership is mandatory for systematic improvement of services. Someone must keep the attention of a group of more-or-less related professionals on such central questions as, "What seems to be the problem? What more do we need to know to arrive at a tentative educational diagnosis and treatment plan? What responsibility will each member of the pupil services and instructional team take?" These jobs are seldom accomplished unless someone in each school system is assigned this responsibility.

Small systems may decide to make this coordination a part-time assignment, but in most communities the demands of the position will warrant a full-time person. This person should be given authority commensurate to his responsibility; he should be directly responsible to the superintendent of schools and be a member of the superintendent's advisory council or cabinet. The administrator should have tenure in the system, probably as a practitioner in one of the pupil services, but he should not have tenure as an administrator. "New occasions teach new duties," but when they do not and other skills are needed the school committee and superintendent should be free to bring in a new leader.

Schools should develop schedules for program development and, before programs are fully staffed, should establish priorities for the functioning of staff already employed within the system. A master plan will enable communities without pupil services programs or with minimal services to initiate or gradually expand services on a planned basis as rapidly as their resources will permit. Such a scheduled approach may help avoid haphazard and expedient decisions. We cannot define schedules or outline priorities for all communities, since they should reflect the unique needs of each community; moreover, when community needs change, priorities should also change.

C. Primary Orientation of Services

1. Pupil Services must expand from a problem-centered to a prevention-oriented approach. Today's schools offer corrective and remedial services at retail, while they create problems wholesale. Services are created and continue to function as reaction to problems rather than preventing problems that responsiveness to student needs and social climate could foresee. Why, Liddle and Kroll ask, have we not really listened and heeded what students have to say, rather than waiting until their frustrations erupt over an issue which specialists then hasten to remediate?

The authors feel that schools in most communities have added pupil services to help meet needs at particular educational levels without taking into consideration the fact that education is a lifelong developmental process. Although the data on planning and organization of early childhood development programs are unclear and incomplete, there seems to be sufficient evidence to justify increased emphasis on program development in the preschool and early school years. Since so many lifelong learning patterns are set by the age of three, bringing children into educational programs in the second and third year of life may be the only way to prevent thousands of children who are capable of being normal from being condemned to unproductive lives.

Pupil services workers should not only take a more active role in building programs to develop positive mental health, but should also continue their more traditional role of facilitating the learning process; medicine, while concerned with prevention, environmental health, and research, does not shut down its hospitals and clinics. In both preventive and remedial efforts, pupil services must become more concerned with institutional structure and the means it does or does not employ to help students learn how to handle problems. The draft, drug use, student protest, racial conflicts, sexuality, and the like confront young people with the necessity for major personal decisions. Pupil services should be vigorously confronting these issues and pressing for organizational and curricular modification where it is needed. It would appear that a variety of conditions in schools which contribute to the production of emotional problems are largely ignored, the assumption being that misbehavior or underachievement results almost entirely from the child's having a lack of motivation or a defect in personality. Tracking is an example of a procedure which has dubious value for the development of students. Pupil services workers, as well as educators in general, must begin to question whether or not the advantages of tracking and similar procedures are worth the price.

D. Support Personnel

1. Individual school systems, training institutions, and the State Department of Education should jointly identify tasks which may be performed by persons with less or different training than professionals. As society becomes more complex and the demand for specialists increases, schools must be willing to experiment with use of support personnel who can free specialists for jobs appropriate to their levels of competency. Liddle and Kroll's investigation has shown that considerable professional time is spent in clerical, routine administrative, and similar duties for which the professional is overtrained and therefore overpaid.

There are presently no national guidelines regarding the use of support personnel, although schools in other states offer excellent precedents for their use. In health services, for example, a support person has been used to screen eyes and ears and perform clerical tasks to free the nurse for more health education activities. In the area of attendance, routine attendance checking and most aspects of the school census can be done by support personnel, leaving activities such as liaison with families and with the court to the professional.

In relation to the particular needs of their community, each school staff must identify the specific tasks which support personnel can perform and, in cooperation with the State Department and training institutions, plan for both preservice and inservice training and see that open-ended career ladders are created. Schools must recognize differences in training, competency, and effectiveness while establishing teams and career lines. To date, personnel policies in education are particularly primitive. If staffing moved toward a more flexible placement of staff according to competencies, with a concomitant flexibility in salary ranges, the retention of more highly skilled specialists would be possible.

E. Staffing Standards

1. Each school system should develop a reasonable schedule for achieving a pupil services worker-student ratio of 1:125 within ten years. The ratio of pupil services staff to pupils is nearly impossible to standardize because of the number of variables involved. Pupil services staffing patterns must be considered in the context of the total needs of a system. The program objectives and goals, the severity and frequency of special needs and problems, and the instructional staffing and facilities available, all influence pupil services staffing decisions.

In the absence of objective evidence regarding staffing criteria, suggested standards for staffing must be based on the judgment of experienced practitioners. The National Association for Pupil Personnel Administrators recommends one pupil services worker for each 125 or 135 students. For a district of 10,000 pupils, NAPPA recommends a pupil services staff of 70–80. Massachusetts cities and towns should establish reasonable schedules for achieving such staffing patterns. Liddle and Kroll suggest as minimal standards the following schedule for achieving staff pupil ratios:
— in two years — 1:400
— in five years — 1:250
— in ten years — 1:125

Since Massachusetts communities are so different in their needs, Liddle and Kroll urge a periodic review by each community of its organization and staffing arrangements to ensure that all pupil services functions are adequately staffed to achieve the objectives of the program. Such reviews should occur no less frequently than every five years.

F. Training and Certification

1. Pupil Services specialists should become certifiable only upon completion of a training program which has been approved by an appropriate accrediting agency.

2. A wide range of short-term, limited focus, nondegree training conferences should be developed through the joint efforts of the school districts, the professional associations, and the State Department of Education.

The authors' conception of the future pupil services worker includes the belief that he will not be acquiring solely a highly specified body of knowledge, but rather a general understanding of social and human processes. No stipulated set of courses has been proven best to accommodate such understandings, although it does appear that intensive on-the-job experience with good supervision is very helpful. Liddle and Kroll would therefore encourage training programs to explore a variety of means which include practical experiences to achieve these ends.

Certification upon completion of an accredited training program is further recommended because Liddle and Kroll feel that course-based certification requirements would only rigidly reflect current practice (which has not yet arrived at a unified set of services of demonstrable effectiveness), instead of encouraging use of a wider variety of personnel and approaches.

G. Financial Support

1. The minimum appropriation allocated to pupil services should be somewhere within the range of 5 to 8 percent of the total budget of a school district.

Although Massachusetts is one of the wealthiest states, because the State Government and the governments of a majority of the towns have assigned low priority to public education, the result has been inadequate education in many Massachusetts schools. In per capita income, Massachusetts ranks ninth in the nation. Only five states have more personal income per child of school age than Massachusetts; only two have a smaller percentage of households with incomes of under $3,000; only three with incomes under $5,000. There are only seven states which have a smaller percentage of their population to educate in either the public or parochial schools; yet, because of the generally low priority given education in the state, Massachusetts ranks twentieth among the states in per-pupil expenditure for education. It spends 1 percent less than the national average and 69 percent less per child than New York State, the leader. In fact, Massachusetts spends the smallest percentage of personal income on public education of any state in the nation. (On the other hand, despite this state's high average income level and small number of poor families, only four states spend more per capita for public welfare; none spends more per capita for fire protection; and Massachusetts ranks eighth in expenditures for police.)

Pupil services is probably affected more by this situation than are the other aspects of education, becuase it came into the schools relatively recently and because it is not in the business of providing the basic foundation for education — a classroom for every child and a teacher for every classroom. As a result, Massachusetts as a state does not meet the nationally recommended level of support for pupil services, and full appropriations for already existing programs would go far toward improving pupil services in the state. In recommending that the minimum appropriation be 5 to 8 percent of the total school budget, Liddle and Kroll underscore the fact that they consider this a minimum support level and hope that many communities will wish to exceed this level.

H. Professional Associations

1. Each of the professional association must be more active in improving the standards of the pupil services they represent and in finding ways of getting those standards adopted.

The associations should undertake an extensive critical analysis of their present relationships with the Department of Education and the State Legislature, and efforts should be made to identify and create means of gaining a more effective voice in establishing professional policies and regulations. The Massachusetts School Counselors Association has taken the lead in recognizing the need for and establishing a strong legislative committee, and it is important that every other organization do the same. Legislative committees should be expected to react to relevant bills submitted by other groups, prepare drafts of needed legislation, and develop closer working relationships with legislative committees on education and mental health.

High standards of competency should be the continuing concern of the professional associations; a practitioner who is judged to be competent by the criteria of his colleagues should be considered to be certifiable by the state. If more flexible and creative programs are desirable, the associations must lessen their concern with course-based certification requirements and focus their attention instead upon the approval or accreditation of training programs, each of which can explore a variety of means to achieve common ends. Training institutions must then be encouraged to take a greater responsibility in screening persons for training and certifying their readiness to practice as professionals.

School psychologists, social workers, speech and hearing therapists, and nurses holding a bachelor's or higher degree are in short supply throughout the state and, in some cases, are in particularly short supply in areas beyond metropolitan Boston. The associations, in cooperation with universities, should endeavor to develop new or enlarged training programs to alleviate these shortages.

Practitioners in all specialties have agreed that a need exists for a spokesman for the entire pupil services team. There is no professional organization which can speak for pupil services as a whole. The Massachusetts Personnel and Guidance Association does have the potential for representing the whole pupil services team if its leaders are attuned to the needs of the larger group and if other specialists are willing to support an association which has its foundation in guidance and personnel work. Professional organizations should discuss the matter with their constituencies and with other organizations to find an effective and practical means of joint representation.

I. Evaluation of Services

1. Pupil services must be recognized as a distinct subaspect of education that must be evaluated by its own distinct criteria. One of the most notable deficiencies in pupil services in Massachusetts has been the lack of evaluation of program efficiency. Nearly all existing services have been granted face validity and considered successful on the basis of the subjective judgments of their proponents. To correct this untenable situation, the professional subgroups in pupil services must develop statements of program objectives which are more tangible, more operational, more subject to measurement.

Some of the state professional associations representing the various pupil services should be commended for developing position statements, preparing certification recommendations, and keeping their membership informed. Local information and stimulation provided by high-quality newsletters such as those distributed by the Massachusetts School Counselors and the Massachusetts Personnel and Guidance Associations are badly needed. Strong future action in promotional activities, public relations, and legislative consultation is recommended. Many pupil services workers claim that their services are vitally important and that they are doing a good job, but these same people also complain that teachers and parents and school committee members do not see the need for such services and don't understand them. While it is true that Americans have been slow to recognize their children's right to a healthy environment and to accept the responsibility for providing it, it is questionable that professional associations have done all they could do to sell their services to the public.

The associations have had minimal impact in influencing program development in laggard communities. Because professional organizations have the most reliable and extensive knowledge on who the most skilled professionals are and which are the best programs, they should assume greater leadership and exert pressure in promoting program development, perhaps by playing a broker role in sending the best practitioners and administrators to systems in need of help. Furthermore, the professional associations should cooperate with such evaluative groups as the National Study of Secondary School Evaluation, groups which up to now have not given extensive recognition or review to pupil services, in developing evaluative criteria. Only then can meaningful evaluative procedures be implemented.

Concern for evaluation should center on ends rather than means; for example, achievement of pupils is more important than attendance of pupils. Involving students and teachers more extensively in determining the types of services to be offered and in evaluating the degree to which the goals are met would help provide the more specific feedback that is badly needed for judging the effectiveness of pupil services.

J. Program Development

1. Attendance supervisors should accelerate their trend toward professionalization and a social work orientation.

2. In order that nurses may become school staff members and equal partners on the pupil services team, they should be paid for out of school budgets, should receive salaries commensurate with their education and experience, and should have training in health education.

3. Secondary counselors should provide comparable services for both college-bound students.

4. Massachusetts counselors are urged to accept the excellent policy statement proposed by the School-College Relations Committee of the Massachusetts School Counselors Association in regard to writing recommendations for college applicants.

5. Research on the effectiveness of pupil services as currently practiced must be pursued more vigorously, and an attitude of experimentation must be fostered if workers are to develop programs based on procedures of demonstrable effectiveness.

Attendance supervisors are experiencing an increasing professionalization in Massachusetts and throughout the nation as better trained personnel are employed and as the profession moves from the truant officer to a social work approach, but there is still much need in the profession for upgrading. For instance, although state law requires each town to employ an attendance supervisor, there are still some towns which have not done so; having an individual responsible for attendance in the new Bureau of Pupil Services will help correct this situation. Also, professional qualifications and certification requirements for attendance supervisors are minimal, and while the level of training should ultimately be that of a social worker, for the present, it should be at least that of a school adjustment counselor; the new Bureau should work closely with the Massachusetts Supervisors of Attendance organization in upgrading skills and providing inservice training. Local supervisors need to develop more creative and systematic procedures for dealing with situations that lead to student suspension and for using the time the student is suspended for seeking new approaches; they need to develop closer relationships with courts and court-related agencies; they need to become more involved in improving student work-experience programs.

Although nurses are potentially qualified for a variety of roles on the pupil services team, they have not been accepted as full members and have, in fact, often been regarded as "second-class" personnel. One remedy for this problem would be for the Departments of Public Health and Education to cooperate in working out a plan of development whereby all nurses will become school staff members, paid for out of school budgets. Since nurses are generally less well paid than other pupil services workers, another solution might be to pay them salaries commensurate with their education and experience. In conjunction with this, the nurse who will be working in the schools should receive preparation different from or beyond that required for general nursing practice; nurse training programs in the state should grant greater recognition to the needs of the school nurse.

Counselors at the secondary level in Massachusetts schools are spending a disproportionately large amount of time on college admissions counseling. In many schools, counselors coordinate school visits from college representatives, process college application forms, write student recommendations, and the like. In some schools, the guidance director hand-carries his students' admissions applications to local colleges to discuss each case with the college admissions officer. Counselors appear to have a much stronger grasp of posthigh school educational opportunities than they have of employment trends and local employment opportunities. The availability and quality of college information in high schools also appears to be much higher than that of occupational information and local employment announcements. Counselors must make their services more equally available and suitable to students of every ability level. Whereas in many communities college admissions counseling is seen as the counselor's "bread-and-butter" work, actually many college admissions concerns now exclusively his domain could be handled quite effectively by paraprofessional information specialists, in conjunction with recently developed technological support systems for assisting in college decision-making. This would free the counselor for working with all students at a level more appropriate to his training.

Liddle and Kroll observe that although many larger school systems are now establishing fulltime research sections, responsibility for research and for modifying programs as a consequence of evaluation typically falls under the auspices of pupil services, because counselors and psychologists generally have more training in research than do other school personnel. Pupil services workers must become more vigorous in pursuing research on the effectiveness of their programs, for students, when questioned, state that they do not perceive those programs as having significant influence on their future plans. Research should be conducted not only on student characteristics and needs and the effectiveness of the pupil services programs designed to meet those needs, but also on the structure and climate of the total educational institution. Evidence on the relative effectiveness of existing practices is badly needed.

Greater program flexibility and experimentation are required if pupil services workers are to develop programs based on procedures of demonstrable effectiveness. Many pupil services programs in Massachusetts have succumbed to the phenomenon which Edwin Bridges of the University of Chicago has called the "Xerox syndrome in educational change." By accepting the basic existing school structure as a "given" and by limiting themselves to one model in providing services, workers have brought about a proliferation of similar programs that reflect little of the environment in which they exist. The very group that holds the greatest promise for affecting institutional change apparently continues to be concerned primarily with helping the child develop within a structure, rather than concerning itself with the relative merits of the structure itself. Pupil services must abandon this "Xerox copying" trend and their contentment with existing, unproven programs and move toward the development of truly creative innovations, i.e., new unproven programs. We have no quarrel with traditions or practices that have demonstrable effectiveness; our quarrel is with the tendency to defend or imitate as-yet-unproven programs.

K. Adult Services

1. Community colleges should develop career-planning information and counseling programs for adults, and Massachusetts schools should become more creative about opening their facilities during nontraditional time periods so that their personnel will be available to adults.

Although a variety of services is available to adults in Massachusetts, educational counseling has not been widely available because continuing education for adults, as we have noted in Chapter 7, has only recently shown signs of stiring. With the continued development of community colleges, Liddle and Kroll urge the establishment of adequately staffed counseling offices and career information centers in these facilities; since they generally must follow an "open-door" admissions policy which results in a notably heterogeneous student body in terms of ability, previous achievement, career goals, age, and motivation, demonstrable effective guidance and counseling programs are needed to help these students toward achieving their educational goals. More specifically, assistance is needed on problems of admission, self-evaluation, career exploration, study skills, program selection, and transferring to other schools.

High school counseling offices might also utilize some of their staff for extended services during the evening hours and on Saturdays. There is little justification for continuing to have all staff members in pupil services work the same schedule; for example, having a small segment of the staff employed from 1:00 to 9:00 p.m. would facilitate service to parents and other interested adults. They recognize the organizational inertia that must be overcome if schools are to employ professional staff for such nontraditional schedules. Yet, the need is present, and heavy evening college enrollment will attest to that need.

First Steps to Implementation

Implementing the major proposals will require the concerted activity of many groups and individuals. Some actions are underway. Others must be started to assure a continuing structure for implementation. The following are specific actions which Liddle and Kroll feel should be initiated.

1. The Commissioner of Education should designate a task force composed of representatives from training programs, professional associations, local communities and the State Department of Education to design specific plans for a Bureau of Pupil Services within the State Department of Education. This task force should convene in the Spring 1970 and should have specific plans ready for presentation by late Summer. Liddle and Kroll encourage the Commissioner to grant financial support to this task force so that it will be able to utilize consultants from the National Association of Pupil Personnel Administrators and the pupil personnel services units in the New York and Connecticut Departments of Education. Within the next three years the proposed Bureau should undertake the proposed development activities outlines in the report. Within five years, the Bureau should be removed from the Division of Curriculum and Instruction and be established as an autonomous Division, headed by an Assistant Commissioner. Special attempts should be made by the Commissioner during 1970 to recruit a vigorous pupil services administrator to provide leadership for these efforts. A salary in the range of $20–23,000 would be required to attract such a person, and the study directors are willing to assist in such a recruitment effort.

2. The professional associations in pupil services should initiate, in conjunction with university training programs, a Task Force on Goals for Pupil Services. This task force should be convened in 1970 to consider issues such as the above, with particular focus on (1) education for the promotion of mental health; (2) potential contributions of the social and behavioral sciences to education; and (3) pupil services programs for preschool and early elementary age levels. Specifically, we urge the president of the Massachusetts Personnel and Guidance Association to accept responsibility for convening this task force.

3. To assist in developing more integrated school and community services, the Departments of Public Health, Education, Mental Health and Welfare will have to cooperate more fully at the state level. The School Health Council which was formed for this purpose and was to be composed of commissioners of each Department is almost defunct as an effective innovative structure; it should be transformed into a Children's Services Council, and the commissioner of each Department should appoint one representative to this policy-making group.

4. Liddle and Kroll urge the Division of Maternal and Child Health of the Department of Public Health to convene, in 1970, a conference of nurse educators, school nurses, public health officials, state-level supervisors, and pupil services administrators to deal with training issues related to school nursing, as well as with the larger issues involving the incorporation of the health services into the pupil services administrative unit. This proposed conference should select a working committee that would be established for a two-year period to formulate policy regarding the future of school nursing.

5. Legislation should be drafted to provide for the transfer of the School Adjustment Counseling Program from the Division of Youth Service to

the proposed Bureau of Pupil Services within the State Department of Education.

6. The proposed Bureau of Pupil Services in the State Department of Education should stimulate universities and cooperating school districts to further pursue training and employment of support workers.

7. The professional associations should initiate cooperative activity with the universities and the State Department of Education to establish better methods for governance of the professional subgroups in pupil services.

8. Existing laws relative to part-time employment of persons under sixteen should be changed to permit students under sixteen to obtain part-time work experience in a variety of work settings from which they are now excluded.

9. All training programs should offer practicum or internship experiences in work settings, and efforts should be made to initiate the development of interdisciplinary internships.

10. Certification of school psychologists should revert to the position maintained several years ago when applicants were certified jointly by the Departments of Education and Mental Health.

11. School systems should arrange for pupil services workers to have access to regular consultation with qualified professionals who are not members of the school staff. Inservice training programs could be determined by the expressed needs of the workers in a community.

So much for pupil services. The reader must realize that pupil personnel services are really a very new enterprise. Few schools went in for such luxuries before the second world war. Massachusetts had eighteen full- or part-time guidance persons in the public school system in 1942.

Pupil personnel workers too often operate in a kind of no-man's land. They are not close enough to students, not powerful with school administrators, remote from parents and often know nothing about the communities in which their charges reside. Meanwhile, the challenge to guide, counsel and serve children and youth grows daily.

The story of much that happens in education is the story of people. We have saved for the last one of the Council's first studies dealing with an age-old problem: how to qualify teachers to enter classrooms.

13 Qualifying the Teacher

All other reforms are conditioned upon reform in the quality and character of those who engage in the teaching profession. – John Dewey

There is no backdoor entry to a genuine profession. – Lucien B. Kinney

A trinity of schoolmen, programs and facilities comprise the educational system to serve students. Of these, schoolmen are by far the most important. Yet, we are little closer in our efforts to assure competent teachers than we were in the days of Socrates.

A succession of societies have, indeed, overlooked few barbarisms in qualifying those who enter classrooms. At times, and often in some weird combination, the privilege of teaching has been dependent upon sex, religion, manners, nepotism, examinations (name all the bodies of water in the United States), or the ability to sing.

Today, we are told that things are better, but recently the voice that says so has lost the timbre of surety. A surprising number of thoughtful people who care really doubt if we've made any progress worth reporting since the hemlock drinking bacchanals in Athens. So much for revery.

Closer to home and the tempo of Lindley Stiles' report, we find the short-comings of the present system of qualifying teachers by certification, described by Roy A. Edelfelt. Dr. Edelfelt, Director of the National Commission on Teacher Education and Professional Standards, an offshoot of the National Education Association, states:

1. The certification of teachers as we presently operate is incomplete and inadequate.
2. We have passed the era when certification based on college credits reported by paper credentials was adequate.
3. Able people are not attracted to or enticed to stay in teaching by present certification standards and procedures.
4. Certification should distinguish levels of competence, and responsibility for it should be fixed with several agencies.
5. The profession itself must become more directly responsible for the certification of teacher competence.[1]

Dr. Alvin P. Lierheimer, Director, Division of Teacher Education and Certification in New York State, reinforces Edelfelt's final point:

297

Today certification means course prescription by the state, completion of which is offered to the public as a guarantee against incompetence in the classroom. If that is really the purpose of certification, is the state the best agency to carry out the function? Certainly, the state is pretty far removed from the individual teacher whose incompetence is being protected against and a Martian observer could well ask why the decision about competence is not made by someone who knows the teacher.[2]

Evidence of thinking and action upon improved approaches to the twin issues of teacher education and certification will be presented in this chapter. Stiles' proposals, shortly to be presented, develop a process which makes sense and should, if fully implemented, help put a better teacher in the classroom.

The Development of Certification

Certification gradually became the way states chose to qualify schoolmen. In New England, certification done on the basis of oral or written examinations began in colonial times. School committees did the certifying and there was no appeal from their decision. Ohio is considered to be the first state to certify teachers, beginning in 1825. Vermont, in 1845, made teacher certification one of the duties of its newly created county superintendents. Arbitrary examination was slow to be overthrown. By 1900, only two states required college graduation in order to teach. Nineteen hundred is viewed, however, as a watershed year as large numbers of normal school graduates began to enter the field. These graduates were certified directly in New York without further examination. Still, high school graduation remained adequate to teach in most states until the 1930s. Not until 1964 did all states require a bachelor's degree to teach.

Meanwhile, certification was becoming a state function. Between 1898 and 1940, the number of states vested with authority for certification grew from three to forty-two. Today the states, usually through the Boards of Education, control the certification system, although in some instances, the authority is shared.

The sense of administrative tidiness, if not complacency, which developed as certification was centralized and certain basic requirements became standard (e.g., a degree) has been questioned by many and held in ridicule by some.

Meanwhile, the quickening pace to state certification remained a casual stroll in Massachusetts. Until 1951, as in colonial times, localities made up their own qualifications. Not until 1956 did certification in the Bay State require various patterns of course work. A grandfather clause exempts thousands of teachers — anyone who had ever taught prior to 1951 — from all subsequent certification requirements. The requirements, as Table 13-1 illustrates, are minimal.

In practice, certification in the Bay State became a real fandango. To teach science in a senior high school requires a bachelor's degree with six courses in science and four in education unless the teacher:

Table 13-1

Ranges of Credit Requirements for Certification

	Secondary School				
	Liberal Arts Courses[a] (Sem. Hrs.)	Major Field (English) (Sem. Hrs.)	Minor Field (English) (sem. Hrs.)	Professional Education – not including student teaching (Sem. Hrs.)	Credit Requirement for student teaching (Sem. Hrs.)
High for Nation	100	48	36	24	8
Average for Nation	54	28	22	14	6
Low for Nation	–[b]	15	6	9	2
Massachusetts	–[b]	18	9	10	2

	Elementary School			
	Liberal Arts Courses[a] (Sem. Hrs.)	Specialization in a subject field[b] (Sem. Hrs.)	Professional Education – not including student teaching (Sem. Hrs.)	Credit Requirement for student teaching (Sem. Hrs.)
High for Nation	100	36	30	8
Average for Nation	50	24	19	6
Low for Nation	–[c]	–[c]	5	2
Massachusetts	–[c]	–[c]	16	2

[a]May include some courses taken for specialization.

[b]Required in eight states.

[c]Not specified.

Source: Lindley J. Stiles *Teacher Certification and Preparation in Massachusetts* Massachusetts Advisory Council on Education June 1968 pp. 51, 52.

1. is covered by the grandfather clause and taught something prior to 1956; or
2. has a minor in science and teaches that subject half time; or
3. has no science course work and teaches that subject one-fifth of his teaching time; or
4. teaches on a waiver; or
5. is employed in violation of the regulations since no enforcement mechanism exists; or
6. is employed in a private school.

Other events have led to another look at certification. Minority groups have felt that certification works against their entry into teaching. A new cadre of teachers called "paraprofessionals" has an unclear relationship to certification. And emerging teaching fields and educational alternatives (early childhood is an example of the first and off-campus vocational experiences of the second) clouds the certification process. Richard Rowe's Study for MACE is helpful in viewing certification for teachers of preschool youngsters (see Chapter 8).

Lindley Stiles entered the scene at a pregnant time. He also decided early to tackle both certification and its partner-preparation for becoming a teacher.

Study Methods

Lindley Stiles felt that certification should serve three major purposes. First, it must protect its historic role against incompetence. Second, it should help in distinguishing levels of professional competence. Last, it ought to protect against professional obsolescence. The study director came to Massachusetts with a vast fund of experience and a number of ideas. But he was not at all certain about how it would all come out. He was, however, determined to treat teacher education, and how it was performed, as a part of certification.

A twenty-five member study committee, drawn from various segments of lay and professional elements, played a key role in all phases of the study. It advised the study staff throughout and helped interpret needs and possibilities. The Committee hald hearings to gain the views of representatives of key educational groups. It also sponsored three statewide Advisory Conferences. The first, held in November 1967, dealt with *Teachers for Massachusetts – 1980;* the second, in December 1967, focused on *The Reform of Teacher Education;* and the third, in February 1968, was concerned with the *Certification of Teachers.* Each of these conferences was attended by about 200 representative leaders from schools and colleges, including academic as well as pedagogical specialists, various education agencies and organizations as well as lay groups. Both public and nonpublic education were represented throughout. The general format entailed hearing the views of selected consultants on each subject and then providing opportunities in small discussion groups for reactions and suggestions. Key ideas and issues were recorded for analysis by the study staff.

A broader effort to obtain ideas and information involved the use of an attitudes inventory that was sent to random samples of educational personnel and citizens in Massachusetts. The following groups were sampled: various public and nonpublic schoolmen, School Committees of public schools, presidents of Parent-Teachers Associations, and college professors of education and liberal arts. In addition, all staff members — a total of 60 — above the rank of supervisor in the State Board of Education were polled.

Numerous personal interviews were held by the study director and staff with individuals and committees who represented a number of public and nonpublic education agencies and organizations. Proposals for certifying and preparing particular types of schoolmen that had been developed by several professional groups and institutions were studied. Also, information was obtained about practices in other states and nation-wide proposals. Stiles writes: "All in all, this is perhaps the most extensive study of teacher certification ever undertaken by any one state. The large-scale involvement of professional and citizen leaders is unique to studies of this type."[3]

Data on the sources, supply, demand and quality of the state's educational personnel came from analyses of trends over five years. Information was obtained from 190 Superintendents of Schools in Massachusetts and also from a study made of the qualifications of teachers certified during this period. In addition, visits were made to fifty-one colleges and universities — both public and non-public — that offer comprehensive programs of preparation for those entering education.

The Findings and Recommendations

The study director and his staff mused over the issues and dilemmas of certification in Massachusetts (and in consequence elsewhere as well). Stiles was much concerned about mastering the full scope of teaching and collected quantities of information to use in mastering the full scope of teaching and collected quantities of information to use in making his final report. His report, in essence, follows.

Massachusetts schools — both public and nonpublic — confront deficiencies in educational personnel that are multidimensional. The quality of preparation is usually minimal and the variety of specialized personnel required to staff different kinds of schools is insufficient. Many teachers do not match the jobs that need to be performed in schools. He indicated that the numbers of experienced teachers available and retainable, are too small to guarantee stability in many school programs.

Predictions, wrote Stiles, suggest that even with the increases in college graduates expected, the competition for the kinds of high-ability persons needed for teaching will perpetuate the shortages of schoolmen. Improved programs of recruitment, certification and preparation, as well as better salaries and working conditions are vital and will help. They likely, he stated, can do little more than to assure that education will not fall further behind in the race for talent. To staff schools in ways that help assure quality education for all pupils ways must be found to tap other sources of manpower, such as paraprofessional workers, specialized technicians, and professionals in cognate fields. In addition, he felt, full use must be made of educational technology to supplement the teacher.

Standards and procedures for certifying educational personnel in Massachusetts are inadequate. They fail to guarantee that all licensed to practice in various educational positions will be competent. Neither do they differentiate between levels of professional performance nor protect against professional obsolescence. The emphasis on specific course requirements tends to block experimental efforts to improve teacher education in colleges and also repels able persons from entering educational work.

Qualified and experienced teachers from other states, and countries, find it difficult or impossible to be licensed in Massachusetts. The present certification system may operate, Stiles sensed, to reduce the supply and in some ways the quality of educational personnel.

Massachusetts was the first state to develop college programs specifically for teaching, and some institutions of higher learning located within the state continue their pioneering. There are plenty who simply replay the past for each new class of teachers-to-be.

In general, Stiles continued, a gap exists between the kinds and quality of educational personnel being prepared and the needs of schools that now confront many new educational problems. Problems of preparation are not eased by the absence of job descriptions and general agreements relating to differentiations in levels of professional performance, as well as the lack of opportunity for advancement of instructional personnel. Failure to devise systems to keep educational programs up to date and self-renewing represents an added limitation on programs of preparation for the educational professions.

Improving the certification and preparation of educational personnel in Massachusetts will require a partnership among all concerned. Strong leadership to pull it together is necessary at the state level. Much can be accomplished within the unique traditions of local responsibility prevailing in Massachusetts, but a state structure is needed to assure minimum standards for educational personnel and to provide colleges with financial assistance to encourage them in improving programs of preparation. The Massachusetts General Court will need to provide appropriate legislation and certain kinds of financial support. A suitable agency needs to be developed by the State Board of Education to provide leadership, to achieve appropriate involvement of various concerned gruops, to develop common minimum standards for certification, to encourage experimentation to improve teacher education and to administer certain kinds of financial support. Authority to act and freedom from politics — both from within and outside the education professions — are essential to its success, along with effective staff leadership.

Stiles' writing style is mild but every so often he indicates that he knows where the thumb-screw is.

This study was predicated on the assumption that it is futile to expect that changes in certification will automatically produce needed reforms in the preparation of teachers. Documentation of institutional apathy and addiction to the status quo was offered by Dr. Alvin P. Lierheimer, consultant to the project, in describing a New York State experiment in pioneering teacher preparation:

> Even when colleges are reminded of their freedom to experiment with new cirriculums for teachers, they appear reluctant to do so. Colleges frequently talk rebelliously about the choking effects of state requirements but few of them ever propose and justify significant departures.[4]

Basing certification on demonstrated performance rather than accumulated college credits, as this study recommends, will release colleges and universities from ineffective state prescriptions for the preparation of educational personnel. Such action, in and of itself, experience tells us, will not automatically bring the reforms needed in teacher education. It can only free institutional faculties to plan together with elementary and secondary schools, as well as the other education agencies, ways to develop the various kinds of professional abilities needed.

Since Massachusetts, perhaps more than other states, depends on both public and private institutions for its supply of educational personnel, cooperation between and among them is deemed imperative. Academic scholars, responsible for the general education and subject specialization of teachers, must collaborate with specialists in education. Close partnerships are required between colleges and elementary and secondary schools if educational progress on certification is to be achieved. Various segments of the teaching professions, especially classroom teachers, are also required to assume greater responsibilities. Organizations that provide leadership in professional affairs should be involved as well as members of school committees and other interested lay groups.

Despite widespread dissatisfactions with present practices in teacher certification and preparation — for differing reasons, incidentally — rather general support prevails for the following basic assumptions upon which Stiles based his report:

> 1. Certification of educational personnel is considered an appropriate and essential obligation of the state. Its function, as in the licensing of professionals in other fields, is to attest the professional competence of various types of educational personnel and to protect the public, e.g., pupils in elementary and secondary schools, from incompetent practitioners. A permit to practice — which is what certification represents — should be a guarantee of performance above defined minimum levels for particular kinds of professional responsibilities. Continuation or renewal of a license should carry with it assurances that professional competence is being maintained.
> 2. The need for educational personnel to be prepared — both by study and

supervised clinical practice — for specific kinds of professional assignments is incontestable. The academic study of a subject in college for given lengths of time is no reliable guarantee of adequate professional performance. Suitable preparation of educational personnel should provide for the mastery of appropriate knowledge and intellectual abilities and also for the development of performance skills. The latter requires extensive supervised clinical practice in assignments for which preparation is aimed.
3.   Those who teach should take major responsibility for establishing and maintaining standards and for judging qualifications for professional practice. In doing so, the objective should be to attract and retain in teaching competent persons, rather than arbitrarily to limit the numbers certified.
4.   The state, in this instance the Commonwealth of Massachusetts, shares responsibilities with local school districts and institutions that prepare educational personnel to define the kinds and qualities of personnel required and to provide a constant and adequate supply of well-prepared candiates to staff educational programs in both public and nonpublic schools.[5]

What Stiles writes is exciting conceptually. He insists on a responsible definition and then he pegs down where that definition leads. It leads to a demanding set of relationships between and among all of those who share in making and needing competent teachers. Above all, teachers must play a key role in determining who will enter the profession. What he begins by shading in, he enunciates clearly in his major recommendations:

A. Staffing Schools in the Future

1. Staffing patterns should be redesigned to make full use of various education specialists, professionals in cognate fields, fully qualified professional personnel, beginning or associate teachers, interns in training, and paraprofessional personnel. Schoolmen making full use of educational technology should be in charge of the diagnoses and prescriptions for instructions of all children with the various teaching services performed by appropriate members of the instructional team.

2. School personnel policies, such as employment qualifications, staffing assignments, salaries, promotion and tenure, should be configured to new differentiated uses of teaching talents. A key objective should be to provide opportunities for appropriate professional contributions, advancement, financial reward and professional prestige within the instructional team.

B. Certification

1. Certification should be based on knowledge — of general background, subject specializations and pedagogy itself — and professional performance, rather

than transcript records, as at present. A citizenship requirement should be dropped or made more flexible, since it denies schools the services of teachers from other countries.

a. In changing the approach to certification, those presently employed and those in preparation should be protected. They should be permitted, however, to seek certification – initial or renewal – under this plan.

b. The present permissive policy regarding certification of teachers in nonpublic elementary and secondary schools should be maintained. It is hoped, however, that the proposed new approach will attract their voluntary participation.

2. Standards of professional performance require development by representative leaders in each field, including scholars in academic and professional areas and teachers in elementary and secondary schools as well as school officials. The objective should be to assure that all licensed to professional practice will have initial and continuing minimum acceptable performance ability at the level certified.

3. Procedures for certification need to provide alternate ways to qualify that while assuring adequate performance by all, will accommodate differences in individual and institutional programs of preparation. Examples suggested in Stiles' report include approved institutional plans for judging knowledge of subject matter and ability to perform, certification by examination that includes performance tests – administered either by preparing institutions or state credentials committees – and professional judgments by qualified colleagues in schools and colleges in accordance with established standard approved procedures.

4. The number of licenses issued for various kinds of professional practice, e.g., teaching, counseling or administration, must be kept to a minimum with specialized qualifications of educational personnel attested by academic, experience and performance records rather than by license.

Four levels of licenses are suggested: *Internship licenses* for those in training; *Associate Teacher Licenses* for beginning teachers; *Professional Licenses* for those who demonstrate ability to handle professional assignments independently of supervision; and *Educational Specialists Licenses* for high-level teachers and those with particular kinds of specialization, such as counseling, supervision, administration or professionals in cognate fields, e.g., sociology, psychology, or systems analysis. (Licenses for paraprofessional workers, Michael feels, will likely be unnecessary unless they are required for employment or otherwise by the practice in a trade field.)

5. Provisions should be made for periodic renewals of licenses, without reference to tenure, based on demonstrated maintenance of scholarship and professional competence. Suggested renewal points are: *Internship Licenses* – annually; *Associates Teacher Licenses* – every three years; *Professional* and *Educational Specialists Licenses* – every seven years.

C. Teacher Preparation

1. The General Court should appropriate and allocate, through the budget of the State Board of Education, funds to provide adequate conditions for clinical training of educational personnel, e.g., for student teaching, internships and practicums. Such funds should be used primarily to reimburse school systems that reduce the loads of interns and personnel who supervise those in training (e.g., critic or cooperating teachers) and to provide state personnel to assist preparing institutions in making assignments of prospective teachers to training stations in schools. Some funds may be needed also to reimburse colleges and universities for training school supervisors of clinical practice.

2. School systems and institutions that prepare teachers should be encouraged, and provided financial help, to experiment with ways to redesign systems for student learning in elementary and secondary schools and the preparation of needed personnel — particularly in situations in which existing programs are inadequate such as in inner-city or rural schools.

3. Academic professors in colleges and universities, with the assistance of specialists in education, as well as teachers and administrators in elementary and secondary schools, should work to redesign the liberal arts and subject specializations of prospective teachers to make such studies relevant to the life of the times as well as a base for scholarly development. Attention should be given to preparing teachers who have mastered new curriculum theories and who are well grounded in the academic discipline.

4. Local school systems, either individually or in cooperation with each other and/or colleges and universities, should provide plans for the in-service development of educational personnel that will ensure continued learning and professional competence.

5. Graduate programs of preparation for specialized educational personnel needs to:

   a. make full use of the academic resources of cognate fields;

   b. avoid the national pattern of overemphasis on professional courses, and

   c. make appropriate use of supervised internships to develop and verify needed professional skills.

In general, the master's degree should be aimed at improving teaching competence.

D. State Leadership

1. The General Court should authorize or request the creation of a new subdivision by the State Board of Education to which should be delegated full responsibility for the certification and improvement of educational personnel Such a mechanism might be termed a "Commission for Certification and Prepar-

ation of Educational Personnel" (see Figure 13-1). It should be accorded quasi-legal powers to perform its duties and given such other protections as may be needed to guard against political pressures. Its composition should provide for appropriate representation of able and respected public school teachers and administrators, various scholars and key laymen representing school committees or possibly other citizen groups concerned directly with education. The commission should have authority to develop standards and procedures for the certification of educational personnel, to certify to the State Board of Education all eligible for licenses, to provide leadership, to coordinate resources for the improvement of teacher education and to administer the plan of support for

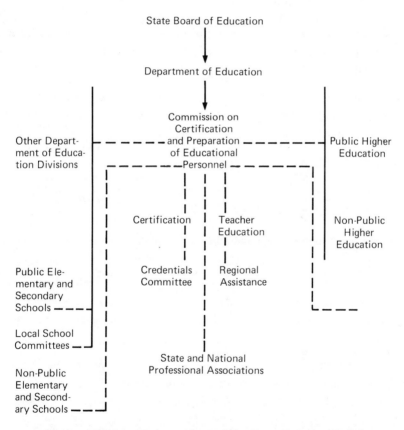

Figure 13-1. Proposed Relationships of the Commission with Other Agencies. Source: Lindley J. Stiles, *Teacher Certification & Preparation in Massachusetts*, Massachusetts Advisory Council on Education, June, 1968, p. 113.

clinical training proposed in the report. In carrying out its responsibilities, the Commission should be empowered to employ professional staff and to create and support various credentials committees needed to establish standards in the different areas of specialization.

2. Departments of the State Board of Education should continue to project the requirements for educational personnel, issue official licenses for various kinds of educational practice, maintain comprehensive data on the personnel licensed, and to assess the effectiveness of educational programs.

3. Increased financial support should be provided for the preparation of teachers in the state colleges and the University of Massachusetts. The objective should be to make the programs of preparation, particularly in the areas of general education and subject specializations, equal to the best in the private colleges. At the present time, Massachusetts state colleges spend less for a student annually to prepare teachers than do better public high schools to educate their students. Compared to the support provided for the preparation of other professionals, teacher education is woefully undersupported, in both public and nonpublic institutions.

4. The Massachusetts Advisory Council on Education should continue to provide assistance to the Massachusetts Legislature, the State Board of Education, the Board of Higher Education, and other agencies to help enact the recommendations of this report. The Committee that has helped with this study might be asked to continue to provide assistance until the new Commission has been activated.

E. Taking Action on the Recommendations

1. The Massachusetts General Court should modify present certification statutes to:

a. discontinue or otherwise provide greater flexibility for the citizenship requirement;

b. authorize or request the State Board of Education to establish the proposed Commission for Certification and Preparation of Educational Personnel, and

c. transfer complete responsibility for certification to a new division within the Department of Education.

It will need, also, to appropriate funds to support the new program of certification and the provision of adequate resources for clinical training and experimentation to improve the preparation of schoolmen.

2. The State Board of Education needs to take the following steps:

a. Establish the Commission for Certification and Preparation of

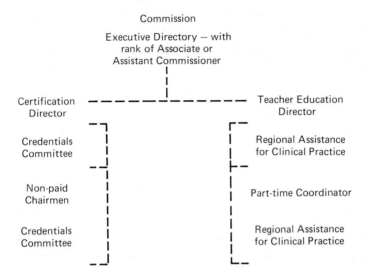

Figure 13-2. Suggested Organization and Staffing for Commission.
Source: Lindley J. Stiles, *Teacher Certification & Education in Massachusetts*, Massachusetts Advisory Council on Education, June, 1968, p. 111.

Educational Personnel as a quasi-legal adjunct service (see Figure 13-2); b. Request funds to support the work of the Commission, including a budget to provide appropriate resources for the clinical training of educational personnel, and

c. Define working relationships between existing departments with the new Commission.

3. Teachers and other educational personnel, individually and through their professional associations, need to take responsibility for supporting the needed legislative action assisting the Commission to establish and maintain suitable performance standards for each field and level of certification, and help school systems and preparing institutions to improve the preparation of educational personnel.

4. Colleges and universities that prepare educational personnel should move to:

a. project preferred approaches to judging performance of candidates for teaching;

b. cooperate with the proposed state-supported program of clinical training of educational personnel, and

c. work with school systems to relate the preparation of educational personnel to new designs for student learning in elementary and secondary schools.

5. School systems should move as rapidly as possible to adapt all personnel policies to the new differentiations of teaching competence. They will need, also, to develop appropriate inservice programs that qualify teachers for higher levels of certification and for the periodic renewal of licenses. So much for Stiles' outline of the study — two parts deserve more detail.

Stiles' Clinical Model

How Stiles views the "clinical" aspect of teacher training merits further discussion. He cites a research study intended to support aspects of his model:

> Research by Bob Burton Brown and Associates, conducted in California, Florida, Illinois, New York and Wisconsin, has indicated that it is possible to judge teacher performance. Of significance is the evidence that professional observer judges can agree fairly closely on who is a good teacher or a poor one provided they hold basically similar philosophical and educational beliefs. Observations of teacher classroom behavior were found to be the most reliable predictor of evaluative ratings.[6]

Suggesting improvements in teacher education in Massachusetts presents limitations in part because some institutions are strong where others are weak. An exception is the problem of providing suitable resources for clinical practice. Practically every institution, public and nonpublic, indicated a need for state assistance to improve conditions essential for good programs of student teaching and internships.

Making the improvement of clinical practice a priority, Stiles feels, offers the best promise of gains in the quality of teachers produced. Already, this phase of programs of preparation, e.g., student teaching or the internship, is rated most popular of all collegiate courses — academic or professional — by candidates for teaching, despite deficiencies that may exist. An inherent value is any opportunity to learn from firsthand experience. Given the chance to deal with pupils, prospective teachers find greater relevance for theories and knowledge about teaching and education. General collegiate preparation as well as specialized knowledge of a subject field also take on added meaning.

The quality of supervised clinical practice makes significant differences in the levels of professional performance candidates for teaching achieve. Of greatest significance, perhaps, is the supervision provided by the clinical supervisor in the classroom. Such individuals need not only to be master teachers, they must know how to guide the development of neophyte teachers. Time must be available to provide the close tutorial help. In addition, supervising teachers must have the kind of commitments that make teacher development a first priority. Other factors that relate to the quality of clinical practice included the kinds of pupils taught, the time devoted by trainees, both daily and overall, and the integration of study about education with actual experience.

Colleges and universities are unable to provide suitable clinical practice for all prospective teachers without considerable help from elementary and secondary schools. Past attempts to do so led to the development of campus laboratory schools which ultimately proved, for a variety of reasons, inadequate.

A strength of the laboratory school, nevertheless, was found in the quality of supervision provided. Staff members made teacher education a first priority, generally were prepared and competent to help teach teachers and usually took time to do so. Another plus for the campus laboratory school was the close correlation between the methods prospective teachers studied and those practiced in the schools. An over-all contribution was the idea that learning to teach required extensive practice under supervision.

As campus laboratory schools proved too small to serve an expanding number of teachers-in-training, and faced with criticisms that they provided unreal conditions, colleges and universities increasingly turned to public and nonpublic schools for clinical practice for their teacher candidates. In moving clinical practice out of the laboratory school, the advantages of variety of student populations and typical school conditions were obtained. Disadvantages were found in the ranges of preparations and commitments of the classroom teachers who cooperated in providing day-to-day supervision of student teachers and interns. Often, trainees had to be assigned to anyone who would accept them, rather than to teachers selected for either their abilities as teachers or as supervisors of those learning to teach. Some student teachers, for example, spend almost all their time observing their supervisors teach with a minimum opportunity to practice. In other situations, trainees taught almost full time with little supervision. Another major disadvantage was a lack of correlation between pedagogical instruction campus and practices in schools where clinical experiences are provided.

Stiles continues:

> The need of teacher education programs in Massachusetts now is for elementary and secondary schools to develop the kinds of resources for clinical practice that the better campus laboratory schools have maintained. To achieve such a goal will require commitments by school systems to serve as training centers, as some already have made. Classroom teachers who serve as clinical supervisors must be carefully selected, professionally prepared to teach teachers and provided time in which to perform such duties. School systems that elect to help prepare teachers must take responsibility for the quality of clinical practice. Colleges and universities might well

concentrate on helping schools to develop high-level clinical supervisors rather than dissipating staff resources by sending professors into classrooms to supervise as has been done in the past. The State Board of Education needs to help with financial support and assistance in placing trainees in assignments. In short, the need is for a three-way partnership between the institutions of higher learning, school systems and the State Board of Education.

As Massachusetts schools move to provide improved conditions for clinical practice certain models of supervisor-trainee relationships may be useful guides. First of all, experience has demonstrated that two student teachers assigned to a class group learn more individually than when one works alone. The reason is that they teach each other through comparisons of ideas. Second, the time of competent clinical supervisors is better employed if each works with several trainees — perhaps four or six — during a semester. Such arrangements permit economies through group instruction as well as a commitment of portions of the supervising teacher's time to teacher training. With six trainees assigned, for example, the supervisor might teach elementary or secondary pupils only two-thirds of the time. The other third would be devoted to supervision. As a third suggestion, team teaching arrangements that include interns as full members of instructional teams under the leadership of the clinical supervisor have proved to be good plans for teacher development. At the elementary school level, one clinical supervisor and two interns may teach two classroom groups, e.g., fifty to sixty pupils. In secondary schools, such a team might carry the teaching loads of two English or mathematics teachers. Larger teams are possible, too, that include both additional trainees, professional personnel, paraprofessional personnel and deal with larger numbers of pupils.

As school systems take greater responsibility for clinical practice, colleges and universities probably will concentrate more on developing personnel competent to serve as clinical supervisors. They will need, also, to provide consultation to schools and clinical supervisors as a continuing type of service. Once relieved of the task of close supervision of trainees, personnel in higher education can give more time to leadership in research to improve pupil learning and teacher development. A key need is to know more about the learning-teaching processes. An example of this type of pioneering research is the microteaching approach some institutions are now testing. Others include program learning, television instruction, sensitivity training programs, instructional teams, nongraded programs, and various approaches to teaching basic skills and knowledges to differing kinds of pupil populations. Helping schools to renew and modify curriculum content and emphasis represents another responsibility college personnel confront.

School systems that elect to become centers for clinical practice have obligations to help select and support the preparation of high-level clinical supervisors. They should also provide the kinds of reduced teaching loads needed to permit time and energy for training teachers. Each center, also, should be prepared to provide certain resources needed by good programs of clinical practice. Perspective teachers should have opportunities, for example, to observe a variety of types of teaching, and at different levels of the school system. This means that the entire faculty should accept responsibility to help trainees as well as those serving as clinical supervisors. Needed in training centers, also, will be certain kinds of equipment such as that for video-tape feed-backs of teaching performance, facilities for using all kinds of educational technology, libraries of sample curriculum materials, conference and trainee work rooms, duplicating equipment and secretarial services.

The role of the State Board of Education, broadly interpreted, is one of leadership and assistance to schools and colleges. It should provide financial support to schools to help make possible quality conditions for clinical practice. Another need is for help to schools and colleges to arrange orderly assignments for trainees in practice stations. Financial support and leadership to stimulate research to improve pupil learning and related teacher development are other responsibilities the State Board of Education should be prepared to provide.

Some Concluding Observations

The present certification process is nothing more than a maze, unconnected to teacher preparation and devoid of accountability. Lindley Stiles knew better than to suggest that all we need in order to get out of the maze is some wallpapering and a better pair of walking boots.

It is not minor reconstruction which he advocates, but a total demolition followed by a planned rebuilding of the total system. In the process, Stiles lays the groundwork for a plausible profession.

Key recommendations with respect to certification call for a complete turnabout in the present system. Certification is to be based on knowledge, not only of pedagogy but of general background and subject specializations. Actual professional performance also will become a licensing criteria if the MACE study is adopted.

The measurement of competence will not continue to be an automatic process based upon the accumulation of course credits. Rather, under the MACE plan the criteria and measurement process will be developed by teachers who are probably representative leaders in various subject areas or levels, or teachers from different varieties of class compositions. For example, under the present system, the training for a twelfth grade advanced placement French teacher in a wealthy suburb is not much different from the training requirements of an eighth grade teacher of Earth Science in a ghetto school. A training system which ignores such vast differences is obviously out of touch with reality.

Although certification procedures would vary, what probably would be common to all systems would be the development of clinical requirements. The MACE plan calls for state reimbursement to school systems willing to develop effective education clinics for the proper training of intern teachers. It is forseeable that whereas now, student teachers are taken into school systems each year with only lip service paid to professional concern, and under the worst conditions, in the near future, some school systems would be proud of their clinics and they would contribute significantly both to the reputation and effectiveness of a school system.

Under the clinical system recommended by Stiles, it is possible, for example, that intern teachers will compete for acceptance to school system "A's" clinic because it is the best mathematics clinic in the state. Another school system may develop the best clinic for the training of teachers of disadvantaged students in the country, etc. Clinics of significant reputation would become Meccas for serious, dedicated, and talented experienced teachers who would look forward with enthusiasm to a professional atmosphere which provides opportunity for real contribution.

The clinics would be similar to hospital clinics: a meeting place for scholars, centers of experiment, research, and development, testing places for newly emerging curricula, methods, and materials. Supervising teachers in the clinics would be provided with money, time, and training, to do the job properly; and enormous prestige would accrue to clinical staffs as learning breakthroughs occur consistently under this design. The clinic would become the rallying point for all the forces involved in education; and the partnership involvement of college teachers, public school practitioners, and student teachers would result in a first-rate system of defense against educational obsolescence at any point in the cycle.

In retrospect, the Advisory Council was pushed willingly into conducting a study of the teacher certification process. The Willis-Harrington Commission made such a study a high priority item for the Council. Both teacher preparation and teacher certification appear to suffer from an anti-social disease. Prospects for recovery are inching forward in Massachusetts.

This concludes Part III, "Revisiting Some Conventional Programs." The final chapter will recycle us through the Council and make a stab at what the future might become for MACE.

14

On Need, Impact and New Ways

Our problem is, in fact, to fit the world to our perception, and not our preception to the world. — Alfred North Whitehead

The first condition of progress is a lively and preemptory dissatisfaction. — Albert Jay Nock

We need to reappraise the uses of state educational R&D management agencies including the Advisory Council. In addition, we should as best we can, look at the impact of the Advisory Council on the state. The final section in this chapter presents certain selected issues and makes proposals for acting upon them.

On Greeting New and Continuing State Educational Needs

The calling cards of educational change are strewn all over the landscape of every state. Some cards call for improvement in the existing system and urge quality, options, expansion and improved access to schools and programs. Others threaten, and sometimes even demand, overthrow of our educational system. And many of the calling cards tell us to shuffle in a system of accountability for all aspects of the educational enterprise before things get out of hand.

An important objective in this section is to indicate that enormous pressures for educational change are building up and that organizations such as the Advisory Council on Education are badly needed to help assure an orderly and sensible change process.

In quieter days, it was no great problem to run schools or to find ways to make adjustments when pressures in a given area made an adjustment advisable. Times have changed and mild-mannered issues of the past have lost their temper. People in all walks of life find it impossible to ignore school, since education, American style, enhances or destroys.

Parents on one hand adjust and mold their lives to schools but on the other hand find themselves in anguish over the issues that do or do not converge on the schoolhouse door. Rightly or wrongly, parents from all walks of life expect much of schools. Parents with high expectations and little say in schools find themselves paying more taxes to keep the educational enterprise afloat.

Meanwhile, today's students view life with great seriousness. They see a world of war, rhetoric, easy morals, drugs, strife and uncertainty. Naturally, they

315

wonder what response they will find to these issues in schools. When the schools disappoint them, it should not surprise us when they adopt aggressive or passive forms of behavior. Like it or not, learners also expect much from schools.

In banding together, teachers have discovered power and its uses and are ready to challenge both old and new ways. Not much changed in education for many years. Now changes on a large scale are beginning to work on the teacher. Disruptions, new staffing techniques, teacher surpluses, and technology keep teachers in a paranoid state.

The demands made on education by society often collide with taxpayers and legislators. Bond issues, schoolhouse construction and expanded educational programs are being rejected when possible and challenged in any case. Taxpayers object to inequitable and unsound property taxes, inefficient and overlapping educational jurisdictions, seemingly expensive teachers and administrators, under-utilized schools, and poor planning. They demand evidence of accountability and in some parts of the country, voters have closed down schools by refusing requests for operational funds.

Meanwhile, state policy-makers including legislators are in a quandary. While they acknowledge that public education falls far short of serving the needs of society, they sense a financial crisis on one hand and a credibility gap on the other.

We therefore propose the need for a state educational research arm with the resources and talents to help in serving students, parents and others. This calls for R&D activities far beyond those usually envisioned.

Over the long haul, the efficiencies and economies suggested by such an operation would be felt. But many proposals made, especially in the early stages, will have high price tags simply because the past has slighted so many areas in education.

MACE, for instance, was tempted into conducting studies of emerging educational needs. Two of them in particular, Levin and Slavet's *Continuing Education in Massachusetts: State Programs for the Seventies,* and Richard Rowe's *Child-Care in Massachusetts: The Public Responsibility,* call for new government offices and considerable sums of money.

Other MACE studies discuss in turn better uses for the educational dollar. The business task force report helped three dozen businessmen, all with executive abilities and special expertise, to learn more about schools while proposing many ways in which funds could be better spent.

In relation to new and more critical audiences, what are the uses of a state educational research agency? What kind of research is necessary and who should do it? Who are the clients? How can a research agency move research studies and planning into the real world of education? We hope this chapter will be helpful in addressing these questions.

We began our book reflecting on the need for a state R&D arm and to advocate the Advisory Council as a model for an R&D agency. At the same time, we presented a grim national picture of inadequate funding and skimpy research efforts. Agencies sponsoring research must therefore prepare themselves for the wisest use of research funds. The public is easily angered when it reads about money being spent on R&D even when the amount is trifling when compared to the millions spent daily operating and maintaining marginal educational programs and services. We continued by suggesting that states coordinate their study and planning efforts, and in fact develop plans for carefully allocating scarce R&D funds.

Above all, in the opening chapter, we attempted to outline how the Advisory Council was put together. The purpose was to illustrate how such a distinctive, permanent research agency, to wit, the Council, is potentially useful beyond the borders of Massachusetts.

A word about who should do what in educational R&D. Does it make sense now to pull it altogether in one agency?

The state of R&D activities is such that it makes little point to insist that they all be performed by one state agency. There is simply too much to do, yet the possibility of planning and research agencies in conflict over who should do what is unattractive.

Is there a transition to this? There is too great a need and too many unresolved issues to consider a one-agency approach at this time. There is, for instance, no over-all agency strategy for sponsoring and conducting educational R&D. Furthermore, data inadequacies and a lack of agreement as to what constitutes R&D, means in part that sharing and comparing R&D activities are possible only through arrangements between those people and agencies in close coordination.

While agreements should be developed about what R&D is all about, coordinating activities should not be used for constraining options or for compromising diversity. Later in this chapter, we will illustrate some of the desired outcomes for cooperation and collaboration.

The central point to keep in mind is that a state needs all the help it can get in clarifying issues, developing new approaches, planning and seeking answers. Changes in education should not be haphazard events which are likely to be costly or misunderstood.

However, not only is educational change unavoidable, it is desperately needed. How, then, can a state agency such as MACE keep a state from being overwhelmed with unanticipated demands and real or imaginary issues? We suggest fourteen reasonable research agenda items to help:

1. Monitoring educational systems to ascertain if priorities are being met.
2. Fostering links and affiliations, both permanent and temporary, between educational systems and other systems.
3. Measuring the status and change in the distribution of educational resources and outcomes.

4. Developing ways to improve efficiency and to avoid waste in educational systems.
5. Assuring vertical and horizontal articulation in educational systems.
6. Stating and defining new educational needs.
7. Exploring the impact and effectiveness of novel approaches to education.
8. Developing standards for new and contemporary educational systems.
9. Defining and setting educational priorities for the state.
10. Evaluating and adjusting priorities, programs and systems as needed.
11. Proposing changes in structures and power relationships when necessary.
12. Seeking to make educational issues publicly known.
13. Measuring rates of progress toward certain goals.
14. Assisting in improving systems within systems (e.g., planning an information system for public higher education).

An agency such as MACE could not and should not try to take on all these agenda items by itself. This is meant as a *state* agenda. It should, however, ascertain what is being done about them and develop some priorities among those that are being overlooked.

Research agencies themselves need some tools. One of the greatest obstacles to MACE's study processes has been the need to start at ground zero with almost every study. This is not to say that many good people and ongoing agencies haven't cooperated with the Council. The cold fact is that much of the information being gathered, and many of the mechanisms and procedures for reporting, are of very little use to planning and research. Information systems, we have found out the hard way, correlate with the general quality of the educational subsystem under study.

The following five points, adapted from Clifford L. Dochterman's *Directions to Excellence in Education,* give a sense of how research agencies in a state can help *themselves.*

1. Establish an information program that can be utilized to clarify issues.
2. Provide social mechanisms at several levels for testing and establishing goals and objectives and for establishing priorities.
3. Map alternative courses of action and show the consequences of each. Determine what forces and events need to be activated in order to make the desired happen.
4. Help assure orderly and systematic procedures for needed changes.
5. Assure feedback of evaluations and possible modification of needed changes. [1]

The implications embedded in these five points for education and for public policy are challenging, to say the least. Perhaps only because the need is so great, will the several agencies that conduct studies and do research and planning in any given state meet around a table to plan cooperatively for their own needs.

Clearly, a state agency so involved in issues will have to be prepared to change itself. In this regard, the Council must be given high grades. The etymology of many issues indicates that they arose because of (a) internal organizational rigidities; and (b) the development of hard and fast lines between government agencies. Warren G. Bennis writes about agencies of the future:

> The key work will be "temporary." There will be adaptive, rapidly changing temporary systems. These will be task forces organized around problems-to-be-solved by groups of relative strangers with diverse professional skills. The group will be arranged on an organic rather than mechanical model; they will evolve in response to a problem rather than to programmed role expectations. The executive thus becomes a coordinator or 'linking pin' between various task forces. He must be a man who can speak the polyglot jargon of research, with skills to relay information and to mediate between groups. People will be evaluated not vertically according to rank and status, but flexibly and functionally according to skill and professional training. Organizational charts will consist of project groups rather than stratified functional groups.
>
> Adaptive, problem-solving, temporary systems of diverse specialists, linked together by coordinating and task-evaluating executive specialists in an organic flux — this is the organization form that will gradually replace bureaucracy as we know it. Organizational arrangements of this sort may not only reduce the intergroup conflicts mentioned earlier; it may also induce honest-to-goodness creative collaboration.
>
> I think that the future I describe is not necessarily a 'happy' one. Coping with rapid change, living in temporary work systems, developing meaningful relations and then breaking them — all augur social strains and psychological tensions. Teaching how to live with ambiguity, to identify with the adaptive process, to make a virtue out of contingency, and to be self-directing — these will be the tasks of education, the goals of maturity, and the achievement of the successful individual.[2]

We are hard put to be facile about achieving the fourteen-point and five-point agendas we have just reviewed unless at least *some* of the agencies called to work on these points are prepared to be flexible. The "temporary" and flexible agency is not a new invention. Top-level executives, including the nation's presidents, have traditionally created mission-oriented groups and kitchen cabinets to get various tasks done.

The adaptive and informal qualities of proposed external universities appear to be similar to Bennis' model. Model Cities programs, as well, have evolved from a complex of multidisciplinary needs.

A recent article in the *Saturday Review* by Henry Resnick[3] describes how the Harvard Graduate School of Education has reorganized itself to view education as not a set of specialities but rather within a "learning environment" and public policy context. Dr. Rowe's MACE study, *Child Care in Massachusetts,* was produced under his direction by an interdisciplinary team brought together to represent "public psychology."

There is, in other words, a respectable group of agencies which (1) have been formed for new purposes; or (2) have a capacity to adapt themselves to new internal and external requirements. We hope the reader agrees that the Council is eligible for membership in both categories.

The Impact of MACE

While we have discussed implementation in the introductory sections in each of the three parts of this book, we should take a moment to re-examine implementation and to add some new dimensions. While MACE has no statutory responsibility for implementation, there is likely to be a time when the Advisory Council will be visited by the tribunes of accountability. The accountability team must realize that not all research endeavors do succeed. The purpose of accountability is not to produce a higher order of virtue. Accountability calls for explicit understandings both of what MACE did in a given study and what the consequences were. A pass-fail grade should not be the objective of the first efforts at accountability. Instead, measures necessary to the improvement of the Council's behavior should result.

What has happened as a result of MACE studies? While certainly not enough, no simple answer is appropriate. It may, for instance, take several years for conditions to be right for major changes in any given area. At the moment, belt tightening is the predominating local and state activity. Legislators, in particular, are in no mood to be known as spenders and many of the MACE recommendations require legislation and funds.

A good part of the job of implementation, however, can be done outside of the legislative halls and with much less visibility. Several of MACE's studies are being implemented in this fashion by committees of concerned individuals or organizations. Furthest advanced in this direction is a committee, which has been in operation for well over a year, seeking to implement the recommendations of the Council's 1970 study of the *Report of the Massachusetts Business Task Force for School Management*. This committee, composed of some of the original members of the task force as well as individuals from various educational associations, has during its short existence:

1. actively participated in regional and statewide meetings and workshops conducted by the Department of Education (MDE) and the Massachusetts Association of School Business Officials (MASBO);
2. supported passage of legislation permitting cooperative purchasing arrangements among school districts;
3. supported MDE's supplemental budget request for establishment of a Bureau of School Management;
4. began preparations for a follow-up project to bring about more active school-business cooperation.[4]

Partly because of the MACE study of the Department of Education, that agency has undergone a drastic organizational overhaul and has prepared a set of goals and objectives. Other major administrative changes have occurred in the Boston school system.

Because so many MACE studies focused on school districting as a problem, a governor-appointed commission has been established, and given Council funding, to recommend ways to develop more rational LEAs. The charge given to the Commission encourages it to work out, in cooperation with caring citizens, an action program to be implemented in part even before the commission's two-year undertaking is completed.

Major new state governmental agencies are recommended by Blatt for special education and by Rowe for early childhood programs. Several bills are presently pending in the legislature to authorize the establishment of these agencies. Recently, the legislature raised the special education bureau to a departmental division to be headed by an associate commissioner.

For three years running, a major, widely supported effort has been carried on to change the certification process. Some variation of the recommendation made by Stiles in his MACE study is almost certain to pass the legislature in the next few years. It is ironic that other states have piggy-backed on the MACE certification study and have succeeded in getting a number of state legislatures or departments of education to modity their teacher certification processes.

It is interesting to look at Governor Francis W. Sargent's "State of the State" address, delivered on January 10, 1972, and to read his seven educational needs:

1. Legislation to provide for a comprehensive tuition-scholarship program in our colleges and universities for Massachusetts residents establishing more equitable distribution of educational costs.
2. Administrative action to examine various options for equalizing educational opportunities through a fairer method of financing school costs.
3. Legislation to establish standards of attendance for all boards governing state colleges and universities including provisions for removal of trustees for failure to meet these standards.
4. Legislation authorizing modular construction and other economical construction techniques for the building of new schools.
5. Administrative action to establish programs in the state institutions of higher learning to prepare personnel to carry out the provisions of the Transitional Bilingual Education Act of 1970.
6. Administrative action to establish, on a voluntary basis, cooperative purchasing, planning and program administration by local school committees to take advantage of financial economies resulting from the use of modern business management techniques.
7. Administrative action to implement an Open University program in the Commonwealth utilizing correspondence courses, television and other media allowing people of all ages and economic backgrounds to receive higher education at low cost to themselves and the taxpayers.[5]

The Council has been, or will be, involved in all of these areas with the exception of numbers 3 and 5. While the Council did not submit material for the governor to use in his report to the citizens of Massachusetts, it is most likely that MACE reports and MACE activities did suggest to the governor's staff several of these issues.

Other achievements can be cited, but our purpose is to give a general sense of the impact of MACE studies. We have not been able to measure to what extent MACE recommendations may have been carried out locally. We know they are referred to constantly by local schoolmen and board members to support an array of administrative and programmatic changes.

MACE has tried to link its studies informally with development as we partly indicated earlier in discussing *The Report of the Massachusetts Business Task Force for School Management.* The Council's central role in such efforts, except in developing the commission to develop a school districting plan as a result of Dr. Donald Donley's preliminary study of the same topic, has left something to be desired. The handicap of being a change-agent at a time when no one wants to invest funds in education should not be underrated. More than in the past, the Council itself must consider using its funds to move into post-study development activities. More on this point later.

Some of the results of MACE's studies are harder to pin down. Few organizations, for instance, have used state lay and professional citizens as extensively as MACE. Perhaps as many as 4,000 to 5,000 persons have voluntarily been involved in the actual work of producing a MACE study. Some studies have literally involved hundreds of citizens in interlocking committees and activities. MACE study teams have visited all parts of the state and have been in countless classrooms.

It has been said that the "best conversations" on educational matters were emanating from MACE studies and references to the Council among the educational establishment are frequent.

Clearly the new Secretary of Education, who himself did a major MACE study, will be a major asset in matters of implementation. He has already begun to swing into action on several MACE reports.

Greater visibility for MACE studies is called for. Efforts have been made to produce a television series on two reports, but they have failed to receive funding.

We can speculate over what layers or slices of the educational enterprise we should study to produce the greatest likelihood of implementation. Perhaps proposals to the legislature which require funding in these locust years are idle. Perhaps MACE should follow federal funding and conduct studies which tap the federal charities. This is another topic to return to later.

Meanwhile, we hope the reader will enjoy a moment of levity as we glance at what happens when a MACE study is completed and greeted by those bureaucracies, private as well as governmental, affected in Table 14–1.

Some Proposals Modest and Otherwise

The time has come to break new ground in educational research. It will have to be done with scarce funds and in a climate suspicious of research and

Table 14-1

A Chronology of Attitudes Held towards a Typical Study by Those Groups Affected (with tongue in cheek)

Date Study was issued to Three Months Later	Three to Ten Months Later	Ten to Sixteen Months Later	Twelve to Twenty-Four Months Later
1. Anger because release of final report not delayed	1. Committe formed	1. Statements made that report has some good points	1. Study now the authorative work
2. Criticism of the handling and dissemination of the study	2. Copies of report running low	2. Those associated with study stress their role	2. Study used to block any other related studies contemplated
3. "Faults" in report stressed 1. "Nothing New" 2. "Expensive" 3. "We're doing it now" 4. "Creates more work"	3. Is mostly ignored	3. Cited	3. Legislature passes a bill with inadequate funding
	4. Study Director in hiding	4. Study Director unpaid consultant	4. Study Director paid consultant

Source: by the author.

development. Stephen Bailey of Syracuse University has told schoolmen that they "must not only be aware of politics, but influencial in politics," and this "may be the key to our survival as a free and civilized nation." Our message is not different. We focus on the role and responsibility of those who decide what will be studied, planned and implemented in a state. There is, we submit, politics and more to getting the job skillfully done. We offer a number of proposals which indicate some fresh views of research and some ways to get moving.

But before we turn to these proposals, let us take a final look at where a research and development organization might be located.

At least eight possible models for a state handling its educational R&D management responsibilities should be recognized:

1.   The present model of MACE.
2.   An R&D agency serving the legislature.
3.   An R&D agency serving the governor.
4.   An R&D agency sponsored by other agencies and groups.
5.   An R&D agency, with a citizen commission in, but not of, the Office of the Secretary of Educational Affairs (applies only to Massachusetts at the moment).
6.   A central agency handling all R&D matters for state agencies — educational and otherwise.
7.   A state agency for the coordination of R&D activities — educational and otherwise.
8.   An R&D agency as part of a monolithic state board of education.

The weakest of these possibilities, it seems to us, is 4. Under a sponsorship arrangement, it appears likely that "R&D" would merely serve the noncontroversial interests of the sponsoring agencies. Versions 2, 3 and 5 are lesser versions of MACE today. All three could lead to staff positions being considered patronage plums. Six and 7 are interesting but contain no citizen element. With number 8, in which *all* public education would be under one board, it can be rationalized that citizens sit in public policy-making positions. (Such a prospect involves far more than we are able to discuss here and should be planned over several years.) The mood of the nation requires citizen groups involved in the formulation of policy-making. We support and recommend, at the risk of immodesty, the first option. Properly operated, the Council can have the citizen-political elements necessary for a research management agency to have acceptance and impact.

The ensuing proposals are based in large part upon the struggles of the Advisory Council to become a vibrant and necessary agency. Much of what follows can be teased out of earlier statements in this book. But some are new and, we would hope, bold. The proposals are not a long way from exhaustive and they deliberately leave room for debate over their exact implications. We hope that our proposals, if followed, will help to thrust the management of R&D endeavors into more useful frames of reference and intent.

Our proposals will, we trust, be viewed as both salient to and necessary for effective action. The time is long overdue for those who would sponsor educational research and development to assume a leadership position and plan a strategy for putting research and development into the forefront of educational matters.

No agency unprepared to assume a share of leadership in a state can lay claim to being a major state agency. There is no substitute for leadership. Research and development which moves a state from one policy to another clearly requires and displays leadership. This point was made in the first chapter as basic to an effective educational research agency. Who will exercise leadership, we said in that chapter, is not so important as that the citizen component, as represented by the members of the Advisory Council, itself be the leading party in deciding what is to be done. Unless those dealing with an R&D agency understand that an internal concensus has been achieved, and that final policy decisions depend upon lay citizens playing a central role, the agency in the long run is going to be ignored.

Proposed: *A research agency, with a citizen board or council, must play a leadership role in which a lay citizen group pass upon final policy decisions.*

A study sponsord by a research agency should be submitted to that agency for whatever use it wishes to make of it. When the study is finally printed for wide distribution, it should be absolutely clear that it is a document of a given research agency for which that agency takes full responsibility. A study director should respond to the wishes of the research agency while doing his study. When the product is finished, the study director should submit 50 or 100 copies of a full and summary report to the research agency. The research agency can then do what it wishes with the final report. This is the only way to make a research-sponsoring agency more than a conduit for funds and to assure the greatest impact from a study on both the public and on schoolmen.

Proposed: *A research agency must take full responsibility for a report released by that agency.*

Educational planning is far broader than the production of a report from which findings and recommendations flow. While a research agency must develop a plan of work leading to measures of implementation, a number of interested parties must be consulted formally and informally. While the agency needs to be independent, it defeats its own mandate when it works in isolation or develops only part of a course of action. Mounting studies using qualified staff temporarily attached to the agency or contracted to produce a product for the agency hardly justifies a talented staff.

Proposed: *A staff* plan of work *should be presented to the citizen council or board at the same time it hears a proposal to conduct a given study. The plan of work should include plans for implementation.*

Since we presume that educational planning is woefully primitive and too much slighted, a major effort must be made to indicate its importance.

At the same time, the several state agencies with a direct interest in state planning and research should strive to strengthen their single and collective positions through close collaboration.

Proposed: *A Committee on Educational Planning should be formed of the heads of state educational agencies and an equal number of citizens. After careful staff work, the Committee should meet no less than three times each year to:*
1. *prepare an agenda for state action;*
2. *prepare an annual report for the* citizens of the state *for wide public distribution;*
3. *ask for presentations and special reports and statements from all interested groups in the state; and*
4. *effect liaisons with Washington, other states, and with groups within the state.*

While the staff should not represent an expanding bureaucratic body, several skills should be represented among them. Each state has different needs and therefore must develop a separate rationale. The Advisory Council presently has three professionals and an administrative assistant. Since it should pay far more attention to liaison activities, to research development and to dissemination, at least two professionals should be added to the staff and perhaps two more administrative assistants.

Some of the guidelines to be considered in staffing should include the following study of the work to be done:

- Helping to encourage citizens and officials of the state in agreeing to appropriate state and national goals and priorities for education.
- Working closely with other agencies, in particular, the state boards of education. Links should also be developed with other states and with the federal government.
- Analyzing the needs of education and assisting in decisions regarding the allocation of resources. The state education R&D agency must be concerned about the most effective utilization of the human and material resources for education.
- Becoming a major force for gaining public acceptance and support for alternative programs in education. The state education R&D agency can help build a climate in the state to encourage needed changes in education.

Proposed: *Staff requirements should be based upon the skills necessary and the amount and kind of R&D to be planned and sponsored by the agency.*

State educational R&D agencies must plan just as they call upon others to plan. Some of the components of the plan should extend over several years while other parts will need to be more short range. Such a plan should include "formative evaluations"[6] based upon information feedback in such a way as to affect and redirect plans and programs being undertaken within the plan. A simple question that needs to be asked each year: Are things being done better this year than last? Formative evaluation should be designed around the plans and objectives of the agency. Outside auditors are necessary to assist in certifying the adequacy of the internal planning and evaluation system.

Particular attention must be paid to the constraints under which the research agency operates. The Advisory Council, for instance, is limited both by statute as to how far it can get into implementation and by its limited funding.

Proposed: *An educational R&D agency must plan and must, in a systematic way, evaluate and adjust its planning and programs.*

We have already proposed each study have a plan of work associated with it. The plan of work should be submitted for approval to the Council along with the study proposal to do a given study. Such a plan would indicate activities within and concomitant to the proposed study and be intended to guide implementation efforts. A *plan of work* should, as necessary, span several months or several years. It should contain a frank discussion of change strategies and should indicate various alternative ways to proceed. It is highly desirable that operating agency staff have a hand in such a document even though this might somewhat delay beginning the research activity.

That part of the plan of work dealing with implementation should consider the four basic techniques that lead to change:

1. the exercise of authority and power by legislators and executives;
2. the involvement and education of citizens who modify their personal
    attitudes, or focus their efforts better to work for change;
3. the involvement and education of schoolmen also to the point where their
    behavior changes and they begin to operate differently, and
4. demonstration and diffusion of a new practice through prototypes and pilot
    programs which can be viewed and tested by the appropriate actors.

Proposed: *An educational R&D agency must prepare a comprehensive plan of work for a study proposal which stresses strategies, and prospects for change.*

Other ways than those presently employed must be used to involve citizens and to press home the importance of studies. State and regional "town meeting" assemblies involving several hundreds of citizens should be arranged on an annual basis. We leave open how often such an assembly should meet. Possibly, it should meet every day for a week or more. Whatever, the assembly should not become a lifeless *pro forma* production. While the asemblies should be open to all, a voting process should be used to elect representatives from each part of the state.

The several state agencies with a stake in educational R&D, including the Department of Education, and a citizen component, should plan the meeting and allow for the give and take of the town meeting approach. At this time, the Committee on Educational Planning could issue its annual report for citizens.

Proposed: *Educational R&D can be important only when treated as important. State educational agencies, with citizen input, should arrange town meeting assemblies, with members elected to the assemblies, to discuss R&D activities with particular emphasis on planning and implementation.*

Proposed: *This should also be the time for the Committee on Educational Planning to report to citizens in general.*

There are other ways for a state R&D agency to avoid the arrogance of believing that it can think of all things that are interesting. Give and take sessions with a number of special interest groups could be helpful. A variety of modestly paid consultants could, on a retainer basis, supply an R&D agency with a variety of insights and practical help. A great deal of communication, with a stress on listening, makes sense.

A formal information system, designed for R&D uses, especially analyzing and planning, is necessary in each state. The Council's study directors have been forced to begin almost from scratch in information gathering when conducting a study. False starts, wasted efforts and poor relationships with a number of agencies, have sometimes been the result.

Proposed: *A joint committee, perhaps the Committee on Educational Planning, should make its data needs known to those whose task it is to* *collect data. Old and new data, and the way it is used, should be evaluated at least annually to determine if and how it is being used.*

A state R&D agency should give serious consideration to extending itself by incorporating a separate and private nonprofit organization to be managed in conjunction with the state agency. This new private organization could perform functions which most state agencies can't do for a variety of reasons including a lack of resources, the sluggishness of state bureaucracies and the constraints of law. Many divisions within institutions, especially state universities, have several nonprofit private organizations associated with their activities which can serve as examples.

Care should be taken to ascertain that such a private venture in no way compromises the state agency. The organization is meant to further the cause of R&D endeavors in imaginative and synergistic ways and to enable the agency to move with new boldness.

Proposed: *A state R&D agency should consider the uses of a related private, nonprofit corporation.*

Further recognition of new state educational agencies conducting studies, planning and coordination must be made by Congress and H.E.W. This recognition should not result in funds going to state departments of education being diverted to emerging R&D-oriented state agencies.

There are a number of ways that recognition could be increased. One possibility is to form an organization of "chief state educational research officers" somewhat similar to the chief state school officers organization which pulls together state commissioners of education.

Proposed: *Educational research agencies must register their existence with H.E.W. and elsewhere.*

Proposed: *A fifty-state organization of chief state educational research officers should be formed and should make further recognition by Congress and H.E.W. a major objective.*

It seems reasonable to suggest that states should collaborate far more than they now do on R&D projects. While many issues are important within a given state, it should be obvious that issues often transcend a state boundary. We need also to realize that few states are prepared to support regular R&D activities beyond a minimum level. This, a collaborative effort may well be the only way to cover increasing educational R&D needs. As the term collaboration suggests, we have in mind much more than an information exchange.

Interfacing state educational R&D activities call for a series of interstate meetings which would develop a set of common objectives and plans to undertake R&D activities on a broad front. Such meetings will, ideally, lead to giving a sense of what state best manages certain R&D endeavors. Perhaps, for instance, a study could be conducted in one state and in some ways tested in another. One state coud do "R" and another "D." In other words, a number of permutations could be tried.

We stress that a state agency clearly must not neglect in any way its state obligations. Other state agencies cooperate and even plan together and it is time state schoolmen learned the uses of interstate collaboration.

Such efforts need not wait or rely upon the suggestion that chief state educational research officers convene. The sooner states come together, in whatever arrangement, the better.

Proposed: *Using needs assessment as a possible basis, state research agencies should begin to forge interstate links. Several objectives should be prominent, such as an exchange of information, but one should be paramount: improving the performance of research and development state by state.*

If educational research in states has been slighted, development has been little more than an idle dream. Studies are relatively easy to do but the development aspect, which involves prototypes, pilot efforts, small-scale starts and so forth, have been grossly underfunded, if funded at all. A research agency, such as the Advisory Council, should be funded on the basis of forging R&D together. By law, the Council is restrained from operations. Operations, however, should not be confused with experimental and small-scale trials after a study has been completed. Unfortunately, the Council is not funded to do more than conduct studies, which is only part of the job. One consequence of this is that implementation suffers.

Proposed: *A research agency should include a development component which should live closely to the operational world represented by SEA's and LEA's.*

In numerous ways, we have indicated a need to communicate and link with others. One product of these activities could be a state registry of key persons and agencies interested in education and caring about improving our means of study, planning and implementation. A research agency could develop and use such a registry. Since the list would very likely overlap with those needed by other state agencies, it might be wise to pool resources in developing a registry. Some thought should also be given to an R&D clearinghouse function at either the state or regional level. Such a clearinghouse function should have on hand detailed information about R&D activities. Who should develop and carry on this activity is secondary to the need.

Proposed: *A research agency should assure itself that such functions as (a) a registry of those interested in furthering educational change; and (b) a clearinghouse of R&D and related activities, are developed and maintained.*

We come finally to the matter of funding state R&D activities. Early in the process we should establish the conviction that money is by no means the only scarce element in R&D matters. Public acceptance of R&D in almost any social science field has been almost nonexistant or negative. Ideas on what to study, and how to study a given problem don't come so easily when the issue of implementation is considered.

The point is that funding is only part of a much larger problem. This section of our book is pointed to that problem and hopefully some of the answers make useful sense.

In the context of major efforts to make R&D important, to involve citizens and to widen the horizons of nascent R&D, we propose one dollar for each student in public and private education at all levels as a reasonable minimum figure for R&D endeavors in the early 1970s in states now starting out in research. States more into R&D should take the time to add up all funding being spent at the state level for R&D activities. Massachusetts, for instance, should record a state-run elementary school, costing several hundred thousand dollars a year, as part of its R&D activities. This inventory of on-going R&D expenditures may lead some states to reconsider present habits of using research funds. The state should also review its capabilities of using the products of R&D. No explicit conclusions may flow from such a review but new perspectives on how educators themselves view R&D when it comes to implementation may be interesting to explore.

Discussions of this kind bearing on the need and uses of R&D funds are hard to stop once started. They are fruitless if they merely lead to protecting interests and in due time avoiding decisions.

You fill in the information. If research, development, planning and studies are to take their rightful place, you really don't have any choice.

Proposed: *The state of _____ has explored fully and openly with citizen, legislative and agency involvement and we deed that no less than _____ per student should be spent annually on research and development intended to improve education and increase the efficiency of the educational enterprise.*

Afterword

The fitful 1960s were unpleasant for many in education and tragic for some. The 1970s find us sober and uncertain. But the present will not go away. Daniel Bell, writing in *Daedalus,* tells us:

> The year 2000 has already arrived, for in the decisions we make now, in the way we design our environment and thus sketch the lines of constraints, the future is committed. Just as the gridiron pattern of city streets in the nineteenth century shaped the linear growth of cities in the twentieth, so the new networks of radial highways, the location of new towns, the reordering of graduate school curricula, the decision to create or not to create a computer utility as a single system, and the like will frame the tectonics of the twenty-first century. The future is not an overarching leap into the distance; it begins in the present.[1]

We must come together for important discussions, and responsible actions, to make today's education a worthy father of tomorrow's world. In consequence, we must find ways to invoke the reconstructive powers of research and development.

Appendix A

Members of the Advisory Council on Education

Past Members

Mr. Norman S. Rabb
Dr. John S. Sprague
Mr. Hazen H. Ayer
Mrs. Bruce C. Benson
Mr. Paul Parks

Current Members

Mr. Morton R. Godine
Dr. Nina E. Scarito
Mrs. Shirley R. Lewis
Mr. J. Norman O'Connor
Mr. Felix de C. Pereira
Mr. Walter Ryan
Mr. Verne W. Vance, Jr.
Mrs. Mary E. Warner
Mr. Philip C. Beals

Professional Staff
Past

Dr. Lawrence E. Fox

Current

Dr. William C. Gaige
Dr. Allan S. Hartman
Dr. Ronald B. Jackson
Ms. Judith Pippen

333

Bibliography

Books

Aikin, Wilford M. *The Story of the Eight-Year Study.* New York: Harper and Brothers, 1942.

Armor, David J. *The American School Counselor, A Case Study in the Sociology of Professors.* New York: Russell Sage Foundation, 1969.

Beer, Samuel H., and Barringer, Richard E. *The State and the Poor.* Cambridge: Winthrop Publishers, Inc., 1970.

Bronfenbrenner, Urie. *Two Worlds of Children: U.S. and U.S.S.R.* New York: Russell Sage Foundation, 1970.

Brown, Larry. *The Way we go to School: The Exclusion of Children in Boston.* Boston: Beacon Press, 1970.

Conant, James B. *The Education of American Teachers.* New York: McGraw-Hill, 1963.

Drucker, Peter F. *The Age of Discontinuity – Guidelines to Our Changing Society.* New York: Harper and Row, 1969.

Drucker, Peter F. *Technology, Management and Society.* New York: Harper and Row, 1970.

Gordon, Ira J., ed. *Early Childhood Education.* Part II, 71st Yearbook. Chicago: National Society for the Study of Education, 1972

Koerner, James D. *The Miseducation of American Teachers.* New York: Houghton Mifflin, 1963.

Ovian, Lawrence A. "A Study of the Independent, Union and Regional School District in Worcester County: Proposals for Reorganization." Doctoral dissertation, University of Mass., June 1968.

Morphet, Edgar, L., ed. *Designing Education for the Future: Emerging Designs for Education.* Denver: Improving State Leadership in Education, 1968.

Morphet, Edgar L., ed. *Designing Education for the Future: Preparing Educators to Meet Emerging Needs.* Denver: Improving State Leadership in Education, 1969.

Morphet, Edgar L., ed. *Planning and Providing for Excellence in Education.* Denver: Improving State Leadership in Education, 1971.

Thomas, Lawrence G., ed. *Philosophical Redirection of Educational Research.* 71st yearbook. Chicago: National Society for the Study of Education, 1972.

Thomas, Lawrence G., ed. *Philosophical Redirection of Educational Research.* Chicago: National Society for the Study of Education, 1972.

Woodring, Paul. *Investment in Innovation: An Historical Appraisal of the Fund for the Advancement of Education.* Boston: Little, Brown and Co., 1970.

Public Documents

Harrington, Kevin B. *Report of the Special Commission Established to Make An Investigation and Study Relative to Improving and Extending Educational Facilities in the Commonwealth.* House Number 4300, June 1965.

Sargent, Francis W. "State of the State," Unpublished address by the Governor of Massachusetts, delivered January 10, 1972.

Reports

Advisory Council on State Departments of Education. *The Federal-State Partnership for Education.* 5th Annual Report. H.E.W. OE 23059–69, 1969.

Allen, James E. *An Open University/External Degree Program for Massachusetts.* Prepared for the Massachusetts Board of Higher Education, October 1971.

Campbell, Roald F.: Stroufe, Gerald E.: and Layton, Donald H. *Strengthening State Departments of Education.* Chicago: University of Chicago, 1967.

Dochterman, Clifford et al. *Designing Education for the Future: Directive, to Excellence in Education.* Denver: Improving State Leadership in Education, 1968.

Edelfelt, Roy A. "Certification and Teacher Competence: Repair or Reform." A presentation given before a study Advisory Conference for Dr. Lindley Stiles, July 1968.

Fischer, John. "Educational Reform in Other States." Unpublished address made at the Governor's Conference on Education. University of Massachusetts, Amherst, January 27, 1966.

Hartman, Allan et al. "Installation Strategies: A Retrospective and Prospective Analysis." Syracuse: Eastern Regional Institute for Education, 1970.

Hodgen, John E. "Regional School Districts." Commonwealth of Massachusetts, Department of Education, School Building Assistance Bureau, 1971.

Jackson, Ronald B. "A Care For Redesigning School Districts and Regions." Unpublished document, Massachusetts Advisory Council on Education, 1971.

Liecheimer, Alvin P. "Give Up The Ship." A Presentation Given before a Study Advisory Conference for Dr. Lindley Stiles, July 1968.

Menzies, Ian, and Forman, Ian. "The Mess in Bay State Education," *Boston Globe,* September 1961. 32 pp.

Reprinted from National Center for Educational Research and Development. *Essential Research and Development in the United States.* U.S. Dept. of H.E.W. GE 12049. December 1969.

Zacharias, Jerrold R. *The Open University.* Prepared for the Massachusetts Board of Higher Education, September 15, 1971.

Articles and Periodicals

Bell, Daniel. "The Year 2000 – The Trajectory of an Idea," *Daedalus,* 96 (Summer 1967): 639–651.

Brown, Bob B. et al. "The Reliability of Observation of Teachers' Classroom Behavior. *Journal of Experimental Education* 36 (Spring 1968).

Hartman, Allan. "Saving Money Through Better Business Practices," *School Management* (December 1970), pp. 25-26.

Jackson, Ronald B. "Early Childhood Education," *Massachusetts Teacher* XLX, No. 2, (November 1970): 9.

Jackson, Ronald B. "Mace – The Critical Mass," *TREND* 5 (Fall 1968): 17.

Kotin, Lawrence. "Equal Educational Opportunity: The Emerging Role of the State Department of Education," *Boston University Law Review* 50 (Spring 1970): 211-29.

Murphy, Jerome T. "Title I of ESEA: The Politics of Implementing Federal Educational Reform," *Harvard Educational Review* 41 (February 1971): 35–63.

Resnick, Henry. "Are There Better Ways to Teach Teachers? *Saturday Review* (March 4, 1972), pp. 46–50.

Scriven, H. "The Methodology of Evaluation," *AERA Monograph Series on Curriculum Evaluation*, No. 1 (1967), pp. 38–39.

Stake, Robert E., and Denny, Terry. "Needed Concepts and Techniques for Utilizing More Fully the Potential of Evaluation," in National Society for the Study of Education, Yearbook 68, part 2, *Educational Evolution: New Roles, New Means*, 1969, pp. 370–90;

Suchman, Edward A. "Evaluating Education Programs," *Urban Review* 3 (February 1969): 15–16.

MACE Reports

A Report of the Advisory Committee on the Schaefer-Kaufman Recommendations, April 1970.

Blatt, Burton, and Garfunkel, Frank. *Massachusetts Study of Educational Opportunities for Handicapped and Disadvantaged Children*, 1971.

Campbell, Aldrich and Nulty, *A Systems Approach for Massachusetts Schools: A Study of School Building Costs*, 1971.

Collins, Evan R. et al. *The People's Colleges: The State Colleges of Massachusetts*, 1971.

Cronin, Joseph M. *Organizing an Urban School System for Diversity*, 1970.

Daniere, Andre. *A Cost-Benefit Analysis of General-Purpose State School Aid Formulas in Massachusetts*. 1969.

Daniere, Andre, and Madaus, George. *The Measurement in Alternative Costs of Educating Catholic Children in Public Schools*, 1969.

de Lone, Richard H. *Massachusetts Schools: Past, Present and Possible*, 1971.

Donley, Donald T. *Organizing for a Child's Learning Experience: A Report on a Study of School District Organization in Massachusetts*, 1971.

Dunsmore, Bruce. *Guidelines for Planning and Constructing Community Colleges*, 1969.

Gibson, John S. *The Massachusetts Department of Education: Proposals for Progress in the 70s*, 1970.

Gove, Samuel. *The Massachusetts System of Higher Education in Transition*, 1967.

Hoffman, Herbert. *Take a Giant Step: Evaluation of Selected Aspects of Project 750*, 1969.

Information Management, Inc. *The Management of Educational Information*, 1968.

Jordan, Daniel, and Spiess, Kathryn H. *Compensatory Education in Massachusetts: An Evaluation with Recommendations,* 1970.

King, Warren, and Associates. *Report of the Massachusetts Business Task Force for School Management,* 1970.

Levin, Melvin, and Slavet, Joseph. *Continuing Education in Massachusetts: State Programs for the Seventies,* 1970.

Liddle, Gordon, and Kroll, Arthur. *Pupil Services for Massachusetts Schools,* 1969.

Michael, Lloyd S. *Quality Education for the High Schools in Massachusetts: A Study of the Comprehensive High School in Massachusetts,* 1971.

New England School Development Council. *Inequalities of Educational Opportunity in Massachusetts,* 1967.

Rowe, Richard R. *Child Care in Massachusetts: The Public Responsibility,* 1971.

Ryan, Charlotte. *The State Dollar and the Schools: A Discussion of State Aid Programs in Massachusetts and Promising Reforms,* 1970.

Schaefer, Carl, and Kaufman, Jacob. *Occupational Education for Massachusetts,* 1968.

Stiles, Lindley J. *Teacher Certification and Preparation in Massachusetts,* 1968.

Notes

Chapter 1

1. Edgar L. Morphet et al., *Planning and Providing for Excellence in Education* (Denver: Improving State Leadership in Education, 1971), p. 43.
2. Ibid., p. 67.
3. Ian Menzies and Ian Forman, "The Mess in Bay State Education," reprinted from *Boston Globe,* September 1961. Also quoted by Richard H. de Lone in "Massachusetts Schools: Past, Present and Possible," p. 3.
4. From the Massachusetts Education Study. June 1965
5. Ibid., p. 220.
6. *General Laws of the Commonwealth of Massachusetts,* Chapter 15, Sect. I H.
7. Edgar L. Morphet et al., op. cit., p. 43.
8. U.S. Dept. of H.E.W., *Educational Research and Development in the United States,* December 1969, p. 117.
9. *Designing Education for the Future: An Eight-State Project,* Project Office, 1362 Lincoln St., Denver, Colo. 80203.
10. N.Y. State Fleishmann Commission on the Quality, Cost and Financing of Elementary and Secondary Education.

Chapter 2

1. Ewald B. Nyquist, "State Organization and Responsibilities for Education," *Emerging Designs for Education, Designing Education for the Future* (Denver: Improving State Leadership in Education, 1968), p. 148.
2. John Fischer, "Educational Reform in Other States," (unpublished address made at the Governor's Conference on Education, U. of Mass., Amherst, January 27, 1966), p. 8.
3. Quote is from John Gibson's report, *The Massachusetts Department of Education: Proposals for Progress in the 70s.* Massachusetts Advisory Council on Education, September 1970, p. 2.

Chapter 3

1. *Report of the Business Task Force for School Management.* Massachusetts Advisory Council on Education, September 1970, p. 3.
2. Ibid., pp. 19–20;

Chapter 4

1. Lawrence Ovian, "A Study of the Independent, Union and Regional School District in Worcester County," doctoral dissertation, U. of Mass., June 1968.

2. The State Department of Education "endorsed" these minimum standards but little has happened as a result.
3. Gordon P. Liddle and Arthur M. Kroll, *Pupil Services for Massachusetts Schools.* Massachusetts Advisory Council on Education, p. 55.
4. Ibid.
5. On Dec. 8, 1971, Governor Francis W. Sargent appointed a 25-member commission: "The Commission to Establish a Comprehensive Plan for School District Organization and Collaboration."

Chapter 5

1. This and other excerpts on the following pages are from Joseph M. Cronin's report, *Organizing an Urban School System for Diversity.* Massachusetts Advisory Council on Education, September 1970, p. vii.
2. Ibid., p. viii.
3. Ibid., p. viii.
4. Ibid., p. ix.
5. Ibid., p. ix.
6. Ibid., p. 4.

Introduction to Part II

1. James E. Allen, Jr., *An Open University/External Degree Program for Massachusetts,* prepared for the Massachusetts Board of Higher Education, October 1971, p. 238.
2. Richard Rowe, *Child Care in Massachusetts.* Massachusetts Advisory Council on Education, February 1972, p. 2–27.
3. Richard H. de Lone, *Massachusetts Schools: Past, Present and Possible.* Massachusetts Advisory Council on Education, Annual Report, 1971, p. 28.
4. Ibid.

Chapter 6

1. Elementary Education Act of 1965, P.L. 89–10.
2. Ibid.
3. Daniel Jordan, *Compensatory Education in Massachusetts.* Massachusetts Advisory Council on Education, March 1970, p. 124.
4. Robert E. Stake and Terry Denny, "Needed Concepts and Techniques for Utilizing More Fully the Potential of Evaluation," *Educational Evaluation: New Roles, New Means* (National Society for the Study of Education, Yearbook 68, Part II, 1969, p. 377.
5. Daniel Jordan, op. cit., p. 249.

Chapter 7

1. James E. Allen and Jerrold R. Zacharias' reports to the Board of Higher Education, p. 299.
2. Jerrold R. Zacharias was commissioned by the Massachusetts Board of Higher Education to recommend needed programs for an open/external university, p. 301.

Chapter 8

1. Urie Bronfenbrenner, *Two Worlds of Children* (New York: Russell Sage Foundation, 1970), p. 347.
2. Rowe, op. cit., p. 9–58.
3. Rowe, op. cit., p. 1–9.

Chapter 9

1. Quoted in Burton Blatt and Frank Garfunkel, *Massachusetts Study of Educational Opportunities for Handicapped and Disadvantaged Children.* Massachusetts Advisory Council of Education, p. 1.
2. Ibid., p. 216.
3. Ibid., p. 218.
4. Herbert Hoffman, *Take a Giant Step.* Massachusetts Advisory Council on Education, September 1969, p. 4.
5. Ibid.
6. Blatt and Garfunkel, op. cit., p. 217.

Introduction to Part III

1. de Lone, op. cit., p. 25.
2. Michael, op. cit., p. 104.
3. Liddle and Kroll, op. cit., p. 33.
4. Liddle and Kroll, op. cit., p. 68.
5. Schaefer and Kaufman, op. cit., p. 27.
6. Stiles, op. cit., p. 53.
7. de Lone, op. cit., p. 34.
8. Stiles, op. cit., p. 25.
9. de Lone, op. cit., p. 34.

Chapter 10

1. Schaefer and Kaufman, op. cit., p. 240.
2. *Occupational Education for Massachusetts: A Report of the Advisory*

Committee on the Schaefer-Kaufman Recommendations. Massachusetts
Advisory Council on Education, April 1970, p. 11.
3. Ibid., p. 3.
4. From a paper by James J. Hammond, "On Teacher Education for Occupational Education," April 1970.

Chapter 11

1. Wilford M. Aiken, *The Story of the Eight-Year Study* (A classic study
completed, unfortunately in 1941 when World War II burst upon the world).

Chapter 12

1. Liddle and Kroll, op. cit., p. 86.
2. David J. Armor, *The American School Counselor: A Case Study in the
Sociology of Professions* (New York: Russell Sage Foundation, 1969), p.
558.

Chapter 13

1. A paper prepared for Lindley Stiles, p. 601.
2. Ibid.
3. Ibid., Introduction.
4. Ibid., p. 56.
5. Ibid., p. 11.
6. Bob Burton Brown and Associates, p. 625. (Cited on p. 62 of Stiles, op. cit.)

Chapter 14

1. Clifford L. Dochterman, *Directions to Excellence in Education, Designing
Education for the Future* (Denver: Improving State Leadership in Education,
1971), p. 643.
2. Warren G. Bernis, p. 645.
3. Henry Resnick, "Are there Better Ways to Teach Teachers?" *Saturday Review,*
March 4, 1972, p. 46.
4. As told to the author.
5. Governor Francis W. Sargent, Annual "State of the State" Message to the
Commonwealth, January 10, 1971.
6. M. Scriven, "The Methodology of Evaluation," *AERA Monograph Series on
Curriculum Evaluation,* No. 1 (Chicago: Rand McNally, 1967)] p. 38–39.
Cited in Richard Rowe's study for MACE.

Afterword

1. Reprinted from Daniel Bell, "Toward the Year 2000 — The Trajectory of an Idea" (Summer 1967), with permission of *Daedalus,* Journal of the American Academy of Arts and Sciences, Boston, Mass.

Index

345

About the Author

Ronald B. Jackson has been associated with educational research for a number of years. Before being appointed Associate Director of the Council in 1968, Dr. Jackson served under Benjamin C. Willis on the Staff of the landmark Willis-Harrington Commission in Massachusetts which evolved an educational master plan for the Bay State in 1965. He has also taught and been a school administrator or a consultant in several states and in Greece, Taiwan, and West Germany.

Dr. Jackson has worked with Navaho Indians, served as a summer ranger in Bridger National Forest in Wyoming, and been a Fulbright Teacher on Corfu.

As an undergraduate Dr. Jackson, after military service with the Air Force in World War II, attended Black Mountain College. Later he received his MA at Montana State University and his doctorate in education from the University of Arizona. He also holds a certificate in linguistics from the University of Michigan.

Dr. Jackson is currently on the Executive Board of Directors at Stockbridge School and Secretary to the Governor's Commission to Establish a Comprehensive Plan for School District Organization and Collaboration. He is active in penal reform and has been successful in obtaining funds for correctional institutions.